Reading Zoos

Representations of Animals and Captivity

Randy Malamud
*Associate Professor of English
Georgia State University*

First published 1998 by
MACMILLAN PRESS LTD
Houndmills, Basingstoke, Hampshire RG21 6XS
and London
Companies and representatives
throughout the world

ISBN 0–333–71406–7 hardcover
ISBN 0–333–71407–5 paperback

A catalogue record for this book is available from the British Library.

This book is printed on paper suitable for recycling and made from fully managed and sustained forest sources.

10 9 8 7 6 5 4 3 2 1
07 06 05 04 03 02 01 00 99 98

Printed and bound in Great Britain by
Antony Rowe Ltd, Chippenham, Wiltshire

For Jacob Simonds-Malamud
(instead of going to the zoo)

Contents

Acknowledgments

For alerting me to various sources, I thank Noelle Baker, David Bottoms, Jimmie Cain, David Galef, Ralph Gilbert, Alex and Nancy Hicks, Michelle Lewis, Judith Malamud, Marilynn Richtarik, Jan Rieman, John Robinson, Bob Sattelmeyer, Sandra Sherman, Malinda Snow, Wendy Simonds, and Allan Tullos. For reading and commenting on sections, I thank Bob Sattelmeyer and David Galef. For reading the entire manuscript and making immensely valuable suggestions on every page of it, I thank my research assistant Noelle Baker – an ideal reader, whose dedication and support over the years have been indispensable. I appreciate Lorraine Dabbs's similarly brilliant help during production. And Macmillan's anonymous reviewer graced my work with sensitivity to what I was trying to say, and editorial perspicacity that helped me say it better, leaving me grateful for the kindness of strangers.

In immeasurable ways I am indebted to my department chair, Bob Sattelmeyer, for indulging me and not worrying about how this would become a book. I thank him for supporting his colleagues' research, and for creating a milieu maximally conducive to intellectual inquiry. Bob and other extraordinary administrators at Georgia State University mean what they say when they talk of their commitment to scholarship. I thank especially Associate Dean for the Humanities David Blumenfeld, College of Arts and Sciences Dean Ahmed Abdelal, and Associate Provost Paula Dressel, for their friendship as well as their leadership. And I want to acknowledge a circle of friends, students, and colleagues at GSU – my most immediate audience – whose contributions to my scholarship have been indefinite and unspecific, but vastly important: Noelle Baker, John Burrison, Patricia Bryan, Patrick Bryant, Shelle Bryant, Tim Crimmins, Lorraine Dabbs, Jennifer Fahey, Meg Harper, Marta Hess, Jim Hirsh, Jane Kuenz, Ralph LaRossa, Elizabeth Lopez, Tom McHaney, George Pullman, Marilynn Richtarik, Matthew Roudané, Bob Sattelmeyer, Paul Schmidt, Shelton Waldrep, Marta Werner, and the participants in my Modern Poetry Seminar (Spring 1996) who indulged my sermons on ecocriticism. Christine Gallant has been a peerless source of assistance, sometimes more confident than I was that this would all come together, for which I am consummately thankful. To three other dear friends, Lauraine Leblanc, Meredith Raimondo, and Kim Springer, I offer my greatest thanks and appreciation.

I thank Boria Sax of Nature in Legend and Story (NILAS), and Virginia McKenna of the Born Free Foundation, for their generous correspondences with me and for providing many useful resources. And I am grateful to Charmian Hearne at Macmillan, for her resoundingly efficient and supportive shepherding of this book.

Wendy Simonds knows that this book could not have been written without her wisdom, insight and love (not to mention world-class editing). Daniel and Judith Malamud and Lisa and Paul Apostol, as always, have my deepest gratitude. And I welcome Benjamin Simonds-Malamud, who came along as this book went to press (and for whom I promise to dedicate the next one).

Copyright acknowledgments

Excerpts from '"Gay" is the captivating cognomen of a Young Woman of cambridge, mass.' are reprinted from *Complete Poems 1904–1962* by e.e. cummings, edited by George J. Firmage, by permission of W. W. Norton & Company Ltd. Copyright © 1991 by the Trustees for the E.E. Cummings Trust and George James Firmage.

Excerpts from 'The Zoo Attack,' by Haruki Murakami, copyright © 1995 by Haruki Murakami, are reprinted by permission of International Creative Management, Inc.

Excerpts from 'The Jaguar,' by Ted Hughes, copyright © 1982, are reprinted by permission of Faber and Faber Ltd.

1

Zoo Stories

... the knowing animals are aware/that we are not really at home in/our interpreted world.

Rainer Maria Rilke, *Duino Elegies*

... hideous, tired, Bank Holiday crowds moronically looking through bars at creatures they could hardly discern, creatures as listless, dragging in their steps and whining in their cries as the children that watched them.

Angus Wilson, *The Old Men at the Zoo*

I don't want to go to the Zoo any more.

Russell Hoban, *Turtle Diary*

I do not like zoos; this book begins from that premise. Most people consider zoos to be socially and culturally unobjectionable – indeed, desirable – venues of education and horizon-broadening: environmentally and ecologically enriching, and especially appropriate for young children. Generally thought to be as important to any city as a good symphony orchestra or a well-developed system of parks, a zoo embellishes a place's perceived appeal.[1] Zoos are high-profile cultural attractions and, as I will argue, this is their key problem: when we consider them a cultural attraction, we mean *our* culture, human culture. We subsume zoos and their captive animals within various anthropocentrist social structures and systems of culture, thus misrepresenting the realities of animals' existence and their role on this planet.

Zoos are valued because they supposedly offer experience of the animal world's natural beauty and wealth to people who have little access to the wild. But a caged animal in the heart of a city, perhaps thousands of miles from its habitat, really offers little insight into the natural condition of that species. Whatever 'awareness' a zoo visitor reaps, I suggest, is undesirable: rather than fostering an appreciation for animals' attributes, zoos convince people that we are the imperial species – that we are entitled to trap animals, remove them from their worlds and imprison them within ours, simply because we are able to do so by virtue of our power and ingenuity. The spectator does not see a zebra in a zoo – a zebra is something that exists on an African plain, not in an urban North American animal collection. People cannot appreciate an animal's essence when it is displayed in captivity alongside a hundred others with which it does not naturally share living quarters, in an artificial compound that they pay to enter. Passive spectatorship is not only not a good way to appreciate a zebra, it is a bad way. It teaches children and other zoo visitors exactly the wrong thing about a zebra: they do not see the creature as it is – an animal that lives its life in a certain way on a different continent – but rather as an amusement, a display, a spectacle in a menagerie. 'To put animals on exhibit as "specimens" and "social groups," torn from the very fabric of their ecosystems wherein they have evolved and have existed as an inseparable part of the seamless web of creation, violates the biological and spiritual unity of all life,' writes Michael W. Fox.

> There can be no communion with our animal kin when they are held captive, no matter what the reasons may be for their 'protective custody.' The zoo is a trick mirror that can delude us into believing that we love and respect animals and are helping to preserve them . . . We cannot recognize or celebrate the sanctity and dignity of nonhuman life under such conditions. There can be no communion: only amusement, curiosity, amazement, and perhaps sympathy.
>
> (153–4)

Dale Jamieson puts it succinctly: 'Zoos teach us a false sense of our place in the natural order' ('Against', 117). And whatever ideals zookeepers may have for the appealing and sensitive display of their animals, actual conditions are more likely to resemble Angus Wilson's pathetically dreary tableau (quoted at the head of this chapter) than cutting-edge prototypes of natural conservation/education centers. Critical appraisals of zoos copiously reiterate Jonathan Barzdo's accusation that 'a good zoo is a rare thing' (19).

Zoos offer a convenient way to indulge cultural appetites for novelty and diversion; but spectators delude themselves if they believe they garner the experience of animals. 'Historically, zoos have presented animals as freaks, as objects divorced from nature, belittled, distorted, out of context' (424), writes David Hancocks. In zoos, 'what the animal is doing is rarely what its free-living kin are doing,' argues Boyce Rensberger. Because zoos offer minimal opportunity for natural animal behavior, habitat, or social grouping, he continues, 'One might even argue that an animal in a zoo is not a whole animal . . . Every animal's existence is more than just flesh and blood contained within its skin; it is this, plus its natural environment, the two linked in a dynamic equilibrium. A person with a mature appreciation of wild animals recognizes this linkage' (258).

Traditional opposition to zoos comes from the perspective of the animal rights movement: activists protest the cruelty of removing animals from their habitats, transporting them to some urban prison decorated with items designed to contrive nature, and subjecting them to the humiliations of crowds as well as numerous other inhumanities consequent upon the unnatural condition of captivity. Tom Regan synopsizes an animal rights attitude toward zoos: animals' lives 'include a variety of biological, psychological, and social needs. The satisfaction of these needs is a source of pleasure, their frustration or abuse, a source of pain' (44). The animal rights position questions solely if animals are treated with appropriate respect for their needs – and if not, the zoo must be unilaterally condemned:

> It is morally irrelevant to insist that zoos provide important educational and recreational opportunities for humans, or that captive animals serve as useful models in scientific research, or that regions in which zoos are located benefit economically, or that zoo programs offer the opportunity for protecting rare or endangered species, or that variations on these programs insure genetic stock, or that any other consequences arise from keeping wild animals in captivity that forwards the interests of other individuals.
>
> (45–6)

While I sympathize fully with such an animal rights view, it is not my main focus. I am more concerned with what the imprisonment of animals says about the *people* who create, maintain, and patronize zoos: what they believe or pretend zoos offer, and how underlying cultural nuances deconstruct their experiences and behavior. Why do people feel the need and entitlement to 'possess' (physically or experientially) everything on the face of the earth? How do we justify such enterprises as laudatory, educational, intellectually and culturally rewarding? Why are zoos largely exempt from accountability for their hegemonic exercise and representation of power?[2] My argument implicitly extends to related institutions – contemporary and historical – that assemble captive animals in artificial contexts for spectators' ease and mawkish amusement. Circuses and carnivals (along with such other genres of animal performances as hippodrama, vaudeville, and magic shows), sea worlds, and 'wildlife centers' where cars or monorails carry people through game preserves, all contribute to shaping cultural representations of animals. But the modern zoo is at the center of my examination, as I attempt to identify institutional forces that illuminate its operative cultural processes. By studying modern depictions of zoos – exploring how literary and other cultural texts portray zoos and their significance to cultural consumers – I plan to present a paradigm of how they reveal the workings and the failures of our aesthetic, cultural, and ecological habits.

I adopt Jamieson's simple but functional definition of zoos – 'public parks which display animals, primarily for the purposes of recreation or education' ('Against', 108) – although at times my analysis extends to include practices of animal captivity and exhibition in earlier avatars, illustrating cultural and historical traditions that resonate in modern zoos. I realize that I expose myself to charges of reductionism – of unfairly critiquing a wide swath of institutions within a monolithic framework. Certainly it is true that all zoos are not exactly alike. Many zoos today differ significantly, physically and conceptually, from those of a generation ago; although, on the other hand (sadly), many zoos today closely resemble those from the previous century. My appraisal of zoos, generically, reflects my conviction that they all fundamentally constitute a common type of institution – inherently similar in terms of their essential workings and the ethos underlying the basic precept of procuring (or breeding) and exhibiting captive animals. I consider differences among zoos cosmetic, or otherwise insignificant in terms of mitigating their collective implication in a culturally retrograde enterprise.

Zoos have generated little scholarship outside of their own zoological and institutional community, as Bob Mullan and Garry Marvin note in *Zoo Culture*: '[W]e were astonished that so little social science or humanities work has been directed towards understanding the zoo, whether historically or sociologically ... The key, we believe, to this lack of interest is that people regard the zoo as an easily understood and essentially unproblematic institution, and the zoo visit as an unproblematic event' (xvii). Like them, I will problematize zoos. Mullan and Marvin's research sociologically examines zoos' institutional practices; my own approach uses what I term 'zoo stories' – a catchall reference to a diverse range of literary and popular cultural artifacts – to generate as many complexities, nuances, implications, and contradictions as possible. I hope to establish the manifold cultural morass zoos present, and to show how people appraise zoos through the mediation of the representations that zoo stories embody.

I plan to use zoo stories in conjunction with accounts of how zoos actually function to develop my argument – a kind of aesthetic exposé: zoos represent a cultural danger, a deadening of our sensibilities. While many extol zoos as sacrosanct, I believe they actually threaten to narrow our cultural faculties. I do not profess to know precisely the *right* way to regard, imagine, interact with, and learn from wild animals – although my final chapter broaches a few possible models – but I want to argue that the ubiquitous institutions of animal captivity are the wrong way. And despite the fervency pervading my analysis (verging – not too often, I hope – on what may seem dogmatic absolutism), I must modestly admit, at least once here at the opening, that I cannot claim to resolve definitively all the issues I raise about cultural representations of animals and nature. The subject of how people and social institutions relate to the natural world is so complex and infinitely regressive that it would be overweeningly ambitious to presume to have unique insight or a single correct dictum. Instead, I hope to lay out an amalgam of illustrations, conjectures, and arguments – ranging from those I consider demonstrably certain to those that a sympathetic, indulgent audience might credit as being not impossible – from an array of diverse perspectives, directly or indirectly emanating from the consideration of zoos. In the end, what I consider the most important element of my project is encouraging readers to think about these issues themselves, and formulate their own range of reactions to my assertions. I expect to elicit many shades of agreement and disagreement; I will consider my work successful as long as I am able to facilitate thoughtful deliberation.

My challenge is to examine links between human culture and nature.[3] I believe that doing so will enrich both realms, and will contribute as well to the emerging discourse of ecocriticism.[4] I hope such fusions will culminate in a vital new cultural awareness: one can think of 'environmental literacy... as a kind of culture,' writes Lawrence Buell, 'with local and historical variations, requiring efforts of study and adaptation' (107). Ecocriticism, as described by Cheryll Glotfelty, promises to embody Buell's vision of environmentally literate culture: in 'the study of the relationship between literature and the physical environment... ecocriticism takes an earth-centered approach to literary studies,' she writes. 'All ecological criticism shares the fundamental premise that human culture is connected to the physical world, affecting it and affected by it... As a critical stance, it has one foot in literature and the other on land; as a theoretical discourse, it negotiates between the human and the nonhuman' (xviii–xix).

Forces within and outside academe implore scholars to demonstrate more clearly the relationship of our work to the world around us, and the relevance of studies in the humanities: Glen A. Love, for example, writes that despite the international prominence of green concerns,

> rather than confronting these ecological issues, we prefer to think on other things... One would hope and expect that our field of English would respond appropriately to the radical displacements accompanying ecological catastrophe... But curiously enough... the English profession has failed to respond in any significant way to the issue of the environment, the acknowledgment of our place within the natural world and our need to live heedfully within it, at peril of our very survival.
>
> ('Revaluing', 202).

Despite the lip service Love suggests most English professors would pay to environmental consciousness and ecological awareness, he lambastes our 'general failure to apply any sense of this awareness to our daily work' (203). As literary criticism

> retreats ever further from public life into a professionalism characterized by its obscurity and inaccessibility to all but other English professors, it seems necessary to begin asking elemental questions of ourselves and the literature which we profess . . . The most important function of literature today is to redirect human consciousness to a full consideration of its place in a threatened natural world . . . [T]he current ideology which separates human beings from their environments is demonstrably and dangerously reductionist.
>
> (211–13)

I hope to help make amends for the past deficiencies among literary scholars, and also to satisfy Andrew Ross's admonition that developing 'a green cultural criticism [is] . . . one of the more pressing challenges for cultural politics in this decade' (*Weather*, 8). I am aware that I am considerably extending – some might say, demeaning or violating – the tradition of literary criticism by meshing it with the unabashed activist advocacy I embrace. I believe our intellectual traditions can stretch to encompass the acknowledgment that art can and should have a direct ecocentric impact; as readers and scholars, we may fruitfully mediate this process. Due to a confluence of various ecological realities and aesthetic, cultural, and intellectual currents, the time seems propitious for a full-front ecocritical assault on *idées reçues* regarding people's relations to the other elements of our world. Mary Midgley writes that people have traditionally attended to aspects of non-human living nature

> as they have thought of drains – as a worthy but not particularly interesting subject. In the last few decades, however, their imagination has been struck, somewhat suddenly, by a flood of new and fascinating information about animals. Some dim conception of splendors and miseries hitherto undreamt of, of the vast range and sentient life, of the richness and complexity found in even the simplest creatures, has started to penetrate . . . For the first time in civilized history, people who were interested in animals because they wanted to understand them, rather than just to eat or yoke or shoot or stuff them, have been able to advance that understanding by scientific means, and to convey some of it to the inquisitive public.
>
> (13–14)

As a professor of literature, I feel a particular claim in culture and the way its consumers process it, value it, position themselves with respect to it. I have a vested interest in sustaining the respect, appreciation, and integrity with which people treat objects of culture; and I think zoos pervert cultural perceptions and practices. It is too easy to experience zoo animals: their existence in caged compounds, and their arrangement for spectators' convenience, encourage imperialistic cultural habits and a lazy, undeserved sense of appreciation/control over these animals. Our ecological desecration of innumerable habitats (human and animal) reveals this supposed mastery to be delusory. The token preservation of animals in zoos allows us to repress the reality of the danger people pose to the natural world. The zoo is a 'diminishing space,' as John Roberts terms it (60); it is not conducive – indeed, it is directly antagonistic – to the broadening of people's imaginative, cultural, or ecological consciousness.

It is difficult, and, of course, important, to learn from animals the lessons they can teach about living in the ecosystem we share with them. These lessons, however, cannot be crammed or modified to conform to the limited amount of time and attention – an afternoon outing – people may allocate for such education. And in fact, this 'education' is probably of minimal efficacy: a study by zoologist Stephen Kellert 'indicates that zoo-goers are much less knowledgeable about animals than backpackers, hunters, fishermen and others who claim an interest in animals . . . One reason why some zoos have not done a better job of educating people is that many of them make no real effort at education. In the case of others the problem is an apathetic and unappreciative public' (Jamieson, 'Against', 111).[5] Further compromising the zoo's potential for effective education is the fact that animals in their natural habitats are strikingly different from the captive animals zoo visitors actually observe. As Peter Batten writes, one would learn from watching zoo animals 'that the chimpanzee, for example, is a neurotic humanoid that cadges food from humans, and throws tantrums and excreta should this not materialize . . . Or that the orang-utan, which by nature seldom descends to the soft forest floor, is a pathetic bundle of matted red fur in the corner of a tiled cell' (22). Mullan and Marvin observe that there is 'usually a sense of disappointment in the visitor when the sleepy and lethargic beasts visible in front of him are not easily imagined as the accomplished hunters of the African plain,' and conclude, 'The zoo cannot but fail in its attempt to give a full understanding or appreciation of natural behaviour and natural relationships for these cannot be displayed in an environment which consists of artificial segments of the whole, all within yards of each other. This is an artificiality that fools nobody' (159).[6]

The attitude that people are entitled to develop our awareness of animals in a way that suits our own habits is part of the problem, not the solution, of our limited perspective that threatens our future on this planet. The ways people behave at zoos support Rainer Maria Rilke's observation in the *Duino Elegies*, quoted above as an epigraph, that 'we are not really at home in our interpreted world.' Zoos provide a fascinating paradigm of people's *interpreted world* (which is, of course, to be strikingly differentiated from the real world, as signifier differs from signified), revealing how we think about the creatures, earthmates, selected as specimens for display. Our cultural spokespeople demonstrate how zoos confirm Rilke's observation: exhibiting our discomfort, our insecurity, our sense of misfitting, our injustice and deceit, in the world as we have interpreted it. Something is rotten in our world, and zoos offer a valuable opportunity to identify what this is and how we confront (or, mostly, repress) the problem.

The ecologist Aldo Leopold observes in *A Sand County Almanac* that art is not separate from nature: 'That land yields a cultural harvest is a fact long known, but latterly often forgotten' (xix). *Reading Zoos* attempts to encompass and conjoin both culture and nature from within a critical stance that situates zoos, animals, and stories in a sphere of interaction, intertextuality, inter-referentiality. My methodology features an ecocritical appropriation of the familiar cultural studies bricolage, what Cary Nelson, Paula Treichler and Lawrence Grossberg call the 'interdisciplinary, transdisciplinary, and sometimes counter-disciplinary' enterprise 'that operates in the tension between its tendencies to embrace both a broad, anthropological and a more narrowly humanistic conception of culture,' and that is 'committed to the study of the entire range of a society's arts, beliefs, institutions, and communicative practices' (4). If 'reading zoos' seems a semantic justification for a literary scholar to conduct an examination of zoos (which it is in part), it is meant to suggest, beyond this:

- Reading about zoos: the most basic thing that happens when a reader takes on a zoo story.
- Reading through zoos: using the complexities and figurative polyphonies of literature, art, and culture to challenge zoos. The zoo projects itself as straightforwardly innocuous within its own simple discourse and context; it endures quietly in a kind of 'cultural default' mode – that is, there's nothing wrong with a zoo if one doesn't think much about it critically, if one doesn't probe for anything wrong. But the more suggestive and richer discourse of zoo stories deconstructs the seemingly stable institutional existence that zoos have enjoyed.
- Reading against zoos: arranging zoo stories in an enterprise of critical/interpretive advocacy to bolster the case against zoos; picking through zoo stories to amass evidence that supports my argument. I embrace Nelson, Treichler and Grossberg's characterization of cultural studies as 'both an intellectual and a political tradition . . . "culture" is simultaneously the ground on which analysis proceeds, the object of study, and the site of political critique and intervention . . . Cultural studies believes that its practice does matter, that its own intellectual work is supposed to – can – make a difference' (5–6).
- Reading beyond zoos: presenting models of experiencing animals in ways that do not necessitate the mediation of zoos.
- And, literally, reading zoos themselves: what language do they use to define themselves and explain their endeavors? A basic way to read zoos, for example, is simply to read the signs outside the cages. In the modern era, writes Thomas Veltre, the print medium guides the design of zoos and the uses to which they are put. 'With the development of long, erudite, museumlike graphics, zoogoing was considered more than ever to be a literacy-based experience' (27). Zoo signs use homogeneous and limiting language to identify and 'authoritatively' contextualize animals. The language writers use to perform their version of the same activity is immensely more interesting. Regarding such dialectically opposite modes of language as thesis and antithesis assists the effort to discover, in an educed synthesis, the reality of the zoo.

Zoos aspire (and, I believe, fail) to accomplish what Stephen Greenblatt calls in *Marvelous Possessions* 'the assimilation of the other' (3). Zoos try to contextualize, comfortably, natural animals within human culture, and to assert that creatures that are so obviously 'other' – caged, fed special diets, identified by signs indicating their unique zoological purview – are nevertheless assimilable. The intent of this attempt at assimilation is to demonstrate the breadth and bounty of our own marvelous possessions.

Greenblatt adapts Marx to help explain the problem of assimilating the other, identifying the crux of this endeavor as *'the reproduction and circulation of mimetic capital* . . . in the modern world-order it is with capitalism that the proliferation and circulation of representations . . . achieved a spectacular and virtually inescapable global magnitude,' marked by 'the will and the ability to cross immense distances and, in the search for profit, to encounter and to represent radically unfamiliar human and natural objects' (6). The representations of animals in zoos and zoo stories are indebted to the machinations of capitalism and the agenda of capitalist hegemony. The energy – physical, financial, cultural – that goes into the acquisition of captive animals and the proliferation of zoos as institutions reflects the 'magnitude' that Greenblatt (following Marx) sees as an essential constituent, or force, of modern capitalist culture.

Greenblatt continues:

> I want to convey the sense of a stockpile of representations, a set of images and image-making devices that are *accumulated*, 'banked,' as it were, in books, archives, collections, cultural storehouses, until such time as these representations are called upon to generate new representations. The images that matter, that merit the term capital, are those that achieve reproductive power, maintaining and multiplying themselves by transforming cultural contacts into novel and often unexpected forms.
>
> (6)

The zoo represents such an archive or cultural storehouse. I see zoos as embodying, in the minds of those who support them, an accumulation of 'capital' in the local culture – evidenced, for example, when a chamber of commerce lauds a zoo's contribution to a region's cultural climate, and when zoo directors vociferously promote the importance of their enterprise to society as an investment in the social and ecological infrastructure.

Finally, Greenblatt writes:

> I want to suggest that mimesis, as Marx said of capital, is a social relation of production. I take this to mean that any given representation is not only the reflection or product of social relations but that it is itself a social relation, linked to the group understandings, status hierarchies, resistances, and conflicts that exist in other spheres of the culture in which it circulates. This means that representations are not only products but producers, capable of decisively altering the very forces that brought them into being.
>
> (6)

Zoos are products and producers: they produce, most notably for my study, zoo stories, a wide range of cultural descriptions of (and often reactions against) their existence. Zoos offer an experience of nature that presents itself as mimetic of a larger animal macrocosm; and zoo stories promise varying degrees of mimetic representation of zoos. In this network of relational representations, then, the zoo and culturally mimetic portrayals of zoos are ripe fodder for examination. I believe, as Greenblatt's model asserts, that representations – zoo stories – are indeed capable of altering what brought them into being (that is, zoos), and this capability is very much what I hope to facilitate. By studying the social relation of production surrounding zoos, I will characterize their role in what Wendy Griswold calls the 'cultural diamond' – a model of cultural creation and duration whose four corners are 'audience' (in this case, zoo spectators), 'creator' (zookeepers), 'cultural object' (zoo animals) and 'social world' (represented here via the world that surrounds the zoo, the contexts in which zoos appear, as put forth in zoo stories). No account of a cultural phenomenon is complete unless it considers all four corners of the diamond and the connections between them, Griswold argues.

Discussing the subject of his research, early European responses to the New World, Greenblatt offers the following caveat:

> The responses with which I am concerned – indeed the only responses I have been able to identify – are not detached scientific assessments but what I would call engaged representations, representations that are relational, local, and historically

> contingent. Their overriding interest is not knowledge of the other but practice upon the other; and, as I shall try to show, the principal faculty involved in generating these representations is not reason but imagination.
>
> (12–13)

In the same vein, I offer not 'detached scientific assessments' of animal captivity or ecology. Instead I present, like Greenblatt, 'engaged representations' – engagements between cultural producers and zoos, between myself and these cultural producers, and between myself and zoos. None of these engagements is objective or value-free; all are interpretively colored by an intricate backdrop of cultural assumptions and limitations. I subscribe to Greenblatt's characterization of such engagements, with one amplification: I consider my representations relational, local, historically contingent, *and especially culturally contingent*. This final contingency depends upon the conviction that zoogoing cannot be considered as an isolated social or cultural practice. My study of zoo stories, thus, infers fundamental relations between zoos and a range of other cultural constructs, including imperialism; consumerism; cultural processing, mediation, and consumption; imprisonment, enslavement, and sadism; and voyeurism and spectatorship, among others. I wholeheartedly embrace the paradigm of zoos as embodying, in Greenblatt's words, 'not knowledge of the other but practice upon the other.'

Animals appeal to their spectators as tokens of a collective unconscious fantasy of Edenic perfection: Walt Whitman makes this point famously in section 32 of *Song of Myself* ('I think I could turn and live awhile with the animals . . .'). Leonard Lutwack suggests the place animals occupy in the cultural imagination:

> Animals must have evoked from primitive human beings a more immediate and telling response than any other feature of their natural surroundings simply because animals were perceived to be so nearly like humans and in many ways superior to humans. As the earliest inhabitants spread out from the limited locales that favored their earliest evolution, they moved into places where they found already well-established animal inhabitants. To struggling humanity the capability and

> beauty of the animal, a result of its perfect adaptation to environment and its single-minded effort to survive, must have seemed especially impressive . . . the animal was venerated because it appeared to have special powers that made it conversant with the more elusive forces of nature.
>
> (ix)

But while zoos represent our compulsion to connect somehow with animals (or, through animals, to nature), they simultaneously embody the frustration inherent in that attempt. For zoo animals, life is manifestly constricted, and by all apparent indications – whether we acknowledge or repress this – unnatural. Ironically, their helpless entrapment may make zoo animals all the more fitting as emblems of the modernist anxiety that pervades human social life. In Duncan Smith's graphic art exhibition 'Images of Captive Animals,' the text frames zoo animals as types of a troubled contemporary *Zeitgeist*:

> Refugees from Nature.
>
> Mad mutant descendants of real animals who die with the destruction of their world.
>
> Zoo animals leave us in the nuclear age with images of extinction.
>
> (42)

'The eyes of an animal when they consider a man are attentive and wary,' writes John Berger (2). Animals are oblivious to our social culture, except when they are undone by us. They are affected, by and large, only negatively by the achievements of which people are so proud. Their obliviousness to human exploits may heighten people's sadistic compulsion to master them, to keep them in captivity. If animals in nature taunt people with their innocence and freedom, zoos represent people's revenge. Our primordial admiration for their power and beauty manifests itself, ironically, as a desire to exercise control over them: to implicate (and then capture, transform, destroy) them in our systems, structures, poetics, epistemologies.

Animals have fallen along with us – by our own doing – and fallen even further than we have. In the wild, people drive species after species to extinction; and in civilization, people capture and breed species after species to embellish zoos. Both zoos and zoo stories exert human control over animals. The feelings that come out of the interaction between people and animals manifest themselves in many different ways: love and admiration for the animal kingdom, and an idealistic sense of its magnificence; resentful determination to drag animals down to our level; empathy, as their increasingly degraded habitats and conditions offer a reflection of our own existence; pathos, when we displace our failures onto them and implicate them in the state of the troubled modern ecosystem. Zoos are neat paradigms, metaphors, not for animals but for *our* animals: for what people have done with them and to them; how we value them; and most essentially, how we observe them, and what this process shows about how we perceive ourselves to relate to them. The Renaissance age of imperialism made it economically, historically, and morally possible to amass animals and squeeze them into the compartments people created for them. The Victorian age accelerated, institutionalized, and sanctified the processes of zookeeping and zoo spectatorship. In our own time, we must confront the ramifications of all this.

In reading zoos, I will present a dialectic that contrasts, on one side, the restricting and artificial appraisals of nature offered within the popular cultural institution of zoos, and, on the other side, the imaginatively incisive and provocative examinations of zoos in literature. It is significant how often – almost always – zoo stories condemn zoos. With striking consistency zoos are seen, literally or metaphorically, as places of cruelty, deadened sensibility. At least, this is what most zoo stories seem to indicate to me – at times I wonder if I have projected my own prejudices too strongly, but I think my range of evidence bears out my interpretations. What are the implications of these aesthetic sensibilities so pervasively antithetical to zoos? Perhaps some people do indeed consider zoos to be fine, palatable places, but do not develop or broadcast their ideas in any culturally expressive medium, simply attending the zoo regularly – and only when the idea of zoos riles someone does the emotion enter into art. Or perhaps, as I believe, the broadly antagonistic cultural representations of zoos indicate that some of the most sensitive, incisive members of society (cultural producers) generally find zoos tawdry, unpalatable, dangerous.

For centuries, writers have decried the constraint of animals.

In the fourteenth century, Geoffrey Chaucer's *The Manciple's Tale* imagines animals' craving for freedom from human control:

> God it woot, ther may no man embrace
> As to destreyne a thyng which that nature
> Hath natureelly set in a creature.
>   Taak any bryd, and put it in a cage,
> And do al thyn entente and thy corage
> To fostre it tendrely with mete and drynke
> Of alle deyntees that thou kanst bithynke,
> And keep it al so clenly as thou may,
> Although his cage of gold be never so gay,
> Yet hath this brid, by twenty thousand foold,
> Levere in a forest, that is rude and coold,
> Goon ete wormes and swich wrecchednesse.
> For evere this brid wol doon his bisynesse
> To escape out of this cage, yif he may.
> His libertee this brid desireth ay.
>
> (225–6)

In Sarah Scott's *Millenium Hall* (1762), a gentleman visiting a communal asylum of women sees an enclosure which reminds him of another he had once seen that contained 'lions, tygers, leopards, and such foreign animals'; he wishes to view the women's enclosure because 'nothing gave him greater entertainment than to behold those beautiful wild beasts, brought out of their native woods, where they had reigned as kings, and here tamed and subjected by the superior art of man. It was a triumph of human reason, which could not fail to afford great pleasure' (22). His hostess rebukes him, informing that her enclosure does not contain animals, and their community finds such captivity repugnant:

> to see a man, from a vain desire to have in his possession the native of another climate and another country, reduce a fine and noble creature to misery, and confine him within narrow enclosures whose happiness consisted in unbounded liberty, shocks my nature . . . Every thing to me looses its charm when it is put out of that station wherein nature, or to speak more properly, the all-wise Creator has placed it. I imagine man has a right to use the animal race for his own preservation, perhaps

for his convenience, but certainly not to treat them with wanton cruelty... it is, in my opinion, criminal to enslave them, in order to procure ourselves a vain amusement, if we have so little feeling as to find any while others suffer.

(23)

Leigh Hunt, in *A Saunter through the West End*, derides animal captivity in the nineteenth century:

> Why can we have Acts of Parliament in favour of other extension of good treatment to the brute creation, and not one against their tormenting imprisonment? At all events, we may ask meantime, and perhaps not uselessly even for present purposes whether a great people, under a still finer aspect of knowledge and civilization than at present, would think themselves warranted in keeping *any* set of fellow-creatures in a state of endless captivity – their faculties contradicted, their very lives, for the most part, turned into lingering deaths?
>
> (In Altick, 318)

Thomas Hardy writes in a 1913 letter to *The Times*: 'It seems marvellous that the 20th century, with all its rhetoric on morality, should tolerate such useless inflictions as making animals do what is unnatural to them, or drag out life in a wired cell' (in Lutwack, 154). Hardy was always, as here, adept at identifying the 'marvellous,' the ironic, the dissonant, the *crux* of our spiritual, moral, and social existence. Along with Hardy, I marvel at the idea of zoos in our modern world, and, further, marvel at those who marvel at them.

Describing the eclectic Bloomsbury atmosphere in which she lived and worked, Virginia Woolf writes in a 1920 letter to Barbara Bagenal, 'Gordon Square is like nothing so much as the lions house at the Zoo. One goes from cage to cage. All the animals are dangerous, rather suspicious of each other, and full of fascination and mystery. I'm sometimes too timid to go in, and trail along the pavement, looking in at the windows' (451). Confronting this passage early in my research, I felt compelled to establish a praxis: how would I use such cultural artifacts and evidence in the service of studying zoos? This quotation struck me as obviously interesting, worthy of examination, but what exactly would I do with it? What does it mean? What do I make it mean? Woolf's characterization of a scene, of her milieu, is – as typically – biting. Leon Edel found it so incisive that he titled his biographical survey of the Bloomsbury Group *A House of Lions*. The cultural presence and impact of zoos in early twentieth-century England certainly inform Woolf's observations – but *how*, exactly?

What was Woolf's attitude toward zoos? Another self-referential zoo metaphor appears in a 1912 letter to Leonard Woolf, when she was in a convalescent home recuperating, slowly, from a breakdown: 'I now feel very clear, calm, and move slowly, like one of the great big animals at the zoo' (in Bell, 1.183). Her letters indicate she visited the Regent's Park Zoo regularly.[7] To her sister, Vanessa Bell, in a letter of 19 May 1926 she uses a zoo reference again, as in her 'lions house' image, to describe her friends with animal symbolism: at the opera, she met 'Ralph and Frances, connubial, furtive; James and Noel, both grey as badgers and sleek as moles (I have just been to the Zoo, and noted these facts accurately.)'

But what do all her metaphors have to do with zoos? The connection is, admittedly, tangential: Woolf was appraising the emotional pulse of her own Bloomsbury life, not zoos, in these various letters. Yet I feel confident that these references are in some way relevant to my study; that they are, somehow, zoo stories. I derive these connections less from contemporary New Historicist theory than from Woolf herself, who spent seven years writing a novel, originally titled *The Pargiters*, and collecting newspaper clippings as part of her work on that project, in the conviction that there was some connection between art and the parade of ideas, facts, and observations that float around in the real world. She eventually separated *The Pargiters* into two entities, the novel *The Years* and the essay *Three Guineas*. In *Three Guineas* she demonstrated how an artist can bring together disparate data, incidents, sensibilities – plumbed generously and idiosyncratically from a swath of the outside world (outside of art, that is) – to make an argumentative case. (Her argument, that war is bad and that it is avoidable, was monumentally important when she published *Three Guineas* in 1937.) Woolf inspires my belief that documentary material from different cultural genres can be brought together productively in the examination of a single topic. Before New Historicism, Woolf showed how the writer can arrange and contextualize the tangential (or, what the subjective determinants of norms and centrality *posit* as tangential) to offer pertinent intellectual analysis. Her process of creation delineates common ground between art and polemic social criticism, and this common ground is, in some ways, both unified and disparate (as Woolf's enterprise began as a unified one in *The Pargiters* but ended as two separate works). In my own writing, I acknowledge a similar ambivalence: the concerns of art and of real life at times will coalesce with a common interest, and at other times will diverge. But they will always remain close, interrelated, and part of the same overall enterprise.[8]

Woolf's thoughts on zoos, while they appear quietly, offhandedly, are nevertheless resonant. Indeed, several sources I will examine present zoos in 'scraps, orts and fragments' (a phrase Woolf uses in *Between the Acts* to connote the overwhelming and often minimally comprehensible panorama of sensory data with which the world bombards us). Some of this material seems more like a fleeting glimpse than a sustained deliberation about zoos; Woolf's occasional epistolary allusions are provocative, elusive, and disappointingly – unless I have missed a reference – hardly reiterated or developed at all in her fiction. Her first novel, *The Voyage Out* (1915), contains a few passing mentions of zoos. When the shipboard party admires two British warships nearby, one woman dissents from the patriotic chorus: 'no one liked it when Helen remarked that it seemed to her as wrong to keep sailors as to keep a Zoo' (69). The implication casually condemns. Later in that novel, the zoo trope appears when Woolf uses unattractive images of captive animals to invoke (as in her letters) an ominous characterization of an assemblage of people. A character watching residents in a South American English colony read their mail observes that their silence

> reminded him of the silence in the lion-house when each beast holds a lump of raw meat in its paws. He went on, stimulated by this comparison, to liken some to hippopotamuses, some to canary birds, some to swine, some to parrots, and some to loathsome reptiles curled round the half-decayed bodies of sheep. The intermittent sounds – now a cough, now a horrible wheezing or throat-clearing, now a little patter of conversation – were just, he declared, what you hear if you stand in the lion-house when the bones are being mauled.
>
> (177)

And in *To the Lighthouse* (1927), as the blundering Victorian patriarch emotionally harasses his family, a brief zoo reference connotes his behavior as ridiculous and disjunctive:

> Already ashamed of that petulance, of that gesticulation of the hands when charging at the head of his troops, Mr. Ramsay rather sheepishly prodded his son's bare legs once more, and then, as if he had her leave for it, with a movement which oddly reminded his wife of the great sea lion at the Zoo tumbling backwards after swallowing his fish and walloping off so that the water in the tank washes from side to side, he dived into the evening air.
>
> (51–2)

People who behave like zoo animals in Woolf's prose appear mean, awkward, unnatural; it seems reasonable to infer that she associates these traits and conditions with zoos *per se*.

However evanescent, Woolf's zoo references confirm the point – perhaps obvious but important – that zoos are metaphorical: more than just pleasure for children, or education about animals. Of course, in the mind of a great artist, everything is potentially metaphorical; one of the things I attempt to discover is what *kinds* of metaphorical opportunities zoos present. A zoo is like . . . what? What makes an artist turn to a zoo, use a zoo, to describe . . . what, about the world around her? (Yet while I eagerly grapple with Woolf's aesthetic implementation of zoo imagery, I acknowledge also Berger's warning against semiotic overdetermination: 'it is both too easy and too evasive to use the zoo as a symbol. The zoo is a demonstration of the relation between man and animals; nothing else' (24). The essential facts of artificiality and marginalization of animals are so omnipotent, Berger feels, that zoos, and those who culturally recycle zoos, cannot transcend these facts by entering into the realm of metaphor.)

Woolf's sporadic mentions of zoos give a sense of what she thought about them, how she transformed them in her mind, and how they could serve figuratively in her writing. Here as throughout her oeuvre, Woolf is prolifically suggestive of the range of emotions that an experience generates as it resonates in her mind: the zoo and Bloomsbury for her are linked through their embodiment of danger, suspicion, fascination, mystery. She describes herself both as actively in control of her observation

('One goes from cage to cage') and also, contradictorily, as overwhelmed and disempowered ('I'm sometimes too timid to go in, and trail along the pavement, looking in at the windows'). Several of her zoo figurations connote, metaphorically, the rich yet ambivalent panoply of sensations she found in the human social culture that surrounded her – in which people were various, exotic, striking, remarkable as spectacles, and yet, at the same time, menacing; somehow inherently (or at least potentially) antisocial, even violent; profoundly constrained, and much worse off as social creatures for this unnatural constraint. I infer that Woolf saw in zoos, as she saw in the people inhabiting her world, an array of creatures full of marvelous potential, but subsisting in conditions that destined them to remain far from actualizing that potential.

In her 'lions house' simile, did Woolf draw the parallel between the society that surrounded her most closely (her treasured and inspirational coterie of friends) and a very different world (the animal assembly on display at the zoo) because the zoo really did seem so similar to her stimulating and tumultuously exotic Bloomsbury milieu, as she overtly informs Bagenal? Or is she being lightly ironic, coy, in comparing her intellectual circle (not exempting herself) to a less flattering group of mammals – dumb, caged zoo animals, as some people regard them – perhaps meaning to bring the human beings down a peg? Woolf's reactions both to the zoo and to Bloomsbury (the latter, of course, documented copiously elsewhere) are paradoxical, complicated, sometimes inconsistent. Love/hate is too simple: but there are definitely pulls of attraction and sources of threat that Woolf felt in her circle, for which she finds the zoo an apt analogue. Woolf sees the zoo as a fascinating, stimulating place to visit and experience, but also as perilous: 'All the animals are dangerous.' When she described herself as feeling like a zoo animal during her convalescence, she was attempting to convey an image of the mostly unspeakable fear, pain, and horror she associated with her periods of collapse and dull, laborious recovery.

Who cares, finally, what Virginia Woolf thought about zoos? Well, add to this thoughts about zoos in the works of Edward Albee, Eugene O'Neill, Sylvia Plath, Ted Hughes, Marianne Moore, Rainer Maria Rilke, Isaac Babel, Jean Stafford, William Carlos Williams, John Hawkes, Franz Kafka, Clarice Lispector, Alberto Moravia, E. F. Benson, James Dickey, e. e. cummings, and dozens more (whose zoo stories I examine), and we have a collection of appraisals of how a famous, talented, and influential group of writers – indeed, one of the oddest literary assemblies imaginable, more power to it – regard zoos. To put it simply, I believe the considerable array of zoo stories I have found scattered throughout modern culture compels us to modify how we ourselves might think about zoos. This, at least, represents my ideal formulation of the point of art. As further justification for using cultural documents to argue a case about the real world institution of zoos and the nature of animals, I cite Marian Scholtmeijer's hypothesis in *Animal Victims in Modern Fiction*:

> Literature has caught the effects of the new status of animals in advance of other fields of thought. While even the most up-to-date among the sciences continue to view animals as inferior beings, and philosophers and anthropologists continue to deprecate them in order to assert human eminence, modern literature treats animals as a genuine problem. In modern literature . . . animals contend with the conceptual devices that seek to subsume them. Their resistance to enculturation influences the nature and profundity of the difficulties literature addresses. In fiction, animals steer the course of events into imaginative complications upon which human powers of resolution falter. In fiction, animal victims do not die passively; they fight back by creating dilemmas that surpass human control. They impress their reality upon narrative, not by the stability but by the instability of their presence. They refuse to be incorporated neatly into the cultural field.
>
> (8)

Scholtmeijer does not explicitly discuss zoo animals as examples of animal victims, but I find her theoretical construct here highly applicable to my study. Like me, she laments the deleterious consequences of people's control over animals, and she turns to culture to examine and critique our treatment of animals.

In her introduction to *The Animal Estate: The English and Other Creatures in the Victorian Age* – another valuable source for my own work – Harriet Ritvo writes that she finds literature minimally applicable or useful in her examination of animals in nineteenth-century English society. Her book presents 'interpretations based primarily on texts produced by people who dealt with real animals – the records of organizations concerned with breeding, veterinary medicine, agriculture, natural history, and the like; the papers of individuals active in such pursuits; and the books, pamphlets, and periodicals produced for these specialized audiences. Canonical art and literature have provided only occasional corroborative examples' (4). I focus more enthusiastically than Ritvo on canonical art and literature, as well as popular culture. The fact that, unlike Ritvo, I find this material so rich in providing 'corroborative examples' for my critical analysis, signifies a subtle but crucial difference in our approaches. Her book focuses on the images and issues surrounding animals themselves – the condition of animals amid human culture. Mine, instead, considers people's cultural appropriation and transposition of animals. Ritvo prioritizes animals in her consideration of how animals function in human culture, while I am more interested in the effects upon human culture in this interaction. Thus, I find cultural documents about people and captive animals more useful than the primary source accounts that Ritvo studies. If, at times, I situate myself at some distance from the zoo itself – more so than in other humanist-oriented studies of zoos such as those by Ritvo, Altick, Mullan and Marvin, Jamieson, and Bostock – that is because my subject is cultural representations of zoos rather than zoos *per se*. But the analytic perspective zoo stories afford is nevertheless keenly relevant to what I regard as the problem of zoos.

Numerous other writers present portrayals of the zoo Woolf visited, which provide a useful and interesting context for her zoo imagery. The Regent's Park Zoo, in central London, is naturally prominent in zoo stories throughout the English literary tradition. Sylvia Plath, who wrote 'Zoo Keeper's Wife,' lived near Regent's Park and visited often, as did Louis MacNeice, whose book *Zoo* recounts his sojourns there. The London Zoo also features in Brigid Brophy's *Hackenfeller's Ape*, Angus Wilson's *The Old Men at the Zoo*, Margaret Drabble's *The Waterfall*, David Garnett's *A Man in the Zoo*, Saki's 'The Mappined Life,' and Russell Hoban's *Turtle Diary* (in which the aquarium housing the turtles lies directly underneath the Mappin Terraces portrayed in Saki's story). In Osamu Dazai's short story 'Monkey Island,' the London Zoo metaphorically represents Western imperial exploitation of Japan. Stevie Smith's poem 'The Zoo' features a lion pathetically caged in the heart of London, and another lion, escaped from its cage, confronts the protagonist of William Sansom's story 'Among the Dahlias' as he walks through Regent's Park – terrorizing him not because it springs but because it considers attacking and finally decides not to, leaving the unmauled spectator feeling isolated, undesirable, and dull. A more classic brand of terror emanates from the London Zoo in Bram Stoker's *Dracula*, when the Count appropriates from Regent's Park a grey wolf to accompany and assist the bloodsucker (himself in the guise of a wolf) as he invades the home of his victim. A polar bear from the London Zoo named Winnie inspired A. A. Milne's childhood classic, which opens with a rhapsodic introduction about the pleasures of visiting one's favorite animal in that zoo. E. F. Benson, on the other hand, begins his essay 'The Zoo' with the observation, 'Some of the saddest sights that I know in the saddest city of all the world, our English London, are to be seen at the Zoological Gardens' (153). In Jan Struther's *Mrs. Miniver*, Badger makes an outing to the Regent's Park Zoo 'to go and look at creatures who only behave grotesquely because they can't help it' (165). The profusion of zoo stories I discuss which are set at this zoo indicates, in part, my own reading habits and background; beyond this, however, it seems logical that the zoo in the heart of the city that was at the heart of the British Empire would play such a prominent role in zoo stories. Imperialist tendencies and sensibilities are at least indirectly (and often intimately) linked with the institution of zoos and zoo spectatorship – so it is no wonder that English literature abounds in this subject, and that the Regent's Park Zoo should feature so prominently. (Whipsnade, the larger suburban zoo that the London Zoological Society opened in the 1930s, appears, by comparison, very minimally in cultural representations.[9])

It is informative to compare and contrast Woolf's image with passages from other zoo stories set in the same part of the same zoo. We may get a clearer sense of what Woolf thinks and intends when she refers to the zoo – a wider, richer perspective – by looking at how other writers reacted to the Regent's Park lion house; we can begin to sense the congruities and interrelatedness of zoo stories. In *Zoo* (1938), MacNeice offers two descriptive accounts:

> Of the older buildings in the South Garden the nicest is the Lion House, finished in 1876, whose long stretch inside suggests a railway station. It is austere without being in any way slick.

> The animals, behind their heavy bars, sail past on only one side of the platform. A heavy cast-iron barrier keeps the visitors clear of the cages. On the other side, above two or three tiers of steps, are waiting-room benches for the public. Dark green tiles and shabby black bricks give an appropriate sombreness. There is no attempt to suggest that this is a jolly place, no euphemism, no glossing over the fact that this is a prison. This house is sure in time to be replaced – by something probably more on the Hagenbeck principle, more light, no bars. This will be much better for the animals (those in the indoor cages do not get nearly enough light or fresh air while the outdoor cages unfortunately face north), but I doubt if the visitors will get the same authentic impression of the big cat as enemy and victim – almost what Aristotle would call 'the pleasure proper to tragedy.'
>
> (54–6)

> [T]he Lion House (for it is cheap day) is crammed with people in mackintoshes . . . The place smells like the Underground. The floor of the house is wet and covered with litter – torn newspapers, brown apple-cores, peanut shells, red wrappers from bars of chocolate, tiny wooden spoons for ice cream. Prams and push-carts jostle . . . a sharp-faced mother curses her three children: 'You'll be sick in a moment; sit down and keep still.'
>
> (168)

Considering that MacNeice's book is mostly effusive about the London Zoo, these passages are surprisingly dreary.

John Galsworthy's *The Man of Property* (1906) places old Jolyon Forsyte at the same site; Galsworthy offers a more sociological appraisal of the scene than MacNeice, and a more extensive descriptive appraisal than Woolf's condensed, stylized, subjective images. All three passages combine to help develop a multi-perspectival appreciation of a single zoo venue (and of various possible ways writers may 'use' it). 'From the stone terrace above the bear-pit his son and his two grandchildren came hastening down when they saw old Jolyon coming, and led him away towards the lion-house' (148). The Forsyte clan gathers at the zoo, which serves them as an enclave of class elitism. '"Let's go to the Zoo," they had said to each other; "it'll be great fun!" It was a shilling day [when higher admission is charged]; and there would not be all those common people' (149). The animals are unappetizing ('tawny, ravenous beasts behind the bars . . . "That's a nasty-looking brute, that tiger!"') and Galsworthy sees the spectators as similarly degraded, suggesting that zoos drag both animals and human visitors down to a low common denominator of festering hostility. Spectators assume the worst of animals' natures, and imbue the caged beasts with their own human deficiencies and sordid drives:

> A well-fed man in a white waistcoat said slowly through his teeth: 'It's all greed; they can't be hungry. Why, they take no exercise.' At these words, a tiger snatched a piece of bleeding liver, and the fat man laughed. His wife, in a Paris-model frock and gold nose-nippers, reproved him: 'How can you laugh, Harry? Such a horrid sight!'
>
> (149)

Animals' most innocuous natural behavior, eating, becomes colored with the depravity spectators impute to it. Such attitudes belie the educational value imputed to zoos: Galsworthy suggests that visitors do not learn, or observe openmindedly at zoos, but rather distort whatever they see there to conform with their preconceptions and prejudices.[10]

The zoo, thus, brings out pretention and distrust. Harry ('hairy,' like the 'brutes' behind bars?) himself represents a type of the 'animal' he derides in the cage – fat, well-fed, presumably greedy and indolent – although he represses recognition of such affinities. Galsworthy's irony implies that Harry's own behavior is likely more blameworthy than the tiger's. The animal eats simply because it is hungry; it is not fat, but tawny. Mired in our own depravities, the decadent, hypocritical social condition that Galsworthy lambastes, people insultingly attribute our own faults to those we abase in the drive to satisfy our spectatorial, elitist cravings. This paradigm recurs often in literary representations of zoos. The animals cannot protest their characterizations, or their being forced to carry the weight of our vices and shortcomings – thus they serve all the better as scapegoats, or objects for our scorn that passes as enlightened educational interest. Harry's laughter emphasizes the cruel delight coloring this insidious scenario.

Galsworthy's zoo provides a forum for Victorians such as old

Jolyon and Harry to expose their stupidity, and for more thoughtful, sensitive, enlightened, *modern* young men like young Jolyon Forsyte (and Galsworthy's ideal reader) to express their sardonic and superior intelligence. Like Woolf, Galsworthy uses the zoo as a way to appraise the world around him, and different ways of reacting to it. Young Jolyon enacts the generational conflict in *The Man of Property* by protesting against the values of his father and those of Harry's sensibility. He revolts against the station into which he was born, the elitists who flock to the zoo on shilling day: 'the class to which he had belonged – the carriage class – especially excited his sarcasm' (150); and he employs this sarcasm to denigrate the institution of the zoo and implicitly those who, like well-fed Harry, enjoy the lion house as a validation of their own prejudices about the barbarity of the other.

> To shut up a lion or tiger in confinement was surely a horrible barbarity. But no cultivated person would admit this.
>
> The idea of its being barbarous to confine wild animals had probably never even occurred to his father, for instance; he belonged to the old school, who considered it at once humanizing and educational to confine baboons and panthers, holding the view, no doubt, that in course of time they might induce these creatures not so unreasonably to die of misery and heartsickness against the bars of their cages, and put the society to the expense of getting others! In his eyes, as in the eyes of all Forsytes, the pleasure of seeing these beautiful creatures in a state of captivity far outweighed the inconvenience of imprisonment to beasts whom God had so improvidently placed in a state of freedom! It was for the animals' good, removing them at once from the countless dangers of open air and exercise, and enabling them to exercise their functions in the guaranteed seclusion of a private compartment! Indeed, it was doubtful what wild animals were made for but to be shut up in cages!
>
> (150)

Galsworthy connotes zoos as barbarous not just for the literal treatment of animals but also for the implicitly ingrained cruelty of human keepers and spectators that the scene elicits.[11] People imprison animals, and pretend that they are bettering themselves by such actions. They even try to rationalize that they are doing the animals a favor by bringing them into their own society, under the aegis of their own human institutions. The zoo in this episode is just one of the vehicles Galsworthy uses throughout his novels to lampoon what he sees as lame social institutions. His zoo audiences' rationalizations eerily parallel the rationalizations of those who took slaves as prisoners back to their own cultures and pretended they were acting for the betterment of those victims, removing them from their 'primitive' and 'barbaric' natural habitats which slaveholders characterized as inferior to even the lowest rung of supposedly enlightened and civilized society.

The image of the zookeeper as a type of the benevolent slaveowner recurs throughout zoo stories – as, for instance, in *The Old Men at the Zoo*, when a curator says of his animals, 'By making them captive we take their welfare on our shoulders for good and all. Otherwise we've no right to deprive them of freedom'; and his director responds, 'have you ever thought how damned lucky the animals are that fall into the hands of the [London Zoological] Society? . . . No ghastly search for scarce food or water in times of drought! No relentless native huntsmen! No jungle rivalry! No old age, tracked down, feeble and desperate!' (245–6). And again in Marie Nimier's *The Giraffe*, the zoo director 'considered zoo-raised animals to be privileged creatures, freed from the challenges of survival and adapting perfectly to the constraints imposed on them. He maintained that the elephant or the chimpanzee had every chance of living a better life behind bars than left to themselves in a natural setting' (68). In *The Dreaded Comparison: Human and Animal Slavery*, Marjorie Spiegel writes that both animals and human slaves have suffered 'moral disqualification on the basis of reason [i.e., the supposed lack of rational faculties] . . . For centuries, black people were called "irrational," and this was used as a reason to both continue their "protective custody" (in the form of slavery) and to open them up to virtually limitless abuse' (23). She finds a common pattern in historical Western attitudes toward animals and disempowered human cultures: 'the oppression of animals . . . was in many cases used as a prototype for the oppression of blacks' (25).

'But what if Jacob never gets to Africa to see a real giraffe?' my mother asks, worrying that her grandson will be imaginatively deprived as a result of his parents' eccentric cultural dogma. If Jacob never gets to Africa, then perhaps indeed he will never get to see a giraffe. I don't know what's so horrible about never seeing a giraffe – throughout time, billions of people have endured that fate, with no evident detriment. Even if my son did go to the zoo, he would still not see what I consider to be a real giraffe, but rather a cultural stylization, simplification, distillation, of a giraffe; a sample of giraffe; a (stinted) representation of a giraffe. Teaching children about animals in the zoo is like exposing them to human cultural and ethnic diversity via Epcot's World Showcase Pavilion. I do not agree unilaterally, as Mullan and Marvin claim, that 'animals are human constructions' (3); however, their observation accurately describes zoo animals. Mullan and Marvin continue:

> This is not to suggest that they are not real physical entities living in a real physical world, but rather to emphasize they are also man-made in the sense that they are thought about by man, and it is the animal as it is thought about rather than the animal itself which is of significance. Animals . . . certainly do not represent themselves to human viewers. It is man who defines and represents them, and he can in no sense claim to achieve a true representation of any particular animal; it merely reflects his own concerns.
>
> (3)

(Greenblatt's model of the social relation of production elucidates these 'concerns,' and the unexamined problematics of mimetic representation in zoos.) Marian Scholtmeijer, too, writes, 'cultural history reveals that conceptions of nonhuman animals have wandered erratically from one extreme to another' and 'each conception, as it emerges, represents itself as the comprehensive truth of the animal' (3). She concludes that these conceptions must be cultural constructs, and that animals 'are the "blank paper" on which human beings write messages to themselves' (94). And e. e. cummings, in an essay called 'The Secret of the Zoo Exposed,' wonders whether people have ever thought

> that what we are accustomed to call 'animals' are in reality living mirrors, reflecting otherwise unsuspected aspects of our own human character? . . . let us try to understand the zoo as

> a concatenation of differently functioning and variously labelled mirrors, all of which are *alive*. These living mirrors, mistakenly called 'animals,' are for the most part grouped in systems or 'houses,' like the 'bird house' and the 'monkey house,' and each house or system furnishes us with some particular verdict upon ourselves. In passing from house to house, from one system of mirrors to another system of mirrors, we discover totally unsuspected aspects of our own existence. At every turn we are amused, perplexed, horrified or dumbfounded. No mere spectacle of monsters, however extraordinary, could so move us. The truth is, not that we see monsters, but that we *are* monsters!
>
> (78–80)

Zoos are not a microcosm of the natural world but an antithesis to it. Scholtmeijer describes 'the physical and mental distance from nature' that began with eighteenth-century progressive urbanization, and the consequent diminution of cultural imaginative faculties (betokened by the avatars of zoos) that this distancing generated: a 'primitive intimacy' with animals was 'past recall. The strange animal monsters of legend shrank drastically to the menagerie's placid and no doubt sickly beasts confined to small cages and displayed for the amusement of the public' (18–19). John Berger, too, relates the way animals are culturally regarded today to the disappearance of a past familiarity and intimacy with animals. 'Public zoos came into existence at the beginning of the period which was to see the disappearance of animals from daily life. The zoo to which people go to meet animals, to observe them, to see them, is, in fact, a monument to the impossibility of such encounters' (19). Jim Mason calls the zoo 'a relic of a nature-alienated culture' (255), noting that as early as the Middle Ages, 'While feudal Europe set about destroying its native wildlife to protect its crops and to advance its efforts with domestic animal breeding, it grew more and more fascinated with bizarre animals from other lands. Jugglers, minstrels, mountebanks, and other itinerant entertainers roved from town to town with their performing leopards, bears, and monkeys' (254–5). Harriet Ritvo describes how 'the defining symbolism' of nineteenth-century zoos emphasized their detachment from natural realities:

It was implicit in the very composition and structure of a collection. Animals that roved free and often dangerous in their native wilds were confined in small cages and placed along well-marked paths, in manicured parks... The horticultural displays that routinely adorned the borders... emphasized the artificiality of the setting, as did the man-made lakes... [Guidebooks] implicitly structured visitors' experience of the gardens. No matter what the shape of the zoo they described, nineteenth-century guidebooks were inveterately linear, prescribing a single route through the exhibits, from the entrance to the refreshment stand. Thus, in their physical design, zoos reenacted and celebrated the imposition of human structure on the threatening chaos of nature.

(217–18)

And similarly, today, zoos remain ineluctably ensconced in human culture to the exclusion of nature; they are, as Alexander Wilson writes, 'models of relations between human cultures and the natural world' – rather than models of the natural world itself (246). He explains how distant contemporary zoos are from nature, offering a modern variant (but essentially an identical reiteration) of what Ritvo characterized as nineteenth-century zoos' implication in human culture:

Today the physical plant of a zoo typically includes electrical transformers and generators, water softeners and dechlorinators, pumping stations, kitchens and commissaries, nurseries, ponding systems, sewers, and boilers. Like the infrastructures of theme parks or shopping malls, these internal workings have themselves become part of the experience of the zoo. On the monorail ride that takes visitors around the Metro Toronto Zoo, for example, narration on the P. A. offers a long list of statistics: how large the zoo is, how many tons of horse meat, fish, and mosquitoes are fed to the animals every year, the capacity of the polar bear swimming tank, the size (in football fields) of the giraffe compound.

(247)

Wildlife becomes an artificial construction as presented within zoo culture, Scholtmeijer writes: the world seems '"man-made";

people could regard in safety a mute Nature' (19). Cosmetic variations on nineteenth-century zoo design have made the artifice of zoos less apparent today: guidebooks may seem more interactive, less authoritarian; landscaping may more closely approximate stereotypes of 'natural habitats'; paths are made to appear less manicured, more ruddy. But the overarching sensibility Ritvo describes – the authoritarian imposition of a human structure on a 'threatening' nature – is essentially unchanged in today's zoos, which offer the comforting delusion that we have mastered and subdued the aspects of the world that threaten us.

A significant part of what an animal is involves its context, its natural state, which zoos cannot provide. I think Jacob can have a better imagination, a better appreciation of the multifaceted magnificence of nature and animals, by not seeing a zoo's giraffe than by seeing one. One *can* understand and respect something without seeing it. One can imagine a giraffe; one can read about a giraffe. But any enriching experience sought from the too easy facilitation of a zoo encounter is likely to be elusive. It is immensely important that Jacob and every other four-year-old learn about animals: how they live and behave, what their relationship to people is, how they are like and unlike us, what we can learn from them, what they contribute to the ecosystem, what dangers threaten them, how close they may be to extinction. It is, indeed, more crucial today than it ever has been before that all people, and especially children, learn about the real conditions of animals, for two reasons – one cultural, and one ecological.

First, unfortunate cultural attitudes from the past toward animals are becoming more firmly entrenched than ever. Cultural history – a sense of how people have traditionally reacted to the world around us – is evaporating, inundated by the prodigious profusion of sanitized, hegemonic novelty that hurtles down the information superhighway. Jacob's generation may never, for example, experience first-hand a main street shopping district, and the sense of community and individual agency it embodies; or an influential local newspaper, and the sense of informed public awareness that written language used to convey before the postliterate era; or a variety of regional milieus, rather than a homogeneous interstate culture, in the landscape that one traverses to get from one place to another. The mall will enter into the realm of what Jacob's peers perceive as 'always already'; the infinite immediacy of CNN will subsume the diversity of local opinion and cultural nuance; and an awareness of gradation, differentiation, heterogeneity in Americans' sense of place will disappear. To today's children, I fear zoo animals may seem completely detached from real animal existence; simply perceived en masse as a bounty of zoo-capital; alienated from any inherent and unique place of habitat; implacably institutionalized within their own zoo-mall. Alvin Toffler argues in *Future Shock* that rapid, absolute change characterized by complete dissociation from the past is culturally, socially, and intellectually hazardous. Consequently, zoos, as elements of popular culture (enmeshed in rapidly and arbitrarily changing currents) are unreliable repositories. Wild animals cannot be effectively preserved or sustained amid our cultural whirlpools – as Paul Goldberger terms it, a 'popular cultural [that] is literally devouring itself, a maw that grinds all in its path.'[12]

Throughout our cultural existence, animals have always been immensely important. Mason laments the fact that few people

> seem to understand how essential animals are to human beings, how they are the most vital beings in nature – the soul and the moving parts of nature. Animals represent and symbolize the various features and forces of nature. They have always fed the human mind and culture; they have given us the means of understanding the cosmos. When seen as kin, as they once were, animals gave us a crucial bond and sense of belonging to the living world . . . We simply will not be able to come to terms with nature unless we come to terms with animals and animality, because, for the human mind and culture, animals are the most important part of nature.
>
> (12–13)

Berger amplifies the significance of animals in human art: 'The first subject matter for painting was animal. Probably the first paint was animal blood. Prior to that, it is not unreasonable to suppose that the first metaphor was animal' (5). Elizabeth Atwood Lawrence writes of people's innate need for animals, citing Edward O. Wilson's belief 'that human beings exhibit biophilia, an inherent tendency to focus on and affiliate with other forms of life. If he is right – and there is considerable evidence to support his hypothesis – human relationships with animals take place at the most fundamental level of our existence'; and she suggests that because of the depth of this relationship, 'the bond we share with animals may be comprehended more clearly through poetry than science' (185). John Elder advances that point when he writes, 'poetry is in ecological terms the *edge* between mankind and nonhuman nature, providing an access for culture into a world beyond its preconceptions' (210). The 2,500 entries in Robert A. Palmatier's *Speaking of Animals: A Dictionary of Animal Metaphors* testify to the enduring potency of animal imagery as a vehicle for figurative expression in contemporary language and culture. It is impossible to overstate the cultural importance of knowing animals *in authentic ways*. The more pervasive zoos become as a mediating institution between people and animals, the more impoverishment and degradation we can expect to characterize any of our numerous cultural practices that interact with the realm of animals. Our track record with regard to the preservation and appreciation of subtle cultural experiences is not a good one; and zoos are predominantly influenced by the sphere of popular culture *as opposed to* that of nature. If we accept that the curators of animals are in the camp of the forces that have created Blockbuster Video and Disney World, Mall of America and Pizza Hut as our cultural venues, we (not to mention the animals) are in trouble.

The second reason it is crucial to learn about the real conditions of animals is the impending prospect of what some have termed a human geocide. Immediate, widespread, and *enlightened* reeducation is necessary, and most urgently for Americans, who are most abusive of the ecosystem.[13] 'To start from the soil again is the task, when human culture has become impoverished,' writes Elder (40). We have dire need of a crash course on how to treat the world, how to behave toward its components. We must confront the challenge Greta Gaard proposes for ecofeminism: 'As the human species approaches the capacity to annihilate all life on this planet, it becomes imperative that we challenge both the ideological assumptions and the hierarchical structures of power and domination that together serve to hold the majority of the earth's inhabitants in thrall to the privileged minority' (10). Similarly, Janis Birkeland writes, 'the sources of the environmental crisis are deeply rooted in modern culture, and therefore fundamental social transformation is necessary if we are to preserve life on earth in any meaningful sense' (13). Lawrence Buell (quoting Vice President Al Gore) assumes as a contemporary commonplace 'the reasonableness of the claim that "we must make the rescue of the environment the central organizing principle for civilization"' (2). I hope that the cultural undertaking I argue for here – reconsidering how we regard zoos; confronting their cultural, social, political, and ecological implications – in some small way advances our environmental sensibilities. The transformation I advocate must enact what Marti Kheel calls a holistic rather than heroic approach to the challenges facing our ecosystem:

> As the destruction of the natural world proceeds at breakneck speed, nature ethicists have found themselves in search of a theory that can serve to bring the destruction to a halt. Just as the prototypical hero in patriarchal stories must rescue the proverbial 'damsel in distress,' so, too, the sought-after theory must demonstrate heroic qualities. It must, singlehandedly, rescue the ailing body of 'Mother Nature' from the villains who have bound and subdued her . . . But is this heroic ethic a helpful response to the domination of nature, or is it another conqueror in new disguise?
>
> (243)

Rather than seeking a monolithic ethical theory, Kheel urges embracing 'a number of theories or stories that, when woven together into a fabric or tapestry, help to provide a picture or "portrait" of the world in which we currently live' (243–4). Since patriarchal images of nature have facilitated the exploitation of nature, 'then, clearly, new ways of perceiving the world must be sought' (244). The fabric of zoo stories I examine can aid in promoting new ways of perceiving the world – ways that enhance our appreciation of a holistic paradigm for coexisting with animals.

Zoos perpetuate a *restrictive* popular cultural sense of nature. Predominantly, audiences experience the zoo's collection of captive animals not as a small sample of much larger and more varied wild populations, but as the best examples of a given species, or nearly the only examples of the species, and certainly the only example they can ever expect to see. This is especially true in light of zoos' recent emphasis on preserving endangered species and their claims that, increasingly, the animals they display exist mainly, or most significantly, in zoos. (But as long as zoos sustain the cutting-edge efforts in preservation that they advertise, spectators need have no utilitarian concern with the condition of wild animals: the creatures' prosperity or disappearance in nature will not affect spectators' continued opportunity to have these animals available in zoos.) For both cultural and ecological reasons, then, it is imperative that our society *expand,* not restrict, our sense of the natural realm. At the end of the twentieth century, it is becoming clear that issues previously relegated to a diminutive nature niche are in fact intimately relevant to our most fundamental social and cultural concerns.

My analysis of zoo stories may seem conditioned by an excessive or untenable conflation of human culture with nature and animals, but even some scientists challenge the once sacrosanct anthropomorphic fallacy. Such researchers are exploring what the scientific community had traditionally rejected: coherences and similarities linking the emotional and perceptual habits of people and animals. In sync with the recent aesthetic, critical, and intellectual movement toward postmodernism, scientists have begun to question the absoluteness of previously established categories and hierarchies, that have traditionally separated 'us' from 'them': absolute boundaries between people and animals are giving way to blurry ones. 'Among researchers who study the behavior and ecology of nonhuman animals,' writes Natalie Angier, an orthodox taboo

> has long been the dread practice of anthropomorphism: to ascribe to the creature under scrutiny emotions, goals, consciousness, intelligence, desires or any other characteristics viewed as exclusively human . . . Lately, however, a growing contingent of animal behaviorists has broken ranks and proclaimed that anthropomorphism, when intelligently done, can accelerate scientists' understanding of the lives and sensibilities of the beasts they are studying.
>
> (B5)

A valuable confluence links my postmodern scholarly approach – which asserts that the boundaries between literary culture, popular culture, and nature are highly permeable – and scientific sensibilities that challenge positivist received ideas about how people and animals relate to each other. I hope this confluence might facilitate dialogue between the two cultures of the humanities and science, allowing humanists and scientists to reach out to each other in a way that will allow us to talk and advance together into the world's next era. Humanists, I think, can explore and expose the conditions of the world we live in, while scientists can work to repair the damage this exploration will reveal. Andrew Ross writes that science faces 'the challenge of providing . . . "better accounts of the world," that will be publicly answerable and of some service to progressive interests' (*Weather*, 29); ecocriticism can play a valuable role in helping the culture of science meet this challenge.

Neo-anthropomorphists argue that 'many species give strong indications of possessing self-awareness, awareness of others and a certain degree of foresight and intention . . . The researchers say that by granting their nonhuman subjects a measure of motivation and desire they end up asking comparatively more compelling questions and devising more revealing experiments.' This new breed of scientists finds 'no scientifically valid reason to assume that some sort of unreachable gap separates humans from the rest of the natural world. The human skeleton, the human body, the molecular workings of the human cell, the nerve tissue that makes up the exalted human brain all look remarkably like those of other species; by what act of hubristic reasoning should it be assumed that human psychology and human behavior sprang up de novo, bearing no resemblance to the behavior of any other being on earth?' (Angier, B5, B8). In *When Elephants Weep: The Emotional Lives of Animals*, Jeffrey Masson and Susan McCarthy detail the vast range of feelings they believe animals experience. Presenting vignettes that illustrate fear, anger, joy, embarrassment, and revenge in various animals, Masson and McCarthy argue that such emotional expressiveness – denied by generations of scientists who derided anthropomorphism as a fallacy – affirms animals' dignity and their right to be treated as our social equals rather than as dumb, unfeeling subjects. (Masson's interest in animal emotions was precipitated by 'the common experience of going to the zoo. We have all seen the look of forlorn sadness on the face of an orangutan, wolves pacing nervously up and down, gorillas sitting motionless, seemingly in despair, or perhaps having abandoned all hope of ever being free' (xvii).) Alan M. Beck, too, suggests that 'sensible use of the concept of anthropomorphism can produce more-humane treatment' of animals; if people deny that animals' emotions, intelligence, behavior and feelings may resemble ours in some ways, he argues, it becomes easier to cause and tolerate their suffering, to exploit them more rampantly, and to ignore the ethical implications of our relationship toward them. My embrace of anthropomorphism includes a caveat: one risks subsuming animals excessively within a human model, and obscuring the distinctive attributes of animals' lives. The anthropomorphism I advocate may best serve as a temporary corrective, to become supplanted at some ideal later stage when people appreciate animals more keenly and treat them more respectfully. But first, modern culture needs to accept how much animals are (in some ways) like people – how they exist as part of our biotic community, and demand to be considered as full-fledged equal partners in our ecosystem. At present, the mass cultural sensibility that zoo culture typifies situates animals as subjects, playthings to amuse people; pragmatically, then, anthropomorphism promises to elevate the status of animals in general cultural regard – compared to the status quo – rather than to diminish or colonize their position.

'Until the 19th century,' writes Berger, 'anthropomorphism was integral to the relation between man and animal and was an expression of their proximity. Anthropomorphism was the residue of the continuous use of animal metaphor. In the last two centuries, animals have gradually disappeared. Today we live without them. And in this new solitude, anthropomorphism makes us doubly uneasy' (9). I hope to surmount the solitude – the distance from nature – that people have created in our culture (by locking animals in cages) and to restore the potential vitality of animal metaphor and animal experience (that voyeuristic exploitation of zoo animals has cheapened). This enterprise, I think, will benefit from a dose of anthropomorphism. To give the most basic illustration: I would not want to live in captivity and on display to the public; and I think it makes sense to infer that a panther in such conditions is unhappy. Artists who share my aversion to captivity are better able than I to express the moving nuances of this aversion as a human mind perceives them. And this expression, I contend, helps to advance the claim that animal captivity is wrong: both for the animal which the human artist perceives to be unhappy, and for the human spectator in the position of watching this pain.

I hope to bypass the zoo (which becomes, if you will, the 'monkey in the middle') as the privileged and preeminent venue for people's experience of animals in our culture, and investigate the conditions of animals and the interaction of animal and human ecosystems as portrayed by zoo stories, which tend to be considerably anthropomorphic. My anthropomorphically indulgent humanism inclines me to believe that Virginia Woolf, John Galsworthy, and company can probably teach us more about people and animals – and can *certainly* teach us differently – than zoos. For example, Saki, in 'The Mappined Terrace,' offers a typical (and, to my mind, eloquently convincing) illustration of anthropomorphic sensibilities attributed to an animal – knowledge, satisfaction, memory, individuality, freedom, and so forth – that are calculated to offer a statement against zoos. Describing the unpleasantness of zoo conditions, a woman tells her aunt:

> Nothing will make me believe that an acre or so of concrete enclosure will make up to a wolf or a tiger-cat for the range of night prowling that would belong to it in a wild state. Think of the dictionary of sound and scent and recollection that unfolds before a real wild beast as it comes out from its lair every evening, with the knowledge that in a few minutes it will be hieing along to some distant hunting ground where all the joy and fury of the chase awaits it; think of the crowded sensations of the brain when every rustle, every cry, every bent twig, and every whiff across the nostrils means something, something to do with life and death and dinner. Imagine the satisfaction of stealing down to your own particular drinking spot, choosing your own particular tree to scrape your claws on, finding your own particular bed of dried grass to roll on. Then, in the place of all that, put a concrete promenade, which will be of exactly the same dimensions whether you race or crawl across it, coated with stale, unvarying scents and surrounded with cries and noises that have ceased to have the least meaning or interest.
>
> (187–8)

The best environmentalist literature tends to be rampantly anthropomorphic. I offer a brief example from Leopold's seminal work, *A Sand County Almanac*:

> A meadow mouse, startled by my approach, darts damply across the skunk track. Why is he abroad in daylight? Probably because

> he feels grieved about the thaw. Today his maze of secret tunnels, laboriously chewed through the matted grass under the snow, are tunnels no more but only paths exposed to public view and ridicule . . . The mouse is a sober citizen who knows that grass grows in order that mice may store it as underground haystacks, and that snow falls in order that mice may build subways from stack to stack . . . A rough-legged hawk comes sailing over the meadow ahead. Now he stops, hovers like a kingfisher, and then drops like a feathered bomb into the marsh. He does not rise again, so I am sure he has caught, and is now eating, some worried mouse-engineer who could not wait until night to inspect the damage to his well-ordered world. The rough-leg has no opinion why grass grows, but he is well aware that snow melts in order that hawks may again catch mice.
>
> (4–5)

Anthropomorphism often signals the initiation of an empathetic consideration for the plight of captive animals. In *Turtle Diary*, for example, when William first encounters the animals he will later become devoted to freeing from the zoo, anthropomorphism foreshadows his concern for and sensitivity to their lives. He contemplates the green turtles which feed along the coast of Brazil and swim 1400 miles to breed on Ascension Island: 'How do the turtles find Ascension Island?' he wonders.

> There are sharks in the water too. Some of the turtles get eaten by sharks. Do the turtles know about sharks? How do they not think about the sharks when they're swimming that 1,400 miles? Green turtles must have the kind of mind that doesn't think about sharks unless a shark is there. That must be how it is with them. I can't believe they'd swim 1,400 miles thinking about sharks.
>
> (13)

In Harold Pinter's screenplay of *Turtle Diary*, a vivid anthropomorphic flourish confirms the success of the zoo liberation. The zookeeper who assists their jailbreak asserts simply, 'They'll be very pleased, you know.' Who, asks William's comrade, Neaera, in tears and dubious of what they have accomplished? 'The turtles,' he responds. 'They'll be really happy' (156). Such anthropomorphism is indefensible by the standards of traditional scientific sensibilities; but for humanists it validates, powerfully, the need for people to help and empathize with animals.

Animals are, I believe, considerably more conscious, and of more importance to the Earth, than our culture acknowledges. We need to become more sensitive to their natures, their sensibilities, their lives. We need to revise our ideas about animals, and the first step is to stop gawking at them in cages. We need to relearn first principles about the natural world, and to rethink, on a *tabula rasa*, the constructs we have built up over the centuries – constructs implanted in self-centered visions of how we might manipulate the world around us, including animals, to serve our pleasures, habits, and vanities. In the universities, ecocritics and cultural studies scholars are beginning to embrace such a spirit. In their essay 'Ethics and Cultural Studies,' Jennifer Daryl Slack and Laurie Anne Whitt argue the need to recognize 'a non-anthropocentric alternative' to main-stream cultural theory: 'an ecoculturalist perspective which acknowledges ecological interdependence' (572). They invite cultural theorists 'to extend their concern for instrumentally reduced and socially subjugated subjects beyond the exclusively human to the other-than-human, to intervene for the land (understood in Leopold's inclusive sense, as embracing soils, waters, plants, and animals)' (588).

To rectify our ecological misdirection, the approach I formulate blends ideals from the competing philosophies of deep ecology and social ecology. Like deep ecologists, I attempt to identify aspects of human chauvinism that create a gulf between people and nonhuman nature, 'listening to the nonhuman world (i.e., treating it as a silenced subject)' and overcoming 'the unwarranted claim that humans are unique subjects and speakers' (Manes, 16, 22). Like social ecologists, I believe that hierarchical social institutions accelerate the exploitation of nature, and that human social relationships involving dominance, subordination, control, and manipulation generate similar unfortunate attitudes toward the natural world. I regard as complementary, rather than mutually exclusive, deep ecologists' call for a more informed biocentrism – an expansion of our perspective to reflect more accurately the place of people within the immense scope of nature – and social ecologists' mission to reformulate the networks of power.[14]

Cultural representations of the natural world (such as, prominently, zoos) determine ways of processing this world in our minds that have very real impact in terms of how we live in the world. 'How we image a thing, true or false, affects our conduct toward it,' writes Lawrence Buell.

> Walden Woods in Concord, Massachusetts, has become a legal battleground because Thoreau's writings have led many to perceive it as sacred space that should be kept in its 'natural' state. Novel-begotten stereotypes of Victorian England's industrial midlands are thought to have influenced internal migration to this day. Land reclamation and preservation throughout Denmark, starting in the mid-nineteenth century, was inspired by literary revivals of saga and folklore that infused erstwhile desolate heathlands with romantic meaning and potential. These are but a few examples of how aesthetics can become a decisive force for or against environmental change.
>
> (3)

Animals have an image problem. The consequence of misperceived images is a range of misperceptions about how this planet functions, and the causes of these misperceptions arise from our culture. People have cultivated a deluded sense of our own ecological primacy. 'Humans may think they are evolution's finest product,' writes William Stevens, 'but the creepies, crawlies and squishies rule the world. Remove people from the face of the earth and the biosphere would perk along just fine, ecologists say. Remove the invertebrates – creatures like insects, spiders, worms, snails and protozoans – and the global ecosystem would collapse' (B5). Although invertebrates are fundamental in supporting human life, a study by social ecologist Stephen Kellert indicates that people have little gratitude for insects: 'for the most part people hate the myriad small, spineless creatures on which their very existence depends and would just as soon see them wiped out' (B5).[15]

People act upon perceptions, and misperceptions induce dangerous ecological conduct. 'Because many people do not know or care much about invertebrates,' Stevens explains, 'they do not worry about conserving them . . . The world is experiencing a "catastrophic loss" of invertebrate life as natural areas are destroyed and degraded, [Kellert] writes. Despite this loss, he continues, "the general public seems largely unaware of its possible impact on human well-being."' Conservation efforts to save whales or pandas have a high international profile and cachet, but 'for all their charisma, they are far less important to the maintenance of life' than insects (B5). Charisma, then – a result of cultural constructs and prejudices – can supplant scientific truths in the popular imagination. Kellert's study found aversion, anxiety, fear, and loathing toward insects and spiders prevalent. 'A majority expressed willingness to eliminate whole classes of animals altogether, including mosquitoes, cockroaches, fleas, moths and spiders' and many 'disapproved of major expenditures or economic sacrifices on behalf of endangered invertebrates,' although 'the best-educated people expressed the greatest conservation concern for invertebrates' (B9). Education is a necessary counterforce to cultural perversion of attitudes toward animals. Fighting fire with fire, fighting culture with culture, I attempt to identify and highlight those cultural voices that embody what I consider to be more appropriate, accurate, and ecologically sound attitudes toward animals than the sensibilities given widespread dissemination via zoos.

It is 'the appearance of many invertebrates, their otherworldly monstrosity' (B9), Kellert finds, that repels people and perpetuates ignorance about their function on the planet. Appearance is not reality *per se*, but appearance certainly affects reality. From insects to zoo animals, from air pollutants to waste management, on dozens of ecological fronts, it is imperative to deconstruct pervasive appearances that threaten the fragile realities of the ecosystem. What zoogoers see in cages actually represent a kind of human contrivance immeasurably distant from real animal life. We must dismantle the cultural constructs surrounding animal captivity in favor of more ecologically reasonable attitudes toward animals. If we challenge the received ideas that previous generations have disseminated about our relationship to the natural world, the ideological reform will serve us well in a vast range of other endeavors to change how we think about the world, and how we live in it. We have to become more respectful of it, less cocky.

My son Jacob will learn not that exotic wild animals are ubiquitous and easily accessible, but exactly the opposite: that they are *rare*, and increasingly so as each generation of our industrial culture continues to batter the ecosystem; that the fascinating aspects of yaks and pandas are a consequence of the fact that they do not live in unnatural proximity to each other in local zoos, but far away from each other, and from us. Children need to be taught about the rarity, specialness, ephemerality, of the imagination – and that this *imagination* (as opposed to physical acquisitiveness and control) often provides a better approach to nature. We don't get the best stuff spoonfed; we have to read, fantasize, work hard, to imagine places and ideas and experiences that are so fascinating precisely because they do not come easily. Jacob will not grow up devoid of exposure to animals: although he won't be consorting with giraffes and hippos, I will show him cows at local farms and woodpeckers in our backyard, to teach him how animals that are part of our ecological and economic sociosystem live with us. I think he will grow up appreciating the splendor and reality of giraffes (and other animals that exist in our culture only in cages) more than if he saw them in zoos; I hope his imagination will be all the richer as he learns about animals he may never see.

I dispute the zoo's usefulness as a means of enlightening people about animals, and I further dismiss what would be their only other arguably valid function, protecting and preserving threatened wild animals. Such protection is highly laudable, but I accept no legitimate connection between preservation programs and zoo culture (aside from the financial backing zoo admissions may provide. Bronx Zoo director William Conway, for example, voices a pragmatic economic imperative that recurs copiously in the current discourse of zoo proponents: the zoo 'bends recreational dollars to conservation purposes. Money otherwise used to go to the ball game, the movies, or a symphony is converted to endangered-species propagation and conservation education programs' (7). I reject the implication that the ends justify the means). While some zoos actively engage in preservationist activities that seem commendable, ecologists and zoologists are divided on the efficacy of such efforts. Common demurrals are based upon qualms about the limited gene pool available to zoo breeding programs, possibly resulting in the preservation of weakened species; the forces that drive zoo-based preservation efforts (public relations, mass crowd appeal), which tend to privilege cuddly species and others with high audience approval quotients instead of those with genuine ecological urgency; uncertainty about whether animals involved in preservation programs are ever returned to their habitats, and, if they are, about long-term prospects for survival. 'The importance of preserving endangered species does not provide much support for the existing system of zoos,' Dale Jamieson writes:

> Most zoos do very little breeding or breed only species which are not endangered. Many of the major breeding programmes are run in special facilities which have been established for that purpose. They are often located in remote places, far from the attention of zoo-goers . . . If our main concern is to do what we can to preserve endangered species, we should support such large-scale breeding centres rather than conventional zoos, most of which have neither the staff nor the facilities to run successful breeding programmes.
>
> ('Against', 116)

A species so tenuously dependent on the kind of human intervention that the zoo provides should perhaps die out – a horrible eventuality, certainly, but the perversely appropriate consequence of the indignities people have wreaked on our planet.[16] In 'The Last Bear,' Andrei Bitov describes 'the absolute safety of the zoo' as 'the kind of safety the condemned have between sentencing and execution' (277). And in *The Great Divorce*, Valerie Martin identifies the fallacy of captive breeding programs: 'There's no place to put the surplus animals [raised in zoos]. Habitats are shrinking by the minute. We can't return them to the wild; there's just no place for them to go . . . Zoos operated as arks, holding animals for the future, but it was a future that would never come' (295). Animals preserved in zoos, I believe, are not really preserved.[17] Whatever stopgap zoos provide is only cosmetic and very limited; extinction (which is, of course, part of the cycle of evolution) may be a more natural path than intervention by zoos. Barry Commoner's fourth law of ecology, 'Nature knows best,' applies here.

In 'New Zoos: Taking Down the Bars,' Cliff Tarpy claims that American zoos have undergone considerable changes during the last two decades, and that interest in conservation and environmentalism has led to more sensitive consideration of these concerns by zoos. Exhibits have become more appealing, naturalistic, and educational; they aspire to give a better sense of genuine animal behavior and of animals' relation to their ecosystem (11–15). Mullan and Marvin, on the other hand, suggest that new trends in naturalistic and open zoo designs 'appeal to the conscience of the zoo-goer in modern industrial western society who might well feel uncomfortable with the idea that animals are locked in cages for his benefit . . . [A]lthough such exhibits, because of their attention to animal needs, do improve the conditions of life of captive animals, the fact that a setting looks natural is something which is for human rather than animal benefit' (78). Jamieson rejects even more emphatically the ethos of supposedly ecocentric zoos:

> Most zoos are still in the business of entertainment rather than species preservation. Despite protestations to the contrary, most zoos are still more or less random collections of animals kept under largely bad conditions. Although the best zoos have been concerned to position themselves as environmental heroes, they have done little to promote this ethic in the zoo industry as a whole. There are many bad exhibits and bad zoos, but not much is being done to shut them down. Even the best zoos have problems with preventable mortality and morbidity due to accidents and abuse and are too often in league, wittingly or unwittingly, with people whose idea of a good animal is one that turns a quick profit. The rhetoric of science, favored by the best people in the best zoos, has not yet penetrated the reality of most zoos and indeed carries with it new possibilities for abuse.
>
> ('Revisited', 53)

Zoos are better now than ever, many advocates would have us believe. We must mitigate this, however, with the standard caveat about temporal relativism: people always tend to think they are doing something better than it has ever been done before, and subsequent developments generally prove their self-congratulatory convictions hollow. The Born Free Foundation's Zoo Check project monitors conditions of captive animals; every issue of its journal, *Wildlife Times*, recounts an international panoply of violations of contemporary ideal standards of zookeeping – at zoos old and new, famous and undistinguished – indicating the entrenched persistence of zoos' supposedly obsolete and rectified shortcomings. Stephen St C. Bostock characterizes the functions of nineteenth-century practices at the Zoological Society of London – similar, indeed, to practices at ancient Egyptian zoos – as 'domestication and acclimatisation . . . introducing animals to new continents' (28). The fact that this 'idea was a scientific mistake of the period, not of the Zoological Society in particular' (28) does not mitigate the fact that it is a mistake, and a mistake perpetuated for centuries under the guise of beneficent scientific and natural practice. Still today, albeit often under the popular guise of environmental conservation, zoos act in ways that have unknown or dubious impacts on wild animal populations and habitats. 'Are zoos playing God . . . when they manipulate and even risk killing individual wild or captive animals to learn or achieve something that will preserve their endangered populations?' asks David Ehrenfeld. 'Can zoos predict the outcomes of their actions well enough to justify such interference?' (xviii). I suggest that zoos have historically demonstrated their unconcern, or incompetence, with regard to achieving any beneficial impact upon the natural world outside their gates and cages.

Modern zoological gardens are 'stocked with a finer collection of animals, more suitably housed, than at any past time in the history of the world,' the *Encyclopaedia Britannica* boasted in 1911; yet today's zoos reject the vast majority of practices of zoological institutions from that period. Any comparative contextualization of historical and immediate conditions, whether the 1911 *Britannica* or Tarpy's 1993 *National Geographic* article, is vulnerable to biased perceptions about the present. These biases and distortions are especially germane to a consideration of zoos because zoos have always served prominently as indications of the cutting-edge, state-of-the-art condition of a society's scientific/naturalistic acumen, and of its power. The zoo advertises: See how many different animals we have! See how far away they come from to be in our collection! See how many cultures and geographies are within our ken! See how long we can keep the animals alive, and how many offspring we can elicit from them! See how many species we are preserving, that would otherwise face extinction! See how well we understand the animals, and how knowledgeable we are becoming about the world around us! See how they favor us with their presence, as if to indicate God's approval that the ark has settled right here! Inherent in the justification for such self-praise is the idea that we are doing a good job ('we' indicating zookeepers, zoo spectators and supporters, and the general populace partaking in the culture at large) in sustaining captive animals. We are keeping them happy – we wouldn't want to think of them as unhappy; watching sad otters wouldn't make a very palatable afternoon outing – and somehow making ourselves better people at the same time, and doing a better job of this than anyone, ever before, has done.

The strong potential for unpleasantness presents itself to anyone who attends any zoo. Masson and McCarthy write:

> There is no reason to suppose that zoo life is not a source of sadness to most animals imprisoned there, like displaced persons in wartime. It would be comforting to believe that they are happy there, delighted to receive medical care and grateful to be sure of their next meal. Unfortunately, in the main, there is no evidence to suppose that they are. Most take every possible opportunity to escape. Most will not breed. Probably they want to go home. Some captive animals die of grief when taken from the wild . . . quite obviously deaths from despair – near-suicides.
>
> (99)

Can a polar bear be happy in a warm climate? Can a tiger live a natural existence in a cage, or even a 'terrain'? Does an ocelot really enjoy the passing crowds looking at it all day? A public relations deluge which zoos have embarked upon during the last decade – aggressively coopting green rhetoric – serves to anticipate and defuse potential resistance to zoos. Whatever negative thoughts may invade the spectator's experience are displaced onto the bad old days. Zoos *used to* be dirty, barbaric, heedless of animals' comforts. Today, we know better than that – our experience encompasses all of history's previous mistakes, which means that today's zoos are better than in the past. We *must* be treating our animals well, and they *must* be happy. As the 1911 *Britannica* testifies, people believed they were managing zoos much better then than ever before . . . and we are doing it today much better than they were then . . . and how long will it be before they are running zoos much better than we are today? If conditions are always so drastically better than those of the previous generation, if there is so much room for 'improvement,' then at some point conditions must have been pretty bleak. 'For advocates of zoos, as for Jay Gatsby, the past is evil but fortunately always behind us,' writes Jamieson, and 'Critics of zoos rightly see this attitude as self-serving and disingenuous' ('Revisited', 52–3).

I think that at some point – and I propose *now* – we have to stop and say that things are not good enough and the enterprise should cease. We should stop putting animals in zoos, and stop looking at animals in zoos. But this admittedly extremist suggestion, reflecting a personal sense of outrage at zoos, recalls Kheel's advice to solicit holistic rather than heroic responses to our ecological challenges. So I modify my call to arms: if we examine the evidence and documents of our own culture, through our representations of zoos, I believe that the inconsistencies, the hypocrisies, the logical fallacies, and the rationalizations that have undergirded the perpetuation of zoos will become readily apparent; the system will deconstruct. The substantial and essentially unchanged reality of zoos is that they remain prisons for animals and quick, convenient, sometimes titillating, but ultimately distorting experiences for people.

Interlude: *The Zoo Story*

In Edward Albee's *The Zoo Story* (1959) the first words are Jerry's desperate and neurotic explosion, apropos of nothing, to a stranger sitting on a bench in Central Park. 'I've been to the zoo.' The play's ensuing dialogue, embodying an offputting absurdist incoherence, alternates between non sequiturs, small talk, and disturbingly unresolvable angst. The audience faces the difficult task of imposing coherence upon nonsense, and at the core of this nonsense lies the zoo itself. The zoo evokes an unsettling weirdness that connects with (or results from) Jerry's weirdness in some vaguely indefinite way. In fact, the play never literally depicts the zoo, only evoking it tangentially through Jerry's deranged perceptions. This ambiguity makes the image of the zoo all the more volatile, troubling, and uncertain, complementing Albee's presentation of a displaced and alienated world devoid of comprehensible landmarks or mores.

When the stranger, Peter, finally takes notice, Jerry explains, 'I went to the zoo, and then I walked until I came here' (12). *The Zoo Story* happens after Jerry has visited the zoo, and thus seems to concern the aftereffects or ramifications of an experience there. Jerry himself figuratively suggests a kind of refugee from the zoo – his physical decline, described in Albee's sketch of the players, approximates what happens to animals removed from their habitats and kept in captivity:

> What was once a trim and lightly muscled body has begun to go to fat; and while he is no longer handsome, it is evident that he once was. His fall from physical grace should not suggest debauchery; he has, to come closest to it, a great weariness. (11)

Albee's characterization of Jerry abstractly but presciently evokes the human equivalent of a zoo animal. Captivity may generate intense stress for animals, as it curtails their patterns of natural behavior. Zoo animals are prone to such abnormal manifestations as pacing and weaving, self-mutilation, manipulation of feces – all this 'has been widespread in captive animals in the past, and is by no means unknown even in some good zoos today' (Bostock, 87–8). Ubiquitous mangy and hapless zoo animals testify with their bodies that captivity is often unkind to their natural conditions. Jerry's physical appearance, then, may foreshadow the tragic fate Albee has in store for him by reference to the traumas zoo animals manifest and the physical indications of their degradation in captivity. While *The Zoo Story* focuses entirely on people – as a parable of fallen humanity – the title invites its audience to regard Jerry's despair as somehow parallel to the suffering of captive animals. His drama occurs at the fulcrum of good and evil, safety and danger, nurturance and cruel self-preservation. The backdrop offers a dialectic situating grace against alienation, community succor against impenetrable solipsism. At the center of these opposing forces is the zoo.

As Jerry and Peter struggle, each alone, amid the confines of an inhospitable modern world, the dramatic atmosphere suggests violence, awkward communication, and the eventual despair of interpersonal connection. A literal zoo story never actually gets told: Jerry builds up to it throughout the play, but repeatedly veers off on digressions or gets caught up in the immediate drama and pathos of whatever he happens to be saying, thus forestalling narrative progress toward his account of what happened at the zoo. His apparent failure to tell an explicit zoo story confirms the play's *Zeitgeist* of absurdist torpor, incommunicability. Jerry offers a series of gauche personal revelations, continually approaching the promised story but faltering each time: Peter tries to pin down Jerry's discursive anecdotes by asking, 'Look here; is this something about the zoo?'

JERRY (*Distantly*)

The what?

PETER

The zoo; the zoo. Something about the zoo.

JERRY

The zoo?

PETER

You've mentioned it several times.

JERRY

(*Still distant, but returning abruptly*) The zoo? Oh, yes; the zoo. I was there before I came here. I told you that.

(22–3)

But Jerry goes on to circumvent the zoo. And again, later: 'Let me tell you about why I went [to the zoo] . . . well, let me tell you some things' (32, author's ellipses), Jerry says, prefatory to discussing his roominghouse, his landlady, and her dog, but not the zoo.

'THE STORY OF JERRY AND THE DOG!' (36) – as he bills it – is as close as Jerry comes to any full-fledged zoo story. Animals do not love Jerry: they 'don't take to me like Saint Francis had birds hanging off him all the time' (37). The landlady's dog proves especially hostile, snarling at Jerry's legs. He had made friendly overtures toward the dog – offering it hamburger meat – but the dog still snarled and attacked. 'So, I decided to kill the dog' (39). Jerry's glib inhumanity, his sense of mastery over the dog, his conviction in his own right to determine whether the dog lives or dies, all reflect an imperially tyrannical construction of people's relation to animals – which zoos reinforce. Zoo animals exist to amuse people. Our claim to capture and control them justifies removing them from their natural habitat (indeed, zookeepers often explicitly congratulate themselves for 'playing God' when they celebrate zoos' role in preserving endangered species from extinction) and refiguring them in circumstances convenient for spectators. Jerry's attitude derives from a cultural sense of absolute power over zoo animals, and a heedlessness about their independent existence, their lives beyond people's line of vision: if animals dare to respond contrary to people's expectations, befitting our purposes or whims, then off with their heads.

Jerry tries to kill the dog by lacing its hamburger with rat poison; the dog becomes deathly ill, but survives. Now, Jerry decides, he no longer wants the dog to die – he wants it to live 'so that I could see what our new relationship might come to' (40). Even more than before, Jerry revels in his exercise of power, whether the power of death or of life, over this creature. Incapable of normal relationships with people, Jerry displaces his social ineptitude onto a realm where he can exert the control he lacks in human society. His discovery: animals exist for us to dominate and manipulate in a way that we cannot do with other people. Jerry transposes his repressed and frustrated urges, that cannot be appeased among his fellow creatures, onto the victimized dog. '[I]f you can't deal with people, you have to make a start somewhere. WITH ANIMALS!' Jerry explains. 'Where better to make a beginning . . . to understand and just possibly be understood . . . a beginning of an understanding, than with . . . than with A DOG' (42–3, author's ellipses).

Trying gamely to rationalize his behavior, Jerry asserts that the dog 'looked better for his scrape with the nevermind' (41). But he realizes that, in reality, he has sundered his relationship with the dog (as, even more clearly, he has estranged other people – his severe social dysfunctionality becomes increasingly evident as the play unfolds). After the attempted poisoning, 'We regard each other with a mixture of sadness and suspicion, and then we feign indifference' (43). This interaction paradigmatically describes the course of a relationship between the human zoo spectator and the caged zoo animal: each is burdened by the falsity of the institutional arrangement. The person is not enlightened at the zoo, but rather, haunted by a lapsarian awareness of imperfection, sin, guilt, cruelty. Finally, Jerry relates, 'We had made many attempts at contact, and we had failed. The dog has returned to garbage, and I to solitary but free passage. I have not returned' (43) – just as Adam and Eve could never return to Eden; 'what is gained is loss' (44), Jerry concludes, evoking the loss of innocence, protection, succor, that accompanied the expulsion in Genesis. The story of Eden is the seminal irony: our species' first, absolute and incontrovertible. So it is fitting that Albee here turns the table on us: people finally become, ironically, the victims of the irony we tried to control and exploit – hoist with our own petard. The dog survives Jerry's psychotic assault by escaping the realm of human authority and oppression; Jerry is left only with 'loss.' For Jerry, as for Adam and Eve, the harmonious coexistence of people and animals proves impossible, to the detriment of humanity.

As the play draws to a close, Jerry attempts one final sally at his zoo story. Promising again to tell Peter what happened at the zoo, he begins,

> I went to the zoo to find out more about the way people exist with animals, and the way animals exist with each other, and with people too. It probably wasn't a fair test, what with everyone separated by bars from everyone else, the animals for the most part from each other, and always the people from the animals. But, if it's a zoo, that's the way it is.
>
> (49)

The fundamental construct of a zoo, Jerry announces, is inadequate and counterproductive, yet it proliferates in our culture. As Albee's metaphor for human society, the zoo provides an inauspicious model for functional interaction. '[T]he zoo, with its bars and cages, symbolizes the disconnectedness of one human being from another,' writes Matthew Roudané; 'the cages function . . . as psychological dividers between people, the effectively convenient separators severing meaningful encounters . . . The entire human condition, for Jerry, is a zoo of people (and animals) forever separated by bars' (39). And Lucina P. Gabbard explains the simple symbolic equation that underlies Albee's metaphor: 'man imprisoned within himself equals an animal caged at the zoo' (365–6).

Before Jerry can proceed beyond delineating the zoo's general praxis, he begins bickering, and then viciously fighting, with Peter over the bench they have been sharing throughout the drama: Jerry repeatedly demands that his listener 'MOVE OVER!' (50). In the wake of their altercation, the zoo story is again forestalled. Any semblance of human civility or compassionate interaction dissolves as Jerry forces Peter to defend himself with a knife – upon which Jerry subsequently impales himself. His death is a nonsensical waste (and in its overarching moral, *The Zoo Story* ultimately professes that all human social behavior must be deemed a wasteful failure if people remain separate from each other), just as a zoo, with bars separating every creature from each other, literally wastes animals' natural lives. The stage direction informs that Jerry's scream, his death cry, *'must be the sound of an infuriated and fatally wounded animal'* (59). Jerry's terminal animal grunts – beyond human language – finally suggest that it *is*, in fact, a zoo story that we have been watching. This revelation becomes unequivocal only at the climactic moment of action, as we see the (human? animal?) victim becoming a slab of dead meat. The significance of the zoo had remained elusive throughout the play, but *The Zoo Story* – like all zoo stories, generically – ultimately coalesces around the phenomena of suffering, tragedy, and the ethical abrogation of a social/natural contract.

The zoo story in *The Zoo Story*, finally, remains literally unvoiced – Jerry could not bring himself to tell it in life, and as he finally approaches it most promisingly in his death scream, he is obviously incapable of proceeding. Jerry's narrative incompletion intimates that the zoo lacks a dramatic power, fecundity, or voice; it falls into the modernist abyss of mute ineffability. It is too horrible, perhaps, or too banal: in default of the narrative, we can never know. Albee suggests (and I concur) that the zoo itself is unstoried: this may seem paradoxical given the profusion of zoo stories compiled throughout the following chapters. But in fact, what happens in Albee's play recurs in other zoo stories: the zoo story situates itself *against* the zoo – resisting it, subverting it, deconstructing it. A zoo story, paradigmatically, does not posit a voice the zoo could claim as it own: rather, it displaces and replaces the zoo in one motion. The zoo story exists instead of going to the zoo. The zoo alleges that it can tell a story, its own story – roughly along the lines of, 'Here is a zebra . . .' The zoo story, instead, more routinely tells something like 'Here is a voyeur'; 'Here is a victim'; 'Here is a sadist'; 'Here is a corpse.'

Albee's audience can educe a zoo story, despite the lacunae and absences that seem to efface it: a story of pathetic constraint; oppressed humanity and animality; and ultimately, pointless exhaustion, failure. Replete with danger, hostility, fear, dementia, and distortion of right relations between the earth's creatures, *The Zoo Story* provides a fitting entrée to the zoo stories that follow. For all its effective provocation, the play finally presents a rather unsatisfying vacancy, more troubling than conventionally entertaining; and indeed, there are not many happy stories ahead – but rather, anguished, contorted expressions of an institution generally construed as unappealing.

If Jerry seems to be a strange and perverse zoo spectator, we will encounter many others cut from the same mold as zoo stories go about undercutting the zoo by (among other strategies) highlighting the frequently bizarre and unsettling sensibilities of their patrons – often, as in Albee's play, culminating in violence. In Steve Watkins's story 'Critterworld' (1991), three adolescents conspire to burn down a shabby zoo – or, in default of that, at least to kill the most mistreated animal – as a perverse gesture of liberation. 'The point . . . was to kill a thing that had compromised itself so much that it no longer had a self. Something that wasn't true to its nature.' They decide to assassinate an elephant that 'represented all those things that had lost their essence' (355). In the same vein, a character in Charles Baxter's story 'Westland' (1990) thinks about liberating animals by killing them: 'What would you do if I shot that lion?' she asks a fellow zoo visitor. To his objection, she responds, 'It wouldn't be that bad . . . You can tell from their faces how much they want to check out' (19–20). Clarice Lispector's story 'The Buffalo' (1960) begins with a woman thinking 'of the carnage she had come in search of in the zoological gardens' (147); she 'had gone to the zoological gardens in order to be sick . . . She sought out other animals and tried to learn from them how to hate' (148). Standing outside the cages, she thinks, 'she would have destroyed these monkeys leaping around inside the cages . . . She would have destroyed them with fifteen sharp bullets' (148).

The zoo as trope arouses such emotional responses as anger, violence, irrationality, depravity, depression, helplessness, fear, sadism, voyeurism, madness, guilt – a wide range of reactions, but generally unified by a common strain of dark pathos. In numerous zoo stories I will examine, as in Albee's, the denouement is death: if not literally (for people and/or animals, as in *The Hairy Ape*, *Setting Free the Bears*, *The Old Men at the Zoo*, 'The Zoo Wheel of Knowledge,' 'The Zoo Attack,' *Zoo: A Zed and Two Noughts*, and *Cries from the Mammal House*, among others), then in the form of a figurative/imaginative/cultural death-in-life (as in 'Axolotl,' 'The Hunger Artist,' 'The Panther,' 'Welcome to the Monkey House,' *Creature Comforts*, 'Zoo Keeper's Wife,' and many more).

2

Exhibiting Imperialism

Human societies in different historical periods have created major social institutions in which living creatures are forcibly contained and controlled. In prisons, mental asylums and zoos, creatures are taken from their natural surroundings and, for differing reasons, held apart. All such institutions . . . demonstrate power relations . . . power relations arise in zoos because in them human beings enforce the containment and display of animals in ways which unconsciously express attitudes usually of superiority and distance toward the natural world.

Bob Mullan and Garry Marvin, *Zoo Culture*

In many ways, the zoo has come to typify the themes of the Age of Control: exploration, domination, machismo, exhibitionism, assertion of superiority, manipulation.

David Ehrenfeld, *Ethics on the Ark*

Repositories of a power conditioned by the imperial mindset, zoos prosper amid the nexus of imperialism. In zoos, people dominate animals, relegating them to bounded and confined habitats, and contextualizing them in ways that reflect how we overwrite the natural world with our own convenient cultural models and preferences. Surmounting nature with human culture reflects the exercise of power, manifested in zoo animals' subjection to the constraints of cages (see Chapter 3), in animals' pain (Chapter 4), in the omnivorous spectatorial gaze (Chapter 5), and in the determination to indoctrinate the next generation, children, into replicating this pattern of subjugating animals (Chapter 6). Here, I turn my attention largely toward the historical and political contexts of real zoos (and antecedent practices of animal captivity), rather than zoo stories. Zoo stories represent how zoos function in societies mediated by the dynamics and aftereffects of imperial development; it is necessary first to consider how zoos themselves operate in the praxes of imperialism, in order to read them through this critical lens. I attempt (as Edward Said describes a comparable objective in *Culture and Imperialism*) 'to show the involvements of culture with expanding empires, ... the connection between the pursuit of national imperial aims and the general national culture' (7, 13).

The zoo's forte is its construction of zoogoers as paramount, masters of all they survey, and zoo animals as subalterns. The zoo's exercise of control and oppression, and insistence on the distant, subjugated subject as other, sustain an imperial hegemony. The zoo is the analogue, in popular culture, to the colonialist text in literary culture. Such a text appropriates and packages the 'native' experience, simultaneously contextualizing and distorting that experience with the inherent biases of the imperial culture. The very fabric of representation itself (in the case of literature, language and other textual givens; in the case of zoos, captivity and other institutional givens) embodies and ensures the exclusive voice of the dominant system out of which it emerges.

No matter how well Rudyard Kipling (or his character Kim) knows his Indians, for example – how convincingly author and protagonist may lay claim to Indians' culture, their stories, their lives – Kipling's Indians can never be other than, precisely, Kipling's Indians (and thus, by implication, England's Indians). Indians and Kipling's Indians are, of course, mutually exclusive. The construct of England's Indians in imperial political reality, or of Kipling's Indians in the parallel narrative enterprise, diminishes Indians' autonomous ability to control or convey their own culture. The accretion of various diminutions – Kipling's plus E. M. Forster's, Flora Annie Steel's, Edward Thompson's, Paul Scott's, and so forth – hinders the indigenous society's cultural expression as the colonizing texts coopt the 'native' experience. The cultural power that writers like Kipling exercised over India forms a constituent element of the imperial hegemony that perpetuated British dominance. Transposing this model to zoo animals: within popular culture, zoo animals serve as a 'text' authored by the people who capture or breed them, cage them, feed them, put them on display, and decide what time to open to the public and how much admission to charge. The absolute control keepers exercise over animals parallels the omnipowerful authority of authors over their characters; the omnibus of the zoo is like a literary anthology; zoo signage may be considered analogous to textual annotation or other forms of supratextual contextualization; the creation and delineation of habitats of captivity is like a kind of editorial arrangement or abridgement. The *tour de force* of zookeepers' 'authorship,' confirmed by the popularity of zoos, establishes the zoo as the authoritative text on its subject. Just as Kipling's success resulted from his implicit contention that he knew India better than the Indians, the zoo's derives from its pretensions that it represents natural animals better than nature itself: it promises better animals (because they are better fed, better tended); better variety; better access; better accompanying texts (signs) offering better means of identification and education; better amenities, souvenirs, refreshments, and so forth. And just as the colonialist text usurps and displaces the 'native culture' itself, the zoo implicitly relegates natural animals to a paltry and primitive position. The imperial sensibility suggests that animals in nature, like the signified Indians that Kipling's signifiers point to, are extremely inaccessible, and would prove not very interesting first-hand even if one could have immediate experience of them. The mediation (provided by the colonialist text, and by the zoo) ostensibly represents a desirable reward of membership in an imperial culture. But just as the colonialist text has been avenged by a postcolonial aesthetic of resistance, subversion, and deconstruction,[1] many zoo stories embody a strategy resembling such counter-discourses.

The zoo itself acts as both a model of empire (where humanity holds dominion over lesser species arrayed for our pleasure, our betterment, our *use*) and simultaneously as a metaphor for the larger, more important imperial enterprises in the sociopolitical hierarchy amid which it flourishes. In an imperialist society, constituent institutions will likely replicate the overarching political structure, and the zoo is indeed fundamentally a construct of imperial culture. 'The race for colonies, to possess in the name of the nation state territories discovered and explored overseas, began as soon as European travellers and voyagers were able to cross land and sea. The initial tendency was to ransack the new areas and take plunder back to the homeland' (Giddings, 1–2). This plunder consisted of tokens and totems of (so-called) discovery, including flora,[2] fauna, resources, and indigenous peoples. For centuries, the appropriation of animals from non-Western locales into Western captivity has played an integral part in the imperial enterprise; the great animal 'collectors' were the great imperialists. It should not be surprising that imperialism has so prominently affected people's relationship with animals: 'The effects of the exercise of power are everywhere,' Yi-Fu Tuan writes; 'In large and complex societies, perhaps the most striking effect is the transformation of nature' (2). The zoo, paradigmatic of such a transformation with free-ranging animals turned into specimens of possession/subjection, resembles what Mary Louise Pratt calls a 'contact zone,' representing 'the space of colonial encounters, the space in which peoples geographically and historically separated come into contact with each other and establish ongoing relations, usually involving conditions of coercion, radical inequality, and intractable conflict.' The contact zone, she writes, invokes 'the spatial and temporal copresence of subjects previously separated . . . whose trajectories now intersect' (6–7). Pratt's image highlights the fact that political and ecological dynamics are played out in miniature at the zoo: it represents the tip of the iceberg, with traditions of imperialist cultural practices and ideologies lying submerged beneath the surface.

It is no longer palatable for empires to grandstand their booty as in ages past, but the zoo remains a potent symbolic perpetuation of such spectacles of geographical/natural dominance and control. Especially within the last generation, zoos have attempted to dehistoricize themselves: their intricate links to imperial confiscation and braggadocio have been repressed. Their semiotic evocations of empire – wildness conquered, fierce native threats subjugated and tamed, homogeneous Western order imposed upon a global array of living creatures via cages, paths, signs, schedules, all mediated by the principle of commerce (i.e., admission) – have been tidied up, sanitized (at least in the cannier zoos), as their exploitative underpinnings have become embarrassingly gauche. Following the stratagem of contemporary postcolonial analysis, I attempt to rehistoricize zoos by deconstructing the myths, lies, and prejudices of imperial history/natural history.[3]

In the nearly two centuries that zoos have existed in their present form, they have played a vital role in the rhetoric of empire, and in the consequent sustenance of a prevalent imperial ethos. Indeed, the founding and operation of prominent zoos serves as a tracking device for the proliferation of imperialism. In the early nineteenth century, when London was the unrivaled seat of imperial authority, the spectacular development of the London Zoo strikingly paralleled that of the British Empire. It was founded out of a desire to surpass zoos in rival imperial countries, and thus reinforce England's own primacy symbolically, writes Harriet Ritvo. 'From the beginning the London Zoo was measured against its European competitors. Indeed, according to the Zoological Society's first prospectus, Britain's shameful lack of an institution for the study of living exotic animals – despite being "richer than any other country in the extent and variety of our possessions"' (231) – provided a primary motive for its establishment. At the end of the nineteenth century, as America challenged Britain's dominance, American zoos emulated the London Zoo's ambitions. Sally Gregory Kohlstedt describes how nineteenth-century American zoos 'featured animals from the American West, such as Rocky Mountain goats and Alaskan black bears, which conjured up visions of Manifest Destiny' (6), just as the London Zoo justified British expansionism. With the diffusion and subdivision of the American empire as the century has progressed – with every region competing for the pride of mini-empire or local boomtown – numerous American cities have founded and developed zoos as a testament to their stature and a stepping stone to greater aspirations: the Philadelphia Zoo, America's oldest (opened in 1874) – modeled after the London Zoo – emerged in tandem with that city's rise to national stature and its self-celebratory Centennial Exposition; Chicago's Lincoln Park Zoo, developing at about the same time, reflected midwestern aspirations to frontier primacy. Washington, DC's National Zoo, founded at the end of the nineteenth century, represented its region's claims as a federalist bastion of power – part of the Smithsonian Institution's ambition to present national scientific omnipotence on display in the nation's capital. The Bronx Zoo advanced the claim for New York's place at the heart of this modern empire in 1899. The San Diego Zoo, founded in 1916, is the showpiece of the twentieth-century California empire (and like the Philadelphia Zoo, its founding coincided with an imperial-type celebration: its first holdings were surplus animals from the 1916 Panama–California International Exposition); in the sunbelt Zoo Atlanta, reiterating the city's fortunes by rising from disastrous conditions to distinction, advances the New South's claims to preeminence.[4]

Captive animals have always represented conspicuous splendor:

they attest to the grandeur of those who keep them captive. 'Potentates demonstrate their power by appearing to sustain a cosmos,' writes Tuan. 'One element of that cosmos is the menagerie. The keeping of menageries is a discriminative trait of high civilization, combining as it does the desire for order with the desire to accommodate the heterogeneous and the exotic' (75–6). From ancient times, rulers enjoyed the possession of unusual animals as a perquisite of majestic privilege: 'The Persian word *paradeisos* refers to a large, walled park where a large number of beasts were kept for the exclusive contemplation and enjoyment of the monarch,' writes Thomas Veltre. 'The earliest record of such a park comes from China (established around 1150 B.C. by Emperor Wen Wang),' and 'evidence of such parks can be found in the empires of Assyria and Babylonia and later in the Egyptian dynasties' (21). Stephen St C. Bostock illustrates the association of captive animals with political power in medieval Europe, when

> large exotic beasts tended to be the property of kings (and were often gifts from one monarch to another), and might be kept in menageries or in deerparks. One famous royal gift was an elephant called Aboul-Abas which Charlemagne (742–814), king of the French, asked for and received from the caliph of Baghdad ... The elephant came with monkeys, perfumes and spices, and was to accompany Charlemagne for thirty years. From other Arab leaders Charlemagne received a lion and a Numidian bear, which were added to the peacocks and ducks already ornamenting the gardens of his numerous residences. (15)

The returns resulting from the display of captive animals generate an almost measurable allure: sensual atmosphere, exotic panache, self-increasing profusion (as the animals ornamenting Charlemagne's many estates prompted others to bestow upon him more of what he already had: evocative of the dynamics of hegemony, the power that generates more power). 'The ownership of rare or exotic wild animals seems to have fulfilled several functions for the rich and powerful who had the resources to build such collections,' write Bob Mullan and Garry Marvin. 'The animals ... indicated prestige, luxury and love of display' (96). Jeremy Cherfas writes that the very earliest incarnations of zoos, from centuries ago, 'represented a tradition – the association of wild animals with powerful rulers – that was ancient then and yet continues to this day. The primary motive was to demonstrate the power and glory of important people, and this sentiment is still part of the zoo world' (17). An empire requires something to show for itself, to demonstrate to its own citizens and to foreign friends and foes its unique significance. Guns and gold can carry only so much of this burden: beyond this, one must venture into the realm of culture, where animal displays (along with numerous other enterprises) serve as semiotic indications of the far-reaching extremes of imperial power. Barry Lopez illustrates how exotic captive animals provide a symbolic but nonetheless powerful currency for geopolitical interaction: 'European royalty received live polar bears as gifts from explorers and adventurers from the tenth century onward. They, in turn, historically found them 'an extremely valued and efficient instrument of diplomacy' in North Africa and the Middle East, where they were sent, along with gyrfalcons, in royal retinues' (112). It is probably not coincidental that as the captive animals became engaged (or, to sustain the image of currency, circulated) at deeper levels of the imperial enterprise – a present from a small band of adventurers to a monarch, subsequently used to pave the way for trade routes and military alliances – they became increasingly geographically distanced from their natural climes: from the Arctic to Europe to equatorial regions. A paradigm here suggests an inverse relationship between an animal's implication in imperial culture and the preservation of its integrity.

Other historical examples of animal captivity as imperial accessory include the British royal menagerie at Woodstock begun by King William II, which transferred to the Tower of London[5] and endured until the nineteenth century; the exchange of animals as tokens of political alliances between England's King Henry III and France's King Louis IX, and also between Henry and Frederick II, King of Sicily and Holy Roman Emperor, in the thirteenth century (reenacted in recent times in President Nixon's giant panda deal with China); and the *pièce de résistance* of imperial animal captivity in the Middle Ages, Kublai Khan's Chinese animal gardens. His palace 'surrounded by animals on a quite ridiculously extensive scale' (Bostock, 17), offered a world-famous testimony to the power of Kublai's Mongol empire. King Philip VI of France had a fourteenth-century menagerie at the Louvre; King Louis

XIV's *ménagerie du parc* at Versailles was maintained for over a century (nearly destroyed by revolutionaries in 1789, who saw it as a symbol of royal decadence). Ancient rulers, writes Dale Jamieson, 'kept large collections of animals as a sign of their power, which they would demonstrate on occasion by destroying their entire collections. This happened as late as 1719 when Elector Augustus II of Dresden personally slaughtered his entire menagerie' ('Against', 108). Generally the power symbolized by animal keeping is now manifested less blatantly (although copious examples of present-day barbarities against captive animals endure); today, zookeeping has evolved into more tactful incarnations and representations of power.

Founding and operating a zoo involves both real and metaphorical appropriative control of the earth: of nature, land, and habitat; and of animals taken from natural habitats, subjugated, and recontextualized in a way that upholds the captors' self-serving ideologies. This violation of natural principles of geography and habitat – of the integrity of place – reiterates the historical enactment of human political imperialism. 'Imperialism,' writes V. I. Lenin in his classic formulation, 'is capitalism in that stage of development . . . in which the division of the world by the international trusts has begun, and in which the partition of all the territory of the earth by the greatest capitalist countries has been completed.'[6] Zookeeping nestles into the space and the concepts established by such macrocosmic workings of imperialism as Lenin describes. When the proliferation of European and American zoos began, the major empires had largely finished carving up the world into a template of imperial territory; the dark spaces on maps of the world had been colored with the appropriate hues to indicate their Western proprietors. The middle nineteenth century defines that stage in capitalist development marked by (re)distributing and exploiting the fruits of imperial partition – 'the division of the world by the international trusts,' as Lenin puts it – by displaying tigers from India, kangaroos from Australia, elands from South Africa.

In England – the most prominent and ambitious imperial power at the time zoos came into existence – the relation between zoos and empire is especially interesting. In the era when the London Zoo was founded, Ritvo suggests how conceptions of animals reenacted English imperial culture: society was constructed as 'a carefully modulated and delicately balanced hierarchy, which might be threatened with social chaos and economic collapse if its members, especially its subordinate members, failed to recognize their places and do their jobs,' and other species were included in this model.

> Thus the animal kingdom (that standard phrase was itself part of the metaphor) was generally compared to the lesser ranks of a domestic commonwealth. Descriptions of individual animals routinely expressed subordination in terms of service. The best animals were those that displayed the qualities of an industrious, docile, and willing human servant; the worst not only declined to serve, but dared to challenge human supremacy. (17)

Indeed, the prevalent sociopolitical ethos always colors cultural representations of animals. Institutions of animal captivity operating amid systems of imperial power become imperial institutions, which relegate animals to subaltern status. People manifest a kind of imperial grandstanding – an institutionalized assertion of power, control, supremacy – at the expense of animals and (loaded) animal representations, according to Jeffrey Masson and Susan McCarthy: 'Humans have historically been much concerned with distinguishing ourselves from beasts. We speak; we reason; we imagine; we anticipate; we worship; we laugh. They do not.' There is a 'historical insistence on an unbridgeable gap between humans and other animals' (24). Human behavior toward animals replicates the processes of the empowered caste's relationship to the colonized:

> Dominant human groups have long defined themselves as superior by distinguishing themselves from groups they are subordinating ... These empirical distinctions are then used to make it appear that it is the distinctions themselves ... that are responsible for the social dominance of one group over another. Thus the distinction between man and beast has served to keep man on top. People define themselves as distinct from animals ... in order to keep themselves dominant over them. Human beings presumably benefit from treating animals the way they do – hurting them, jailing them, exploiting their labor,

> eating their bodies, gaping at them, and even owning them as signs of social status.
>
> (27)

'At the most basic level, zoos are institutions of power,' write Mullan and Marvin,

> in that they reflect the unique human capability to hold in captivity and dominate large numbers of diverse wild animals for the purpose of human enjoyment and human benefit. The zoo constitutes a gallery of images constructed by man. The fact that he is able to arrange around him living creatures from all parts of the world, to make decisions with regard to the quality and conditions of their lives and to give shape to the world for them in terms of his imagination and desire is, in the end, an expression of power.
>
> (160)

Jim Mason delineates an intellectual sensibility that preceded (and enabled) animals' subjugation in zoos as well as other forms of animal oppression. He traces Western theories that legitimize human domination over animals back to Aristotle – who wrote in *Politics* that animals exist for the sake of people – and cites Bacon and Descartes as laying the foundation for exploiting animals as inferior beings. From religious sources such as the description of Eden in Genesis

> we got the notion that conquering nature is permissible, but from Bacon we got the notion that it is *desirable*. Human ambition makes us want to do it, said Bacon . . . 'Knowledge is power,' he said, which legalized and elevated the vigorous pursuit of both. Pursuit of power, especially power over nature, became an obsession, an end unto itself, in the scientific age . . . Descartes published ideas that further strengthened the case for humanity's conquest of nature. Descartes's major contribution was to completely sever any connection between man and nature and to place an absolute gap between them.
>
> (37)

Humanity was established as a ruling class, immensely superior to the rest of the supposedly insensible and inert natural world, and thus essentially unrelated to it. Cartesian thinking 'justified the elevation of humans over nature' (38) and rationalized people's exercise of domination over animals. Such ideas mesh with political and mercantile imperialism to create an ethos that celebrates on all fronts the captivity and display of wild animals in the zoo, which Mason characterizes as an institution promoting 'the reinforcement and recycling of human supremacy, mastery over beasts, victory over nature' (255). Mary Midgley cites other philosophical traditions that exclude moral consideration for animals, thereby rendering them subordinate: Hume's exemption of animals from justice or the possession of rights, property, and social claims, and Kant's denial of duty to animals (48–52).

Even reading the zoo's function through what would seem a relatively innocuous lens – as a place where people may develop affectionate appreciation for our furry cousins – embodies an imperialist subtext: discussing people's attachment to domesticated animals (specifically pets, but zoo animals are so tamed and withdrawn from nature that these observations equally fit them), Tuan writes that our affection

> mitigates domination, making it softer and more acceptable, but affection itself is possible only in relationships of inequality. It is the warm and superior feeling one has toward things that one can care for and patronize. The word *care* so exudes humaneness that we tend to forget its almost inevitable tainting by patronage and condescension in our imperfect world. (5)

Throughout history, animal collecting and exhibition have embodied the cultural pretensions that provide the justification, the manifest destiny, for empire. A culture capable of maintaining an exotic array of captive animals and demonstrating exquisite naturalistic cravings deserves to rule over heathen outposts. A culture that 'keeps' (owns, preserves, nurtures, displays, values) captive animals so well, by implication, can keep with similar proficiency the native trusts (people and other resources) that are the charges of empire. English imperialism was predicated upon 'a sense that British government was good government,' writes Robert H. MacDonald, 'and that the rest of the world would be better under English rule' (4). An empire bolsters itself with what MacDonald terms 'myths of legitimation, stories which work to justify conquest and colonisation' (5). Zoo culture embodies such a myth. Zoos symbolize the benevolent proprietorship of myriad disparate entities: consolidating far-flung species in seemingly harmonious unity mimics the empire's amalgamation of far-flung races and nations.

Bostock catalogues a historical tradition of animal captivity that represents imperial conquest and provides the cultural currency of power. For example:

> Queen Hatshepsut, of the [15th century BCE Egyptian] 18th Dynasty, sent five vessels to Somalia to collect ebony, ivory and gold, and also animals. They returned with monkeys, leopards, a giraffe, cattle and numerous birds.
>
> (8)

> The first exotic animal spectacle recorded at Rome was the appearance in a triumph of four elephants captured from Pyrrhus, who was defeated in 275 BC. Twenty-four years later more than a hundred elephants captured from the Carthaginians were similarly brought to Rome.
>
> (12)

> It is usually assumed that Aristotle's remarkable biological writings were assisted by observations in a Greek zoo stocked by animals sent back by his famous pupil Alexander the Great from his military expeditions ... It is probable that animals were actually available for observation in Greece following Alexander's military exploits.
>
> (11)

For the Egyptian queen, captive animals celebrate the enterprise of commercial trade; the animals she acquired symbolize her country's ability to sail to Somalia and back and to appropriate living specimens along with inanimate natural and mineral riches. These animals both reinforce the taking of ebony and gold, and testify to a 'higher' type of acquisition of Somalian resources – that is, it is more complicated to *sustain* monkeys and giraffes than ivory and gold. And while the gold and other resources may circulate within the economy, and/or undergo some sort of industrial transition that quantifies their value, the animals represent a more intricate (unspendable, non-circulating) status symbol. Tokens of trade with realms of exotic otherness, captive animals both consecrate and transcend the circulation of a commercial imperial economy.

In Bostock's illustrations of Roman animal captivity, the elephants function like slaves or booty – as vulgar tokens of conquest and subordination – but, apparently, with an especially appealing sense of novelty and phenomenal array. Anyone can parade people and jewels in a triumph, but elephants comprise a striking and unique display. It is probably not coincidental that while the first spectacle consisted of four elephants, a later one was vastly increased to 100. These parades suggest the extent to which the imperial operation is a show, and each performance must necessarily outdo preceding ones.

And finally, in the case of Aristotle, the 'remarkable biological writings' in *The History of Animals* figure as epistemological currency representing the fruit of expansionism. Alexander's exploits directly benefit Aristotle's science. The advance of biological study was certainly not a primary inspiration for Alexander's imperial appetite, but it provides a palatable rationale for monumental military undertakings. Captive animals and the knowledge they generate legitimize the brutality of Greek imperialism.[7]

The interlacing of war with the accumulation of animals for captive display endures beyond the distant past: 'the spoils of war made their way into America's first zoo,' writes Bernard Livingston. 'General William T. Sherman tarried long enough on his march through Georgia to seize three African Cape buffalo from the estate of some Confederate bigwig and pack them off to Central Park. Likewise General George A. Custer,' whose 'trophies were American buffalo seized in the Indian Wars' (239–40). The relationship between Washington's National Zoo and the armed forces dates to 1899, when the zoo made a 'request to the Secretaries of War and of the Navy that their officers bring back live specimens from foreign postings and tours'; this relationship has 'proved most fruitful. The services have been a never-ending source of animals and, on occasion, particularly from their Antarctic stations, have provided some prize exhibits' (Zuckerman, 118).

Imperialism relies upon the accumulation and control of knowledge. As Thomas Richards writes, physically occupying a vast empire is much more difficult than positing control via an archive of information, which serves 'not as the supplement of power but as its replacement in the colonial world' (5). For Richards, this imperial archive embodies 'a fantasy of knowledge collected and united in the service of state and Empire' (6). A century earlier, Joseph Conrad anticipates Richards' notion about the primacy of the intellectual and imaginative (rather than literal) essence of empire. 'The conquest of the earth,' he writes in *Heart of Darkness*, 'is not a pretty thing when you look into it too much. What redeems it is the idea only. An idea at the back of it . . . something you can set up, and bow down before, and offer a sacrifice to.'[8] Conrad shows that 'the idea' – however far removed from the reality of imperialism – is fundamental to making the enterprise tolerable and repressing 'the horror'; the idea, indeed, must be distant from the reality, because the reality is inherently ugly and morally objectionable. Aristotle's zoology, and zoo holdings generally, represent an imperial idea, or archival holding, in which animals embody data – material that can be transformed into knowledge. The concept of owning, or controlling, an array of far-off lands is abstract and elusive; however, the concept of a Tibetan yak or an Indian elephant in a zoo, or of concrete knowledge about the animals in Aristotle's treatises, offers a more tangible imperial representation. Aristotelean scientific discourse, embellishing the treasures of Alexandrine imperialism, provides a template to perpetuate and sanctify imperial culture.

And the imperial sensibility proliferates in reciprocal, symbiotic, dynamics in the interaction between Alexander's (military) and Aristotle's (scientific) expansionism. Aristotle reifies Alexander's imperial prowess (that bestowed specimens upon Aristotle). The knowledge that emerges from Aristotle's science replicates the sensibility of its culture, producing a model replete with imperial chauvinistic prejudices, representing animals as subordinate to people: 'Aristotle's *scala naturae* . . . puts man on top and has traditionally been used as a justification for exploitation,' writes Roger Fouts. The Aristotelean ethos obfuscates our natural relation to animals, he argues, for it embodies a seductive justification of domination: Aristotle's 'patronizing point of view . . . basically says that mankind is special and above the defective have-nots who make up the rest of the animal kingdom'; he 'held that creatures without a rational soul were inferior' (281).

Thousands of years after Aristotle and Alexander, today's zoos reiterate the anthropocentric biases of the *scala naturae*, transforming captive animals into (supposedly) apolitical specimens of universal interest and benefit, to abet the sustenance of an omnipowerful imperial culture. Zoos incorporate imperial subjects – including, besides animals, an array of entities related to the places where the animals naturally exist, or symbolically evoked by their display: people, resources, biotas – in a system of representation which integrates the following presuppositions:

(a) 'We' (representing institutions and people who found, support, administer, and patronize zoos) can take animals from 'there' and exhibit them in zoos 'here.'
(b) We can see animals more conveniently and marvelously here than there, so here is culturally *better* – more stimulating, more varied, better modulated, richer in natural knowledge – than there. Especially with zoos' recent emphasis on conservation, a subliminal message zoos project is that 'we' *must* confiscate animals from other places and nurture them here because the people in whose countries they naturally exist are incapable of sustaining them. Such an implication meshes with what Chris Tiffin and Alan Lawson describe as a fundamental imperialist praxis: 'Inscribing the natives as primitive and unable to make use of the natural resources around them [in this case, wild animals] allowed first the biblical parable of the ten talents, and then the Darwinian theory of natural selection to justify their dispossession as part of the plan of Destiny' (5).
(c) One need not go there at all in order to experience the essence of there, because here subsumes there (and consequently, the existence of there is less valuable than the existence of here) – here includes the only valuable, unique aspects of there. We can represent there here, in ways that diminish or eliminate the necessity for there. 'As more and more animals are taken out of the wild,' writes Dale Jamieson, 'the case for preserving wild nature erodes. Why save a habitat if there is nothing to inhabit it?' ('Zoos Revisited', 62). It is unnecessary to travel to Africa to see an elephant. It is, then, so much less necessary – perhaps completely unnecessary – to go to Africa at all. Consequently, following the logic of imperialism, it is only minimally necessary for Africa to exist, except to supply Western

> zoos with elephants (and Western industry with cheap oil, and so on for all the other constituent categories encompassing the functions that 'outposts' provide imperial society). As long as Africa can supply the West with elephants, oil, diamonds, it seems to be suitably fulfilling its role in the imperial world; there is no need for concern about what other unfortunate or unsavory things may be happening with regard to its environments, its societies, its economies, its politics.

Several important animal collections gave rise to the modern zoo. The menageries of imperial rulers figure as a backdrop, but these precursors lack an important element, mass public exhibition, which is fundamental to my analysis of the cultural significance of zoos and zoo stories. The London Zoo stands as institutionally seminal in terms of its ambitions, its public presence, and its relation to national, cultural, and imperial history. From its founding in 1826 (and its opening two years later), that zoo was explicitly intended as a national cultural repository dedicated to public animal display. 'Unlike Paris and Vienna,' writes Cherfas, 'London Zoo – the first menagerie to be described as a zoological garden – was founded expressly as a zoo, rather than emerging haphazardly from other animal collections' (35). The practical and ideological underpinnings of every modern zoo are indebted to the London Zoo. 'As self-proclaimed leader of the pack, London Zoo has set the standards,' writes David Hancocks; it 'was the first public zoological park. It provided edification and entertainment for the day, and immediately enjoyed great success. Public zoos soon began spreading all over the developing world. London Zoo set many other precedents: the first reptile house, the first insect house, and so on' (424).

Thomas Richards suggests that 'the symbolism of the British Empire was built on an extended foundation of national symbols,' which manifested themselves, for example, in 'the steady extension into the colonial world of domestic institutions like the British Museum' and an array of other knowledge-producing institutions such as the Royal Geographical Society, the India Survey, and the universities. The London Zoo functioned par excellence as such a symbol, and thus as an instrument of imperial hegemony, 'len[ding] the Empire the sense of symbolic unity that it so often lacked in practice' (3). Animals in cages proved where Englishmen had been, what they had done while there, and what they brought back to enrich the capital. The gathering of animals from the corners of the earth in the heart of Regent's Park signified the favor bestowed upon the British Empire and everything it stood for – its supremacy over any other place or people – just as the assembly of animals in Noah's ark proved God's favor for that just man over all other people on the face of the earth. The 'two sides of imperialism, the acquisition of territory and a campaign of propaganda [geared toward] making imperialism "popular," went hand in hand' in nineteenth- and early twentieth-century England, writes Robert H. MacDonald (2); the London Zoo served importantly in the popularization of imperial exploration and conquest, thus playing a central role in what MacDonald terms 'the metaphorical construction of empire' (3).

In its entry on zoological gardens, the eleventh edition of the *Encyclopaedia Britannica* (1911) boasts that the collection of the Royal Zoological Society 'has always been the finest in existence' (28.1019). The *Britannica* presents itself as the finest assembly of knowledge ever, compiled at a time when Britain considered itself the finest empire ever (the entry for 'London' begins: 'The capital of England and of the British Empire, and the greatest city in the world'). 'Partly because of the extensive possessions of Great Britain throughout the world,' the entry on zoological gardens continues, 'the Zoological Society of London has been able to exhibit for the first time in captivity a greater number of species of wild animals than probably the total of those shown by all other collections' (28.1019). Note the quiet qualifier 'probably,' technically excusing any possible quantitative errors, or niggling concerns for factual precision, in the writer's presumption. (The author commissioned to produce this effusive prose, incidentally, is the Zoological Society's secretary, Peter Chalmers Mitchell.) The language unconsciously inflates with grandiose assertions that do not need to be supported because it is assumed (within English culture) that such generalizations must be true – that, indeed, nearly any generalization an Englishman might make, no matter how vast, would 'probably' be true, or at least true in the sense that everyone else in England would affirm it. The encyclopedia's rhetoric betrays the glib pride of the powerful British Empire, and by extension of such constituent institutions as its zoo.

The *Britannica* account highlights the direct relationship between a country's imperial (political, military, economic) power and its zoos, when it attributes the zoo's splendor to the empire's 'extensive possessions.' A subsection, 'Sources of Animals,' reinforces the relationship between animal captivity and imperialism, describing the procurement of animals in terms that bespeak all the resources of a vast commercial empire:

> The most promising sources of new animals for collections are young creatures which have been partly tamed by hunters, traders or natives, and which have been acquired by travellers. Many of these find their way to the great shipping-ports, where there have grown up establishments that trade in wild animals. Occasionally special expeditions are arranged to procure numbers of particular birds or mammals.
>
> (28.1020)

A great zoo seems to be an obvious consequence of the commercial infrastructure (procurement, shipping, trading, consumer market development) that accompanies an imperial society. To contrast what animal procurement might look like from the animal's own vantage point, as opposed to the macrocosmic imperial perspective, I like e. e. cummings's terse, fractured, anthropomorphically resonant image from poem 30 of *50 Poems* (1940):

> the silently little blue elephant shyly(he was terri
bly
warped by his voyage from every to no)who
still stands still as found some lost thing
>
> (516)

The *Oxford English Dictionary* – with an arrogant sense of authority rivaling the *Britannica*, and a similar stake in propagating Anglocentric cultural hegemony – colludes in establishing the primacy of the London Zoological Gardens. The English language anoints that institution as the seminal zoo, according to the primary reference in the *OED*, and identifies other institutions as etymological offshoots of the ur-zoo:

> **Zoo** (zu) *colloq*. (The first three letters of ZOOLOGICAL taken as one syllable.) The Zoological Gardens in Regent's Park, London; also extended to similar collections of animals elsewhere.

Similarly, the Victorian music hall disseminates in English popular culture the idea that the London Zoo is *the* Zoo: 'The Zoological Gardens' became 'the Zoo' one night in 1867 when the Great Vance (a music hall artist) sang: Weekdays may do for cads, but not for me or you, / So dressed right down the street, we show them who is who . . . / The O.K. thing on Sundays is the walking in the zoo' (Bostock, 27–8).

With such culturally pervasive reinforcement, it is unsurprising that the English should have been convinced of their zoo's unparalleled grandeur, and of the flattering testimony this animal emporium offered to their society. The sun never set on the British empire and here were the animals garnered from around the globe, exhibited in the heart of 'the greatest city in the world,' to prove it. 'Situated as it is in a royal park,' writes a recent president of the Zoological Society of London, Solly Zuckerman, the zoo 'has always had to live up to the high standards expected of a national institution which graces the capital of a country that, until the Second World War, was regarded as the dominant power in the world' (11).[9]

History confirms the London Zoo's manifestly imperialist roots: its founder, Sir Stamford Raffles, was one of nineteenth-century England's most notoriously successful imperial traders and administrators. No one better embodies the link between imperialism and the collection, imprisonment, and display of animals. Raffles represents the prototype of the adventurer who journeyed abroad for the empire, made his mark, demonstrated his power by accumulating all the necessary credentials, and finally directed the exhibition of exotic plunder in the empire's capital.

As an East India Company explorer, Raffles traveled extensively in southeastern Asia. His accomplishments included the founding of Singapore, the conquest of Java, the administration of Sumatra, and the advancement of English commercial interests (against those of the Dutch) throughout the region. His economic-political imperialism went hand in hand with what I would call his naturalistic imperialism:

> [W]hen his official duties permitted, Raffles had devoted himself to zoology and botany. He discovered many new species, several of which, including a gibbon with black fur and an enormous parasitic flower that smelled like rotting flesh, were named in

> his honor; he also amassed a substantial private museum of animal and plant specimens as well as a small domestic menagerie containing tigers, bears, orangutans, gibbons, and monkeys.
>
> (Ritvo, 205)

The man who made his reputation by conquering and administrating England's imperial outposts in Asia ended his career by establishing the Zoological Society of London. The talents and sensibility required for the former proved ideal preparation for undertaking the latter. The London Zoo benefitted overtly from Raffles's imperialist exploitation and conquest: his personal collection of animals (mainly from Sumatra) became part of the zoo's opening endowment.

Raffles's leadership of the zoo reiterated his imperialist habits and training. Harriet Ritvo writes that his

> activities as a naturalist echoed his concerns as a colonial administrator: he made discoveries, imposed order, and carried off whatever seemed particularly valuable or interesting. The maintenance and study of captive wild animals, simultaneous emblems of human mastery over the natural world and of English dominion over remote territories, offered an especially vivid rhetorical means of reenacting and extending the work of empire, and Raffles intended to continue his colonial pursuits in this figurative form after returning to the center of English power and enterprise.
>
> (205)

Raffles hoped the Zoological Society would present and maintain what Ritvo characterizes as 'a collection of captive wild animals that would serve not just as a popular symbol of human domination, but also as a more precise and elaborate figuration of England's imperial enterprise' (206). And celebration of geopolitical predominance was not limited to the echelons who actively participated in imperial undertakings; the entire nation shared in the empire's good fortune and prowess, partaking vicariously in the adventures Raffles experienced first-hand. Exotic animal displays were presented 'as evidence of British ability to subdue exotic territories and convert their wild products to useful purposes' (Ritvo, 217).

The zoo that was originally stocked with Raffles's trophies continued to develop in a similar mode, in tandem with the proliferation of England's imperial glory. For example, as Wilfrid Blunt describes: 'In the nineteenth century, British royalty were constantly receiving splendid gifts of wild animals from miscellaneous Oriental potentates and Indian princes: they were the obvious presents for them to make . . . The most spectacular single collection was that brought back by the Prince of Wales (Edward VII) after his four months' tour of India in the winter of 1875–76' (189). The bounty, which the Prince deposited at the London Zoo, included tigers, leopards, elephants, bears, deer, goats, wild dogs, monkeys, zebus and sheep. Several animals bore injuries from inhumane collection and transport: one of the young bears, for example, 'whose mother had been shot by the Prince, spent most of his time in the gloomiest corner of his cage' on the trip to England. A pangolin 'died during the voyage of wounds probably received at the time of its capture'; a Kashmir deer escaped after the ship docked at Portsmouth and was found dead (192–5). The surviving animals were displayed in Regent's Park alongside other souvenirs of the Indian tour, such as 'Sixteen tiger skins, with dates affixed to them, bear[ing] witness to the Prince's marksmanship' and 'the four feet of an elephant shot by the Prince in Ceylon' (196). Every aspect of this expedition illuminates the inextricable entwining of imperialism and zoos: the tribute from native subjects to the imperial Prince; the display back home of souvenirs from the empire's exotic distant reaches; the prevalence of cruelty, whether attributable to the overlord's imperious neglect or the willful maiming or slaughter of wild animals (represented as sport). In the display of captive animals adjacent to pelts or other animal parts, the grandee intimates his power to adjudicate between life and death. The living animals survive by the grace of the benevolent patron; the dead ones warn of the imperial figurehead's fierce skills.

Lingering traces of the imperialist sensibility endure in today's zoos, which retain a legacy of acquisitiveness, exploitation, and the self-flattering exhibition of captive exotica. Angus Wilson's fictional portrayal of the London Zoo in *The Old Men at the Zoo* (1961) includes an episode showing the modern zoo's posthumous homage to a dead empire. A carnivalesque extravaganza,

'British Day,' celebrates the spirit of the zoo's Victorian heyday. The spectacle features 'a show of fireworks with two set pieces – a British lion and an Indian elephant' (261). A *'chef-d'oeuvre à la* Paxton ... this great glass palace' (evoking the 1851 Crystal Palace exhibition that celebrated British imperial prowess)

> housed birds from every corner of the earth that was now or ever had been British ... five separate roads led off each to a separate continent – to Stanley's Africa, to Botany Bay, to a Hudson Bay fur station, to the jungle of the British Raj, and, a little incommensurately ... to the Apes of the Rock. Strictly European animals or those creatures such as lemurs, armadillos, Brazilian tapirs, sloths and manatees whose species had never known the glories of British rule, were temporarily banished to a remote corner.
>
> (261–2)

Even if the Victorian glory days have passed, zoos can revive their semiotic spirit by parading the animals that once betokened England's glory; indeed, the animal exhibits survive as a memento even after most of the physical remains of empire have crumbled. Wilson's keepers set out a tableau as if the entire world were constituted to advance the British empire's greater glory. Africa, in this vision, becomes 'Stanley's Africa'; North America becomes a fur station, a token of its function in the commercial trade that flourished under imperialism; Asia is characterized as a British possession; and animals from European countries which had the misfortune never to experience British imperial rule – which indeed had the temerity to *challenge* that rule with competing imperial aspirations – are 'banished,' and later, in a flourish of revisionist fantasy, 'slaughtered.' Wilson illustrates how zoo animals may serve as pawns in zookeepers' cultural mythography of imperialism. At the end of the novel, this vision of British Day is shown up as a pathetic nostalgic travesty, blind to present reality. The backdrop for Wilson's story of squabbling zookeepers is a fictitious political contretemps simmering across Europe. On the brink of a horrific conflagration, the zoo director responsible for organizing British Day switches on the lights and fountains; he conducts his fête, in the mode of Nero, as the attack explodes over London, while the zoo is being bombarded and the animals killed. Wilson suggests that such annihilation is the fitting culmination to the fantasy that the British Empire endures into the present.

Wilson's parodic imperial nostalgia indeed permeates actual zoos. The prominent American zoo designers Jones and Jones 'are now interested in developing storylines for zoos,' write Mullan and Marvin, and their zoo stories uncannily replicate Wilson's fantasia, the only difference being that they offer an internationalist smorgasbord of world imperialism rather than the home-grown English variety depicted in *The Old Men at the Zoo*. 'At the Blue Ridge Zoological park, Virginia, they duplicate Livingstone's treks and also the Lewis and Clark journey . . . future exhibits could focus on Humboldt in South America, Burke and Wills in their crossing of Australia, perhaps even Marco Polo on the steppes of Asia' (59–60). Habitats in many contemporary zoos, especially 'safari parks,' feature African themes. Alexander Wilson confirms the zoo's situation as a metaphorical/vicarious homage to imperialism, and the endurance of an appeal dating back generations when he suggests that 'the African reference has to do with the stature of African animal species, both physically in the savannah and culturally in imperial myths about Africa and "big-game hunting"' (251).

Some zoos today are working ardently to obscure unpalatable associations with their historical forebears. 'The New York Zoological Society, deciding the word "zoo" had become an urban pejorative with a limited horizon, announced today that it was dropping the word from the Bronx Zoo, the Central Park Zoo, the Queens Zoo and the Prospect Park Zoo,' according to a 1993 *New York Times* report. 'They are to be called Wildlife Conservation Parks,' announced society president William Conway. The public needs to realize, Conway states, that 'the society runs much more than zoos, with 158 conservation and research projects flourishing worldwide.' Conway hopes to revise how people regard zoos by changing the terminology, the language, with which they think about zoos. His public relations maneuver acknowledges that the public's traditional conception of zoos is undesirable; he aims to substitute a new and improved perception: 'it's really too late for the simple idea of conventional zoos. We need a sea change' (Clines, A1).

Conway complains of pejorative linguistic associations surrounding the word 'zoo': it connotes a place of confusion and disorder. He offers an example of such usage in an anecdote about a friend who 'asked a taxi driver to take him to the Central Park Zoo and the guy said, "Which zoo? The whole city's a zoo"' (B10). As Conway realizes, 'zoo' indeed often evokes derogatory imagery, in the vein of the taxi driver's comment. The entry for 'zoo' in Robert A. Palmatier's dictionary of animal metaphors reads: 'A crowded, confused, and boisterous assemblage of people . . . A human zoo is a home or workplace in which the people behave like animals in the zoo: pushing, shoving, yelling, and fighting' (429). According to e. e. cummings, 'the word "zoo" . . . generally speaking, suggests little more than a highly odoriferous collection of interesting and unhappy animals' ('Secret', 78). In K. B. Laffan's 1968 play *Zoo Zoo Widdershins Zoo*, the characters live in a commune metaphorically resembling a zoo, unmotivated and unable to do anything meaningful. Laffan's 'zoo' inmates live a paralyzed, immobile existence, like caged animals. The commune's zoo-like attributes stultify its inhabitants and lead to feelings of indolence, restriction, deprivation; it is an oppressively dysfunctional setting. A character named Zoo in Truman Capote's *Other Voices, Other Rooms* (1948) – with an elongated neck that made her 'almost a freak, a human giraffe' (59) – suffers horrific violence, knife assaults, and gang rape, as if her very name sentences her to victimization. In *Howl* (1956), Allen Ginsberg depicts 'the best minds of my generation destroyed by madness, starving hysterical naked' as people 'who chained themselves to subways for the endless ride from Battery to holy Bronx on benzedrine until the noise of wheels and children brought them down shuddering mouth-wracked and battered bleak of brain all drained of brilliance in the drear light of Zoo' (9–10). The end of the line, Ginsberg shows, is Conway's own Bronx Zoo – a place of exhausted dreariness. Like so many other images of the zoo which Conway aspires to suppress, Ginsberg's symbolizes cacophonous, fetid, tawdry constraint.

Conway seems to believe that negative zoo imagery inheres only in the linguistic signifier and that the institution itself can prosper, shorn of the connotative taint, if he simply divorces the offending term, by fiat, from the 'wildlife conservation park' that will remain. I believe, however, that the unfortunate associations go beyond the word and relate rather to the thing itself. It is not the word but the *essence* of the zoo that is unappealing, and that leads to the word's use as an indication of unpleasantness or disorder. Throughout this book I catalogue various descriptions of zoos' unpleasantness, and consequent service as metaphors for unpleasantness. In *The Old Men at the Zoo*, for example, a character comments about Harriet, the psychologically tormented daughter of Zoo Director Leacock who creates horribly inappropriate scenes in public and makes passes at all her father's acquaintances in private: 'Oh, God! I've heard extraordinary things about her . . . Anyhow she seems to go rather far if the stories are true. I must say I never thought Leacock would have a Messalina for a daughter. In fact she seems to start where the Empress left off. As I said she couldn't be better placed than in a zoo' (208–9). The zoo is connoted as a fitting venue – perhaps a refuge, perhaps more of a prison or asylum – for dysfunctional outcasts unfit to roam freely in human social settings. As this chapter's epigraph from Mullan and Marvin suggests, a latitude of interplay exists between various institutions of confinement, places where the empowered constrain the disempowered. And in the same vein, John Berger writes, 'All sites of enforced marginalisation – ghettos, shanty towns, prisons, madhouses, concentration camps – have something in common with zoos' (24). So when acquaintances consider Harriet's unusual demeanor mad and criminal, but cannot cite any specific certifiably insane or criminal behavior, they figuratively consign her to the zoo. As Berger, Mullan and Marvin, and numerous zoo stories indicate, 'the zoo' as a bundle of images and associations embraces misfitting, undesirable, slovenly creatures that skulk around in our world.

Part of Conway's agenda for the erstwhile Bronx Zoo seems to be delineating a class divide: cab drivers, exemplifying stereotypically proletarian New Yorkers, use the word in a way he characterizes as wrong; people will show themselves to be more educated, scientifically and ecologically enlightened, if they adopt Conway's discourse and refer to zoos as wildlife conservation parks. People who think of zoos as unpleasant, he implies, are like mere cab drivers; those who use *his* language, which he implicitly situates as superior, will regard zoos not as 'zoos' but as more rarefied institutions.

There's nothing new under the sun: Raffles intended the London Zoo as a stately venue for studying animal life, not one that pandered to popular mass tastes (such as might exist in nineteenth-century approximations of cab drivers). He differentiated his zoo from more vulgar spectacles of travelling menageries and animal displays; exactly like Conway, he attempted to elevate the image of *his* zoo above what are projected as lower and less dignified institutions of animal captivity.

Conway believes the word 'zoo' embodies an unmerited image of disorder. But ecologically, it seems obvious that the institution of the zoo inherently and literally wreaks disorder – that is, it disrupts the natural order (whereby hyenas, for example, would live only in Africa and Asia, not in the Bronx). Popular cultural slang and colloquial usage often have their own immutable logic: people use the word 'zoo' to suggest unpleasant conditions because they consider zoos (at least in some ways, or potentially) unpleasant. Conway's spin-doctoring can do little to change the essential reality of people's perceptions.

Indeed, public response confirmed the transparent inefficacy of Conway's linguistic sleight of hand. In an editorial (headlined 'A Zoo by Any Other Name . . .'), the *New York Times* ridiculed the name change.

> No longer will there be a Bronx Zoo; as of Monday, it's the International Wildlife Conservation Park. Gone is the Central Park Zoo; it's the Central Park Wildlife Conservation Center . . . Why the multisyllabic mayhem? The society believes that it has outgrown its old names . . . Thank goodness the new appellations will never stick . . . a citizenry wise enough to reject 'Avenue of the Americas' [the official name for what every New Yorker knows as Sixth Avenue] will surely reject Wildlife Conservation Parks as well.

In a *Times* column titled 'Fear of Zoos,' Charles Siebert writes, 'one has to wonder what zoo officials are trying to hide.' He suggests a manipulative rationale underlying the name change: 'we're being told that we've discovered and displaced too much of the animals' world to feel anything but guilt about keeping them in such a clear-cut rendition of our own.' And he accuses zoo administrators of hypocritical duplicity: 'The message from the zoological society is that we shouldn't have zoos even as we go on having them.' For generations, zoos have been trying to distance themselves from disreputable origins. Again and again, the refrain echoes: zoos have a bad name because of the flaws of previous generations of zookeepers; now we are redressing their errors and improving the practices governing animal captivity. Yet surely today's state-of-the-art institutions – whether called zoos or wildlife conservation parks – will appear just as inadequate in the tradition of retroactive castigation.

The display of exotic subaltern people occurred commonly in past centuries. Those on display may or may not have been technically enslaved, but at least metaphorically, such dehumanizing displays celebrated the essence of mass slavery – confiscation of freedom in the service of the empowered group's advancement – as the ultimate signifier of imperial rule. The dynamics of exploitation, oppression, and cruelty lurk implicitly in such displays of people. A South African woman billed as the Hottentot Venus, for example, in an early nineteenth-century London exhibition (whose attraction lay in what was advertised as her grotesque savagery) was 'produced like a wild beast, and ordered to move backwards and forwards and come out and go into her cage, more like a bear in a chain than a human being' (Altick, 27); spectators were allowed to pinch and poke her. The impulses to exhibit and view 'exotic' people resemble the impulses that motivate zookeepers and spectators today. Human displays, often similar in many particulars to captive animal displays, inform the historical/cultural legacy of modern zoos.

Animal captivity recurrently accompanied the keeping of people in zoo-like settings, or occurred in parallel types of ventures. When Pope Leo X expanded the Vatican's animal collection in the sixteenth century, for example, 'The cardinals followed the Pope's example . . . one cardinal, a Medici, kept a troop of exotic foreigners, who spoke more than twenty different languages and were all chosen for their good looks – Moors, Tartars, Indians, Turks, and African negroes' (Bostock, 21). A 1519 account of Montezuma's zoo in Mexico describes, in addition to the vast animal assembly, a 'strange collection of human monsters, dwarves, and other unfortunate persons' (Mullan and Marvin, 32).

The English habitually exhibited people under obviously exploitative conditions, for the purposes of education, entertainment, and profit, in settings more or less like zoos. In *The Shows of London,* Richard Altick details an extensive history of people put on display in the world's great imperial power at the height of its reign – beginning in the sixteenth century and culminating in the nineteenth. Blockbuster nineteenth-century exhibitions of people from around the world included a Botocudo Indian from Brazil, billed as 'the Venus of South America,' in 1822; a troupe of Laplanders in 1822; Eskimos in 1824; American Ojibbeway Indians in 1843; African 'Bushmen' in 1847 and 'Kaffirs' in 1850; 'Natives of the Polar Regions' in 1854; and Canadian Lake Huron Indians in 1856 (Altick, 268–87). A popular 1853 exhibition of 'Aztec Lilliputians,' just over three feet tall, combined the fascination of exotic foreigners with the well-established allure for 'freaks' or 'human curiosities.' Their exhibitors reaped large profits from showing them in various settings, including the Liverpool Zoo, where 18,000 people crowded in to see them during a three-day engagement (Altick, 285).

Human shows abated by the late 1850s, when 'Londoners' taste for samples of primitive races from the corners of the earth had been abundantly satisfied, and showgoers once more were seeking new sensations' (Altick, 287). But while they endured, they were intertwined with captive animal displays. 'Many of the menageries in England in the eighteenth and nineteenth centuries exhibited strange and unusual humans as well as rarely seen and exotic animals,' write Mullan and Marvin. Such human exhibits included 'giants and giantesses, bearded women, boneless children, fireproof people, humanoid animals and midgets' (32). These exhibits moved to circuses and carnivals in the later nineteenth and early twentieth centuries, before humanitarian objections and chastisement from the medical community brought the practice to an end by around 1940 (Bogdan, 62–6). During their heyday, freak shows frequently exhibited – as variants of physical 'freaks' (people with abnormal physiology, unusual bodily characteristics, or retardation, for example) – people from disempowered lands. Robert Bogdan explains:

> It was a standard sideshow practice from the days before Barnum through the 1930s for people from the non-Western world to climb on to the freak show platform . . . These non-Westerners were not necessarily individuals with disabilities, or who were unusually tall or short, or who performed some novelty act like fire eating. Such unusual people were indeed displayed; but those whose only difference lay in the fact that they belonged to an unfamiliar race and culture had value as

> show pieces as well. Dexter Fellows, exalted press agent of the amusement world, explained: 'The Borneo aborigines, the head-hunters, the Ubangis, and the Somalis were all classified as freaks. From the standpoint of the showman the fact that they were different put them in the category of human oddities.' (176–7)

Zoos, carnivals, freak shows, and other traditions of human displays represent a continuum of spectatorial attractions with a related heritage. The connection between zoos and human displays is sometimes explicit, as when the 'Aztec Lilliputians' played the Liverpool Zoo or Montezuma displayed deformed people along with animals. People were sometimes displayed with animals – as, for example, the 1822 Laplanders were displayed along with reindeer and elks – or with other artifacts constituting a sort of miniature 'habitat.' After her popular London run, 'an animal showman exhibited [the Hottentot Venus] for fifteen months' in Paris (Altick, 271) – showing how marketing and logistical skills used for exhibiting animals were readily applicable to human exhibitions. A newspaper writer confirms the popular perception that people on display were regarded essentially like specimens in a zoo, describing them as 'sullen, silent, and savage – mere animals in propensity, and worse than animals in appearance' (Altick, 281). Bogdan cites the simultaneous development in nineteenth-century America of the travelling animal show and the travelling human freak show: 'Announcements for human and animal exhibits,' he writes, 'used the phrase "To the Curious" to grab patrons' attention. Animal and human oddities were referred to jointly as "living curiosities"' (26). During the heyday of these shows, the boundary between animal and human displays blurs.

Animal and human exhibitions each demonstrate the tenacious cultural compulsions to reify imperialism: they celebrate the power and conquest necessary to acquire specimens for exhibition; integrate the dynamics of commercial trade and economic exploitation; and engage crowds in the imperial enterprise by vicariously confirming their place in the empire, and thus their consequent empowerment. Modern zoos replicate imperial traditions of displaying the other, constructing a subjective, privileged sense of spectatorial *positioning*; viewers inherently occupy a superior perspective with respect to the exhibition – deciding when to come, look, and depart, while the subject must stay. In exhibitions of 'freaks,' 'primitives,' 'natives,' or 'noble savages,' spectators gape at the objects of interest, making disparaging comparisons to the dominant 'normal' culture; celebrating power over the subjects; mocking their barbarity.

People who observe other people in such settings are hardly likely to develop any cross-cultural understanding or appreciation – just as zoos are not conducive to learning about animals' natural conditions or integrity. Both nineteenth-century human exhibitions and modern zoos confirm the prejudices of cultural superiority, dialectically oppositional in nature: 'they' differ from 'us,' and if they are on display and we are watching, the implications of superiority/inferiority are self-evident. Cultural bias, Altick speculates, provided the essential attraction for Victorian human shows: 'Although the showmen deemed it advisable to stress the intellectual value of the exhibitions – their contribution to the ongoing discussion of ethnological subjects in the press and the learned societies – in practice their fortune lay not in the scientific implications of the creatures on display but in the vigor with which these creatures confirmed the spectators' prejudices' (279). In modern zoos, similarly, we should be wary about the extent to which claims of educational enlightenment may mask more ignoble instincts. If cultural prejudices from the Age of Empire persist in zoo spectatorship, then non-human creatures figure as less valuable, subordinate. The ecological implications are devastating, encouraging audiences to regard animals as imperial Europeans regarded their subjects – with *carte blanche* to pillage the animals' world for the betterment and convenience of our own.

By and large, zoo-like displays of people ended with the nineteenth century, but notable exceptions link human exhibitions with modern zoos. In 1907, Carl Hagenbeck – a German animal collector and trainer and a seminal figure in the development of modern zoos – founded an extensive zoo at Stellingen, near Hamburg, that included displays of Laplanders, Sudanese 'wild men,' Eskimos, Somalis, Indians, Kalmucks, Cingalese, Patagonians, Hottentots, and others (Mullan and Marvin, 87). 'What Hagenbeck liked to call anthropological-zoological exhibitions were introduced in 1874,' writes Herman Reichenbach. 'Over the next fifty-five years, Hagenbeck's Tierpark would organize some seventy performing ethnographic shows with groups ranging in size from three to four hundred, featuring three dozen "tribes" and races' (56). Hagenbeck describes meeting his imported Lapps for the first time:

> Here was a truly interesting sight. On the deck the three little men dressed in skins were walking among the deer, and down below we found to our great delight a mother with a tiny infant in her arms and a dainty little maiden about four years old, standing shyly by her side. Our guests, it is true, would not have shone in a beauty show, but they were so wholly unsophisticated and so totally unspoiled by civilization that they seemed like beings from another world.
>
> (In Mullan and Marvin, 86)

The lack of sophistication Hagenbeck condescendingly imputes to 'our guests' disqualifies them from the dominant society's appreciation or respect and simultaneously demotes their ethnographic interest to a significantly lesser plane.

Hagenbeck was one of the European stars of late nineteenth- and early twentieth-century zookeeping, and Bronx Zoo director William T. Hornaday was a contemporary American counterpart. Hornaday also resembles a New World incarnation of Sir Stamford Raffles – an American equivalent, as this country crafted its variant of the imperial power that Raffles's England had enjoyed. Like Hagenbeck, Hornaday displayed people in the zoo. Ota Benga, a pygmy from the Congo who had attracted international attention while on exhibition at the 1904 St Louis World's Fair, served an infamous month-long booking at the Bronx Zoo two years later that illuminates the intersection of zoos, animals, people, and imperial culture. In St Louis, Benga enjoyed prominence because of newly awoken public interest in anthropological science; he was displayed along with other 'natives' including a dozen neighboring pygmy tribesmen, a hundred Zulus, a hairy Japanese Ainu man and his tattooed bride, Filipino Igorots, native American Kwakiutl, and Geronimo, an aged prisoner of war, who made and sold bows and arrows (Bradford and Blume, 14, 113–26).

Benga returned to Africa after the Fair, in company with his American agent, guide, and friend, Samuel Phillips Verner (who was also in some sense his owner, having purchased him at a slave market run by a rival tribe that had raided Benga's village). Benga and Verner travelled in Africa, and then returned together to America. When Verner got to New York, he tried, with mixed success, to cash in on his adventures as an explorer. Benga was a possible attraction in this enterprise, but also a burden for a man with limited funds drifting around trying to stir up interest in his African wares and experiences. So, at least partly to get Benga off his hands, Verner placed the pygmy in the New York Museum of Natural History. When this proved to be an uncongenial residence, the museum's director suggested that Verner contact Hornaday at the Bronx Zoo.

Hornaday eagerly took in Benga (who had brought a chimpanzee with him from Africa as a companion, sweetening Hornaday's interest in him). At first the African wandered the zoo freely, in Western clothes, aiding the keepers with their chores, observing the crowds, and helping the chimpanzee acclimate in the Monkey House (170). But Benga's presence 'activated dormant plans,' write Bradford and Blume; 'conversations were being held and calls were being made. A trap was being prepared, made of Darwinism, Barnumism, pure and simple racism' (174). When the trap sprang shut, Benga 'was propelled into maximum visibility. His story became the stuff of headlines, his name a household word' (175). Benga 'was encouraged to set up his hammock and sleep in an empty Monkey House cage,' and

> Hornaday let the crowds know something special was going on at the Monkey House, 'something,' as he had once put it, 'new under the sun.' Crowds tended to wane with the passing of summer. The director had found a way to keep them coming. They came and gathered at the Monkey House. On September 9 [1906], the *New York Times* carried the first headline: 'BUSHMAN SHARES A CAGE WITH BRONX PARK APES.' He didn't have to do much. He just had to be short and black.
>
> (178–9)

During the month he spent on display, Benga lived a degrading existence. Condescending press accounts betrayed racial and cultural prejudices: 'It is probably a good thing that Benga does not think very deeply,' the *Times* editorialized. 'If he did it isn't likely that he was very proud of himself when he woke in the morning and found himself under the same roof with the orang-outangs and monkeys' (in Bradford and Blume, 259). The *Times* drew the fairly obvious conclusion that the display suggested a similarity between the caged man and caged animals: 'the pygmy was not much taller than the orangoutang, and one had a good opportunity to study their points of resemblance. Their heads are much alike, and both grin in the same way' (in Bradford and Blume, 181). Later, however, when the implication that Benga was a lesser creature provoked controversy and protest, Hornaday claimed he never meant to suggest that the pygmy was like an animal; Benga stayed in the cage simply to help care for the animals, he said. (In the Victorian era, Ritvo writes, animals brought from distant realms to the London Zoo 'were often accompanied by exotic human attendants' regarded as 'equally curious if not equally lovable' (230).)

The display accentuated Benga's distance and difference from the Bronx crowds: bones were 'scattered around the cage to increase the impression of savagery and danger' (181). Bradford and Blume describe the appearance of Benga cavorting with the orang-utan, Dohong, in the cage they shared:

> The orangutan imitated the man. The man imitated the monkey. They hugged, let go, flopped into each other's arms. Dohong snatched the woven straw cap off Ota's head and placed it on his own. Ota snatched it back. He picked up the monkey and let him drop, then turned his back to walk away. Dohong jumped up on his shoulders to hold him back. Ota shrugged him off, turned again to walk away. Dohong grabbed an ankle with one arm. Ota took big, limping steps around the cage, shackled to the ape. The crows hooted and applauded. Dohong and Ota hugged. If Hornaday had thought to supply them with canes and Derby hats, they might have obliged with an old soft-shoe.
>
> (181)

As soon as he entered the cage, Benga became like an animal to his audiences. He suffered the indignities of display in captivity: not just the invisible ones but also the physical dangers that befall zoo exhibits – 'he was always in danger of being grabbed, yanked, poked, and pulled to pieces by the mob' (197), necessitating that a police officer guard his cage.

Some expressed outrage at the display: 'Rev. R. S. MacArthur of the Calvary Baptist Church was an unsmiling face in the light-hearted crowd at the zoo . . . "The person responsible for this exhibition," he said, "degrades himself as much as he does the African"' (182); MacArthur joined other African American clergy in working to end the zoo exhibit. 'They had heard blacks compared with apes often enough before,' write Bradford and Blume; 'now the comparison was being played out flagrantly at the largest zoo on Earth' (183). (Marjorie Spiegel explains commonly aired prejudices that confirm protestors' perceptions: 'racist authors propagandized against blacks by comparing them to negative stereotypes of non-human animals'; she quotes Sterling A. Brown: 'The stock Negro' in what Brown calls Ku Klux Klan fiction 'is a gorilla-like imbecile, who "springs like a tiger" and has the "black claws of a beast"' (31–2).) Finally, after a month of publicity, protest, and mobs of visitors, Benga's stint played itself out. Hornaday became exhausted with the affair, and Benga came to resent the crowds' constant scrutiny. His picaresque odyssey continued with various adventures and hardships, ending with a despondent suicide in Lynchburg, Va., in 1916: the result, Bradford and Blume surmise, of his lonely alienation amid an American culture that had objectified him as a bizarre attraction.

Chapter 3 examines several *literary* manifestations of people in zoo cages. Such depictions seem, generally, not an explicit commentary on the historical situations of Ota Benga, Hagenbeck's Lapps, the Hottentot Venus, or other human displays, but rather, they suggest a more *immediate* (as opposed to historical) reaction to zoos themselves. Rarely do twentieth-century depictions of people in zoo cages acknowledge that earlier eras actually featured such displays; yet it seems unlikely that the distasteful history I have described does not somehow underlie zoo stories of people in cages.

Exhibitions of marginalized people demonstrate the paradigm for spectators' latent contempt of what is on display. Displayed subjects reinforce viewers' flattering prejudices, and reify their hegemony. Modern zoogoers' attitudes toward other species evoke imperial audiences' attitudes towards the exhibited subaltern. As our planet hurtles toward ecological catastrophe, as it becomes clearer how tenuous nature is and how ruthlessly we are desecrating it, it makes sense that we would crave cosmetic assurance of our place at the top of all species (implying that we reign over a stable natural kingdom). Facing increasing signs of danger about the ecosystem and our place in it, we seek some way of asserting human supremacy. The modern zoo fulfills that role: it soothes and settles anxieties consequent upon our contamination of nature, as, perhaps, earlier zoos' tributes to imperialism soothed their societies' anxieties about exploitative domination. To counteract guilt and remorse in an exploitative society, the collective unconscious demands a token that indicates that everything is all right out there (despite all rational evidence to the contrary): zoos perform this service.

In modern Western culture, the political and economic conditions of imperialism that accompanied the first century of public zoos' existence have disappeared – or, more accurately, have become transformed into something with a different appearance and composition, but a comparable underlying ideology. 'The extraordinary global reach of classical nineteenth- and early-twentieth-century European imperialism still casts a considerable shadow over our own times,' writes Edward Said. The networks established by today's technological, commercial and cultural infrastructure 'have joined together even the most distant parts of the world,' he argues, in a 'set of patterns . . . first established and made possible by the modern empires' (5–6); the contemporary strain of imperialism 'lingers where it has always been, in a kind of general cultural sphere' (9). As Linda Hutcheon explains, 'The twentieth century has seen the end of official colonial rule in much of the non-European world and, as many have argued, the simultaneous recolonization or neocolonization of the globe by multinational economic forces' (7). Today, the legacy of the imperialist zoo consorts with the predominant and familiar late twentieth-century supraimperial vehicle of commerce. If the nineteenth-century sun never set on the British Empire, today's never sets on McDonald's. The successful modern zoo in a successful modern society positions itself to *buy into* the contemporary sensibility – a geocommercial economic culture – that occupies the place vacated by the demise of manifestly geopolitical imperialism.

In the same way that the nineteenth-century London Zoo was designed to make visitors proud of vicarious engagement in their culture's imperial prowess, today's zoos are marketed to flatter spectators' roles as active members of a gloriously affluent consumeristic society. Contemporary zoos condition the public to savor its participation in the thriving Western commercial culture of the late twentieth century; its privileged charge of keeping/possessing/experiencing the zoo's exotica; its luck to possess the funds that support such infrastructures. The responsibilities that, we are told, accompany our society's consumer prosperity are strikingly similar to the responsibilities that citizens in British imperial society took upon themselves in light of the power and talents that they believed their empire betokened ('the white man's burden'). Zoos appeal to a sense of the dominant power's public responsibility, *noblesse oblige*. Zoo visits are not primarily about having fun watching animals, according to the luminary directors at the cutting edge of today's zoos – who evoke the culture of the CEO as much as Raffles, Hornaday, Chalmers Mitchell, Hagenbeck, et al., evoked the persona of the imperial explorer – but about saving the planet. (From whom are we saving the planet? one wonders, remembering that Americans exact so much more of a toll, inflicting more damage per capita on the planet, than anyone else. We might recall the epiphanic words of Pogo: We have met the enemy, and he is us.)

Bostock offers an eloquent ethical argument: our mission demands we realize that 'it is not just a matter of not destroying something of value. It is a matter of caring for it, in the appropriate way. This caring is what we mean by conservation' (125). He continues, 'caring for valuable things . . . is moral . . . and we deserve credit for engaging in it, and discredit for neglecting it' (127). Zoos provide a vehicle for people to express their ecological morality, specifically as they may help to advance animal preservation. Extolling the importance of social wealth and financing as a factor in the role zoos play, Bostock writes:

> Zoos' raising of money for wild habitats is an example of a supplementary conservational role . . . Zoos can act as a powerhouse of motivation for concern about conservation; namely, enlisting the interest and concern of the public as well as actually raising money for conservation in the field. People are more likely to be concerned about the survival of animals of which they have experience and, while they can see them in their natural habitats on film and television, they can also be powerfully influenced by the more direct experience available in a zoo. (153)

Bostock takes the moral high road in encouraging citizens to attend and support zoos, and to assist a conservationist agenda via the pathways of commercial culture. He urges people to vote with their pocketbooks for ecological preservation. Zoo Atlanta Director Terry Maple, on the other hand, takes the low road. He speaks of successfully promoting a zoo as if it were a sneaker or floor wax, with a praxis embedded in American capitalism. He has learned from observing the public at zoos: 'No person should ever leave the zoo without a peak, personal experience, a unique insight, a new idea, or some unusual memento' (79). His consumeristic modulation of zoogoers' experiences embodies images and discourse more appropriate to advertising and accountancy than zoology or ecology. Referring to spectators' experiences and insights as 'transactions,' he writes:

> People multiply these transactions many times over as they recollect and recite the details of their zoo visit. To do this right, we must be prepared to provide our supporters, partners, and guests with specialized bumper stickers, pins, T-shirts, ties, and coffee mugs. The successful zoo must be carefully and constantly marketed to its public.
>
> (79–80)

Maple's commercial models bespeak his aspirations toward pure, raw, capitalist success. He proudly admits, 'we adopted some of the techniques and methods commonly used by entertainment and amusement enterprises, such as Disney World and Six Flags' (89).

Both Bostock and Maple suggest that the modern zoo inhabits a realm where commercialism meshes with what I see as the fad of feel-good ecoactivism. Consumers are cajoled to buy a product and save an animal. It might seem as if animals could benefit from this interaction – that money thrown at nature helps, whatever strings and contexts are attached. But the danger in this equation is that the culture of commerce is certain to overwhelm and coopt nature when zoos become implicated in the processes of capitalism. The tenuous state of animals and their habitats throughout the world today affirms the harsh toll that market forces exert upon the planet; occasionally lip service is paid to the importance of preserving animals and treating them considerately, but the record of actions overwhelmingly gives the lie. In the nineteenth century, the culture of imperialism – with its Eurocentrism, its insensitivity to the cultures and ecosystems of disempowered people, its cocky bravado that destroyed the integrity of animals' lives – predominated in zoos. In the twentieth century, animals cannot prosper, or even survive, if they are beholden to capitalism and its ways – forced to play by its terms, its practices.

In recent years, as the scope of danger to nature has become impossible to ignore, a profusion of successful business enterprises has emerged, tapping into (and, of course, exploiting) a green market. Ubiquitous New Age crystal shops prosper by spiritualizing fetishes of nature: rocks, fossils, shells. A chain called The Nature Store (with identical competitors, such as The Discovery Store) sells books, CDs, posters, tools, and sundry gizmos for our better appreciation of nature – really, of course, to commodify nature: to offer something to buy that makes us feel as if we are participating in nature, and advancing the cause of preservation, excusing us from the less compelling (and less materialistically tangible) menial labor of environmentalism. The Nature Store touts the joy of tramping around in nature with lots of fun merchandise that they sell.

Comparable ventures abound. A line of clothing called The Daily Planet sells 'global products' featuring 'the colors of earth and sky' and offering items that come with a catalogue description suggesting an affinity closer to the unspoiled primordial natural world than to the urban industrial fashion industry that they actually represent. Mail-order catalogues target demographic groups likely to buy products marketed in the halo of environmentalism. 'Serengeti, A Wildlife Apparel and Gift Catalog' features such items as a rainforest afghan ('this stunning throw turns any sofa or chair into a lush, relaxing refuge') and an underwater reef umbrella ('No need to dive the Caymans to see underwater. Our finely silkscreened umbrella or sunshade gives you a canopy of a marine life experience'). Another mail-order concern, Seventh Generation: Products for a Healthy Planet, explains its name in a quotation from the Great Law of the Iroquois Confederacy printed on the catalogue's cover: 'In our every deliberation, we must consider the impact of our decisions on the next seven generations.' This company markets a few accessories to facilitate conservation (reusable carry-all bags, furniture made out of recycled wood, phosphate-free laundry powder) combined with a larger assortment of home decor items typical of any upscale design store (planters, oriental rugs, CD stands) that have no discernible ecofriendly function, but might look nice in the home of someone who really cares about the environment. The green marketing approach combines a few items that are actually ecologically beneficial with a great deal of other flotsam, ecokitsch, tailored to the design aesthetic – yet with little discernible difference from any other consumer products – of people who fancy themselves environmentalists.

Another attempt to exploit consumer appetites by invoking a connection to ecological concern comes from a business called Rent Mother Nature. That mail-order firm markets the standard range of greenish products, all advertised as representing a direct line to the earth (and a nonexploitative one, in that they only rent, not sell, the productive aspect of nature): a five-pound sack of stoneground flour is advertised as a Minnesota Wheat Lease: 'Rent a rolling acre of nature for wholesome, healthful Minnesota Red Wheat.' A wool blanket is packaged as 'Rent-a-Sheep: Adopt a lovable Dorset lamb or sheep for a season: we'll custom weave a wool heirloom for you.' Jars of raw natural honey: Rent-a-Honey-Hive; baskets of apples: Apple Tree Lease. Each purchase includes 'a handsome, personalized lease document, suitable for framing.'

A group of American businesses including Ben & Jerry's, Rhino Records, and Patagonia outdoor clothing banded together as the Social Venture Network, supporting an array of causes. Perhaps most successful at the commodification of nature is Anita Roddick's chain of stores called The Body Shop. Her first store opened in Brighton, England, in 1976; by 1990 the chain included 600 franchises in 38 countries, worth £280 million (Roddick, 86, 245). The stores feature skin care and hair products (lotions, scents, soaps) and a few gift items and trinkets from other cultures. Roddick and her husband, Gordon, virulently condemn the predominant cultures of capitalism, the business world, and the cosmetic industry, in favor of a more folksy, humanistic approach toward their workers and customers. They refuse to advertise or to use traditional marketing departments; forbid animal testing of their products; and make social and environmental activism part of the company's mission. In her autobiography, Roddick proudly describes the values by which The Body Shop operates, and her rejection of mainstream commercial practices: 'I am mystified by the fact that the business world is apparently proud to be seen as hard and uncaring and detached from human values. Why is altruism in business seen as alien to the point where anyone claiming to be motivated by it is considered suspect?' (16). She has committed her company to be a force for social change and environmental protection.

> Not a single decision is ever taken in The Body Shop without first considering environmental and social issues. We do not, for example, sell any products which consume a disproportionate amount of energy during their manufacture or disposal, cause unnecessary waste, use ingredients derived from threatened species or threatened environments, or adversely affect other countries, particularly in the Third World. We have an Environmental Projects Department which monitors the company's practices and products to ensure they are environmentally sound and up-to-date, organizes campaigns, coordinates global projects, gives guidance and support to local activities and liaises with other pressure groups. We have a vigorous 'Trade Not Aid' policy, encouraging local communities in the Third World to utilize their resources and trade with us to help alleviate poverty. We use our shops worldwide as 'arenas of education' to proselytize among staff, customers and passers-by on issues as diverse as the destruction of the rainforests and the spread of Aids. Every shop has its own local community project run by volunteers from the staff. (23)

Delivery trucks bear Roddick's motto: 'Education is at the very heart of The Body Shop. We encourage the development of the human spirit as well as the mind. We transmit values as well as knowledge: we want to educate our people to be good citizens' (124).

Roddick has committed The Body Shop's funds, resources and employees to numerous campaigns, including human rights movements, but most prominently to environmental activism. Working with other organizations (Friends of the Earth, Greenpeace) and on her own, she has tackled deforestation, acid rain, and animal cruelty. Roddick donates personal and company funds; allows employees to do green work (canvas for signatures, demonstrate, engage in specific projects) while on her timeclock; uses her stores as a clearing house for activist efforts; lends her status as a compelling business celebrity; engages in trade that supports ecologically beneficial programs; and displays posters in her shops' front windows to draw attention to a range of issues.

Roddick has prominently embraced what I characterize as environmental consumerism. She has commodified ecological awareness, as if it were one more product line on her shelves (or, more accurately, as if it underlies all the products on her shelves – buy the lotion, and earn a bonus green point . . .). I admire Roddick's ethos, certainly compared to that of any other billion dollar firm's CEO, but one probably cannot, finally, save the planet through skin cream. I remain skeptical about the environmental impact of Roddick's brand of commerce, and the overlapping of human commercial culture with the natural world that seems so easy – too easy – as she describes it. Inevitably, commercial culture will overshadow nature, replicating the dominance of imperial culture over the subaltern. The Environmental Projects Department of which Roddick is so proud (charged with saving the planet) employs four people as compared with the 5,300 who staff the company's main enterprise of selling merchandise (118, 245). For all her ebullient activist prose, her primary aptitude and orientation are finally in the arena of commerce; she freely admits that her *sine qua non*, her bottom line, is trade:

> we could only undertake social welfare work or environmental campaigning by the gift of our profits. But every now and then we had someone who got it all about face and thought her primary job was to love the world rather than to trade. (Sometimes people get us entirely wrong and apply for jobs thinking we are an environmental protection organization or a charity; they are quite taken aback to learn that working in a Body Shop means selling and cashing and wrapping.)
>
> (154)

And again: 'Although both Gordon and I wholeheartedly support all our campaigning we would never sanction any of it if we could not afford it, or if it somehow endangered the future prosperity of the company' (221). She takes pride in her business acumen that exploited the appeal of environmentalism: describing her canny intuitions regarding expansion, she writes, 'I believe time will show that we probably arrived in the United States at about the right moment, when Americans really started taking the environmental message seriously and were very sympathetically disposed to a company which demonstrated its concern for environmental and social issues' (139).

Roddick's ethos lulls her clientele into thinking that things are OK, or nearly OK and capable of improving within the discourse, sensibilities, and practices of the commercial-imperial status quo. She defuses environmentally informed skepticism about consumerism and its toll on the planet. Roddick's success indicates a disturbing aspect of commercial culture's relation to environmentalism: you have to *buy in*. In this relationship, nature is in the position of subaltern; and the history of imperialism has irrefutably demonstrated that the subaltern can never prosper in that role, however attractive the claims of membership in the imperial culture – whether the fruits of affiliation with Britain (for India et al. in the nineteenth century), or of green commerce today. No matter if we allocate a few percent of credit card charges or phone expenditures (on Working Assets) to salving our consciences: the 'green' that prospers in this relationship will always be, predominantly, that of greenbacks rather than chlorophyll.

Zoos, especially as marketed today, are a variant of the consumer product lines exploited in ecocommerce – promising that people can meet their obligation to the planet by spending a few dollars and a few hours. But even in the hands of the most enlightened emperors of commerce, consumer culture cannot beneficially mediate people's relationship with animals, and nature can prosper only to the extent that it can be divorced – rescued – from consumerist forces. Terry Maple provides a case study of what happens to a zoo in the throes of consumer culture. In *Zoo Man: Inside the Zoo Revolution*, Maple details Zoo Atlanta's transformation under his leadership in the 1980s from a badly run institution that treated animals barbarously to what he characterizes as a stellar modern zoo. It is a success story, as he presents it – his accomplishments verge on miraculous. Maple's language evokes the tenor of Horatio Alger or Dale Carnegie – American capitalist pulled-up-by-the-bootstraps prose. He writes of the zoo's 'transition to excellence' (17) under his reign; he calls the chapter about his appointment as director 'The Ascending Phoenix'; he dubs his domain, 'The world's next great zoo' (20).

Maple touts the virtues of canny management and entrepreneurialism. If he seems to celebrate his triumphs in a shamelessly self-laudatory fashion, this is because he has, in fact, written an autobiography rather than an account of the zoo. The perspective spotlights the keeper: it is the man who matters here, and whose experiences solicit the reader's praise. Probably unintentionally, *Zoo Man* illustrates how zoos tend to concern the *people* involved in them more prominently than the animals – they are so largely about people, in fact, that little space or function remains for animals, which are consigned simply to sit in their cages, to inhabit the small space people have carved out for them.

Describing his quest to rebuild the zoo, Maple sometimes broaches an ecological sensitivity: he writes of how '[o]ur vision of the zoo was based on the wilds of Africa . . . we all talked about how to recapture the experience of communing with wildlife' (73). But two pages later, a photograph punctures this idealism: 'Professional soccer star Pelé dribbles with Starlet the elephant in a 1986 match arranged by the Ford Motor Company,' as the caption describes (75). Starlet is draped with the sort of smock circus elephants wear; in a gaudy typeface befitting a carnival advertisement, the embroidery reads, 'I'm Starlet. Visit me at Zoo Atlanta.' Maple takes credit for such fund-raising promotions as enthusiastically as for his vision of communion with wildlife, but the two are incompatible – the capitalistic discourse must trivialize, patronize, and ultimately destroy the natural discourse. The elephant's full name is Starlet O'Hara; Maple is proud of the publicity garnered by such clever names (which further situates the animal in the human culture of the local zoo – Starlet O'Hara is, of course, an Atlanta elephant – and distances it from natural animals which lack clever names).

The picture of Starlet playing soccer with Pelé does not merely mitigate, but absolutely belies, any vision Maple claims of homage to Africa and African animals. He might argue that the ends justify the means, but such public relations nonsense – manipulating images of animals to implicate them in our cultural practices, subordinating their integrity to the ethos of promotional hucksterism – disqualifies zoos from facilitating honest experiences of animals. Zoo visitors cannot dismiss the semiotics: a zoo animal is demonstrated to be important because it is engaged in a human activity with a human superstar, who anoints the animal with a second-hand distinction by association that implies it lacks any compelling significance on its own. The value and function of this animal are further identified via its implication in commercial imperialism: it is helping to sell Fords. Deeply rooted in the system of American capitalist values is the idea that what's good for General Motors (or, here, Ford) is good for America. Ford likes elephants, Ford sponsors zoos, Ford is good so zoos are good. The ideas are simple enough to be expressed in Orwellian Newspeak – a testimony to their impregnable 'logic' within the discourse of American commercial culture. Everyone likes Coke, Levis, and other ubiquitous trademarks of American commercial culture; in the Communist world, people used to risk death to attain these icons, at least according to the mythos of cultural hegemony. Therefore, these products must be inherently, unassailably valuable. Therefore, everything wallowing in our cultural production systems (Starlet O'Hara, Ford, zoos, whatever else shimmers in the photographs Maple presents for his audience) must be similarly valuable. Zoos are very American, very educational, very wholesome, very family-oriented, very much linked to everything that is supposed to be good about the Free World; they prove their mettle by promoting the forces of Consumerist Democracy.

Maple enjoyed media prominence with the long-running saga of Ivan, the mall gorilla. For 26 years, the 500-pound western lowland gorilla lived in a concrete cage in a Tacoma, Wash., shopping center, serving as a gimmick of commerce. When the B & I Shopping Mall went bankrupt in 1992, it no longer required Ivan's services; several zoos sought to acquire the animal. After two years of negotiations, Zoo Atlanta lay claim to Ivan, and newspapers produced a spate of articles celebrating the 'rescue' of an oppressed animal and Ivan's exciting future prospects in the zoo. A typical illustration is one story with a headline that glibly mocked Ivan's past tribulations while looking forward to the future: 'Mall rat goes ape: Ivan the Gorilla heads to Zoo Atlanta';[10] the article focuses on the brave new world that cutting-edge zoos offer.

As zoo officials prepared to move the animal across the country, continuing news accounts described the battery of preparations, and the zoo's publicity machinery made the most out of the unusual angle. In the coverage lingered a sense of the unique, the bizarre – partially, but not wholly condemnatory – surrounding the notion of a gorilla that had lived in a mall. Perhaps this coverage reflected a perceived desire on the part of the public at large to see a gorilla in a mall (anyone can see one in a zoo). Or perhaps it anticipated that the allure of seeing Ivan on display in Zoo Atlanta would derive, specifically, from its provenance of acquisition: that is, from seeing a gorilla in a zoo that had once been in a mall. (Ivan had lived in Tacoma since the age of three – it was one of seven captured in the Congo in 1964; the others all died in transit to America – and much was made of the fact that it really was a bona fide mall gorilla, having spent essentially its entire life there.)

Traditionally, much of a zoo animal's semiotic attraction is its place of origin: spectators are invited to regard an animal that once roamed the plains of (*fill in the exotic terrain*), and was masterfully trapped, transported, reacclimated right here in our own backyard. Even for zoo animals bred in captivity, the resonance associated with their free-ranging ancestors endures. If audiences have become jaded by the extremities of Madagascar or Tibet, Maple cannily realizes that a Tacoma shopping mall represents the twentieth century's last frontier. He has acquired something that must have been a compelling element of earlier zoos' attraction, but which is a very scarce commodity in today's age of ubiquitous zoos: the unique display specimen. What does a mall gorilla look like, people must have wondered? Reflecting Maple's marketing philosophy of creating a buzz about a specific, striking circumstance regarding an animal, the press featured stories about every stage of Ivan's settlement in the zoo: its arrival in October 1994; its transfer from a holding cage and introduction to what the zoo called a natural habitat (a cageless enclosure) in March 1995. The celebratory coverage peaked when keepers introduced two other gorillas to share Ivan's habitat in June 1995, ending 28 years of isolation from other gorillas. 'Not since Charles wed Di has the selection of a mate for a celebrity bachelor received so much public attention as today's union of Ivan the gorilla with Kuchi and Molly at Zoo Atlanta.'[11] Adolescent leering colored media reaction, as the next day's story indicates: headlined 'Ivan a bit awkward on first date,' it begins, 'They eyed each other and chattered angrily. They chased each other around. The girl slapped the guy, and the guy lay down to think things over.'[12]

On the editorial page, somewhat loftier discourse (headlined 'Here's looking at you, Ivan') lauds the zoo:

> In providing Ivan a more appropriate home, Zoo Atlanta is fulfilling several of the functions of a first-class zoo. It is providing a refuge for an animal that had been deprived of space, outdoor air and companionship. It also will use Ivan to teach zoo visitors about our responsibilities to our fellow creatures and about the fragility of life.[13]

Ivan's cross-country relocation brought the animal out of the frying pan into the fire: from one type of constrained exhibition to another, more appealing but essentially comparable situation. Ivan was not rescued so much as moved laterally from one venue of captivity amid commercial culture to another. As such, the gorilla represents the perfect mascot for Maple's zoo. The pedestrian commercialism of a tacky mall plays off the brilliant commercialism of Zoo Atlanta – a place just about as far from Ivan's African habitat as Tacoma (and not merely geographically). Ivan's attraction lies in having traversed the breadth of a cultural spectrum: from a seemingly inappropriate venue for the display of animals in consumer culture to what is touted as a superlative and nurturing niche of that same culture. Maple thus replicates Stamford Raffles's enterprise in bringing back unique specimens from the other side of the world – the wild, raw, primitive margins of civilization; the lowest rung of the British Empire, yet still a part of the same imperial enterprise as the heart of the highest reaches of culture, Regent's Park. Nineteenth-century zoos celebrated the display of living artifacts from so far away and so unusual, yet still constituent elements of the dominant culture – possessions of the empire.

For both Raffles and Maple, such acquisitional transactions testify to otherness, but otherness within a single overarching cultural enterprise: geopolitical imperialism in the nineteenth century, and commercial imperialism today. Raffles celebrates Britain's sway over Asia as he appropriates foreign oddities for display, to great acclaim, back home. Britain is thus demonstrated to be an imperial power, and Asia an imperial outpost. By the same process, Maple situates Zoo Atlanta at the top of the enterprise in which Tacoma's B & I Mall is at the bottom: he validates his cultural triumph, the sublime celebration of commercial imperial prowess, with a token from the outposts.

A coda to the commercial empire of zoo culture in the late twentieth century features, perhaps inevitably, the American emperor of culture, Walt Disney. I might have been tempted to invent this, or construct its hypothetical likeliness, if reality didn't cooperate. In 1995, the Disney Company announced plans to construct its largest park ever, an 'animal adventure park,' combining amusement rides with 'real wildlife' (Navarro). Slated to open in 1998 near Orlando and estimated to cost close to a billion dollars, the Wild Animal Kingdom will display over a thousand animals in a compound five times the size of Disney's Magic Kingdom. The park was planned with the advice and support of prominent zoo experts (including bumper sticker maven Terry Maple and William Conway of the Bronx Zoo cum Wildlife Conservation Park) 'who have embraced it as an opportunity to excite the public about wildlife.' It will feature three areas – displays of real animals, mythical animals, and extinct animals – 'to offer visitors encounters with live giraffes and make-believe unicorns, journeys like an African safari and a Jurassic Park-type trip to the dinosaur era.' In the hands of Disney, the zoo disregards nature even more than usual, relegating extant natural animals to a mere one-third of the display range, and supplementing this with a majority – mythical and extinct animals – that a paltry natural world cannot offer.

Because of Disney's preeminent stature in the modern American empire, I see its zoo venture as a tremendously significant phenomenon in terms of the future role, and direction, of zoos in Western culture. I second Alexander Wilson's assertion that 'Disney World is a good place to take stock of how the dominant culture of North America . . . makes sense of both historical and ecological change' (11). What we see here is Disney leading the way as it brings zoos into the twenty-first century: bettering zookeepers at their own game; taking the display of captive animals into the realm of hyperreality; accelerating the technology and discourse of representation up to the speed limit of turbocharged American commercialism; giving people even more variety, more fun, more fantasy, more guidance and pampering as they interface with animals in a ritual anointed with the mantle of vintage Disney style, consummately canonical mass/pop culture.

The lowest common denominator pathways of American culture will encourage millions to come to this zoo to experience the Disnified American experience of controlled, processed, eloquently homogeneous, predictable, buyable culture at which the Florida habitat excels. Certainly the Disney Zoo will succeed wildly, complementing Orlando's existing attractions with captive animals arrayed for mawkish observation. Disney will cheapen all the more the experience of nature, and inscribe it even more indelibly in the indolent and inextricable comforts of commodified American culture. Satiating Americans' entertainment cravings with a brilliantly packaged experience, Disney will offer one expensive pass which admits the bearer to theme parks *ad infinitum*: *Kingdoms* (where each ticket holder becomes deputized into the empire's forces) that cover the world from soup to nuts. The experience of nature becomes all the more enticing of a tourist attraction given the consumeristic appetites that Disney stokes and the accompanying fetishes (proximity to carnival rides, movie studios, high-tech fantasias of the Orlando popular cultural complex, and, of course, the incomparable right-from-the-source line of licensed Disney souvenirs). An imperial panoply of cultural fascinations – the wonders of the modern commercial empire – are all arrayed together for a simultaneous moment of gluttonous spectatorial immersion, all feeding into each other and reinforcing their cultural primacy, desirability, supremacy, like a modern Crystal Palace. If our cultural baubles cannot all be displayed under one roof, as in Paxton's nineteenth-century imperial showcase, then they are at least concentrated at one exit off the Florida Turnpike in Walt Disney's twentieth-century version. With its zoo, Disney will expand its empire, further remove animals from nature, and forcefully convince spectators of how wholly corporate America can appropriate nature as a subsidiary of Mickey Mouse. It's the logical culmination to the cultural history of captive animals during this American century.

3
Cages

Cage, from the Latin cavja/cavea, *hollow, cavity, dungeon, cell, cave. A box or place of confinement for birds and other animals (or, in barbarous times, for human beings), made wholly or partly of wire, or with bars of metal or wood, so as to admit air and light, while preventing the creature's escape.*

Oxford English Dictionary

They pay for their beauty, poor beasts . . . Mankind want to catch anything beautiful and shut it up, and then come in thousands to watch it die by inches.

David Garnett, *A Man in the Zoo*

unlock
the ugly gadgets of the zoo: release
the leopard, lemur and the kangaroo:

so that the eagle finds again his perch,
the polar bear his berg . . .

the flopping seals become sea-
cats again, torpedo-shaped with whiskers

and lions stretch & roll their golden thunder down
the quivering river of the crocodiles

Edward Kamau Brathwaite, 'The Zoo'

Animals' cages in zoos are unpalatable. Visitors watching caged animals may ignore or repress the fact of confinement; they may somehow rationalize the need for the cage, or they may on some level enjoy the sadistic spectacle. Guilt or defensiveness about caging animals pervades zoo stories, as when a keeper in Marie Nimier's *The Giraffe* describes a research project, '"On the integration of *Giraffidae* in a protected environment" . . . scrupulously avoiding the word "captivity." The Director was most punctilious about the use of terms designating the concepts of confinement and freedom' (68). Besides euphemistic or periphrastic avoidance, language demonstrates in other ways an uncomfortable awareness of what cages imply. The simile 'to be nervous as a caged lion,' for example, means 'To be nervous, anxious, frustrated and frantic . . . The King of Beasts does not enjoy being kept in a cage at a circus or zoo. He paces back and forth, paws at the bars, charges at the onlookers, and roars with rage. People behave much the same way when they are denied participation in an event' (Palmatier, 60).

For Brigid Brophy, zoo cages typify people's general insensitivity toward animals, and heedlessness of their dignity: 'It is rare for us to leave wild animals alive; when we do, we often do not leave them wild. Some we put on display in a prison just large enough for them to survive, but not in any full sense to live, in' ('Rights', 15–16). Zoo stories abundantly relate the indignities caged animals suffer, often draped in heavy pathos: typical is this passage by Felix Salten (the author of *Bambi*) in 'Prisoners' (1942):

> These [zoological] gardens fenced in many prisoners. They were all sentenced to lifelong loss of liberty, yet they were all innocent. Some of them seemed reconciled to their existence; some were done in by their fate. One huddled in apathetic despair; another paced in wild desperation . . . Llamas, antelopes, mufflins, ostriches, zebus, little deer, zebras. Pitiable, unhappy creatures that were born to live in the free wilderness and shun man, to flee his very scent with dismay – now they denied their own natures and sought him because his presence was less terrible than unnoticed solitude in caged confinement. A magnificent white ass trotted around in small circles behind his bars and raised the cry which always touches me. It sounds like the sob of a man who cannot weep; in it are longing and accusation and painful renunciation.
>
> (100–1)

Boria Sax describes a traditional resonance of cages: 'Many early menageries appealed to a taste for horror by stressing, and exaggerating, the savagery of their animals. The bars were a symbolic acknowledgment of this ferocity . . . Zoos and menageries of the Victorian era . . . tended to dramatize the increased dominion of man over nature, by keeping large animals such as tigers in extremely cramped cages.'

A fashion for more naturalistic zoo settings instead of steel-barred cages may seem to alleviate the unpleasantness inherent in the display of caged animals – providing comfort at least to human spectators, if not animals – but their essential function is equivalent to that of the standard zoo cage.[1] (The *OED* defines 'cage' as 'Anything resembling a cage in structure or purpose' [entry 4].) 'A new concept called "landscape immersion" puts people into the animals' home rather than vice versa,' writes Allen W. Nyhuis. 'Modern technology has provided fog machines, convincing artificial rocks and trees, and recordings of wildlife noises that allow visitors not only to see animals in a realistic rain forest setting, but also to feel as if they are actually in the rain forest themselves. The exhibits look, feel, sound, and even smell like the real thing' (6). To the people, perhaps; but to the animals? . . . doubtful. Nyhuis suggests that an animal's 'home' can be replicated with accessories and landscaping; yet the captive creatures remain just as far from their real homes as if they were in concrete and steel cages. Trendy replications of habitats mislead zoo spectators to believe that wild animals can be at home in alien compounds; people thus become less rather than more appreciative of what a habitat actually is, and what relation an authentic biota has to the life forms that inhabit it.

The pretense of cagelessness is an attempt at self-delusion about what cages and zoos signify in our society, both in terms of people's position as spectators and in terms of the general conditions of animals in our world. Valerie Martin's novel *The Great Divorce* (1994) describes a cageless zoo as a faux 'Zoo Eden,'

> the final irony: a false paradise in which the last representatives of soon to be extinct species are displayed to a public eager to be absolved for their extinction. The expensive exhibits conjure up a world that never did, never will, exist, in which predator and prey gaze stupidly at one another across invisible but effective barriers, while plant life flourishes, water supplies are stable, and all of nature is benign.
>
> (1)

We remove the cages, Martin suggests, because the animals are so close to elimination, to non-existence, that cages are superfluous, and are, further, embarrassing reminders of what we have done to animals.[2] If the architecture and semiotics of nineteenth-century zoos served to tame a threatening realm of nature, then the modern 'natural' zoo habitat as Martin contextualizes it is a refinement – a culmination, a logical consequence – of the zoo's historical signification. Nature is now so incontrovertibly harmless that the zoo's very cages may be eschewed. Animals roam 'free' as confirmation that they pose no threat to any element of the human setting in which they are ensconced; like eunuchs in a seraglio, their freedom is a humiliating indication of their impotence.

While many of the most dramatic restraints on animals, particularly the bars of cages, are being removed, Sax argues, the lives of animals are subject to increasingly complex and sophisticated regulation. The semiotic and literal facts remain: the assertion of captivity and subjection, the delineation of enclosure and confinement. 'The lions weren't caged, exactly,' the narrator of Charles Baxter's 'Westland' observes of two animals he sees lying on fake rock ledges; 'they just weren't free to go' (19). In 'The Mappined Life' (published posthumously in 1919), Saki examines whether or not cageless enclosures are any more humane than traditional cages:

> 'These Mappin Terraces at the Zoological gardens are a great improvement on the old style of wild-beast cage,' said Mrs. James Gurtleberry, putting down an illustrated paper; 'they give one the illusion of seeing animals in their natural surroundings. I wonder how much of the illusion is passed on to the animals?'
>
> (187)

In answer to Mrs Gurtleberry, Saki's story asserts that the delusion does not embellish the animals' lives; it turns out to be even more cruel than conventional cages because it taunts the inmates with the delusion of an attainable freedom. ('London's Mappin Terraces, which house the bears and sheep, were opened in 1913 and used some of the same principles' as Carl Hagenbeck's designs for zoos, writes Jeremy Cherfas. 'Hagenbeck was an immensely clever landscaper, and instead of putting his animals behind bars he put them into moated enclosures. Carefully planted trees and shrubs, artificial rockwork, paths that meandered between the exhibits all conspired to give a feeling of freedom. The animals were still captive, but their captivity was well hidden' (39–40).)

Jeffrey Masson and Susan McCarthy find 'natural habitats' in zoos minimally amenable to the residents: despite the innovations, 'most zoo animals, particularly the large ones, have little or no opportunity to use their abilities. Eagles have no room to fly, cheetahs have no room to run, goats have but a single boulder to climb' (99). John Wuichet and Bryan Norton agree that, even if naturalistic enclosures are not obviously restrictive, they may still leave animals no better off than in cages. 'Stimuli that evoke species-typical behavior,' such as cageless zoo displays are supposed to facilitate,

> do not necessarily entail real autonomy or authenticity of experience, and attempting to justify captivity on the grounds that behavior in captivity and behavior out of captivity are roughly indistinguishable falls short of the authenticity criterion. Simply because humans tend to sleep in the same place every night does not mean we would be just as well off sleeping in prison. Similarly, the fact that some migratory birds elect to return to the same territory every year or that other animals stake out rather limited territories does not . . . justify their confinement.
>
> (241)

It seems paradoxical at best, deceptively hypocritical at worst, for the zoo – fundamentally a place of confinement – to promote the idea of cagelessness for its captive animals and to dupe spectators thereby into believing they are watching real animal life. In *Zoo*, Louis MacNeice expresses this disjunction when he voices his preference for traditionally delineated captivity because it makes him feel more comfortable in his role as a zoo spectator: he discusses a new elephant house being built in the London Zoo where the animals 'are to have no bars. I feel a little about unbarred animals as I feel about the stage experiments of Mayerhold and Vakhtangov after the Revolution in Russia. These producers insist on mixing the actors up with the audience, emphasizing their unity. This seems to me wrong. The audience are there to look at the actors and that is as far as their "co-operation" should go'; if actors (or zoo animals) and audience are not separated by some clearly perceived construct,

MacNeice concludes, 'you don't know where you are' (108). Charles Siebert, too, prefers his zoo animals in cages:

> Somehow, by the end of a day of peering into deep, landscaped 'natural habitats' – looking for the animals we've brought from so far away only to place too far away to really see – I'd decided that it was far less depressing to proceed, as one did in an old zoo, from the assumption of the animals' sadness in captivity than to have to constantly infer the happiness we've supposedly afforded them in our new pretend versions of their rightful homes. The former premise, at least, seems less of a lie about what a zoo is.
>
> ('Gone', 54)

CAGED

Although cages are not funny, I begin by examining a humorous representation of caged zoo animals, Nick Park's 1989 animated (claymation) short feature *Creature Comforts*. The film consists of interviews with zoo animals that explain with polite, genteel English decorum why they would prefer *not* to live in a cage, all things considered. Park describes how he assembled the film's script and soundtrack: 'With *Creature Comforts* I decided not to use actors, and not to write a script as such, but to go out and record ordinary people in their homes, ask them questions which would somehow get the kinds of answers that animals in the zoo would give if you were able to go into the zoo and interview the animals' (Interview).

Despite manifestly oppressive situations the animals remain soft-spoken, almost apologetic about having to complain. The creatures seem bored and weary in their cages, but never rude or hostile. It is clear, however, reading through Park's satire, that he imagines the animals must be considerably more outraged than their propriety betrays. Indeed, the film's title emphasizes the ironic understatement: 'creature comforts' are 'The basic needs of life: food, drink, warmth, security . . . those things that are necessary to sustain the life of all "creatures"' (Palmatier, 101). Obviously, though, what people determine to be creature comforts create far-from-comfortable creatures.[3] Park's interviewees try to explain as clearly as they can why their cages are unpleasant – speaking in simple detail, as if to an audience who for some reason cannot discern what should be painfully manifest. 'Most of the cages are a bit small, and kind of grotty and everything,' says a wild boar. 'Well it's reasonably comfortable, I s'ppose, this place,' adds a terrapin, 'but, uh, I mean, I've been in more comfortable rooms, yes . . . I can't actually get out and about.' A rabbit sticking its head out a small hole in a box, surrounded by a dozen baby rabbits, complains about the enclosure: 'My room is, is a bit too small, really, and I've got so much stuff in it, and if I get anything new there's just nowhere to put it.' A large baboon, sitting on the floor in a corner of its cage, explains, 'Well, sometimes you can't get out and about as much as you would like to, you're *stuck in* for some reason, like I'm stuck in today. And um, then, yes, you get bored, and you get fed up with looking at the same four walls.' A South American-accented jaguar is the most eloquent spokesanimal:

> They try to make you comfortable, they try to put you in, in, in, in a quite, uh, nice situation, which is still, the food that look more like, uh, dog food than food proper for wild animals, all right? . . .
>
> If you try to compare the situations in the environment that live here with the environment that live in Brazil, there is a big difference. Here, you live in a *very small* place with all the technological advances possible. You have, uh, everything sorted out, double glazing, you know, your heating, and everything. In Brazil – But you don't have space. In Brazil, you have the space, although you don't have all this technological, you know, double glazing and things like that, and, uh, you know, uh, but you have the space, and uh, we need the space to *live*, we need the space to feel that we are part of the world and not a kind of, uh, piece of, uh, object in a box . . .
>
> I miss a lot the food; I miss the fresh meat. You know, because, in Brazil we are predominantly carnivores. We are not, you know, vegetarians. And, uh, we don't like potatoes. We like meat. We like fresh meat . . .

> Where I would like to live and to spend most of my life, in a hot country. You know, in a hot country, that I have a good weather, and that I have the *space*, and that I have *trees*, you know, that I don't have only grass, with . . . hayfever every day. I need a space with blue skies, without that I can't see the sun every day, all right, that I have nice weather, that I can just have nice water, you know, to dive, to swim in, it needs a tropical country, not in an island, a cold one. It's easy, any part of the world, but hot, name it and I go.

Although initially amusing, the film is, upon reflection, unsettling. The imprisoned animals talk just like people: they seem similar to us, indeed *too much* like us. Park depicts zoo animals suffering the kind of constraint that (we would hope) could never befall human beings; yet their blasé expression – never tragic, just mutely depressed – sounds as if it could come from our parents or shut-in neighbors. The quotidian grouses in regular people's voices remind us that similar deprivation of freedom and 'comforts' could happen to any of us (and in fact often befalls the elderly). Park cajoles his audience to accept that we *should* empathize with zoo animals: if they could talk to us, he suggests, they would be saying the same kinds of things people say when they are cooped up in depersonalized institutional settings, literally or metaphorically caged.

Other zoo stories that give captive animals a high degree of expressiveness reiterate *Creature Comforts* by suggesting even more accusingly what zoo animals would say to people if they could. Daniel Quinn's *Ishmael* (1992) relates the thoughts of a gorilla about its fellow sufferers in the zoo, who

> cannot help but sense that something is very wrong with this style of living . . . the tiger you see pacing its cage is nevertheless preoccupied with something that a human would certainly recognize as a thought. And this thought is a question: *Why?* 'Why, why, why, why, why, why?' the tiger asks itself hour after hour, day after day, year after year, as it treads its endless path behind the bars of its cage . . . this question burns like an unquenchable flame in its mind, inflicting a searing pain that does not diminish until the creature lapses into a final lethargy that zookeepers recognize as an irreversible rejection of life.
>
> (11)

In 'The Heaven of Animals' (1993), Alison Baker similarly evokes zoo animals' perpetual antipathy toward their cages: ' "Free us," whispers the Stanley Crane, sidling up to the fence. "Free us."' The spectator observes, 'other birds are moving toward me, nodding, their eyes fixed on me, on my hands, their beaks curved down, moving toward the fences of their private and shared enclosures. "Free us," they whisper and hiss' (64). And in Edward Kamau Brathwaite's 'The Zoo' (1989), the entire assembly of animals proclaims their cages' discomfort; they

> cannot conceal the fact
> that where they play or flap
> is merely minor freedom for them
> (47)

By bringing animals' situation as close to human perceptions as possible – by depicting zoo animals with a consciousness and intellectual fluency similar to people's – Park, Quinn, and Baker try to make people realize how life in captivity would feel if it ever happened to us: to appreciate, as Masson and McCarthy write, that an animal 'needs room to wander over a range appropriate to its species ... No cage is big enough for a polar bear or a cougar' (123). In this regard, such zoo stories more effectively spark empathetic interaction between people and animals than a zoo visit is likely to do.

Caged animals appear profusely throughout zoo stories, of course, and I will return to consider this important motif in further detail. But first, the method Park uses to give voice to his zoo animals – appropriating the words of people – suggests a segue to an important tangent to animal captivity: incidences of *people* in zoo cages. *Creature Comforts* invites people to identify with animals' lives in cages, to put ourselves in the animals' place. Numerous other writers, depicting people instead of animals inside zoo cages, force us more explicitly to consider the relationship among species and between different types of captivity. A man in a cage indicates, to begin with, an automatically ironic situation: animals are 'supposed' to be inside the bars, and people outside, so the reverse prominently intimates that things are not right in the world. What else do these men – usually that sex – in cages signify? Chapter 2 surveyed the historical proclivity for putting people in cages (or comparable venues of display connoting control) – 'specimens,' generally, from imperial outposts, contextualized as 'inferior natives' of scientific or ethnographic interest; but modern depictions of men in cages almost totally lack any reference to such human displays. (David Garnett's *A Man in the Zoo* briefly alludes to a display of people that resembles ones from the past,[4] though these are not explicitly associated with his novella's caged man.) The caged men in modern zoo stories are essentially a literary construct, without explicit historical reference.[5] Does the scenario simply use the zoo cage as a metaphor for the image of *human* constraint (which is presumably more important to most people than animal captivity)? Does it attempt to enlighten people about the cruelty of caging animals, showing how it would feel to get a dose of our own medicine?[6] Does the depiction of a man in the zoo somehow, explicitly or subconsciously, set up a bridge, a commonality, between the condition of human captivity and that of animal captivity in zoos, inciting opposition to all forms of constraint of any species and embrace of the struggle for universal freedom?

Or do portrayals of men in zoos legitimize the degradations of animals in zoos, consigning those people who have the misfortune to end up in zoo cages to the status of 'dumb beasts' – suggesting that men who end up in zoo cages deserve what they have gotten? Such an interpretation affirms Palmatier's metaphorical connotations of 'beast': 'a human (esp. a male) who behaves like an animal. A human beast is brutal, coarse, contemptible, cruel, and lacking in intelligence, morality, reason, and self control – i.e., is bestial' (20). Steve Baker finds that animal metaphors embody 'overwhelmingly negative connotations,' cultural expressions of contempt. He asks whether such rhetoric offers 'evidence that animals are generally held in contempt in the contemporary imagination, and, if so, is it the same contempt which is more dramatically apparent in the culture's toleration of such practices as vivisection and factory farming?' (89–90). He concludes that there is indeed significant correlation between the way our language denigrates animals and the oppressions they suffer at our hands. By the same reasoning, when we connote any creature, human or nonhuman, as a 'beast,' we imply that it belongs in a cage.

Remember Palmatier's definition of being 'nervous as a caged lion': 'The King of Beasts does not enjoy being kept in a cage . . .

He paces back and forth, paws at the bars ... *People behave much the same way* when they are denied participation in an event' (emphasis mine). *Do* they? Exactly how closely do caged people correspond to caged animals? A man in a cage offers a potentially useful vehicle for transcending anthropocentrism – that is, allowing people to appreciate the horror of captivity that tends to be somehow trivialized, or rationalized, or sublimated when the victims are nonhuman. On the other hand, while people who are metaphorically caged like animals may provide a convenient vehicle for the depiction of human distress, there may be minimal reference to the actual conditions of caged animals *per se* – as in Paul Laurence Dunbar's 1913 poem 'Sympathy,' a moving poem about human constraints, but one that seems relatively inattentive to the consciousness of captive animals except as a poetic conceit:

> I know why the caged bird sings, ah me,
> When his wing is bruised and his bosom sore, –
> When he beats his bars and he would be free;
> It is not a carol of joy or glee,
> But a prayer that he sends from his heart's deep core,
> But a plea, that upward to Heaven he flings –
> I know why the caged bird sings!
>
> (102)

Bob Mullan and Garry Marvin explicitly link the conditions of people in mental asylums and animals in zoos. In both institutions, 'inmates cannot live normal lives: they do not have to engage in behaviour directed to maintaining themselves in the world, and this contributes to lethargy together with an apparent lack of interest in the world about them' (38). Both zoo animals and asylum residents are separated from their natural habitats in the outside world and from interaction in normal social groups; consigned to enforced idleness; subject to authoritarian institutional regimentation; perhaps drugged, and/or biologically and behaviorally manipulated to facilitate institutional convenience; kept in a ward with 'poor furniture, decoration and lighting, poor diet, noise, unpleasant smells' (in the case of people) or 'caging, a totally alien environment with artificial infrastructures, lighting, artificial diet, unusual noise, strange odours' (in the case of animals) (38). Mullan and Marvin find parallels in the organizational cultures of zoos and asylums, such as the traditional tour of inspection by the institutions' directors at the beginning of the day and the imposition of strict timetables (for feeding, for example, and transferring charges from areas of night confinement to places where they spend waking hours) that structure the inmates' reality. Yi-Fu Tuan, too, notes that the rowdy behavior of some zoo spectators who taunt or physically attack caged animals

> bears a close resemblance to how, in an earlier time, people acted toward caged mental patients. In the early modern period (1600 to 1750), Europeans viewed the lunatic as the lowliest human creature, someone reduced to almost a state of pure animality . . . not only the rabble but the most refined members of society flocked into London's Bethlehem Hospital for the insane (popularly known as Bedlam) for entertainment. Just as people in the early part of the twentieth century might cruelly tease animals caged in the zoo, so in this earlier era visitors to Bedlam deliberately tried to enrage the animals chained to their cells or intoxicate them with gin so as to obtain a wilder performance. Before its doors were finally closed to the public in 1770, Bethlehem Hospital came to admit 96,000 visitors annually. (83)

In zoo stories, are the men in cages somehow crazy? And would this characterization of crazy men in zoo cages then help to explain the ethos of caging animals, which are treated in zoos like insane people? (Palmatier lists four animal metaphors indicating insanity: 'Crazy as a bedbug,' 'Crazy as a coot,' 'Crazy as a loon,' and 'Crazy like a fox'; Elizabeth Atwood Lawrence notes that insects' perceived monstrosity is 'associated with insanity, as terms like *going buggy* and being sent to the *bughouse* express contempt' (183). When people project our insanities onto animals in these metaphors, do we really believe they're all crazy? What must they think about us?) A recurrent strain of madness haunts men in cages; does this suggest zoo spectators subliminally perceive caged animals as being nuts, too? Or, if the zoo animals are not literally and certifiably crazy, then they are at least definitively *other* than us in their rational capacities (according to human standards, which we anthropocentrically posit as the norm). Cages evoke people's belief that those deranged animals would attack us if they could, biting the hand that feeds them; because they are so divorced from (*our*) reality, they do not understand how lucky they are to be in the cage. Such reasoning confirms that it makes sense for animals to be inside the cages, subject to people and our imposition of the conditions under which we determine they should exist.

Besides the asylum, another obvious human institutional parallel to the zoo is the prison. Zoo animals, like human prisoners, experience what Michel Foucault calls 'systems of punishment' that are

> situated in a certain 'political economy' of the body: even if they do not make use of violent or bloody punishment, even when they use 'lenient' methods involving confinement or correction, it is always the body that is at issue – the body and its forces, their utility and their docility, their distribution and their submission.
>
> (25)

Stories of men in zoo cages highlight the ironies and indignities visited upon the subject human body; such degradations, certainly, engage the reader intimately. Other zoo stories tend to be less explicit regarding the corresponding toll on the body of an animal – perhaps because representations of corporeal suffering are presumed to be less accessible or less compelling to members of a different species, or perhaps because animals' constraint is so much more commonplace, and thus less aesthetically interesting, than human captivity. As Foucault writes, the constraints of a cage invoke *systematic* dynamics of oppression – dynamics that prosper in tandem with the cultural processes that enable the zoo's unchallenged proliferation – which, essentially, have the function of victimizing the body. This is no less true of zoo animals (in any conditions of captivity, whether concrete and steel or 'cagelessly natural') than of human prisoners. What Foucault says of the prison – that its primary significance inheres not in its operational details, but rather in 'its very materiality as an instrument and vector of power' (30) – applies equally to the zoo.

Critics conventionally regard Franz Kafka's 'A Hunger Artist' (1922) as an allegory of art – about the decadence of the artist, the obtuseness of his audience, the aesthetics of existential depravity – that might concern zoos only incidentally. But a zoo story need not necessarily express an explicit commentary about animal captivity to contain useful insights on the topic; and Kafka's memorable depiction of a caged man offers provocative insights into zoos and caged animals. The title character travels from city to city, performing (in a loose sense) on display in a 'small barred cage' (268). While he is not literally in a zoo, his environment strongly suggests one: for example, when annoyed by spectators' unappreciative ignorance, 'he reacted with an outburst of fury and to the general alarm began to shake the bars of his cage like a wild animal' (272). And after the popularity of hunger artists has waned, the man – no longer able to attract audiences on his own – joins a circus as a sideshow attraction (alongside captive animals on display, and eventually subordinate to them). By the end of the story the hunger artist's milieu, if not precisely denoted as a zoo, evokes at least a variegated conflation of zoos, menageries, carnivals, and general entertainment spectacles involving animals; and the character's condition is comparable to a zoo animal's.

What a hunger artist does is, simply, fast; people turn out to stare at him in his cage, to watch him abstain from food. He is caged to ensure that he takes no nutrition and also, presumably, because the cage is the conventional semiotic indication that contextualizes a specimen on display: it signifies that whatever is inside is being kept there to facilitate its examination by those outside. The cage guarantees that whenever a spectator should choose to walk by, the creature on display will be nowhere other than, of course, inside it. The story's most striking absurdity is the idea that watching someone fast would interest anyone – what could be less remarkable or spectacular? We can transpose the same irony to zoos: the caged animals aren't doing much of anything either, by comparison to their natural behavior. Just as Kafka's hunger artist is denied food – symbolically evoking other physical and intellectual sustenance – zoo animals are deprived of freedom, many behavioral routines, and other 'nourishing' aspects of their natural habitats. Both cases provoke the question: what kind of perverse spectators would find the deprivation of a caged creature's natural conditions so compelling?

Kafka's artist thinks of the 'honor of his profession' (269), the code of conduct, ideals, and aesthetics governing hunger artists, but the story satirizes this. Despite the artist's pretensions to be engaged in a noble endeavor, there is nothing honorable about the pathetic spectacle he presents. He is miserable in his cage: unable to sleep, melancholy in spirit, devoid of any enduring cultural potency. Similarly, people pay lip service to the nobility of zoo animals, the splendor of their character – as, for example, when the *Encyclopaedia Britannica* claims zoos offer the opportunity of 'viewing at close range the curious and beautiful living products of nature,' or when a zookeeper states that the zoo's function is to 'communicate the wonder and diversity of wildlife' (Mullan and Marvin, 116). But the conditions of caged zoo animals resoundingly belie propaganda or clichés about their dignity. Kafka's character is *called* an artist, just as zoos are called cultural attractions – but both pander to lurid voyeurism, cloaked in the mantle of art and culture.

A creature in a cage may call itself an artist (or be called by its keepers wondrous, 'curious and beautiful') – may purportedly embody whatever refinements it had under happier circumstances. Indeed, the hunger artist's obsession with being appreciated as a maestro suggests a mad attachment to the conceit that his career is meaningful and valuable: thus, according to Mullan and Marvin's association of human insanity with animal captivity, he may belong in a cage for this reason alone. By the end of the story, fanatically committed to preserving the traditions of an art no one else cares about, he grows increasingly detached from normal social perceptions – insane. But however determined (or insanely impervious to reason) its delusions of grandeur, a creature in a cage, whether animal or human, cannot ultimately sustain the charade of dignity. It must become deflated, humbled; it must capitulate to its environs. The cage essentially and wholly defines, subordinates, whatever is inside. There is nothing apparent that the hunger artist's spectators could be looking at: Kafka reveals no compelling attraction other than the lowest common denominator of a caged specimen. One infers that the crowds who come to see the hunger artist may be reveling in the displacement of their miseries, inadequacies, and insecurities, onto him – gloating over the less fortunate because it reinforces their sense of their own superiority; the hunger artist is caged, and they are not.

If the artist's appeal lies in the crowd's opportunity to flatter themselves at his expense because they differ from him, the display reiterates an attraction of zoos. Caged creatures are always imbued with a sense of otherness: in zoos, this sense is highlighted by its self-advertisement as a repository of rare, exotic, odd animals, and by signs that proclaim how far away the animal's natural habitat is, how unusual its behavior is, how unique its climate and diet and habits are. Constructed as absolutely other, zoo animals are thus the quintessential victims. 'The victimization of animals is in all likelihood foundational to culture and civilization,' writes Marian Scholtmeijer. 'The persistence of aggressive behavior [toward animals] suggests that humans have not transcended the need to prove their distinctiveness by means of the domination of animals' (52). Keith Tester writes that in the early modern period, 'aggressive behaviour towards animals was an active way for humans to define themselves as the centre of the universe and the zenith of God's work,' since oppressed animals defined human supremacy by antithesis; 'establishing animals as a distinctive other' ensured that 'virtually anything could be done to them' (51).

As the audience's enthusiasm wanes, the hunger artist becomes more like an animal. At the end of the story, completely dehumanized, he can barely speak; people outside his cage hardly recognize that he belongs to their own species. The decline of his career parallels his increasingly zoolike conditions: people coming to see him, he realizes, 'without exception, were all on their way to the menagerie' (275). He sees that he is becoming closer – too close – to the animals, which worries him: 'Perhaps, said the hunger artist to himself many a time, things would be a little better if his cage were set not quite so near the menagerie' (275). He deplores the caged animals' torpor (despite his increasing affinity to them): 'he suffered from the stench of the menagerie, the animals' restlessness by night, the carrying past of raw lumps of flesh for the beasts of prey, the roaring at feeding times, which depressed him continually' (275). But he feels a debt to the animals for his continued livelihood: 'after all, he had the animals to thank for the troops of people who passed his cage, among whom there might always be one here and there to take an interest in him, and who could tell where they might seclude him if he called attention to his existence and thereby to the fact that, strictly speaking, he was only an impediment to the menagerie' (275–6). Devolving into animalism, the hunger artist is finally ejected from his cage – judged to be a waste of valuable exhibition space – and replaced with a panther. The panther performs easily for the crowds – without the self-reflection, self-obsession, and self-pity that consumed the hunger artist:

> Into the cage they put a young panther. Even the most insensitive felt it refreshing to see this wild creature leaping around the cage that had so long been dreary. The panther was all right. The food he liked was brought to him without hesitation by the attendants; he seemed not even to miss his freedom; his noble body, furnished almost to the bursting point with all that it needed, seemed to carry freedom around with it too; somewhere in his jaws it seemed to lurk; and the joy of life streamed with such ardent passion from his throat that for the onlookers it was not easy to stand the shock of it. But they braced themselves, crowded around the cage, and did not ever want to move away.
>
> (277)

The spectators themselves are figuratively caged at the end: technically outside the bars, but captivated through their compulsion, as if fated to remain there forever. Kafka suggests the condition of caged captivity is contagious: people who stand just outside the cage looking in for too long risk becoming themselves imprisoned, enthralled ('thrall': Old English for serf, slave, one who is in bondage) by the banal and degrading spectacle; stimulated by whatever happens to be displayed in a cage; reduced to spectatorial zombies who have lost the ability to experience anything real, meaningful, challenging, uncaged.

The story's last words illuminate the interplay between a caged man and a caged animal, as one gives way to the other. What has been for most of the narrative a parable of a man in a cage, at the end comes to resemble a zoo story more obviously. Kafka's conclusive vision depicts the animal as happy and fulfilled in the cage. The panther retains its dignity, Kafka informs, and seems not to miss its freedom; but Kafka's parting image of the caged panther must be considered as ironic. The animal seems noble at first glance, a flattering reflection upon both institutional animal captivity and the culture that patronizes such spectacles. But the story's context indicates that the noble panther reigns amid a thoroughly degraded world: if it is some sort of cultural prodigy, then it is a prodigy among wretches, and so implicated in Kafka's existential wretchedness itself.

Kafka allegorically portrays the dangers consequent upon falling away from true art, from the delicacy of the intellect and the aesthetic. When human arts and passions atrophy (as has befallen the hunger artist), the artist increasingly resembles a zoo animal, which is depicted as the endpoint of degradation. Allen Thiher sees the final vision of the panther as an 'image of animal self-sufficiency,' an antithesis to the emaciated hunger artist (90); despite the literal accuracy of this analysis, I dispute Thiher's implication that the panther represents a replacement for the debased art of people, or a viably renewed source of stimulation for the masses. Rather, I think Kafka suggests that the animal, although temporarily appealing and effective as a caged exhibition, will eventually go the way of the hunger artist; the cage itself dooms whatever it constrains to wither. The burst of energy emanating from the cage at the end of 'A Hunger Artist' is only a dithyramb, portending immanent cultural exhaustion. What will happen to the panther when its novelty fades? Stephen St C. Bostock describes the fate of zoo animals whose services are no longer required: 'Of course, not all the animals in zoos live to old age, or, sadly, can be allowed to . . . the killing of surplus animals is likely to be necessary' (65). And what will happen to the spectators – what will remain for them to look at when the panther has gone the way of all zoo flesh?

Although indirectly, Kafka's story valuably addresses the link between zoos and other human cultural endeavors. He portrays the zoo as not absolutely separable or isolated from society's artistic heights, but rather as the termination of a continuum betokening the failure of culture. Kafka represents the zoo's otherness, but not the inevitability of such otherness: depressingly and existentially, he makes it impossible for people to dissociate ourselves from the zoo totally, or to eliminate the hunger artist's indignity as a possible outcome in our own lives, as a symbol of encroaching devolution in the modern world around us. The hunger artist simultaneously resents and embraces his contextualization as a caged zoo animal, aware of its necessity for his continued cultural existence. The audience, too, is effectively as constrained as anything inside the cage. Kafka depicts the zoo (and especially its operative artifact, the cage) as an emblem of the inescapable and ubiquitous force of cultural deadening. If and when the sensibility of 'A Hunger Artist' becomes pervasive, Kafka warns – when cultural producers and consumers are compromised by their acceptance of cages and consequent models of cultural experience and spectatorship – then all is lost.

If Kafka's representation of a man in a cage is one of the most prominent in modernism, David Garnett's in his 1924 novella *A Man in the Zoo* is the most detailed consideration of this motif. It features John Cromartie and Josephine Lackett, a tumultuous couple sorting out romantic conflicts during a date at the London Zoo. Annoyed and frustrated by her companion's constant bickering, Josephine lashes out at him: 'you ought to be shut up in the Zoo. The collection here is incomplete without you . . . You ought to be shut up and exhibited here in the Zoo – I've told you once and now I tell you again – with the gorilla on one side and the chimpanzee on the other. Science would gain a lot.' Impulsively, to shock and humiliate Josephine, Cromartie accepts her absurd suggestion: 'Well, I will be. I am sure you are quite right. I'll make arrangements to be exhibited' (7). In a letter to the Zoological Society, Cromartie lays out his proposal to be inducted into their gardens which contain

> specimens of practically the whole fauna of the terrestrial globe, only one mammalian of real importance being unrepresented. But the more I have thought over this omission, the more extraordinary has it appeared to me. To leave out man from a collection of the earth's fauna is to play Hamlet without the Prince of Denmark . . . Firstly, it would complete the collection, and, secondly, it would impress upon the mind of the visitor a comparison which he is not always quick to make for himself. If placed in a cage between the Orang-outang and the Chimpanzee, an ordinary member of the human race would arrest the attention of everyone who entered the Large Apehouse. In such a position he would lead to a thousand interesting comparisons being made by visitors for whose education the Gardens do in a large measure exist. Every child would grow up imbued with the outlook of a Darwin, and would become aware not only of his own exact place in the animal kingdom, but also in what he resembled, and in what he differed from the Apes.
>
> (10–11)

Cromartie's appeal invokes the two most common justifications for zoos' existence: the collection's comprehensive breadth and inclusiveness (implicitly celebrating the greatness of the society sponsoring the zoo); and the educational betterment of the society's citizens, especially children, who are presumed to be enriched by having access to as many caged specimens as possible. The human being should be displayed, Cromartie's letter concludes, 'as far as possible in his natural surroundings as he exists at the present time, that is to say in ordinary costume, and employed in some ordinary pursuit' (11).

Upon receipt of the letter and after an initial disinclination, the Zoological Society's Chairman finds the idea innovative and attractive, as well as potentially lucrative. He interviews Cromartie, who states conditions for his service concerning 'food and drink, clothing, medical attention, and one or two luxuries which he was to receive. Thus he was to be allowed to order his own meals, see his own tailor,' and so forth, and 'neither was objection to be raised to his having a library in his cage, and writing materials' (13).

Cromartie enlists himself as a zoo animal, but with two significant differences from the other fauna: he has committed himself to the cage of his own freely given accord, and he retains control over at least some of his habits, needs, and desires. Although the Society hopes he will stay for life, 'because the public readily attaches itself to the individual animals in the Zoo, and is not to be consoled when such a favourite dies, or disappears,' Cromartie presumably 'would have been given his liberty whenever he asked for it, without his having recourse to extreme measures such as refusing food or imploring the aid of visitors in rescuing him' (43) – so he is not literally captive. Eventually Cromartie and Lackett become engaged and plan to live together in the cage; but the Society invokes secret contingency plans made in the event of Cromartie's decision to marry, canceling the contract. The lovers walk out of the zoo hand in hand in the final scene, passing unnoticed into the crowds, presumably to live happily ever after.

Zoo stories featuring men in cages suggest that this unusual circumstance makes the zoo man just like a zoo animal. Cromartie may indeed believe this, making his adventure all the more authentic and exotic to him; but at the same time, we note – as George Orwell's discourse of hypocrisy put it – that some animals are more equal than others. Cromartie's voluntary 'captivity,' and the fact that (despite his gentlemanly commitment to carrying out the deal) he can rescind his decision at any time, mitigate the total constraint a zoo cage normally imposes. With his books and letters, Cromartie does not risk the interminable ennui voiced by Park's animals in *Creature Comforts*. (Humane Society zoologist Sue Pressman considers such monotony a serious hazard, noting the danger to animals of 'The stress that comes from boredom in the zoo . . . now being recognized as a medical pathology and being treated as such' (Livingston, 237).) While Cromartie presents himself as capable of experiencing the most extreme constraint imaginable, putting himself in the position of caged zoo animals (and enduring such captivity demonstrating the fortitude of the English stiff upper lip), he cheats by alleviating its worst aspects. Garnett implies that people could not possibly endure what zoo animals do, even if we flatter ourselves otherwise. In the evenings, for example, the keepers release Cromartie to stroll around the zoo, which, of course, the other animals are forbidden to do. Garnett depicts a human character getting as close as possible to the conditions of zoo animals in captivity, and yet finally unable to capitulate fully to the cage's absolute confines. It follows that zoo animals, if similarly given the chance to negotiate their own conditions of captivity with the Chairman of the Zoological Society, would opt for less restrictive circumstances. As the exception who proves the rule, Cromartie confirms the sarcastic observation offered by Masson and McCarthy: 'most animals are not held captive by people who are asking what it would take to make the animal happy' (122).

In 'A Hunger Artist,' Kafka shows how a man in a cage becomes increasingly like a zoo animal (to his detriment, since the caged animal's lot is not enviable). Cromartie faces the same danger. He tries to distance himself from the other animals – for example, inspecting them in their cages during his evening walks, he asserts that he is at least partly spectator as well as exhibit. The animals, however, reject his status as different from their own. They do not give him the attention they give the keepers or spectators, but treat him as they treat each other, with indifference: 'in their eyes Mr. Cromartie was not a man. He might smell like one, but they saw at once that he had come out of a cage' (21). Garnett's animals perceive that the cage is the definitive characteristic that delineates a creature's existence . . . *any* creature's.

Cages are the ultimate equalizer. (Garnett notes 'the often recorded fact that it is particularly easy for convicts to make friends with mice and rats in prison' (21).) Despite Cromartie's attempts to differentiate himself with his library and tailor, all caged animals are finally alike. His special privileges affect his own sense of his caged existence; but others, fellow zoo inmates as well as spectators, see a creature in a cage as wholly circumscribed by that circumstance.

Garnett explores what a captive animal feels like and thinks about in its cage (which people cannot normally know, but can at least approximate by examining the condition of a man in a cage). He characterizes Cromartie's experience as (not drastically, but discernibly) unpleasant, artificial, disoriented, detached:

> As he looked through the meshes of his cage at the excited faces watching him, it cost him an effort to listen to what was being said of him, and after a while his attention wandered even against his will, for he cared nothing for mankind and cared nothing for what they said.
>
> (22)

> the moment that he stepped into his cage in full view of the public . . . he became at once quite calm and self-possessed and showed no trace of any feeling.
>
> (24–5)

> perhaps because thinking so much of Josephine made him withdraw into himself, he became shy, was annoyed by the spectators.
>
> (36)

> he most steadily repulsed all overtures . . . and betrayed an obvious reluctance to enter into conversation with anyone . . . he was so utterly cut off from the ordinary run of humanity that he would not care to risk having any intercourse with his fellows lest he should be exposed to pity, or to an offensive curiosity.
>
> (45–6)

Cromartie becomes a poseur, masking his real personality and feelings. The longer he remains in his cage, the more unhappy and suspicious he becomes: increasingly distanced from normal social and psychological behavior. Detached from his normal habitat, Cromartie becomes introverted; he refuses to interact with the crowds, or even acknowledge the presence of those outside the cage. This strategy of withdrawing into himself seems to help salvage what little self-determination and integrity may endure.

Cromartie's most explicit helplessness derives from his lack of control over whether and when Josephine comes to look at him. When he tries to alleviate his disempowerment by forbidding Josephine to drop in on him, she reacts with uncompromising derision, mocking a caged specimen's tenuous claims to dignity:

> 'Forbid! You forbid!' cried Josephine, who was now furious with him. 'You forbid me to come! Don't you realise that you are being exhibited? I, or anyone else who pays a shilling, can come and stare at you all day. Your feelings need not worry us; you should have thought of that before. You wanted to make an exhibition of yourself, now you must take the consequences. Forbid me to come and look at you! Good heavens! The impertinence of the animal! You are one of the apes now, didn't you know that?'
>
> (55–6)

Because the specimen's removal from its habitual environs makes it a very different sort of creature, Garnett suggests, zoo visitors cannot see natural behavior or experience a real animal. Spectators cannot know what the caged creature is thinking, since it is concerned with something far away and resists awareness of its immediate context. Zoo audiences have a complete and penetrating control over the caged animals – they can look as much as they want, whenever they want. But they are not looking at something they respect – and so, as a consequence of their inherent derision toward a creature in a cage, they are not likely to connect or to interact closely or authentically with the displays. The reactions of the only spectator who actually *knows* the caged creature are drastically different from those of strangers: when Josephine first visits her erstwhile lover, she finds the display shocking and grotesque: she feels 'sick with disgust and weighted down with shame ... She was ashamed of the spectators, of herself, and of the dirty world where such men, and beasts like them, existed' (30). Josephine's unique emotional reaction emphasizes the fact that every other spectator comes, watches, and leaves without experiencing any vital insights or rapport with the caged subject on display.

The experience of seeing a man in a cage, as Garnett depicts it, is basically a cheap thrill; it is at first highly unusual, but finally amounts to just more of the same. Cromartie's exhibition does not strike crowds as radical, or force them to question the basic institutional constructs of captivity – on the contrary, it affirms the status quo, presenting man as a specimen previously missing from the collection and now included, to the betterment of the zoo. Initially Cromartie draws hordes: 'Thousands of people paid for admission to the Gardens and waited patiently for hours in order to catch a glimpse of the new creature which the Society had acquired' (21). Subsequently, however, the crowds recede: 'from four policemen, two were soon thought to be enough to regulate his visitors. After another week the two were reduced to one . . . the crowd was scantier each day' (35); as the novelty fades, Cromartie's aloofness puts off zoogoers. But later, after the zoo embellishes the display by adding a caracal to his cage, he 'suddenly became, what he had not been before, extremely popular. The tide turned, and everybody found charming the person who had so scandalised them. Instead of ill-natured remarks, or even insults, Mr. Cromartie's ears were assailed with cries of delight' (52–3). The phenomenon of a man in the zoo is a fad, like Kafka's hunger artist. However stunning the spectacle may be at first, its allure eventually wanes, implying that the exhibition lacks serious inherent or durable merit. Spectators' vacillating devotion proves traumatic for both Kafka's and Garnett's characters: when a person's entire life involves being on display, diminishing affection annuls his identity and dignity. An audience is on some level a caged creature's *raison d'être,* but also – when people's fickle interest cools – its doom. Garnett provokes us to wonder whether all zoo animals are similarly buffeted by the arbitrary whims of the crowd's approval, subject to such psychological turbulence as Cromartie experiences sitting in his cage at the mercy of those who may choose to stop and look, or may pass uninterested; who may regard the specimen displayed with favor or with scorn.

Josephine comes to believe that John is mad, or at least she tells him so several times (whether because she believes it to be true or simply to hurt him). After she first sees him she thinks, 'I have been in love with John, now I find he is mad' (34). Later, she tells him directly: 'I was very worried about you, because I thought at first that something I had said to you might have made you behave in this idiotic way, but it is now quite clear to me that even if what I said did have any influence, you are quite mad, and that I need not think about you any more' (40–1). Cromartie rejects her diagnosis, although he reveals at least some qualms about his psychological composure in overly elaborate attempts to justify his behavior to himself. Later, following a grisly fight with his neighbor the orang-utan, Cromartie develops a case of blood poisoning and nervous shock that results in hallucinations and delirium for several days. While his affliction is physical rather than psychological in derivation, it reinforces the prevalence of mental derangement in zoo stories – the recurring incidence and confluence of people, cages, animals, zoos, and madness (evoking the parallel organizational cultures of zoos and asylums Mullan and Marvin describe).

When insanity infiltrates zoo stories, it may implicate those outside as well as inside the cage. Like the medical incidence of madness with its vague demarcations, the motif of literary madness, once introduced into a text, tends to disperse rampantly (as in *The King of Hearts*, or *One Flew Over the Cuckoo's Nest*, or *Hamlet*, or Edgar Allan Poe's stories). Who's to say who's mad? Insanity becomes universal; distinction between the mad and the sane becomes impossible, irrelevant as the narrative eruption of madness infests the entire scenario. In the psychologically troubled milieus pervading such zoo stories as Garnett's, Plath's 'Zoo Keeper's Wife,' Albee's *The Zoo Story*, Stafford's 'In the Zoo,' Thomas's 'The Hunchback in the Park,' and Vonnegut's *Slaughterhouse-Five*, it is pointless to identify a specific victim. (Each story presents a loose metaphorical rendition of the person-in-a-cage trope: Plath's wife, for example, is figuratively 'caged' within the authoritarian domain of her tyrannical husband/keeper; Albee's Jerry and Thomas's hunchback suffer in the constricting cages of their own alienation, dementia, social dysfunctionality; Stafford's sisters have been raised in what might colloquially be regarded as a madhouse, imprisoned by their foster mother's constrictive regime.) These works feature a general proliferation of insanity, implicitly indicting the zoo, at least imagistically, for fostering this madness.

Peter Greenaway's 1985 film *Zoo: A Zed and Two Noughts* reflects the pattern of pervasively contagious madness. A surreal, elusive narrative integrates death, obsession, sadism, voyeurism, and sexual fetishism, comprising a rich panorama of insanity that defies diagnosis of any discrete sources or subjects. The protagonists, twin brothers who are the film's most deranged characters, are zoologists so obsessed with their work – the pathology of corporeal decomposition – that they spend most of their lives in the zoo. In the end they commit suicide to facilitate the study of the human body's decay, thus becoming zoo specimens themselves. (So again, as in so many zoo stories that involve psychological derangement, the film depicts people in cages.) The spectacle Greenaway situates in the zoo demonstrates that he sees it as a rampantly mad place; insanity festers there with infectious reach and potency.

Along with Greenaway's film, Marie Nimier's novel *The Giraffe* (1993) and Jacques Tourneur's film *Cat People* (1942) are the most pronounced portraits of derangement found in zoo stories. Nimier's protagonist spends a great deal of time in a cage (reiterating the association of human cage-dwelling with madness): Joseph, a keeper assigned to minister to a giraffe named Solange, soon becomes obsessively attached to it. Under the guise of conducting behavioral experiments and observations, but in fact simply consumed with the animal, he contrives to spend most of his days and nights in Solange's enclosure in Paris's Bois de Vincennes Zoo. His attachment blossoms into a perverse relationship featuring fetishism, voyeurism and exhibitionism, sadomasochism, and an insane jealousy which leads him to kill other animals that vie for the giraffe's attention. Finally when Solange loses her virginity to another giraffe, Joseph kills Solange herself, furious at the betrayal of what he had conceived as their pure and transcendent relationship.[7] In *Cat People*, the main character, Irina, obsessively haunts the black panther's cage at the zoo: she believes that the cat embodies the cursed legacy of her Serbian ancestry, and that the animal's spirit has the potential to infect her and incite her to murderous rage. As the film develops, it becomes apparent that Irina is correct about her identification with the zoo animal and its capacity for unbounded violence. Simultaneously, she becomes increasingly regarded as insane. A psychiatrist and her husband plot to have her committed to an asylum, although she kills the doctor before he can accomplish this. Once again, the motifs of person-as-zoo-animal and madness meet in a volatile confluence that culminates at the locus of the cage: Irina unlocks the cat's cage to let it loose (hoping to wreak vengeance on a world that has tormented her by regarding her as mad). The uncaging is fatal for both: the panther mauls and kills Irina as it flees the cage, and moments later, the cat itself is killed when hit by a car just outside the zoo.

At the end of John Irving's *Setting Free the Bears*, an incidence of a man in a cage again suggests madness, but on an immensely larger social and moral scale. O. Schrutt, the zoo's night keeper (who must be overcome to achieve the plan of releasing the animals), ends up locked in a cage as the animals are freed. He had been a member of Vienna's Nazi youth during the Second World War; Irving depicts his caging as a kind of Dantean *contrapasso*. Hannes, the liberator, prods Schrutt into the giant anteater cage and forces him to grovel in the sawdust of the pitlike enclosure. Becoming delusional with fear of the cage, the captor, and the seven-foot rodents circling him, Schrutt imagines he is the victim of revenge at the hands of the Jews he had persecuted decades earlier; he tries to identify his persecutor: '"I'm sorry, Zeiker," he moaned. "Really, that was a terrible time for us all, you know." And when I didn't answer, he said, "Please Zeiker, is it you?"' (319). Later, as the animals snarl at him, 'old O. was naming names, or asking them. "Zeiker?" he called. "Beinberg? Muffel? Brandeis? Schmerling? Frieden?" Name by name, O. Schrutt was leaving his mind behind' (327). Irving inserts into the locus of a man in a cage, the zoo, and madness an allegory for the moral insanity of the Nazi regime. Irving's treatment of the Holocaust in *Setting Free the Bears* is a rare inscription of the modern world's most barbarous madness into the construct of a zoo story.[8]

Kurt Vonnegut, Jr's *Slaughterhouse-Five* and Eugene O'Neill's *The Hairy Ape* feature other notable occurrences of men in zoo cages. In *Slaughterhouse-Five* (1969) Billy Pilgrim, a shell-shocked Second World War veteran, lives out the years after the war in a semi-delusional haze, given to hallucinatory travels through time and space. Among his adventures, he believes he was abducted by aliens from the planet Tralfamadore who took him to their zoo, displayed him in the nude, and mated him with a fellow Earthling, a porn star named Montana Wildhack. The Tralfamadorian zoo display features specimens exhibited in what the captors perceive to be the captive creature's natural surroundings: he 'was strapped to a yellow Barca-Lounger which they had stolen from a Sears Roebuck warehouse ... to furnish Billy's artificial habitat' (77). In addition:

> There was a color television set and a couch that could be converted into a bed. There were end tables with lamps and ashtrays on them by the couch. There was a home bar and two stools. There was a little pool table. There was wall-to-wall carpeting in federal gold ... There were magazines in a fan on a coffee table in front of the couch. There was a stereophonic phonograph. The phonograph worked. The television didn't. There was a picture of one cowboy killing another one pasted to the television tube.
>
> (112)

The outer space zoo is as homey as a roadside chain motel. The Tralfamadorians have tried, laudably but ludicrously, to reproduce a human being's natural environs. When we see a member of our own species in a cage, it becomes especially clear how unlikely it is that a few items (chosen by the captors) can comprise an authentic 'natural habitat' in which the caged creature will feel comfortable. The point applies equally to animal habitats people create in zoos: however hard zookeepers contrive to imitate something as complex and organic as a habitat, can they know what is appropriate or desirable for other species?

The advanced Tralfamadorians – two-foot-tall green creatures shaped like plungers who can see in four dimensions – are destined to destroy the universe, but experience no anguish over this since they can travel in time and choose to dwell on happier moments. Their motive for abducting, caging, and displaying Billy and Montana is to learn about what they consider our planet's incomprehensibly limited society. But zoo spectatorship is not depicted as a successful way for a dominant culture to learn about others, and the Tralfamadorians never really understand what makes Billy and Montana tick. They have no context for a specimen's existence, and erroneously assume they can become enlightened by watching a very small sample of a species that is tremendously different from themselves, for a brief time, in the zoo's unnatural conditions. Misconceptions are inevitable: for example, 'Most Tralfamadorians had no way of knowing Billy's body and face were not beautiful. They supposed he was a splendid specimen' (113).

The Tralfamadorians are benevolent to the caged couple – or, as benevolent as captors can be; this paradox inherently applies to all zoos, however considerately captors treat the animals they claim to be nurturing and preserving. But despite the zookeepers' magnanimity, the Barca-Lounger and wall-to-wall carpeting, Vonnegut's aliens use what they see as the Earthlings' primitive, crude ignorance as a benchmark to confirm their own advanced sophistication – a sensibility embodying a speciesist bigotry that is ultimately more cruel than the dreariest conditions in the most oppressive cage. It condemns not just a few individual creatures, but all members of all captive species, to remain in continual oppression – in zoos and whatever other constraints the self-affirmed dominant culture chooses to impose. When the zoo guides try to explain metaphorically how limited Billy's temporal perspective is, they ask a crowd of spectators to imagine

> that they were looking across a desert at a mountain range on a day that was twinkling bright and clear. They could look at a peak or a bird or a cloud, at a stone right in front of them, or even down into a canyon behind them. But among them was this poor Earthling, and his head was encased in a steel sphere which he could never take off. There was only one eyehole through which he could look, and welded to that eyehole was six feet of pipe . . . He was also strapped to a steel lattice which was bolted to a flatcar on rails, and there was no way he could turn his head or touch the pipe. The far end of the pipe rested on a bi-pod which was also bolted to the flatcar. All Billy could see was the little dot at the end of the pipe. He didn't know he was on a flatcar, didn't even know there was anything peculiar about his situation . . . Whatever poor Billy saw through the pipe, he had no choice but to say to himself, 'That's life.'
>
> (115)

This account of zoo education amounts to the sentiment: How pathetic to be one of them. Vonnegut describes the subjective imposition of the captor's standards onto the captive. The zoo affords prejudiced affirmation of spectators' presuppositions about themselves. They see what they want to see, rather than the thing itself. They cannot help it: the hegemony of cultural conditioning cannot be eschewed when one looks into a cage. Indeed, the zoo's discourse of guidance, education, contextualization provides no assistance or inspiration to transcend parochialism, but just the opposite. It encourages spectators to see others through their own lens: to see caged creatures only in terms of how different – and implicitly, inferior – they are.

From inside the cage, Billy perceives the irreconcilable gap between the captive species and the one outside: when he speaks to them, 'he saw the Tralfamadorians close their little hands on their eyes. He knew from past experience what this meant: He was being stupid' (116). The danger of this gap, which the zoo concretizes, is that once the caged subjects have been so definitively cast as other, one can do anything to them – they no longer have any moral claim to be treated fairly, or to be governed under whatever standards of justice and reason a society applies to its enfranchised members.[9] Further, the gulf established between species forestalls any possibility that the creatures outside the cage will learn anything from those inside. It does not occur to the spectators, for example, as they pityingly appraise Billy, that the Earthlings, unlike themselves, will *not* destroy the universe, and that Tralfamadorians might learn from Billy how not to destroy the universe. From this observation, it is easy to extrapolate an application of Vonnegut's science-fiction ethos to the situation on our own planet: when people observing zoo animals bask in the glories of human culture as compared with the furry beast inside the cage, do they reflect whether the species should be considered more advanced which did, or did not, create such habitats as Auschwitz, Hiroshima, Soweto, and Love Canal?

Like Garnett in *A Man in the Zoo*, Vonnegut offers his appraisal of how it feels to be caged from the perspective of a fellow human being. Montana is at first terrified when she sees the crowds of little green Tralfamadorians, but she acclimates to her situation. And Billy is asked by a zoo visitor, '"Are you happy here?" "About as happy as I was on Earth," said Billy Pilgrim, which was true' (114). Billy and Montana are not tremendously distraught at their captivity, finally, because it is not much more deadening than the alternative on Earth in the twentieth century. Vonnegut's pessimistic allegory of modern life evokes the behavioral condition psychologists term learned helplessness:

when a caged and tormented creature realizes its powerlessness to alleviate its misery or control its own destiny, it curls up in a corner of the cage and stops protesting. (The depression, alienation, passivity, and dysfunction that accompany Billy's resignation connote at least garden-variety issues of mental disturbance, relevant to the themes from other zoo stories of madness surrounding people in zoo cages.) Vonnegut suggests that his contemporary audience, inside and outside the allegorical zoo, faces a milieu in which one can expect no more than acquiescence to such learned helplessness. It's not that zoos are all right, but the rest of the world is so corrupt that zoos aren't much worse by comparison. Vonnegut's refrain throughout the novel is a capitulation to quiet desperation: 'so it goes.'

The zoo in *Slaughterhouse-Five* ultimately serves less to explore animal captivity than to provide a vehicle for Vonnegut to expose the limitations and misguidedness of our society's conceptions about our culture. In the mode of 1960s Vietnam-weary liberal cynicism, Vonnegut – much like Irving in *Setting Free the Bears* – imbues the zoo with the spirit of narrow-minded hypocrisy. It is implicated in hegemonic cultural chauvinism, asserting the empowered caste's self-importance. Vonnegut's zoo represents a setting where distortions proliferate – where spectators wallow in uncontextualized error and caged creatures resign themselves to abasing depersonalization.

Yank, the protagonist of Eugene O'Neill's *The Hairy Ape* (1922), is pejoratively characterized with the titular metaphor. Once again, the constructions of man as animal and man in the zoo indicate degrading prospects for the caged victim; specifically, O'Neill's zoo imagery illuminates the stultification of the American working classes. The play begins in an ocean liner's depths: '*The effect sought after is a cramped space in the bowels of a ship, imprisoned by white steel*,' the stage directions inform, where bunks and upright supports '*cross each other like the steel framework of a cage*.' The seamen '*cannot stand upright*' in their living quarters, and display the '*stooping posture which shoveling coal and the resultant overdevelopment of back and shoulder muscles has given them*'; their eyes are '*fierce, resentful*' (121). Even before the first words are spoken, O'Neill has sharply drawn these men as caged animals, dehumanized and resentful of their constraint.

The ship is the sailors' home, simply because they have been displaced from anywhere else they could call home, but they detest its cagelike quarters. When Yank rebukes a shipmate for recalling the girl waiting for him at home – 'T'hell wit home! Where d'yuh get dat tripe? Dis is home, see?' (124) – another crewman, Long, responds,

> Yank 'ere is right. 'E says this 'ere stinkin' ship is our 'ome. And 'e says as 'ome is 'ell. And 'e's right! This is 'ell. We lives in 'ell, Comrades – and right enough we'll die in it. (*raging*) And who's ter blame, I arsks yer? We ain't. We wasn't born this rotten way. All men is born free and ekal. That's in the bleedin' Bible, maties. But what d'they care for the Bible – them lazy, bloated swine what travels first cabin? Them's the ones. They dragged us down 'til we're on'y wage slaves in the bowels of a bloody ship, sweatin', burnin' up, eatin' coal dust! (124–5)

Long depicts the shipmates as caged against their will, deprived of a basic right to freedom, miserably oppressed by the wealthy who are their figurative captors. As in other zoo stories with men in cages, O'Neill's bestows his captives with moving expression to voice how they strain against their cages; as in Park's *Creature Comforts*, the people-as-animals seem to say exactly what animals themselves would if they could.

A shipman named Paddy recalls the elegant tall-masted clippers that are sailors' more natural settings, and bemoans their present disorientation in modern ships with 'black smoke from the funnels smudging the sea, smudging the decks – the bloody engines pounding and throbbing and shaking – wid divil a sight of sun or a breath of clean air . . . caged in by steel from a sight of the sky like bloody apes in the Zoo!' (127). With this first explicit reference to the zoo, O'Neill advances the analogy between these men and captive animals: the sailors suffer considerably in their removal from more comfortable environs. The change from their accustomed nautical habitat is connoted as unpleasant and deleterious, and the 'zoo' where they now find themselves is especially distasteful. Zoo stories often depict such drastic contrasts between zoos and natural habitats – smoke, noise, and dirt instead of wind, sea, and air – as if the captives have fallen from top to bottom on a wheel of fortune. Once again, the complaints of these metaphorically caged men reiterate those of Park's animated animals: Park's baboon, for example, complains, 'I'd like to live somewhere a bit hotter. I don't like getting rained on and I don't like being cold, and I find that here I often get rained on and I'm often cold'; the dank cage in an English zoo is the antithesis in every respect of the habitat it desires. O'Neill's sailors, similarly, in the worst possible conditions, figuratively feel as if they are in a zoo.

The catalyst of action in *The Hairy Ape* concerns an issue common to other stories of men in zoos: people's reaction to being on display in a way usually reserved for 'lower animals.' Although able to manage the physical toll of living in a caged hell, the sailors crumble when faced with the added psychological humiliation of being gawked at like zoo animals. Mildred, a first-class passenger (whose father is chairman of the steamship line), wants to see the ship's inner workings – partly to learn how the other half lives, but mostly just for a new experience, a thrill to punctuate her jaded life of luxurious lassitude. But when she actually catches sight of Yank and hears his rough, raw, violent dialogue in the stokehole, she faints in alarm. As the engineers carry her back above deck, Yank *'feels himself insulted in some unknown fashion in the very heart of his pride. He roars* God damn yuh! *and hurls his shovel after them at the door which has just closed. It hits the steel bulkhead with a clang and falls clattering on the steel floor'* (137–8).

Long is incensed at the supposition that Mildred regarded the sailors as brute animals:

> Hinsultin' us, the bloody cow! And them bloody engineers! What right 'as they got to be exhibitin' us 's if we was bleedin' monkeys in a menagerie? . . . [Mildred's father] owns this bloody boat! And you and me, Comrades, we're 'is slaves! . . . And she's 'is bloody daughter and we're all 'er slaves, too! And she gives 'er orders as 'ow she wants to see the bloody animals below decks and down they takes 'er!
>
> (139–40)

The workers' outrage at being considered zoo exhibits implies that they consider zoos inherently degrading; zoo spectators presumably scorn those inside the cage. This is reinforced as the workers later recount the humiliation of the moment when, as the subjects of voyeurism, they became too much like zoo animals to endure it any more: Paddy recalls 'her pale mug when she shriveled away with her hands over her eyes to shut out the sight of him! Sure, 'twas as if she'd seen a great hairy ape escaped from the Zoo!' (141). (Note the affinity to Vonnegut's image of the Tralfamadorians with their hands over their eyes when they could not bear to regard the caged creature's stupidity.)

As offensive as Yank finds Mildred's snobbery, and as much as he tries to reject her characterization of him as a hairy ape, the degradation becomes a self-fulfilling prophecy – as if the monied, powerful woman has the authority to project onto him whatever vision she chooses. As a metaphorical zoo spectator, Mildred has considerable power of determination over the men who eventually conform to her image of them as zoo animals. The earthy charisma and dignity O'Neill bestows upon Yank are undermined by Mildred's snub, her figurative caging of him by looking at him as if he were a zoo animal. Although Yank and Mildred never meet again, the damage is done: once one has suffered the consummate indignity of being seen as a zoo animal, O'Neill suggests, there is no undoing the experience; Yank's subsequent fortunes are in continual descent. Outraged with the affluent, obsessively seeking general retribution against them for Mildred's particular offense, he assaults wealthy strangers on Fifth Avenue and quickly ends up in jail. In society's eyes, Yank has run amok (like an escaped animal), and even O'Neill starts to characterize him as paranoid-delusional. Evidencing strains of madness – in the mode of all the other zoo stories that associate insanity with men in cages – Yank is being preened for the place in the zoo that awaits him.

Jail is another cage for Yank: 'Dis is de Zoo, huh?' (150) he remarks of his new surroundings, provoking clamor among his cellmates. 'I musta been dreamin',' he continues. 'I tought I was in a cage at de Zoo – but de apes don't talk, do dey?' Like a captive animal, Yank furiously rattles the bars of his cell; the other inmates warn him to stop the noisy display – 'You'll have the guard down on us!' – and he responds, 'De guard? Yuh mean de keeper, don't yuh?' (150–1). O'Neill's heavy-handed steel and cage imagery (as when the shovel Yank throws at Mildred clangs against the ship's steel bulkhead and clatters on the steel floor) is further accentuated by the revelation that Mildred's father's fortune derives from steel. In his jail cell, Yank raves: 'Sure – her old man – president of de Steel Trust – makes half de steel in de world – . . . and cage me in for her to spit on! . . . He made dis – dis cage! Steel! . . . Cages, cells, locks, bolt, bars – dat's what it means! – holdin' me down wit him at de top!' (154). The steel that is the cage's essence provides O'Neill with a far-reaching symbol for Yank's constraints. The worker is wholly and oppressively circumscribed by the rich. As representatives of all wealthy people, Mildred and her father exert power over Yank both literally and in their more abstract ability to humiliate him, to keep him in his place. Steel embodies the imagery of the absolute control that the rich exercise over the poor: the material that made Mildred's father wealthy constitutes the bars of the cages that keep Yank permanently imprisoned, whether in the ship's bowels or the city jail (or, by implication, anywhere else he could go in this modern world – steel is everywhere). O'Neill's trope evokes not only the physical qualities of strength and control inherent in the metal, but also the resonances of capitalist hegemony: as America's industrial keystone, steel reinforces the power of Mildred and her father at the same time it molds the ubiquitous cages that stymie Yank. (Max Weber used the same trope, although with a different metal, when he called capitalism 'an iron cage.')

After the play's many symbolic evocations of zoos, the final scene is literally set in one. Desperate after his humiliating experiences, and rejected even by an egalitarian Industrial Workers of the World local because he seems too erratic and bestial, Yank ends up at the monkey house in the zoo. Having been labeled a hairy ape by the world, Yank comes to see the original. Like Jerry in *The Zoo Story*, Yank is drawn to the zoo as a refuge of last resort – a sign that all traces of humanity have disappeared from his world, and that he deserves no better than to be treated as a caged animal. Like Jerry's, Yank's trip to the zoo at least subconsciously reflects an acceptance that he will end up worse off for the visit, and that he deserves whatever befalls him there.[10]

The scene, a single monologue, offers perhaps the most incisive depiction in any zoo story of the man-in-a-cage motif, because the moment at which Yank enters the cage is shown so intricately. O'Neill provides a keen vision of the man's psyche, his feelings, his reactions to the zoo cage, and the significance of the episode as it culminates the course of his entire life. O'Neill presents a microscopic focus on the relationship of a man to a zoo cage as he shows, first, the man outside looking at the animal inside; and then, powerfully, the transposition of their situations. (The moment reverses the scene at the end of 'A Hunger Artist' where the caged man vacates his premises to make way for the animal.)

When Yank approaches the cage, he banters with the ape as he might with a fellow worker. Indeed, the dramatic tension derives from the question of whether or not the animal *is*, as Mildred suggested, Yank's peer, and if so, what exactly this means. Yank's tenor shifts frequently throughout this scene, as if he is constantly adjusting or tuning his demeanor in his uncertainty about how he and the ape relate to each other and what their interaction signifies. Yank's quandary microcosmically addresses central concerns of my study: how does the person at a zoo looking at a caged animal relate to it? What does the person think about? How does the experience affect the person? What does the animal show us about ourselves? Contrary to Mildred's conception of Yank as a savage, he is actually one of the most thoughtful zoo spectators I have come across. The extent to which he grapples with the troubling questions posed by a zoo encounter between human and animal is matched by few other characters. Yank's death at the end of the play is the price he pays for asking the most difficult questions – as with deaths in other zoo stories (such as Jerry's in *The Zoo Story* and the twin brothers' in *Zoo: A Zed and Two Noughts*), Yank's signals that he has ventured too close to the heart of darkness, the horror.

Yank's attitude toward the ape shifts from rowdy collegiality to a friendly, sympathetic, admiration for its physique and demeanor: 'Say, yuh're some hard-lookin' guy, ain't yuh? I seen lots of tough nuts dat de gang called gorillas, but yuh're de foist real one I ever seen. Some chest yuh got, and shoulders, and dem arms and mits! I bet yuh got a punch in eider fist dat'd knock 'em all silly!' (161). Yank sees in the ape a kind of empowered self-determination that, he realizes, he lacks himself. But from here Yank's mood becomes bitter, as he realizes that looking at the ape is like looking at himself in the degrading way the world sees him; the unflattering image breeds self-hatred. (Like Kafka's hunger artist, Yank becomes disgusted at the zoo animals as he approaches their condition.) Bitterness gives way to confusion at the crux of this scene, when Yank comes as close as he ever will to anagnorisis, and to discovering what it means to be caged:

> So yuh're what she seen when she looked at me, de white-faced tart! I was you to her, get me? On'y outa de cage – broke out – free to moider her, see? Sure! Dat's what she tought. She wasn't wise dat I was in a cage, too – worser'n yours – sure – a damn sight – 'cause you got some chanct to bust loose – but me – (*He grows confused.*)
>
> (161)

Yank becomes bewildered as he contrasts the ape's real cage with the more figurative constraints that have pervaded his life. Metaphor is difficult – especially in the confusing, alienated, steely world of modernism. Yank has gone to the zoo hoping to relate metaphor to reality, by attempting to talk at/to the ape about the play's pervading symbol, the cage. But finally, overcome by confusion, Yank falters, unable to ask the overwhelming question; unable to learn from an authority, a zoo ape, how one can survive in a cage on display as an inferior specimen. It is perhaps a consequence of this inability to discover the answers he sought, the answers he needed, that Yank must die.

The mixture of admiration, envy, bitterness, confusion, that the ape evokes in Yank reflects the vacillation any spectator might experience between appreciating an animal on its own terms and seeing it through the blinders with which people (mis)construe animals appropriated in human cultural processes. Yank hovers between really being able to see an animal in a zoo – relating to the ape as a fellow creature (without Mildred's derisive imputations) – and being influenced by deprecatory cultural habits of seeing captive animals as savage beasts who deserve what they get. His final resolution of his muddled experience with the ape in the zoo is to assert their fellowship: 'Bot' members of dis club!' (162), he tells the ape, and then offers it the chance to get even with its captors.

> We'll put up one last star bout dat'll knock 'em offen deir seats! Dey'll have to make de cages stronger after we're trou! (*The gorilla is straining at his bars, growling, hopping from one foot to the other. Yank takes a jimmy from under his coat and forces the lock on the cage door. He throws this open.*) Pardon from de governor! Step out and shake hands!
>
> (162)

But instead of affirming Yank's overture of camaraderie and shaking hands, the ape *'wraps his huge arms around Yank in a murderous hug. There is a crackling snap of crushed ribs – a gasping cry'* (163). Yank has tragically misperceived the relationship between man and animal – an inevitable outcome, I believe, since the interaction occurs in the zoo. This is an extreme metaphor, but still a valid one, for people's failure to understand how animals relate to us amid the falseness and distortions endemic to the zoo. The gorilla drops the crushed body, throws it into the cage, shuts the door, and wanders off to fulfill the escape Yank planned. (Several zoo stories present animals' escape from their cages. *The Hairy Ape* offers the most unpromising version of this, as it appears to be a zero-sum enterprise: for the animal to go free, a man has to replace it in its cage.) With his dying words, Yank announces that he is finally where he belongs. While the animal goes free at the end of this zoo story, the man suffers indignity and death. However unpalatable zoos are for animals, they imprison people in ways that are, by some measures, even more constraining. In *The Hairy Ape*, as in most zoo stories, zoos foster misunderstanding between species; the toll for people, as O'Neill depicts it, is our demise.

'ONE GOES FROM CAGE TO CAGE'

Representations of caged animals, of course, feature prominently throughout zoo stories. I will examine four poems in detail (touching on other works in passing) which exemplify many of the ideas about cages, and images of cages. Two poems, Stevie Smith's 'The Zoo' and Rainer Maria Rilke's 'The Panther,' depict how animals appraise their cages; both poets seem convinced that zoos and cages are cruel, and both their poems resonate with a consequent pathos. Two other poems, James Dickey's 'Encounter in the Cage Country' and Ted Hughes's 'The Jaguar,' depict people's states of mind as they stand outside cages regarding animals within. Dickey and Hughes do not challenge the ethos or cultural authenticity of the caged animal as subject, and their poems evince a kind of manly sadistic demeanor toward the animal stuck inside. They suggest that zoo spectatorship has changed little since the first public zoos where, according to Harriet Ritvo, visitors 'enjoy[ed] simultaneously the thrill of proximity to wild animals and the happy sense of secure superiority produced by their incarceration' (219). The poets outside the cage engage in contemplative introspection at the expense of the animals inside. Somewhat akin to O'Neill's construction of animal captivity as a zero-sum contest at the end of *The Hairy Ape,* it seems imperative for both Dickey and Hughes that the animal be inside the cage and the man outside; inconceivable that man and animal could simultaneously be free. The insights their personae glean from encounters with caged animals are figuratively sucked out of the animals, which are left vacant and drained. Comparably, men in some cultures ingest potions containing animals' paws, teeth, penises, bones, or horns to appropriate their power and essences; for the men to take on the power, the animals must die.

Smith's subject is a lion, Rilke's is a panther, Hughes's is a jaguar, and Dickey's is indeterminate, either a lion or a leopard. All these seem, even more than other animals, unsuitably consigned to cages given their size, speed, and natural proclivity for expansive spaces. It is dangerous to entertain arbitrary speciesist prejudices and the claims of human cultural charisma – I believe it *is* just as inappropriate to cage a turtle or a rabbit as a panther. Yet because these large animals' popular images connote such unfettered freedom, readers of all four poems may feel instinctively that they are especially poor candidates for zoo cages. Depicting the zoo in *The Voyages of Doctor Dolittle,* Hugh Lofting similarly decries caging large cats. (Dolittle, who respects animals, keeps a zoo with cages and locks, but 'the doors open from the inside, not from the out. The locks are only there so the animals can go and shut themselves *in* any time they want to get away from the annoyance of other animals or from people who might come here' (60).) The Doctor's young friend Tommy Stubbins asks if the zoo has any lions or tigers:

> 'No,' said the Doctor. 'It wouldn't be possible to keep them here – and I wouldn't keep them even if I could. If I had my way, Stubbins, there wouldn't be a single lion or tiger in captivity anywhere in the world. They never take to it. They're never happy. They never settle down. They are always thinking of the big countries they have left behind. You can see it in their eyes, dreaming – dreaming always of the great open spaces where they were born; dreaming of the deep, dark jungles

> where their mothers first taught them how to scent and track the deer. And what are they given in exchange for all this? . . . Why, a bare cage with iron bars; an ugly piece of dead meat thrust in to them once a day; and a crowd of fools to come and stare at them with open mouths! – No, Stubbins. Lions and tigers, the Big Hunters, should never, never be seen in zoos.'
>
> (62–3)[11]

Nevertheless, tradition dictates that any zoo worth its salt must possess large cats: Ritvo writes that 'the lion house, where the abject captivity of the king of beasts provided the most conclusive evidence in the zoo of the human triumph over nature, was an essential component of any successful zoo or menagerie' in the nineteenth century (223), and this seems no less true today.

The opening stanza of Smith's characteristically simple and frank poem 'The Zoo' (1942) expresses, anthropomorphically, how she thinks an animal feels about its cage:

> The lion sits within his cage
> Weeping tears of ruby rage,
> He licks his snout, the tears fall down
> And water dusty London town.

The animal regards those outside the cage who have come to observe its misery:

> He does not like you, little boy,
> It's no use making up to him,
> He does not like you any more
> Than he likes Nurse, or Baby Jim.
>
> (172)

Animals hate being in zoos, Smith suggests, and hate the people watching them. Similar accounts of outraged and humiliated animals pervade zoo stories. In William Carlos Williams's story 'The Zoo,' an animal in the monkey house 'leaped directly at the crowd! . . . the beast was furious. He hated the crowd. He wanted to kill them . . . The beast was waving its arms and now it spit. It spit into the crowd' (342). Velimir Khlebnikov's 1910 poem 'Menagerie' depicts a rhinoceros that 'holds in its red-and-white eyes the unquenchable fury of a toppled tsar; he alone, of all the animals, regards mankind with the unconcealed disdain which tsars reserve for slave rebellions' (7). Khlebnikov's rhinoceros resembles Smith's lion in its sense of noble natural majesty laid low. Both animals, although abased in their cages, retain a haughty demeanor. Such arrogance might seem inappropriate in light of their present ignominy, but it reflects habitual instincts that the degradation of zoo life cannot wholly suppress.

Those who promote zoos refute (or anticipate and defuse) indications that animals may not like their cages and may suffer in them. London Transport posters advertising the zoo – which have an obvious stake in supporting its harmless innocence since they encourage people to take the underground to Regent's Park – offer several examples of pro-zoo propaganda. The text for a 1965 poster, beneath a stylized portrait of a lion, contradicts Smith's lion: 'WE ANIMALS are really well-off in London. Take the London Zoo – smart new Elephant House, brilliant and unconventional new aviary (not quite finished), classic-of-modern-architecture Penguin Pool, all in the setting of Nash's Regent's Park' (Riddell and Denton, 86). Highlighting the zoo's physical plant (in terms obviously more compelling to people than to animals – are penguins likely to be impressed by the cachet of Nash's landscape?), the advertisement perhaps protests too much and evokes the implicit presumption that it opposes: the possibility Smith raises, that wild animals are *not* really well off in London. A 1953 poster includes the text: 'The lion and the improbable giraffe are almost Londoners. They live a life of ease in the corner of Regent's Park or high on the downs in the holiday air of Whipsnade. Their visitors are a tonic for boredom' (78), rebutting the common suggestion from zoo stories that visitors are a source of torment for animals. A 1934 poster features a photograph of a man walking a reptile on a leash, above the text: 'THE KOMODO DRAGON "At Home" Weekdays 9 a.m. till dusk – at the Zoo' (64). The reptile is connoted as being at home in the zoo and welcoming visitors' calls, in the mode of social engagements from Victorian novels. (Nineteenth-century hosts, however, made themselves available for unannounced dropping in only a few hours a week, not from 9 until dusk.) All three posters assert exactly what Smith's lion, Park's animals from *Creature Comforts*, and copious other zoo story inmates reject: the idea that animals find captivity palatable, inoffensively cozy.

For Smith, zoos mediate the animal–human relationship in a way that is unequivocally wrong.[12] The lion's tears watering dusty London, besides generally signifying its incompatibility with the cage, indicate (in the vein of *Creature Comforts*) that a wild animal's condition in an urban zoo is particularly objectionable. 'The Zoo' elicits the pathos of an animal forever wrenched out of its native habitat. After evoking the lion's natural predatorial behavior in the wild, the poem concludes with the animal's tormentingly sad memories of how its life should have been lived. That ideal contrasts with the static existence that it now faces: 'All this' (that is, recollections of its natural life)

> the lion sees, and pants
> Because he knows the hot sun slants
>
> Between the rancid jungle-grass,
> Which never more shall part to let him pass
> Down to the jungle drinking-hole,
> Whither the zebra comes with her sleek foal.
>
> The sun is hot by day and has his swink,
> And sops up sleepy lions' and tigers' stink,
> But not this lion's stink, poor carnivore,
> He's on the shady shelf for ever more.
>
> His claws are blunt, his teeth fall out,
> No victim's flesh consoles his snout,
> And that is why his eyes are red
> Considering his talents are misusèd.
>
> (173)

The poem features the same ironically extreme juxtaposition of habitats O'Neill used in *The Hairy Ape* to express his sailors' distance from their 'natural' seafaring life amid the smoky, noisy modern steamship. Smith allows nominal affinities amid the extremity – both the jungle-grass and the cage are rancid; both the jungle and the zoo are hot. But finally the zoo is a very different locale than the jungle, and very inferior for the lion.

The first line of 'The Zoo' directs immediate attention to the cage as the focus of iniquity, and the poem's most striking images concern the cage's restrictions and physical attributes: its dust, its rancid smell, its 'shady shelf' antithetical to 'jungle-grass.' But the poem's ultimate import transcends the cage, which is a metonymic springboard for a more general statement against zoos. The cage is a microcosm of the problems with zoos, animal captivity, and human spectatorship. A zoo story focus on an animal in a cage represents the individual unit, the fundamental construct, through which zoogoers encounter zoo animals. A viewer takes in one cage, watches for a few moments, then moves on to the next. Virginia Woolf, in her Bloomsbury metaphor discussed in Chapter 1, epitomizes every zoo spectator's experience when she describes how 'One goes from cage to cage.' This simple formulation (which, interestingly, describes a zoo expedition without making reference to animals – the metonymy of cage for animal represents animals in terms of their subjection) encapsulates the standard experiential process that occurs at the zoo.

Smith's resolution – the lion's talents are misused – is casually understated in a way typical of her poetic, but nonetheless didactic. She forces an intentionally contrived, unnatural pronunciation as the accent expands the last word to three syllables. Her prosody highlights the sometimes awkward artifice of poetry, an artifice that can be extrapolated to indict the artifice of human culture generally: just as the final word's affectation perverts the language that comprises the 'culture' of poetry, human culture embodies an artifice that changes (and ruins) the nature it attempts to integrate in a zoo. The poem ends on an off-note, leaving the reader feeling unconfident of the power that poetry promises, perhaps overpromises, to subsume everything it appropriates within its ken and to impose order upon it. Smith's final judgment offers an ecocentrist rallying cry: all creatures have certain 'talents' to contribute to our ecosystem; people use them or, as in this poem (and as in zoos), misuse them. It is simply improper, by definition, to misuse something. Smith's poem is finally uncompromising in the verdict it renders on the zoo scenario: an animal has been wasted, treated ignobly, and it is our fault. We must decry the lion's abuse with the determination Aldo Leopold expresses in *A Sand County Almanac*: 'A thing is right when it tends to preserve the integrity, stability, and beauty of the biotic community. It is wrong when it tends otherwise' (262). Every creature has a right to a dignified existence, and what people do to our comrades in the biotic community when we put them in cages abrogates that right.

Rilke's and Hughes's poems feature men watching animals that must look relatively alike in their cages. Yet the two poets' attempts to discern the animals' thoughts generate diametrically opposed results: Rilke casts his subject in 'The Panther' (1903) as exploited and victimized, while Hughes's jaguar is transcendent. Writers' ability to do whatever they want with the subjects they observe – making them sad or noble, pathetic or triumphant – suggests that zoo spectators do not see any precise thing, any *quidditas*. In addition to the caged animal's other travails, it is stripped of an objective identity. Paul Simon's song 'At the Zoo' presents a humorously far-fetched representation of the arbitrary way people construct animals, heedless of their literal nature:

> The monkeys stand for honesty,
> Giraffes are insincere,
> And the elephants are kindly but they're dumb.
> Orangutans are skeptical of changes in their cages
> And the zookeeper is very fond of rum.
> Zebras are reactionaries,
> Antelopes are missionaries,
> Pigeons plot in secrecy,
> And hamsters turn on frequently.
> What a gas! You gotta come and see,
> At the zoo.

Like Smith's lion, Rilke's panther is contextualized in close-up, painful juxtaposition with its cage in the first image, and the end of 'The Panther,' like Smith's 'The Zoo' and Lofting's *The Voyages of Doctor Dolittle*, portrays the animal decaying against the tantalizing backdrop of its natural freedom (that is only vaguely remembered, never recoverable).[13]

> His vision, from the constantly passing bars,
> has grown so weary that it cannot hold
> anything else. It seems to him there are
> a thousand bars; and behind the bars, no world.

As he paces in cramped circles, over and over,
the movement of his powerful soft strides
is like a ritual dance around a center
in which a mighty will stands paralyzed.

Only at times, the curtain of the pupils
lifts, quietly –. An image enters in,
rushes down through the tensed, arrested muscles,
plunges into the heart and is gone.

(25)

The tragic account offers a keen focus on the pain, weariness, paralysis, claustrophobia that a zoo animal suffers.[14] As throughout Rilke's poetry, the curse of stasis is the great evil: unable to see beyond the bars of its cage, the panther finally goes blind, metaphorically representing the toll of its imprisonment. The magnitude of the panther's constraint seems free of hyperbolic excess even when Rilke asserts that the cage seems to the panther like a thousand cages and has wholly obliterated the rest of the world. Rilke's vision of the panther's 'mighty will' shows he appreciates its potential grandeur. Hughes and Dickey, likewise, appreciate the nobility of the animals they regard; Rilke, however, realizes that a caged animal's natural dignity can only flicker and disappear, while the deleterious effect of captivity upon an animal's nature does not trouble Hughes and Dickey because of the presumptions that undergird their zoo stories: once the animal's grandeur enters their mind, it is no longer tethered to the captive creature – it flourishes in them, as they have coopted it; and *they*, after all, are free.

Rilke's poem is the sort of work I think people should create if they go to a zoo for artistic fodder, but moral questions nevertheless arise. What is he doing at the zoo? (Rilke's biographer writes that the sculptor Auguste Rodin had 'advised him to go to the Paris zoo so that he might learn to see. Rilke, who was an animal lover anyway, did not have to be told twice. During the following years, he spent many hours in the Jardin des Plantes, to which he had access through an *autorisation d'artistes*, a special pass for painters and other artists, from 8:00 to 11:00 in the morning before the general public was admitted' (Leppmann, 214).) Does his spectatorship implicate him in the constraint he depicts? (I think it does, and I think he knows it does – but how? The poem seems to leave this question unresolved.) Is Rilke's attendance at a zoo justified because he has written a poem challenging the ethos of animal captivity and enlightening his readers about how zoo culture affects the caged panther? The poem's subtitle identifies the setting as the Jardin des Plantes in Paris.[15] Another poem of Rilke's, 'The Flamingos,' carries the same subtitle, and a third, too, 'The Gazelle,' is probably (but not explicitly) set in a zoo: its subtitle is the gazelle's zoological nomenclature, connoting a zoo sign. But 'The Gazelle' and 'The Flamingos' lack a sense of sympathetic resistance to caged oppression. As morally charged as 'The Panther' seems, other poems indicate that sometimes Rilke is able to ignore the dynamics of animal captivity when he goes to the zoo. The flamingos, in fact, do exactly what the panther cannot: they 'one by one / stride into their imaginary world' (67), reflecting a spiritual empowerment I find unlikely for zoo animals. Perhaps this inconsistency reflects the conceit that a zoo *seems* less cruel to a flamingo than to a panther; or, perhaps, Rilke reveals that my expectations regarding a monolithic logic and rhetoric – that is, the hypothesis that zoo stories will unilaterally advance the case against zoos – may sometimes extend farther than the texts themselves justify.

In 'The Jaguar' (1957), Ted Hughes begins by depicting a zoo where most of the animals are ridiculously undignified – the apes 'adore their fleas in the sun,' parrots 'shriek as if they were on fire, or strut / Like cheap tarts,' and the whole zoo 'Stinks of sleepers.' The speaker's unbridled scorn for the animals suggests that he blames the victims of captivity: complacent in their slovenliness, they deserve whatever they get. 'Cage after cage seems empty,' although the enclosures are not actually unoccupied – but since the animals offer (to the poet's mind) lazy, boring displays, they are invisible to him. But he finds one cage that does merit his attention, a single exception Hughes uses to show how meritless the other animals are: 'a cage where the crowd stands, stares, mesmerized' – as at the end of 'A Hunger Artist.' Hughes focuses on the crowd before noticing the animal itself, but the speaker finally sees, inside the cage, a jaguar

hurrying enraged
Through prison darkness after the drills of his eyes

On a short fierce fuse. Not in boredom –
The eye satisfied to be blind in fire,
By the bang of blood in the brain deaf the ear –
He spins from the bars, but there's no cage to him

More than to the visionary his cell:
His stride is wildernesses of freedom:
The world rolls under the long thrust of his heel.
Over the cage floor the horizons come.

(3)

The speaker admits that the jaguar's condition is undesirable: he sees the animal as 'enraged 'in 'prison darkness,' but he raises no moral protest. (This darkness, and the blindness in the following stanza, seem likely allusions to the blind animal in 'The Panther'; Hughes, then, seconds Rilke's contention of the sensory deprivation, symbolized by blindness, that caged animals suffer.) Indeed, by the end of the poem, the jaguar's constraint seems not to matter much – to the poet, that is. The animal's reactions are irrelevant because the poet is clever enough to imagine away the zoo and its cages. Hughes attributes to the jaguar the conceit that 'there's no cage to him'; the poet's self-absorption undercuts the empathy between the human writer and the caged animal that appears much more trustworthy in most other zoo stories.

Hughes attributes to his jaguar a stock of empowering anthropomorphic sensibilities that I find unpersuasive, because the poem works more prominently to reinforce than to alleviate the animal's captivity. (The word 'cage' appears five times; 'prison,' once; 'bars,' once; 'cell,' once.) Hughes imbues the animal with an aura of fiery resplendence, I think, not as a sign of homage to the animal, but as a testament to himself – as if describing how the poet can imagine the captive jaguar free: for the moment he does so it will be unfettered and see far horizons. But the liberation granted the jaguar is temporary and conditional; the poem projects the caveat that Hughes is in control. Its poetic, its eloquence, and its spirit are all those of the man rather than the animal. The poet keeps the jaguar in its place or bestows a brief fantasy-escape from the cage (for the time occupied by the poem).

Ultimately the cage ensures Hughes's safety, power, and control of the situation – his monopoly on freedom and horizons. The presence of an animal that envies such freedom, but cannot attain it because of the cage, seems to increase the poet's own delight in his possession of this freedom. It is as if he imagines he has more of freedom for himself because the jaguar (which, in nature, ranges widely and makes quantitatively better use of its freedom than a man) has less.

For the type of spectator Hughes represents, the zoo animal is most useful, and most striking, when it is most distanced from its natural life. The cage's starkness, its profound dissimilarity from the animal's native environs, foregrounds the animal and (de)contextualizes it in a way that makes it especially amenable to Hughes's poetic consideration, his aesthetic treatment. In conventional zoos (before the recent fashion of cageless enclosures), Charles Siebert writes, people's visits to see animals were arranged on 'our terms alone and unabashedly. Little effort was made to re-create natural habitats. We were asked to conjure up images of each animal's home by virtue of its starkly arrested presence in ours' ('Gone', 52), exactly as Hughes does in 'The Jaguar.' Siebert analyzes the consequences of people's spectatorship in such zoos, where stark cages 'unabashedly' predominate, in a way that precisely illustrates Hughes' demeanor toward the jaguar he watches: 'the old zoo's arrangement was an open invitation for us to find in animals analogies to our own lives, there being so little detail about theirs to interfere' (53).

'Encounter in the Cage Country' (1966) features a meeting between man and animal that turns into a showdown mediated by the zoo cage. The animal James Dickey depicts 'hiding / His spots in his black hide. / Unchangeably' (274) is probably a leopard (recalling the maxim that it never changes its spots). As in most zoo stories, the cage and the zoo are described unappealingly: the speaker confronts the caged animal in a 'cellblock . . . In the stinking sun of the beast house' (274). In the vivid encounter, spectator and captive animal share an equal allotment of drama and power:

> Among the crowd, he found me
> Out and dropped his bloody snack

And came to the perilous edge
Of the cage, where the great bars tremble
Like wire. All Sunday ambling stopped,

The curved cells tightened around
Us all   as we saw he was watching only
Me. I knew the stage was set.

(274)

The spectator, oddly, begins to perform – pacing in front of the cage like a soldier, pretending to break into a run, acting as if he is drawing a gun – eliciting laughter from children who are watching. But the animal is impassive: 'none of this changed his eyes.'

He waited for what I could give him:

My moves   my throat   my wildest love,
The eyes beneath my eyes. Instead, I left,
Him, though he followed me right to the end

Of concrete.

The speaker realizes that he is in a contest with the animal, and that his trivial clowning is irrelevant. He knows that more important things, significant experiences, should occur between himself and the animal. But this potential cannot be fulfilled at the zoo, certainly not in *this* encounter. The man leaves, walks away: simply because he can, it seems.

The speaker thus exhibits a common sensibility among zoogoers: why bother confronting something momentous, quite possibly difficult, when the path of least resistance is simply to walk on to the next cage? (O'Neill's Yank certainly would have fared better had he chosen such a course.) The speaker had contemplated an evenhanded encounter bedecked with challenging intensity, but finally plays his trump card, denying the animal any possibility of equal participation. The man can walk away from the cage at any time that suits him, and the animal, of course, can never do so. Dickey seems to relish taunting the animal that faces unremitting subjection, with the conspicuously deflationary runover line – 'Of concrete' – reinforcing where it is destined to remain, and what boundary restricts its imaginative potential. The poem concludes with the resumption of the man's cogitations, a sort of imaginative continuation (sans animal) of the encounter:

> I wiped my face, and lifted off
> My glasses. Light blasted the world of shade
> Back under every park bush the crowd
>
> Quailed from me I was inside and out
> Of myself and something was given a life-
> mission to say to me hungrily over
>
> And over and over *your moves are exactly right*
> *For a few things in this world: we know you*
> *When you come, Green Eyes, Green Eyes.*
>
> (274–5)

The speaker has experienced something emotionally arduous: confronting an intensity of light, heat, and metaphysical fervor; entering into a surreally heightened consciousness. Dickey replicates the dynamics from Hughes's 'The Jaguar': the man sees an animal and is stimulated by it; the animal then becomes superfluous, and the man is not going to stand outside the cage all day because he has better things to do. The poet observes, absorbs, uses, then leaves the raw material behind as he goes off to grapple with the fascination of his own mind and think profound abstractions. The prominence of the cage (in the title and in references to 'cellblock,' 'bars,' 'wire,' 'cells,' 'concrete') reinforces the spectator's power, the imaginative strength that the viewer parasitically leeches from the animal. References to the animal's eyes in this poem (a recurrence of the trope from 'The Panther' and 'The Jaguar') seem to ironize and undercut the sight of the animal inside the cage: as if to stress that the animal is there to be looked at, not to look itself; people's and animal's powers of sight are mutually exclusive. Human spectatorship is imagistically enhanced in their versions of the animal–human zoo encounter, which celebrate people as the only creatures capable of seeing – people do *all* the seeing, that is, unthreatened and unchallenged by the animals, from which the poets have eliminated the faculty of vision (or at least, in Dickey's poem, highly compromised the visual energies of 'Green Eyes' to the point of insignificance).

Both 'The Jaguar' and 'Encounter in the Cage Country' dismiss caged animals in favor of the human intellect. It is unfortunate that human culture can be constructed as separate from, even antithetical to, the world of animals; and the zoo, with boundaries clearly separating people from all the captive species, fosters rather than challenges this oppositionality. Glen A. Love describes a common cultural sensibility (which Hughes and Dickey embody when their poems transcend animals) that privileges people above nature:

> It is one of the great mistaken ideas of anthropocentric thinking, and thus one of the cosmic ironies, that society is complex while nature is simple . . . That literature in which nature plays a significant role is, by definition, irrelevant and inconsequential. That nature is dull and uninteresting while society is sophisticated and interesting . . . If we are to believe what modern ecology is telling us, the greatest of all intellectual puzzles is the earth and the myriad systems of life which it nourishes. Nature reveals adaptive strategies far more complex than any human mind could devise.
>
> ('Revaluing', 206)

The ecocritical challenge Love advances is 'to examine this complexity [of nature] as it relates to the human lives which it encompasses' (206). The majority of zoo stories display such examination in some form, but Hughes and Dickey opt instead to reify an isolated and ennobled human presence.

UNCAGED

In Russell Hoban's 1975 novel *Turtle Diary* (adapted in Harold Pinter's 1985 screenplay[16]) two lonely people, William G. and Neaera H., saddened by the plight of three sea turtles that have lived at the London Zoo's aquarium for decades – 'Two or three hundred pounds the big ones must have weighed. Looping and swinging, flying in golden-green silty water in a grotty little tank no bigger than my room' (8) – conspire to arrange their escape. Perhaps the quintessential zoo story, *Turtle Diary* contains nearly every theme about captive animals and spectatorship in zoos that arises piecemeal in dozens of other texts, combined in a single narrative.

Beyond just compiling a comprehensive range of thoughts about zoos, Hoban carries them to an ethical resolution: the conviction that zoo animals must be freed. The turtles are sneaked out of the zoo in crates, driven to the Cornwall coast, and released into the sea in the middle of the night to rediscover their natural habitats and cycles. It is not coincidental that this novel which addresses so many aspects of zoos presents the most radical response possible, the liberation of captive animals.[17] For Hoban, examining the totality of zoo culture ultimately reveals the imperative need to release the animals. 'It seemed to want to happen,' (145) William says, bespeaking the logical inevitability of Hoban's anti-zoo sensibility.

One may question whether aquariums should be considered like zoos, and whether tanks are the same as cages. The aquarium and its reptile house depicted in *Turtle Diary* are actually part of the London Zoo; this, combined with themes regarding the captive aquatic animals that so closely parallel those concerning other animals, justifies considering aquarium scenarios as zoo stories. Several other stories about aquariums seem to be bona fide zoo stories, including Julio Cortázar's 'Axolotl' and Lofting's account of the 'Fidget' in *The Voyages of Doctor Dolittle*. The fish tells Dolittle its story of being captured off the coast of South America and transported to an aquarium:

> Of course we had never lived inside glass walls before; and at first we kept on trying to swim through them and got our noses awfully sore bumping the glass at full speed. Then followed weeks and weeks of weary idleness. They treated us well, so far as they knew how . . . But oh, the dullness of that life! It seemed we were a kind of show. At a certain hour every morning the big doors of the house were thrown open and everybody in the city who had nothing special to do came in and looked at us . . . And the crowds would go from tank to tank, looking in at us through the glass – with their mouths open, like half-witted flounders.
>
> (208–9)

The Fidget pines for its freedom: 'Every night as I lie awake on the floor of this evil-smelling dungeon I hear [the sea's] hearty voice ringing in my ears. How I have longed for it! Just to feel it once again . . . To jump, just to jump from the crest of an Atlantic wave' (211). (It finally escapes – pretending to be dead, it is tossed into the garbage and dumped back into the sea.) Representations of captivity, constraint, and exhibition in stories about fish and reptiles confirm that aquariums, for all practical purposes, function as zoos.

Cages are simultaneously the literal physical embodiment, and the ultimate symbol, of much that is wrong with zoos. *Turtle Diary* and a similar novel about rescuing and releasing captive animals, John Irving's 1968 *Setting Free the Bears*, represent the consummate rebuke.[18] In both stories, the animals are uncaged; the zoos are undone. In Irving's novel three characters, Siggy, Hannes, and Gallen, plan the release of animals from Vienna's Hietzinger Zoo. Their motivation is partly, as in *Turtle Diary*, sympathy for the animals' miserable captivity: the Rare Spectacled Bears serve as the magnets of sympathy, parallel to Hoban's turtles. Partly, too, the liberation is a symbolic gesture of anarchy against social constriction and a reaction against Austria's fascistic history.

Both these writers assail zoos; yet both stories, although inspirational in their activist sensibility, remain at least partly indeterminate. Irving and Hoban unlock the cages, but in neither zoo story is it completely clear where the animals go from there, what the releasers have finally achieved, literally or ethically, or what happens beyond the ending. Nevertheless, the novelists affirm the fundamental idea that zoo animals long for and deserve their freedom. As Masson and McCarthy write:

> Freedom gives joy . . . many well-fed, well-treated captive animals regularly try to escape over and over again . . . One of the joys of freedom is surely the ability to control one's own destiny, and a few scientists have argued that animals feel the need for such control . . . Even if a zoo animal is supplied with all material wants, there may be something vitally lacking, something it needs to be happy. One of the joys of freedom may simply be the ability to evade compulsion.
>
> (120–1)

Among Hoban's themes that recur in other zoo stories: first, *Turtle Diary* simply and straightforwardly condemns zoos as venues for interacting with animals, and expresses the inauthentic, tawdry banality of observing animals in zoos. Neaera muses:

> The fish all look bored to death but of course fish aren't meant to be looked at closely, will not bear close examination . . . The leopard shark they have is so small that his vacant stare and receding chin make him seem nothing more than a marine form of twit rather than a representative of a mortally dangerous species. Rays I think ought to be seen not at all outside their natural habitat, too many questions arise.
>
> (30)

Hoban exposes zoos as infelicitous places to learn properly about animals. Spectators who see animals too easily, Neaera realizes, cannot appreciate their proper, natural contexts:

> Oyster-catchers were what I'd come to see and there were two or three of them mooching about but there was something wrong that made the seeing of them flat and uneventful. I'd never been that close to them before, part of their character had been that they were always seen from a distance on the open mudflats with a wide and low horizon far away. These oyster-catchers were so accessible as to be unobservable.
>
> (27)

The final sentence neatly encapsulates the sensibility I am attempting to elucidate throughout this book. (In the same vein Chris Rawlence writes of wild animals in 'Jungle Lore,' 'the closer we get the further away they are' (12).)

Hoban connotes zoos as unmitigatedly, morally bad, as is anyone who patronizes them. Neaera thinks: 'I wanted to see an oyster-catcher so I went to the Zoo, not feeling at all good about it. The Zoo is a prison for animals who have been sentenced without trial and I feel guilty because I do nothing about it. But there it was, I wanted to see an oyster-catcher and I was no better than the people who'd caged oyster-catchers for me to see' (26). *Turtle Diary* is a call to arms for readers to acknowledge and resist the turpitude of zoos; it suggests that we are culpable if we fail to act against them.

As authors do in other zoo stories, Hoban 'reads zoos,' using zoo signs to subvert the presumptive dominance of one species over another (asserted by the sign's inscribed delineation of captor/captive). The stinted dryness of the sign's language contrasts with Hoban's more engrossing narrative. 'The sign said: "The Green

Turtle, *Chelonia mydas*, is the source of turtle soup"' (13). The novelist flaunts his confidence in the greater power of his language in his character's mocking retort: 'I am the source of William G. soup if it comes to that. Everyone is the source of his or her kind of soup' (13). William's reaction to the zoo sign reminds us that the discourse of zoological/scientific objectivity does not ensure the positivistic legitimacy of human behavior, such as boiling an animal's corpse for the resulting broth. The sign embodies a covert dominionist agenda: people envision zoo animals as existing for their own use – whether a nutritive use, as soup, or a cultural use, as zoo exhibit. What first seems objective fact – the idea that turtles comprise turtle soup – comes to appear ludicrous, noir, barbaric.

The zoo sign's language evokes the rhetoric of Orwellian 'Newspeak': zookeepers constrict the range of discourse on animals in captivity (as the zoo sign is constricted by its terse scientific discourse and by the bounded 'page' of the physical sign itself); they concurrently squelch the ability to explore that discourse critically on its own terms. Newspeak-style terseness announces: nothing more to be said. But the author can deflate that rhetoric, as Hoban does. There *is* more to be said, which is why zoo stories exist. Hoban stretches the language of the zoo sign and breaks through its static and impregnable tenor. He shows how simple it is (for an *imaginative* wordsmith) to make the sign, and its language, and implicitly the ethos of zoo captivity, ridiculous – to hoist it with its own semantic petard. The satire is triumphant: the zoo's cultural sensibility instantly appears as absurd as Hoban's mockery is amusing. The soup becomes a running joke, repeatedly reinforcing the futile and silly reductionism of labeling any species, animal or human, with a few supposedly definitive words. Of a person who enters the bookshop where he works, William thinks, 'Today one of those women who never know titles came into the shop. They are the source of Knightsbridge lady soup' (34); his boss is 'Mr Meager, manager of the shop and the source of Meager soup' (14).

David Garnett's *A Man in the Zoo* offers a model of zoo sign and zoo story as thesis and antithesis. Two people stand before a caged animal; the novella presents, first, the zoo sign (highlighted on the page, centered and set off in a margin-to-margin black-bordered box that graphically approximates a sign): 'DINGO / *Canis familiaris var.* / NEW SOUTH WALES, AUSTRALIA.' The sign's drily authoritative discourse asserts the legitimacy of captivity, but the characters' dialogue challenges and deconstructs the sign, its claim to a scientific absolutism, and the zoo's unexamined entitlement to constrain animals: '"Poor little Dingo," said Cromartie. "They do shut up creatures here on the thinnest pretexts. He is only the familiar dog"' (2). In 'Monkey Island,' Osamu Dazai's talking animal itself makes the point that the zoo sign (which it cannot see) likely demeans its integrity:

> 'There's a long, narrow signboard over there. You see it, sticking above the stone wall? The back side is facing this way – just a piece of weather-beaten wood. But the other side's got something written on it. Maybe it says "The Japanese Monkey, known by its glossy ears." Or else, something even more humiliating.'
>
> (89)

Zoos have one way of contextualizing animals, embodied in the sign; but the sign, as Dazai's monkey informs, probably mistakes and occludes the animal's actual nature.

At the beginning of *Setting Free The Bears*, Irving demonstrates the tension between zoo sign and zoo story in Vienna's Zoo:

> It was the Famous Asiatic Black Bear, crouched in a back corner of his cage ... There was a little printed history of the bear, fixed to a map of the world, with the species' roaming area shaded black and a red star to mark the spot where he was taken – in the Himalayas – by a man named Hinley Gouch. The Asiatic Black Bear, the history explained, had his cage facing away from the other bears because he was 'enraged' when he saw them ...
>
> 'I wonder how old Gouch got him?' said Siggy.
>
> 'Nets, perhaps,' I said.
>
> 'Or maybe he just talked him into coming to Vienna,' said Siggy. But we didn't think Hinley Gouch was a Viennese. More likely he'd been one of those misplaced Britishers, in league with a hundred brawny Sherpas who'd routed the bear into a ready-dug pit.
>
> 'It would be fun getting him and Gouch together again,' said Siggy, and we didn't look at the other bears.
>
> (13)

Irving illustrates the discourse of signage and in response, opposing the sign's dry language, the narrative's engaging vitality. His characters subvert the sign and its language (only paraphrased – 'a little printed history of the bear' – thus further marginalized); they suggest (in the author's own voice and style that is obviously privileged) an iconoclastic hostility to the sign's intended objective dignity. They read beyond the sign's information, assuming that it omits significant material and probing to elicit the background of cruelty (routing the bear into a pit) that they suspect underlies the display of captive animals. They expose the zoo's unwritten history, the traces of imperialism (by 'those misplaced Britishers') that comprise its legacy; they challenge the zoos' very pretext of capturing animals and claiming a monopoly on processes of knowing them. They figuratively reverse the dynamics of captivity, in which people exploitatively domineer animals, by fantasizing a reunion – a rematch – between the captor and his victim.

The way Irving's language undercuts the zoo sign offers a paradigm of how the signifying text can undercut the signified institution when we read zoos. The zoo story has the power, figuratively and imaginatively, to vanquish the zoo: as Irving writes at the end of this scene, 'we didn't look at the other bears' – case closed. The writer stacks the deck in favor of language *about* zoos being vastly superior to the language of the zoo itself. Thus, in the contest on the playing field of language/art/culture/aesthetics, the zoo itself comes in a poor second place to the zoo story. The zoo's language is swathed in inefficacy: many studies 'show that visitors rarely read detailed informational panels, nor do they generally read exhibit-related brochures. In the National Zoological park, Washington DC, nearly all visitors said that they read signs but when actually observed they were found not to do so' (Mullan and Marvin, 135–6). In 'Among the Dahlias,' William Sansom depicts a zoo spectator who gamely reads the signs as visitors are supposed to do, but finds that their meaning and information prove ephemeral, unconvincing, irrelevant:

> Sometimes he stopped and read with interest a little white card describing the bird's astounding Latin name and its place of origin. Uganda, Brazil, New Zealand – and soon these places ceased to mean anything, life's variety proved too immense, anything might come from anywhere.
>
> (384)

In *The Great Divorce*, Valerie Martin depicts another failure of the zoo sign to communicate its intended educational message: two boys 'stood before the two young snow leopards on loan from a zoo in Ohio. One boy read the educational sign on the rail – "Only five hundred left" to the other, who replied, "Well, that's a lot"' (59). Zoo stories constantly deconstruct zoo signs. Even when the sign implies something important about the relationship between people and animals, as in *The Great Divorce*, the author suggests that the medium of the sign simply cannot effectively embody and convey its information, however elementary, to spectators. The subversion of the sign's language, conducted within the language of the story, represents the simultaneous symbolic deconstruction of the zoo itself – or, at a minimum, the prevalent *urge* to challenge zoos and supplant them, displace them, via zoo stories.

The overload of animals in the zoo – the problem of too many animals being gathered, unnaturally, in a single compound and artificially made to exist as neighbors – is another recurrent zoo story theme Hoban presents. However convenient for the spectator, Neaera realizes that the zoo assembly negates the genuine experience of animals:

> There were all sorts of waders in the Waders Aviary, not all of whom would ordinarily have been seen in the same place I think. The sign showed pictures of a red-shank, guillemot, razorbill, eider duck, oyster-catcher, ruff, kittiwake, white-breasted waterhen, rufous laughing thrush, curlew, laysan duck and hooded merganser. They had their concrete pool to wade in, they had reeds and bushes and a strip of sand. The Zoological Society had pieced together a habitat that was like the little naif towns one sometimes sees in model railway layouts. The elements of it were thing for thing a rough approximation of reality but the scale wasn't right and the parts of it didn't fit together in a realistic way.
>
> (28)

The contrived proximity of various animals betokens an unsatisfyingly artificial environment, a vast oversimplification of the natural world's complex geography of habitats and interacting species. The attempt to make the setting seem more realistic (via pools and bushes) actually produces the opposite effect: it only indicates the intrusive artifice of a fabricated human presence.

Hoban's most resonant zoo story motif is the metaphorical association of depressed, unfulfilled people with captive animals. These people project their pain onto the animals in an attempt to concretize their own feelings of despair, and to connect with animals as they cannot with other people. The people may be unable to comprehend fully their affliction; visualizing another creature who suffers a parallel constraint may help them better confront their own situation. Jerry suggests this type in *The Zoo Story*, as does Yank in *The Hairy Ape*, Janice Elliott's Felix in 'The Noise from the Zoo,' and Plath's titular persona in 'Zoo Keeper's Wife.' In 'The Woman at the Washington Zoo' (1960), Randall Jarrell's persona expresses such a projection of personal angst and metaphorical feelings of captivity onto caged zoo animals: the speaker peers 'In the eyes of animals, these beings trapped / As I am trapped,' and apostrophizes, 'Oh, bars of my own body, open, open! / The world goes by my cage and never sees me' (2).

In *Turtle Diary*, the turtles offer a personal metaphor for both William's and Neaera's trapped, stinted humanity. William's family has dissolved and disappeared; his job and his life are mundane, passionless. Neaera, while more professionally successful, shares a similar emptiness, fear of engagement, alienation. Both are unable to venture beyond their neuroses. Their lives are as uncomfortably and awkwardly constrained as if they were in a cage; so it is fitting that they should identify with the plight of zoo animals and, in freeing the turtles, attempt to free themselves. The screenplay, with its short, detached snatches of dialogue and interaction, projects a constant air of inadequacy. Pinter makes explicit the connection between the turtles and the liberators, and the zoo-break's vicarious attractions for William and Neaera: when they first meet to consider freeing the turtles, he tries to ascertain her interest in the enterprise.

WILLIAM: You like turtles, do you?
NEAERA: They're in prison.
WILLIAM: They're not alone in that.

(119)

And again, when William asks Neaera if she has any animals herself:

NEAERA: I have a water beetle.
WILLIAM: Does she want to go to Polperro [where they plan to release the turtles into the sea]? She could ride on the back of the turtles.

WILLIAM: Perhaps we can ride on the back of the turtles.
NEAERA: Bum a ride on the turtles?
WILLIAM: Is that what we're doing?
NEAERA: I don't know. I haven't really... thought.

(140–1; author's ellipsis)

A motif that occasionally (but only infrequently) occurs in zoo stories is talking animals, which indicates that something unusual and significant is going on: the author is making a point about the communication between people and other species. Hoban's animals 'talk' in a version of language that is both human and nonhuman, partly comprehensible and partly elusive. Listening to some of the zoo's birds talking, William hears 'More than one voice, some sort of a controversy: kleep kleep kleep. Kleep kleep' (21). Their speech, although rendered phonetically into English, is semantically gibberish. Hoban thus indicates that an insurmountable obstacle must remain between people and animals in the zoo.

'Kleep it and have klept with it for God's sake,' said one.
'I don't have to kleep it just because you klawp I should,' said the other.
'Then don't kleep it,' said the first one. 'It's no klank off my klonk.'
'Oh aye,' said the second one. 'You klawp that now but that's not what you klawped a little klink ago.'
'I klick very klenk what I klawped a little klink ago,' said the first one. 'I klawped either kleep it or don't kleep it but stop klawping about it. That's what I klawped.'
'It's all very klenk for you to klawp "Kleep it,"' said the second one. 'You're not the one that has to kleggy back the kwonk.'
I didn't want to hear any more.

(22)

One can partly decipher from the context (just as one makes stabs at Lewis Carroll's 'Jabberwocky') what some of the 'klanks' and 'kleeps' might mean, but finally, one cannot discern what these birds are saying. The zoo will not serve as a United Nations (or United Species) where members of different realms come together for facilitated interchange. In *Setting Free the Bears*, Irving depicts similarly elusive animal 'speech': as Hannes and Gallen stroll through the zoo, the animals they are planning to liberate begin talking: '"BROP!" said the walrus.' Gallen asks what the noises mean. '"Something must have startled one of them," I answered, defeated. "BROP!" said the walrus, rising again. BROP yourself, I thought. "BROP!" he repeated . . . the terrible Asiatic Black Bear deafened the zoo. "God, what's *that*?" said Gallen. "BROP!" said the endlessly belching walrus' (307). Zoo animals are depicted communicating to people in something resembling our own language, but only up to a point: beyond a certain low level of communication, the interaction is as meaningless as endless belching. Keith Tester discusses the notion of talking animals:

> Wittgenstein once remarked 'If a lion could talk, we could not understand him.' He was making the largely philosophical point that the world of the lion and the world of the social are totally unconnected and, therefore, communication between them is impossible . . . All of us would rather a lion did not suddenly start up an intelligible conversation because we have taken it upon ourselves, as a mark and a vindication of our difficult, double-faced, and yet privileged status within the world, to speak on the lion's behalf.
>
> (207–8)

Yet despite a linguistic barrier, zoo stories may posit a kind of supralinguistic relationship between animals and sympathetic people. In *Turtle Diary*, such communion occurs only outside of zoos (obviously implying that it is impossible within the zoo itself). The main empathetic relationship is between William and Neaera and the turtles they uncage. A bond is created whereby William and Neaera learn a lesson (about the potential freedom that can exist after, and despite, a long period of captivity) at the end of the novel from animals in the ocean, which they could not have learned from animals in the zoo.

Other brief but meaningful moments of communion occur in

the background; in a fit of depression, for example, William resists returning to his room:

> I didn't go straight home. When I changed from the Bakerloo Line at Paddington I went up into the Main Line Station. I felt like being with a lot of people in a big open place. Ordinarily I don't like pigeons but I like them under the glass roof of Paddington Station. Mingling with the rush of people the pigeons are quite different from the way they are when plodding about in squares and being fed by people who have nothing better to feed.
>
> (109)

William is not a tree-hugging green: he is capable of being as crotchety to animals as he is to people. But here he experiences an important moment of communion – a respite from isolation – with pigeons. There *are* times when people need to be around animals: watch them, share our space with them, learn from them, somehow be healed by their presence. Leo K. Bustad describes the enduring bonds people and animals have always shared:

> Early in our history, we identified intimately with . . . animate elements of our surroundings. Some of the first drawings and paintings depicted people with animals. There is every indication that people adopted pets or animals not only as helpers, but as companions. Primitive people found that people-animal partnerships were important to their well-being, if not vital to their survival. Many of the earth's early inhabitants formed a strong alliance, even a symbiotic relationship, with animals.
>
> (233–4)

Hoban shows this necessary alliance between people and animals occurring in a train station rather than a zoo, and involving one of the most common, unspectacular creatures (by the zoo's standards of exotica) in our ecosystem, a pigeon. It does not require the glamor of a spotted or furry creature, Hoban indicates, to stimulate the essential faculties involved in the authentic interaction between people and animals. Similarly, in several other zoo stories, significant things happen in people's relationships with animals *other than* zoo animals (as with Jerry and the dog in *The Zoo Story*). While people need to observe and commune with other animals, this does not justify zoos' existence; such communion happens with less spectacle but more sincerity and effectiveness outside of zoos.

Turtle Diary features other brief but interesting recurrent zoo story themes: one of these is the idea that children may experience negative feelings toward zoos but be unable to act on these feelings until they are adults, when they go back and recast their childhood experiences. At the novel's opening William notes: 'I thought: when I was a child I used to like the Zoo' (8); but when he returns as an adult, his intricate plot to subvert zoos and free animals seems in part an act of atonement for having liked zoos in his youth. It is significant that the animals he frees have lived in captivity for up to 30 years – he may imagine they could be the very same animals he had visited as a child. Another passing theme is the scientific use of animals, and the way zoos conjoin the cruelties of vivisection and captivity in tandem.[19] Neaera reads a newspaper story about a spider carried into space on a *Skylab* flight; although disoriented at first, Arabella eventually managed to weave a nearly normal web. Neaera thinks:

> That Arabella should have spun any sort of web, should have made the effort at all, overwhelms me. In her place I should have sulked or been sick I am sure. She didn't even know which way was up let alone where she was or why and yet she spun a reasonably workable web out there in space. I hope they had the decency to bring along some flies for her to catch, I can't think they'd make her eat tiny frozen dinners squeezed out of tubes or whatever astronauts subsist on. And if they did bring flies those flies must appear somewhere on *Skylab-2*'s manifest: *Flies, 12 doz.* If there are flies up there no mention is made of them or how they adapted to weightlessness. Perhaps they'd use dead flies just as they use dead mice to feed the owls at the Zoo.
>
> (110)

Neaera humorously empathizes with all the animals, the flies as well as the spider, innocently caught up in scientific quests irrelevant to their own lives. Hoban challenges his audience to regard animals not as insensate tools whose function on the planet is to advance human goals, but as creatures that have their own individual perceptions, and that must be dumbfounded by what we do to them. Antagonism to scientific exploitation of animals complements the opposition to cultural exploitation that *Turtle Diary* and many other zoo stories embody. When animals are construed as pure and detached subjects, whether in the zoo or on Skylab, people are a great remove from them.

The zoo story tropes in *Turtle Diary* include a direct reference to a seminal modern zoo story. Neaera recalls her first encounter with William, conceiving him as:

> A tall hopeless-looking man with an attentive face and an air of fragile precision like a folding rule made out of ivory. There was something in my memory: *The Man in the Zoo* [*sic*], the David Garnett novella about the man who had himself locked up in a cage and exhibited as *Homo sapiens*. Not that he seems part of such a story but the idea of him has something of hapless patience in it.
>
> (54–5)

On the contrary, William is very much 'part of such a story,' as is Neaera herself: they inhabit an intertextual and supratextual story yoking together a variety of themes that combine to shed light on the nexus of zoo culture. To appropriate John Steinbeck's apothegm, there's only one zoo story. Any character in this narrative topos might burst onto the scene just as Albee's Jerry does (at the beginning of the play that actually happens to be called *The Zoo Story*), oddly, unsettlingly, tragically: 'I've been to the zoo. I said, I've been to the zoo. MISTER, I'VE BEEN TO THE ZOO!' (12).

Hoban's network of zoo story themes culminates in the turtles' liberation. Their release is wildly exhilarating – a coup for justice, liberty, and the rights of animals – and at the same time somewhat plodding, quotidian, anticlimactic. Unusually, the keeper, Mr Fairbairn, is in league with the conspirators: he, too, considers the turtles' captivity inappropriate. This seems to be a marginally plausible portrait: no other zoo stories feature keepers who think their charges should be released (other than the zoologists in Greenaway's *Zoo: A Zed and Two Noughts* – but they are so depraved that their liberation of animals seems insignificant). If the keeper thinks the captivity of these turtles is wrong, how does he justify the captivity of the other animals in his displays? Why help to free these few creatures while keeping the rest in captivity (and even replacing the liberated animals with new baby turtles, although he says he plans to free them, too, when they get older)? Hoban leaves unexplored many intricate ethical issues surrounding the keeper's role, in what may be a provocative enigma, or may simply be a weakness in the novel. The keeper's cooperation defuses potential excitement and suspense. In *Setting Free the Bears*, by contrast, much of the action deals with the intrigue of the liberation plan, and the antagonism between the freers and the keepers. But Mr Fairbairn walks William and Neaera through their plan step by step, giving instructions on how to build the crates to transport the turtles from London to Cornwall, and even loading them into William's rented van himself. (Mr Fairbairn ends up romantically involved with Neaera after the liberation, bringing her out of her own 'shell' and back into the world of human society. Even within an ethical fantasy, he strains credulity.)

As they execute the liberation, William and Neaera vacillate between tedium and neurotic anxiety: they worry about the size of the van, wider than what William is used to driving (he fears he will scrape against another car and incur a charge from the rental company); about whether they will be able to get fuel during their long night drive; about staying awake; and absurdly, about being discovered and even imprisoned. Hoban diminishes any valiant aspects of their actions on all fronts. This deflation complements Marti Kheel's call for a holistic rather than heroic approach to our current ecological quagmire; we must not reenact obsolete ways of conceiving the world around us – what Kheel calls the model of Mother Nature as a damsel in distress – in our attempt to reform. The heroic ethic cannot counter ecological difficulties, she suggests; it embodies simply another destructive sensibility. *Turtle Diary* inspires readers to ecoactivism – but not to be a hero, just because it is the right thing to do. Such activism may change one's life, as it does Neaera's when she finds love with Mr Fairbairn, or just as easily may not, as is the case with William. (Indeed, by the measure of romance – the classic yardstick in the genre of the novel – William's outcome is the opposite of his collaborator's: he had initiated a romance as the liberation plan was taking shape, but it broke off because he had been unwilling to share his secret with his girlfriend; realizing his concealment, she resented his introversion.) Similarly, in *Setting Free the Bears*, the three liberators experience radically different outcomes. Hannes and Gallen, stunned by their adventure at the zoo, go their separate ways with the prospect of a possible future reunion. Siggy dies in a freak accident involving motorcycles, bees, and provincial Austrians. Irving makes the same point as Hoban: life may be either good or bad for those who liberate animals just as for those who do not. One shouldn't reenact Hannes, Siggy, and Gallen's actions in the expectation of receiving any automatic reward. What they did, as in *Turtle Diary*, simply had to be done; their lives continue afterwards (or not, for Siggy), for better or worse.

While the liberation in *Turtle Diary* is in many ways underplayed, it remains finally resplendent when it actually happens: William

> up-ended the crate on the edge of a step, he tilted it forward and with a great splash the turtle hit the water and dived. We hugged and kissed each other, ran back for the next turtle, launched it, then the next. Each one dived under the wild water and was gone. It was done, it had actually happened. Three empty crates and the turtles safely off.
>
> (158)

At the end, however, Hoban leaves two large issues unresolved: What finally happens to the turtles? And what finally happens to the people? These are vital questions to address as consequences of the liberation that, Hoban implores, simply must be executed. To amplify the enigma with more questions: What follows from such liberation? What comes next, if anyone heeds Hoban (and me) and radically challenges the zoo's imprisonment of animals? If turtles – or, as in Irving, bears – why not all animals? (Hannes mulls this question over and eventually decides to release most of the animals.) If these animals, what about the ones in other zoos? (Hannes and Siggy do, in fact, contemplate a European tour: 'there's an interesting place I know of in Naples. They've a big aquarium where they keep all the wondrous fishes, in stale sea water under glass . . . In fact, it would be an easy job. We wouldn't have to wriggle the fishes very far, or keep them out of the water too long. Just across a street or two . . . And then we'd launch them free in the Bay of Naples' (259); indeed, Irving's sequel would resemble *Turtle Diary*.) A plethora of philosophical conundrums results from probing the surface of the status quo, from looking at a zoo and making the simple ethical observations that animals should not be caged and people should not be looking at them.

Can liberated zoo animals fend for themselves after spending their lives in captivity? Neaera wonders: 'where is there for them to go really? To what can they navigate? . . . Would they have to swim with signs and slotted boxes begging for protection and support?' (39). William asks Mr Fairbairn about the turtles' restoration back into nature: 'isn't the Channel too cold for them?' The keeper responds, 'I don't think the water'd bother them. Cold water makes them a little sluggish but I think they'd backtrack up the North Atlantic Current till they hit the Canary Current or the Gulf Stream. I bet they'd be in home waters in three months' (53). Despite Mr Fairbairn's supposed expertise, his assessment of what awaits the turtles in nature is only conjectural: 'I *think* . . . I *bet* . . .' After the turtles' release, William remains uncertain about their fate: 'I thought about the turtles and I couldn't believe they'd got out to sea against that heavy tide. Surely they'd been beaten back against the break-water or swept into the harbour . . . They were probably in the harbour now, they'd probably been picked up by fisherman' (164). Confirmation of the turtles' escape and survival can come only (and unsatisfyingly) inferentially, by negation – that is, by not learning of their capture or demise; they will not send a postcard from Ascension Island. The next morning William thinks, 'No one said anything about turtles and there were none in sight. They must have got out to sea all right' (165) – again, this hope is indefinite: William cannot say, 'they *have* gotten out to sea all right.' And in Pinter's script, when Neaera visits the zoo to recount the adventure for the keeper:

NEAERA: They went. They went into the sea . . . and they went off.
GEORGE: Wonderful.
NEAERA: Unless you've had any reports – I mean of turtles being picked up, off the Cornish coast.
GEORGE: No reports.

(156; author's ellipsis)

Even after William is convinced the turtles have been safely launched, he worries, 'I'd never know whether they'd got to where they were going' (199).

Accounts of an actual zoo escape validate William and Neaera's fears about freed animals' viability in nature. In February 1995, after the roof of the Bronx Zoo's nineteenth-century aviary collapsed during a snowstorm, dozens of rare gulls and terns flew away. Bird curator Donald Bruning said in the *New York Times* that chances of recovering the birds were slim because high winds could carry them anywhere across the region; 'the likelihood of finding and recapturing them appeared to be as dubious as their chances of survival in the urban wild. "Most of them were hatched and raised in the aviary and have no experience outside," he said. "The cold will not bother them, but it will not be easy for them to find food. They will have to compete with local gulls and birds, and this is not the best time of the year for trying to find food"' (McFadden, B12). The next day's news story reported that, despite a few isolated sightings, most of the birds had vanished and were expected to survive 'at most a few days without food before they weaken and die . . . "I think it will be very tough," said Peter Joost, head of the Linnaean Society of New York, a naturalist society that specializes in birds. "There's a lot of attrition with all sorts of birds in winter. They couldn't have escaped at a worse time."' There was hope that the birds might return to the zoo for food, the *Times* reported, but 'On the other hand, "if they feel this heady freedom, who knows where they will go?" Mr. Joost said' (Nossiter, A9). Joost's final observation touches just briefly upon the potential exhilaration of liberation. William and Neaera's concerns are complemented by more sanguine hopes – but the real-life zoo escape suggests that their hopes may be no more than fantasy. It would be unreasonable to overlook the likelihood that acculturated zoo animals are simply unable to survive in freedom. Hoban offers a feel-good parable, but perhaps not one that should seduce readers into believing that his novel embodies a valid solution to the problem of zoos. The ultimate fate of freed animals is complicated, and involves circumstances that seem to exceed the scope of Hoban's narrative.[20]

Setting Free the Bears, too, relates irresolution about what happens after cages are opened. Irving's chaotic liberation scene differs from Hoban's sedate triumph. As the animals leave their cages,

Hannes thinks, 'the primates I released were not quiet . . . I could hear my primates smashing ashtrays off the tables in the *Biergarten*' (322). He worries, like William and Neaera, about what the animals will do when free and whether they will survive. But Irving's animals face more unpromising immediate prospects than Hoban's. The turtles were released into the sea, if not their native waters, but the Vienna animals face nothing even remotely resembling their natural habitat. They are left to filter, helter-skelter, into a suburban neighborhood. At first they are merely befuddled and nervous as they stumble through the dark: an elephant 'moved off at a steady, sideways trot, gathering speed, crushing shrubs and flattening down the iron rails along the paths' (323). What ensues becomes macabre: aroused by wild screeches emanating from the released animals, a crowd gathers outside the zoo: 'Through the shrubs, I saw them hiding. Anonymous men with ancient weapons – with fireplace tridents, grub hoes and gleaming bucksaws; pitchforks, sledges and moon-shaped sickles' (329). Shots are fired; injured animals fleeing the zoo course into the streets, where they suffer real physical pain as bad as, if not worse than, what they suffered in their cages. Gallen is

> bumped by a Siberian ibex, stumbling blindly and goatlike over the curb – a chunk of his hide torn open and flapping down over his shoulder; the gash was sort of hoe-shaped . . . I saw the snow leopard panting and licking one paw. And in Sarajevo Platz, I saw a team of five successful hunters trying to crouch down out of my passing headlight, thinking I was a police cycle; behind them, they attempted to conceal the dragged, bloodied and unprotesting gaur. Who, when he was upright, was six-foot-four . . . the last of the pickup trucks to pass us had a load in the back – a lump under a tarp, hanging down off the tailgate. I saw a bit of leg and hoof protrude; I recognized the brownish-red and creamy-white striping, running from hock to shank.
>
> (330–2)

Irving suggests people are fanatically determined to cause pain to animals and to keep them subservient. If animals escape the cages meant to keep them in subjection, then throngs of people will maul them with guns, hoes, or whatever other instruments of violent brutality are available. In 'The Rights of Animals,' Brigid

Brophy denounces the masochistic implications of people's relations to animals evoked in Irving's mob scene:

> The relationship of *homo sapiens* to the other animals is one of unremitting exploitation. We employ their work; we eat and wear them. We exploit them to serve our superstitions: whereas we used to sacrifice them to our gods and tear out their entrails in order to foresee the future, we now sacrifice them to Science and experiment on their entrails in the hope – or on the mere off-chance – that we might thereby see a little more clearly into the present. When we can think of no pretext for causing their death and no profit to turn it to, we often cause it nonetheless, wantonly, the only gain being a brief pleasure for ourselves, which is usually only marginally bigger than the pleasure we could have had without killing anything; we could quite well enjoy our marksmanship or crosscountry galloping without requiring a real dead wild animal to shew for it at the end.
>
> (15)

Irving's vicious posse seems to assault the animals merely to oppose their freedom: out of a will to control them – if not caged, then decimated. The mob's cruelty evokes the racist backlash during the Civil Rights era. Vigilantes bombed, shot, and lynched African Americans apparently for no other reason than to protest oppressed peoples' escape from the constraint, the 'cages,' of segregation; racists attacked in a last-ditch effort to assert (despite all evidence to the contrary) that the status quo could endure, and that they could remain in control while their victims remained in constraint.

Clearly, Irving's animals will not flourish in the Austrian countryside any more than in the zoo. Their emancipation seems only nominal, and the liberation futile: an abstract paean to freedom, overshadowed by its apparent inability to transcend the zoo's legacy of oppression. Irving's animals are damned if they're caged, and damned if they're freed – or, to marshall another cliché, they escape out of the frying pan into the fire. Pessimistically, Irving suggests that the brutality people inflict upon animals (in zoos and elsewhere) represents habits so entrenched in our culture that they cannot be simply undone. Again, human historical analogies come to mind: descendants of American slaves, nominally freed from oppression in 1863, endured another century of discrimination; and freed from segregation, still suffer disproportionally the indignities of poverty and violence. Postcolonial societies, liberated from imperial exploitation, continue to face political turmoil and economic deprivation. The condition of freed zoo animals, as Irving depicts it, resembles those of postcolonial and postenslavement cultures: after generations of evil, merely evicting the captors or opening the cages cannot restore justice. No single momentary action can redress the iniquities of history.

Yet I do not argue (nor do these stories) that the ambivalent 'freedom' implies the acts of liberation ought not to have occurred, nor that the subjects were better off in their cages; that is not a morally valid response. The post-liberation difficulties show the enormousness of the problem, which may be these stories' most pressing revelation. The quagmire highlights the importance of confronting oppressive dynamics rather than letting them drag on for generations and become increasingly intractable. Frustration at the lack of narrative closure (or confirmation of our moral impulse) in even the most activist zoo stories should impel us to determine what other oppressions proliferate unchallenged, and what other moral and environmental desecrations we need to address.

Irving does offer one exception to his bleak vision, mitigating his cynical appraisal of people's efforts to help zoo animals. The animals that first attracted Siggy and Hannes's attention, the bears with which they achieved a special rapport, escape the massacre that befalls the rest. It may be a fairy-tale ending, the stuff of fantasy (or perhaps just the stuff of literature, with a glimmer of the order and moral fairness so often elusive in real life), to inspire people to hold out hope. The day after the disastrous zoo-break, as Hannes sits by the woods nursing his wounds, 'the shoulder-to-shoulder pair of Rare Spectacled Bears tumbled out of the forest and huffed across the road, not more than twenty yards from me' (338). Hannes starts his motorcycle and rides off. 'I suddenly didn't dare stay there any longer' (339). As thrilled as he is to see the bears, he doesn't stare for more than an instant: he freed them precisely so they could escape people's gaze. Instead of looking, Hannes indulges in a conjectural account of what awaits them in the future:

> I was able to sincerely imagine coming this way again, some Wednesday. And meeting someone from the area, who would tell me: There are bears in Klosterneuburg.
> Really?
> Oh yes. Bears.
> But they've done no harm?
> Not these bears. They're strange bears.
> Rare Spectacled Bears?
> Well, I don't know about that.
> But they're multiplying?
> I don't know about that, either. But they're very friendly with each other, you know.
> Oh yes. I know.
>
> (339)

When the bears cease being on display in the zoo, they live on in Hannes's imagination. Zoo stories frequently feature this oppositional construct: people can *either* experience animals via the richness of our imagination, or stare at them in cages, not both. For Neaera, too, the freed turtles live on in an imaginary encounter:

> The turtles would be swimming, swimming . . . Thinking about the turtles I could feel the action of their swimming, the muscle contractions that drove the flippers through the green water. All they had was themselves but they would keep going until they found what was in them to find. In them was the place they were swimming to, and at the end of their swimming it would loom up out of the sea, real, solid, no illusion. They could be stopped of course, they might be killed by sharks or fishermen but they would die on the way to where they wanted to be. I'd never know if they'd got there or not, for me they would always be swimming.
>
> (189)

Neaera appreciates the sea turtles in a real, deep, and satisfyingly graspable way, *as if* they were swimming right in front of her, although of course they are not. Eminently convincing sensory detail and precision prove that people can have meaningful interaction with *un*caged animals – as Hannes and Neaera do, and as we do through them. Neaera's final vision of the animals, like William's and Hannes's, is conjectural, imaginary, unreal (*'I don't know . . . for me* they would always be swimming'), which is the way people must learn to experience and appreciate most animals. It is not a less perfect way than literal, immediate knowledge: it is a better way – both because it does not constrain animals, and because our imaginative faculties are immensely more stimulated than when we see captive animals in the zoo.

If the liberation of zoo animals from their cages is successful, the denouement will be uncertain: we cannot know what happens to the animals because we can no longer see them. As much as Hannes, William, and Neaera wanted to uncage the animals, they grapple, finally, with the quandary of indeterminacy: not knowing exactly what their actions have wrought. It is an enormous challenge for people to act without palpable reward or acknowledgment. (It is not such a problem for ants, Marianne Moore reminds us in 'Critics and Connoisseurs.') The liberators wonder and worry. But they ultimately accept that proper interaction with animals necessitates not knowing exactly where they are. The animals' elusiveness heightens their fascination. Irving's and Hoban's novels typify nature's principles, if not those of a less visionary human society: validation comes by instinct (the liberation feels like the right thing to do to William, Neaera, and Hannes) – an ecological moral for our times – rather than formal confirmation documented in triplicate. Lacking knowledge, one is forced to fall back on *faith* – faith that it is right to do right, even in the absence of explicit and immediate verification.

It is clear enough in the end, despite some equivocation, what the liberators have done for the animals – they have let them out of their cages. But what does it mean for the *people* to have uncaged the animals? What have the liberators done for themselves, and for their fellow human beings? Have they helped us free ourselves from the ultimately degrading position of captor/voyeur – and if so, how? In real life, escape or liberation fundamentally subverts the institution of animal captivity and the trope of human control over natural savagery: Ritvo discusses several incidents involving captive animals that escaped or threatened to escape in the nineteenth century, concluding, 'The uneasiness provoked by the idea of wild animals loose in civilized Britain was not simply a prudent response to their capacity for doing harm; it inversely figured the domination symbolized by their captivity' (226). At least inferentially, Irving and Hoban embody this sense of escape as an inverse figuration of domination, a frontal assault upon zoo culture.

Yet it is profoundly unclear to William and Neaera, on a conscious level, why they are engaged in their liberation, and it seems fuzzy to Irving's characters, too; all seem to feel a vague, deep, primitive urge. For Siggy, Hannes, and Gallen, the liberation is a paean to youth culture antiauthoritarianism, and also a symbolic revenge on the Nazis (via Schrutt, who ends up in a cage while his prisoners are set free). For William and Neaera, the liberation enacts a necessary if elusive moral deed: helping creatures that need help, in a way that affirms a connection to the world which neither person is able to achieve elsewhere; as such, the liberation is somehow therapeutic for them.

William expresses a simple but quintessential function of the mission: 'I think the turtles are better off,' he tells Mr Fairbairn, 'which was after all the object of the exercise' (192). This bespeaks an eco-utilitarian vision of our obligations, to do the greatest possible good for the greatest possible number, all animals included. And again, in reviewing what the liberation has meant, William thinks, 'At first I'd been obsessed with setting them free. Then it had become a heavy task I was committed to. Then we did it and afterwards it seemed a blank and empty thing. Now it felt a good thing again' (199–200). In the last analysis, he appreciates that the enterprise has been ambiguous and inconstant, but nevertheless genuine, *echt*. The sensibility both novels invoke is an inchoate beginning to an immensely large venture that lies ahead: setting free all the turtles, and bears, and others; setting ourselves free, in tandem, from imperialist, dominionist, imaginatively sterile and commodified/institutionalized ways of regarding nature; letting go of misguided attempts to control animals, and giving ourselves over to less concrete and omniscient ways of relating to the world. It is impossible to say how this may play out, but the liberators finally realize that they have taken the first step of a thousand-mile journey, and a step in the right direction.

4
Pain

... the young keeper appeared with a rifle on the rocks above. He fired and the beautiful animal coiled back for a second in the air, gave a faint mewing cry, and fell dead.

Angus Wilson, *The Old Men at the Zoo*

She is mangy, perhaps half her weight when her ordeal started, and she barely has the strength to stand upright against the rusting bars of her cage ... A putrid odor pervades the concrete building, and cage after cage is littered with the carcasses of lions, tigers, leopards and pumas.

New York Times, 'In the Sarajevo Zoo, Only a House of Horrors'

The zoo is a locus of pain. Its cruelty reveals itself most obviously through the range of barbarities that captive animals suffer. Strains of psychological torment and cultural sadism (directed mainly against animals, but sometimes afflicting human bystanders as well) often accompany this physical anguish directly, or emanate metaphorically from the zoo. The pain may or may not be immediately apparent – certainly, it would disturb audiences to have to confront it consciously and ubiquitously, so zoos hide much of the pain that attends animal captivity. Nevertheless, this pain proliferates behind the scenes – sometimes literally so (hidden from spectators looking at public displays during the zoo's hours of operation), sometimes more figuratively concealed. Institutional, cultural, and historic aspects of zoo practices conspire to screen or marginalize zoo animals' pain, making it easier to ignore. Those who inflict this pain are adept at rationalizing, trivializing, or denying its existence. Zookeepers possess extensive traditions of oppressing animals without being called to account; the voiceless victims cannot expose them.

Pain figures prominently in many of the works I examine, and remains understated or sublimated in others. But it can be scented and distilled in every zoo story: it underlies the fear Virginia Woolf embeds in the zoo metaphor she applies to her Bloomsbury compatriots ('All the animals are dangerous . . . I'm sometimes too timid to go in') and the longing and deprivation of natural life evident in Rilke's 'The Panther,' Smith's 'The Zoo,' and Hughes's 'The Jaguar.' The awareness of pain informs and explains spectators' guilty, anguished introspection in Hoban's *Turtle Diary* and Doctorow's *World's Fair*. Pain lurks behind the resistance and antipathy to the zoo visit in Doyle's *Paddy Clarke Ha Ha Ha* and Allende's *The House of the Spirits*. Proximity to animal captivity provokes the painful and infectious angst of inadequacy and impotence affecting people in Jarrell's 'The Woman in the Washington Zoo,' Albee's *The Zoo Story*, and Stafford's 'In the Zoo.' Pain underscores the political/cultural alienation that marks the zoo as metaphor in Guillén's 'Great Zoo of Havana,' Schklovsky's *Zoo*, and Burgin's *Zoo 78*; and the unsettling psychological disruption in Cortázar's 'Axolotl,' Nimier's *The Giraffe*, and Kafka's 'A Hunger Artist.' The pain in zoo stories exhibits manifold representations: it may disclose a repository of irony; a rallying point for empathy with captive animals and activist opposition to zoos; a burden to be confronted (and either endured or overcome); an emblem of modern torment (as, especially, when it takes the form of a gratuitous, existentially vacant sadism). Fundamentally, the pain that infuses zoo stories poses a constant moral challenge: how will the reader confront it?

Elaine Scarry constructs pain as an opposing force to the imagination:

> [P]hysical pain is exceptional in the whole fabric of psychic, somatic, and perceptual states for being the only one that has no object. Though the capacity to experience physical pain is as primal a fact about the human being as is the capacity to hear, to touch, to desire, to fear, to hunger, it differs from these events, and from every other bodily and psychic event, by not having an object in the external world . . . desire is desire of *x*, fear is fear of *y*, hunger is hunger for *z*, but pain is not 'of' or 'for' anything – it is itself alone . . . While pain is remarkable for being wholly without objects, the imagination is remarkable for being the only state that is wholly its objects. There is in imagining no 'state,' no experienceable condition or felt-

> occurrence separate from the objects: the only evidence that one is 'imagining' is that imaginary objects appear in the mind. (161–2)

Although Scarry discusses *human* experiences of pain and imagination, I see no disjunction in adapting her paradigm to support my argument that *animals'* pain in zoos thwarts *people's* imaginative experience of animals. In this construction, as in Scarry's, the potential value of the imaginative realm is infinite, while the prevalence of pain in the zoos 'is itself alone,' as she writes. That is to say: pain remains untethered, ungenerative, unassimilable into any meaningful entity. Imagination – for my purposes, the authentically enlightening intellectual experience of animals as opposed to the captive oppression inherent in zoos' voyeuristic exploitation – is a condition of plenitude. I believe the ethically valid exercise of imagination is impossible in zoos: inconceivable within an institution so intricately associated with pain. Imagination indicates creation, and pain deconstructs creation. What Scarry calls the objectlessness of pain – its disembodiment and its limiting self-referentiality – must forestall the imaginative attempt to make anything of (to learn from, or to interact with) a creature suffering in its grips.

The pain of captive animals is, of course, deplorable; for animal rights activists, it is the decisive reason why zoos should be abolished. In this regard, Dale Jamieson, discussing the scope of pain inflicted upon zoo animals, cites Peter Batten's 1974 study of 200 American zoos which 'documented large numbers of neurotic, overweight animals kept in cramped, cold cells and fed unpalatable synthetic food. Many had deformed feet and appendages caused by unsuitable floor surfaces. Almost every zoo had excessive mortality rates, resulting from preventable factors ranging from vandalism to inadequate husbandry practices.' Another study, reviewing necropsies at the San Diego Zoo during the 1970s and 1980s, discovers

> widespread malnutrition among zoo animals; high mortality rates from the use of anaesthetics and tranquilizers; serious injuries and deaths sustained in transport; and frequent occurrences of cannibalism, infanticide and fighting almost certainly caused by overcrowded conditions. Although the zoo has learned from its mistakes, it is still unable to keep many

> wild animals in captivity without killing or injuring them, directly or indirectly. If this is true of the San Diego Zoo, it is certainly true, to an even greater extent, at most other zoos.
> ('Against', 117)

While I applaud Jamieson's exposition of the pain zoo animals suffer, my focus is on the cultural consumer, the spectator of pain. I shall examine how spectators confront pain in zoos; how it is processed, or repressed, or transformed; how it affects the zoo visitor ethically; and how it finally manifests itself within zoo culture. Fear is an emotion 'that humans often elicit from animals, and may even enjoy eliciting,' write Jeffrey Masson and Susan McCarthy (47). If they are correct, then spectators might similarly enjoy zoo animals' pain, as confirmation that they have elicited fear. While Masson and McCarthy do not explain why they believe people may enjoy animals' suffering, Sigmund Freud suggestively connects the pleasure of watching and the pleasure of pain: his 'discussion of voyeurism links it with sadism – the "drive to master" is a component of scopophilia (sexually based pleasure in looking)' (Burgin, 78).

'The earliest known illustrations of a kind of zoo' depict that of the Egyptian nobleman Mereruka from the sixth dynasty (2345–2181 BC), writes Stephen St C. Bostock: 'Some unfortunate geese and a hyena are being force-fed . . . probably being fattened for eating' (7). (The slaughter and consumption of zoo animals continues even in modern zoos and zoo stories.) The painful force-feeding clearly indicates Mereruka's unconcern with the animals' well-being; he anticipates centuries of zookeepers whose traditions of captivity bring animals pain and death. His behavior lies historically behind the scenes of present-day zoo practices.

The infliction of pain has always accompanied exotic animal exhibitions. Ancient accounts of animal captivity confirm Masson and McCarthy's observation: throughout history, spectators have had no qualms about animals' subservient suffering. In fact, animals' pain may contribute to the spectacle's pleasures. Ancient Greeks and Romans kept leopards, lions, bears, elephants, antelopes, giraffes, camels, and rhinoceroses, to kill at gladiatorial shows. Roman barbarities included 'the slaughter of twenty elephants in 55 BC in a show laid on by Pompey . . . Augustus recorded that 3,500 African animals, mostly lions and leopards, were killed in his twenty-six *venationes* . . . and this appalling level of slaughter continued into the first century AD' (Bostock, 12). The Romans 'succeeded in transforming their interest in exotic creatures into a depraved and brutal cult,' writes Solly Zuckerman (4). Gladiatorial games celebrating Trajan's conquest of Dacia, in AD 106, lasted four months, during which time 'eleven thousand animals were slaughtered, including lions, tigers, elephants, rhinoceroses, hippopotami, giraffes, bulls, stags, crocodiles and serpents' (Jamieson, 'Against', 108). The historic excesses of Roman exploitation exemplify the connection between animals' pain and people's pleasure: 'Augustus, who ruled between 31 BC and AD 14, ran through about 3500 animals . . . Nero, in the middle of the first century, once set a company of horsemen against a collection of 400 bears and 300 lions. The Colosseum was sometimes flooded so that gladiators could kill hippos, crocodiles, and seals. Titus, in the three years between AD 79 and 81, kept (which means killed) about 5000 animals' (Cherfas, 19). Compounding their assault upon nature, the Romans often tortured captive animals in the process of massacring them. 'Countless thousands of animals, maddened with red-hot irons and by darts tipped with burning pitch, were baited to death in Roman arenas' (Ryder, 22). The Roman Empire 'best exemplifies the imperial use of animals,' writes Thomas Veltre, with its 'spectacles of animal slaughter . . . Such sights were considered fitting for a martial people. Not only did they reinforce the idea of blood lust as popular entertainment, but by exhibiting such spectacles as battles between bears from Germany and lions from North Africa, they stood as vivid reminders of the power and extent of the empire' (24).

Marianne Moore depicts the Romans' offenses to captive animals in 'He "Digesteth Harde Yron"' (1941). In the middle of a poem about the ostrich, which mostly describes the quirky bird's natural habits and images in human mythology, she recounts a banquet given by the emperor Elagabalus:

> Six hundred ostrich-brains served
> at one banquet, the ostrich-plume-tipped tent
> and desert spear, jewel-
> gorgeous ugly egg-shell
> goblets, eight pairs of ostriches

> in harness, dramatize a meaning
> always missed by the externalist.
>
> (100)

Moore portrays Romans orgiastically devouring a plucked, aesthetically debased, and enslaved beast of burden. The poem offers disturbing juxtapositions: first, between the animal's natural existence and its lot when it is unfortunate enough to come into contact with people; and second (especially pertinent to animal exhibition), between the bird's cultural image of noble stateliness and the sadistic underside to this representation. Pain necessarily attends the treatment of spectatorially alluring animals, Moore indicates. Contact with people is not *always* detrimental; the poem's mythic characterizations show how some people find it possible to appreciate the bird uninvasively. But Moore suggests that respectful attention by most people will be accompanied by the infliction of pain on the part of a few. And thereby, the ostriches, in the degradation to which some people have subjected them, 'dramatize a meaning.' The 'externalist,' responsible for the degradation, misses this meaning, seeing only facades and surfaces. An ostrich inspires the externalist to pluck plumes for his own ornamentation and aesthetic pleasure, or, if he is as deranged as Elagabalus, to appropriate the ostrich to satiate incontinent hedonism.

However, Moore implies that encounters with animals potentially offer more than such surface perceptions. What is this meaning that is *always* missed by the externalist? It is an understanding caught by what we might call (extending Moore's discourse) an 'internalist' – one who probes more deeply, exercises reflective resources, experiences animals fulfillingly without bashing their brains out. To conjoin Scarry's schema with Moore's, pain inheres in the external; imagination, in the internal. Moore and Scarry interpret pain and imagination as mutually exclusive entities. In Moore's own words, 'He "Digesteth Harde Yron"' states after describing the ostrich banquet: 'The power of the visible / is the invisible.' People's interaction with captive animals is generally restricted to the visible, as spectators gawk at plumage or hides. But a better way to appreciate the animals with which we share this planet depends upon the invisible: upon our imagination of animals – our thoughts about their nature, their dignity, their traits, their behavior, their place in our mutual ecosystem, *when they are not immediately present*. We must learn to take a crucial leap of imaginative faith: to admire what is not directly in front of us, because the alternative necessitates *pain*. It is painful – explicitly or covertly, immediately or eventually – for animals to be in people's presence, to be in captivity, to be visible to us on our own terms. It is possible for some people to be in some contact with some captive animals some of the time without harming them, but the encounters will eventually generate pain. The only way to avoid this pain is to eschew the array of cultural barbarities that Moore characterizes as the trademark of externalists with their demand for the visible. Instead, we must seek the power of the invisible – of the imagination, and the soul – that is more difficult and ephemeral, but ultimately more valuable and kind.

In the modern era, evidence continues to document people's infliction of pain upon captive animals. When King Henry III of France had a nightmare about his animals devouring him in 1583, 'the next day, after hearing mass, he shot his whole collection with an arquebus' (Bostock, 24). Animals kept for exhibition and amusement were assaulted as boundaries blurred between animal keeping and hunting; medieval English deerparks, for example, served both as reserves where animals were admired and enclosures where they were hunted for food and sport (Bostock, 18–19). Animals were commonly set upon each other for entertainment: Bostock writes of 'fights between lions, bears and dogs provided as a court amusement' in the reign of King James I (24), and of 'a series of animal fights between bulls, lions, bears, an ape and wild boars,' in the Elector Augustus II's menagerie in Dresden, featured in a royal wedding celebration (25).

Animals' pain persisted as private collections and menageries gave way to public zoos and other animal displays in the nineteenth century. The popular Indian elephant Chunee, a star of London's Exeter Change Menagerie, offers a prominent example: after years of exhibition, it began having furious fits that frightened its keepers. 'Once he had been defined as a threat to public safety, his fate was sealed,' Harriet Ritvo writes. The elephant's execution illustrates the range of painful assaults that could beset animals:

> [H]is death sentence proved agonizingly difficult to implement. He refused a proffered dose of arsenic, and the shots of three rifles only maddened him further. Soldiers were called in, and they discharged volley after volley without killing him; the coup de grace was finally administered by a keeper with a sword. The struggle lasted over an hour, during which the elephant roared and lunged constantly. A young eyewitness remembered that the noise of his agony had been much more alarming than that made by the soldiers' guns.
>
> (226)

The Exeter Change Menagerie represents the sort of venue that evolved into the modern carnival or circus. A comparable elephant torture occurred at Brooklyn's Coney Island amusement park in 1903. Like Chunee, Topsy earned a death sentence because it had become unmanageable after revolting against the extended indignities consequent upon its conditions of captivity. After Topsy killed a man who had fed it a lit cigarette, promoters feared further problems from an animal that threatened to become inconvenient and unprofitable. Phillips Verner Bradford and Harvey Blume describe how a doctor fed Topsy cyanide-laced carrots, but without effect. Next, men working for Thomas Edison

> clamped the electrodes on her where she stood, and threw the switch. Topsy raised her trunk aloft as if to make one last remark, then commenced to smoke and sizzle while Edison's Vitascope cameramen preserved it on film. (The resulting short – *Electrocuting an Elephant* – was popular in the early days of cinema.) Ten seconds later, she 'shook, bent to her knees, fell, and rolled over on her right side, motionless.' Her organs were donated to Princeton University. Her feet were made into umbrella stands.
>
> (157)

Animals recruited for human culture may be painfully dispatched when they cease to function expediently. The phenomena of suffering which Chunee and Topsy endured resonate behind the scenes of zoo operations. Zoos do not habitually abuse animals quite so cruelly, or allow themselves to be seen doing so as blatantly. But in deciding how to treat their animals, zoos operate in an ethical context in which such cruelty forms one possibility, one model in the realm of ethical considerations affecting such decisions as when animals remain on exhibit, when the terms of exhibit are terminated, and how animals are treated at the termination of serviceability.

Zoos do not offer animals havens from pain. In the early years of the London Zoo, 'the life expectancy of the big cats ... was about two years, because of their poor housing.' Decades later, a newspaper account tells of 'the dismal menagerie cages. The [animals'] cramped walk, the weary restless movement of the head ... the bored look, the artificial habits' (Bostock, 29). Paris's Jardin des Plantes, in its late eighteenth-century inception as a public zoo, straddled the line between professional zoological standards and displays more closely resembling Exeter Change or Coney Island: 'Many specimens came from travelling sideshows that offered people the entertaining spectacle of fights between wild and domesticated animals' (Cherfas, 34–5). Zoos today must confront this legacy of traditions involving animals' pain; historically and culturally, zoos bear collective culpability for the philosophies that inhered at their origination and endure at least palimpsestically (sometimes more explicitly). Heini Hediger admits in his classic monograph on zoo management, *Wild Animals in Captivity*:

> Zoological gardens cannot have isolated existence today. They are necessarily linked up with the long history of development which the keeping of wild animals has undergone in the course of centuries ... Every zoological garden is a part of the whole system and must fit into the picture along with all other zoos ... the keeping of wild animals in captivity implies responsibility, historically conditioned.
>
> (169)

Hediger and other advocates of zoos believe keepers can fulfill such responsibilities by working to ameliorate the unfortunate practices of the past. I argue, more radically, that the centuries-old practices involving pain visited upon animals undercut the possibility that the 'responsibility' Hediger invokes can be met consistently in modern zoos. The common thread in the keeping of captive animals, under whatever conditions hold for different societies and periods, is the infliction of pain – widely enough to suggest that such cruelty is inherent in the institution of zoos.

In the early twentieth century Carl Hagenbeck, a German animal trader and trainer considered a founder and innovator of the modern zoo movement,

> accepted the need, for example, to kill accompanying adults when young elephants were captured, and, worse, allowed local Nubian tribesmen who were assisting him to use their own, cruel methods. Giraffes and antelopes would be chased by the Nubians 'until the young, lagging behind, can be isolated from their parents.' ... half of those [baboons] captured failed to survive the stress of transportation.
>
> (Bostock, 30–1)

Hagenbeck's practices provide examples of cruelty that are institutionally behind the scenes – technically not suffered by zoo animals in the zoo itself, but inflicted upon animals as a consequence of zoos. Four years before it even opened, the London Zoo offers an example of widespread pain, again institutionally behind the scenes, associated with animal collection. Its founder, Sir Stamford Raffles, was departing Asia to return to England in 1824, with a trove of animals intended to stock the future zoo.

> A few hours out of Bencoolen the ship caught fire and he lost everything ... After the disaster, he wrote: 'There is scarcely an unknown animal in Sumatra, whether bird, mammal, or fish, that we did not have on board. There were among them a live tapir, a new clouded leopard and a set of splendid pheasants, which I had specially tamed for the voyage. In short, we had in this respect a perfect Noah's ark. Everything, absolutely everything perished.'
>
> (In Blunt, 24)

We cannot relegate such abuses to a comfortable historical distance. A 1995 *New York Times* article investigates a traveling circus suspected as a front for illegal animal collection and smuggling; conservationists accused the Akef Egyptian Circus of being 'a link through which chimpanzees, pythons, falcons, gray parrots and perhaps even lion cubs make their way from the central African jungle to the private zoos of Saudi Arabia' and elsewhere (McNeil, A1). Circus poachers replicate the painful procedures of Hagenbeck's collecting expeditions generations earlier: since adult chimpanzees can maul people, 'poachers take only babies – by shooting the nursing mother out of the tree. If the baby survives the fall, the whole family group may attack to rescue it, and the poachers will shoot them all. For every baby captured, the Jane Goodall institute estimates, 10 adults are killed' (A13).

Society at large still nurtures customs echoing the Romans' savagery toward captive animals. 'Massive organised animal slaughter may have died out,' Jeremy Cherfas writes,

> but traces of our passion for it remain throughout the world. The Spanish bullfight is an obvious example, one in which the old tradition of man killing animal in front of spectators is maintained. From time to time stories of other forms of similar entertainment find their way into the newspapers. Badger-baiting, in which dogs despatch badgers, is enjoying a resurgence in the north-east of England, and it is still possible to attend dog-fights and cock-fights.
>
> (20)

Such pain inflicted upon animals may be regarded as culturally behind the scenes of zoo pain: activities such as cock-fighting do not directly implicate the institution of animal exhibition, but they do illustrate a sadistic attitude toward animals generally in our culture, and a willingness to cause pain to animals in the pursuit of human pleasures.

Indeed, brutality against animals flourishes inside zoos. The most extreme case concerns zoo spectators who, 'from malice or a morbid disposition, deliberately maim or kill animals,' writes Hediger, providing numerous accounts of poisoned animals, a seal that had its eyes poked out with a walking stick, a bird whose beak was smashed with a hammer, an elephant given an apple full of pins. The assailants 'have a pathological desire to torment, injure, or even kill the animals. They are the ones who stick knives, hatpins and similar instruments into the unsuspecting animals, offer the animals pieces of meat with fish hooks, open safety pins etc. hidden in them, push a stick or an umbrella through to put an animal's eye out or injure its sexual parts' (174–5). Such literal sadism by spectators is a facet of the operational status quo at zoos: 'Experience shows that no zoo in the world is safe from such regrettable incidents,' Hediger concludes. 'In all ages and places menageries and zoos have attracted not only men with a healthy interest but all kinds of abnormal ones upon whom the zoo seems to act like a magnet' (174).

While most pain in zoos is less explicit, simply consigning animals to exist in zoos invites the potential for their suffering. Earlier this century, New York Zoological Park Director William T. Hornaday 'admitted that creatures taken from the wild often objected to life in the zoo. One perverse polar bear refused to swim in his "fine, big pool," becoming "a sore trial to those responsible for his personal appearance before visitors." Elephants, too, sometimes proved to be troublesome to Hornaday. When these animals became "unruly," he did not object to their receiving "a sound whack"' (Mighetto, 69). Bradford and Blume describe the treatment of an elephant, Gunda, during the onset of musth (sexual desire): 'his keepers began whipping him to get him to obey, which set off a public outcry. Director Hornaday was compelled to explain. On a large sign posted outside Gunda's stall he proclaimed, "Whipping an elephant *does not hurt him*; but he *thinks* that it does." It was, and remains, one of the more subtle explanations in the annals of the zoo' (171). After nearly killing a keeper, Gunda followed in the footsteps of other prominent elephants such as Chunee and Topsy that had exhausted their keepers' goodwill:

> [I]t became apparent that Gunda, like many a New York elephant before him, would not die of natural causes. Carl Akeley, who had hunted big game . . . was summoned. He was asked to bring his elephant gun . . . When the shot had been fired and Gunda crumpled to the ground, the *Times*, which had followed his career closely, declared, 'Gunda is a "good" elephant at last.'
>
> (172)

Some contemporary zoos, led by directors who 'realize that they must compete with a wide variety of leisure-time activities,' feature animal exhibitions akin to carnival amusements, writes Michael W. Fox. 'As we demean animals in making them perform unnatural acts, so we demean ourselves. The training . . . is often brutal, and the [animals'] socialization to the trainer . . . is unnatural' (146). In 1995, Washington's National Zoo opened an exhibition of orang-utans that demonstrates how even the most prominent zoos stoop to such demeaning, and potentially painful, carnival-like animal displays. An 'Orangutan Transit Line' features six animals swinging, hand over hand, across a 400-foot route of cables, 45 feet above the ground, directly above the heads of zoo spectators (offering a novel spectatorial experience that officials hoped would attract and dazzle audiences; keepers had contemplated with concern, but dismissed as unlikely, the possibility of orang-utan droppings spattering the crowd below). According to the keepers, the high-wire act better allows the animals to perform their natural behavior, mimicking the swinging from tree to tree that they would do in their native Indonesia. Electrified skirts surrounding the towers that hold the cables – designed to prevent the orang-utans from climbing down the towers and escaping – indicates the pain associated with this sort of exhibition; originally set at 6,000 volts, the power was increased to 9,000 volts after one animal escaped (Molotsky). While touting the exhibition as an opportunity for orang-utans to experience circumstances akin to their native ones, the zoo offered no explanation for a natural equivalent that approximates or justifies an electric skirt.[1]

Even in the most humane zoos, the condition of captivity is itself a source of pain: 'Zoo keepers report that captive elephants are subject to "sudden-death syndrome" or "broken-heart syndrome," which happens (most often with young elephants) when they are separated from their social group or put in a new enclosure by themselves,' write Masson and McCarthy (52). Jonathan Barzdo describes the common occurrences of stereotypy, neurosis, or frustration afflicting zoo animals:

> They may fail to breed, inflict wounds to themselves, or lose condition, perhaps dying as a consequence. The number of bald-fronted parrots, and monkeys that bite their own limbs still bears witness to this. They are not attractive to look at, even though many zoo-visitors find them a source of amusement. To the modern thinker on wildlife, they symbolise what is morally unpalatable about most zoos; that in this relatively enlightened age cruelty through starvation of behavioural requirements is still common.
>
> (20)

And speaking for zookeepers, Hediger concedes the enormous suffering animals face in the transition from freedom to captivity (although he does not examine the ethical implications of his observations). Many animals taken from the wild, especially older animals,

> may often be kept in captivity for a time, but they never become properly adapted to the new situation. If they survive capture they usually linger in a chronic state of excitement generally caused by their uneasiness in the presence of man, and with a basically rigid attitude of mind, so to speak. This prevents any suitable treatment, even the taking of food; it may result in nervous disturbances, reduce resistance to disease and lead to death, psychologically caused.
>
> (27)

In instances of present-day zoo cruelty, a recurring motif is zookeepers' ineptness – which, of course, cannot excuse the infliction of pain. For example, Barzdo describes a 1982 symposium on elephant management where 'the curator of mammals from one of Britain's biggest zoos told of how elephants had four times fallen in the concrete moat, but he still thought moats were the best barrier to use'; while zoos commonly use such moats to separate elephants from spectators, 'tales of elephants falling into these, sometimes breaking limbs, are widespread' (20). Or again: an African bull elephant at the Los Angeles Zoo was being moved to a Mexican zoo in 1992, provoking the protests of animal rights groups. He 'was tranquilized before being loaded into a special crate. He went down on his knees in the crate, and the next morning . . . he died from heart failure' (Tarpy, 33; the writer, an apologist for zoos, concludes, 'The incident was a zookeeper's nightmare'; I submit that it seems more like an *elephant's* nightmare.)[2]

Some of the pain zoo animals suffer might seem unintentional – acts of God, in the discourse of insurance adjusters; yet I insist that animals' consignment to zoos bespeaks a conscious act of ethical conduct (on the part of captors, keepers, and spectators alike), with consequent responsibilities and moral culpability. A 1995 fire in the Philadelphia Zoo's primate house provides a case in point: six western lowland gorillas, three Bornean orang-utans, four white-haired gibbons, and ten lemurs died of smoke inhalation. As usual, the keepers can be charged with ineptitude, if not outright slaughter. The *New York Times* reported that employees smelled smoke three hours before the animals died, but did not investigate or report their discovery; further, the cage was found to be hazardous – faulty electric wiring caused the fire – and the alarm did not function ('Philadelphia Zoo Guards').[3] But I regard the keepers' blunders and the deficient mechanical infrastructure as merely secondary, or contributory, causes to the animals' deaths; primarily, the institution of the zoo *per se* is inherently always a potential source of pain.

In a supposedly humane culture, zookeepers often attempt to relegate the pain concomitant with zookeeping to the discrete past. Thus in his book about the 'revolution' (as he terms it) he led at Zoo Atlanta, Terry Maple can write about animal pain that occurred in the mid-1980s, only a few years before his tenure, and still dissociate it from current practices at the zoo. It did not happen on his watch, so it belongs to that distant era in which insensitive keepers treated animals with sadistic cruelty. Indeed, Maple seems all the more salacious about these details because they accentuate his own beneficent reign. Among the past abuses Maple documents: in 1984, 'the zoo's ailing elephant, Twinkles, had died, while supposedly resting and recovering at a farm near Alpharetta. A week later, the public and members of the zoo society learned that the ailing elephant had in fact been turned over to a traveling circus in North Carolina, where it died' (12). Soon after, newspapers reported 'prairie dog burrows mistakenly plugged with cement, mysterious deaths of several old cats and bears, and the selling and eating of surplus rabbits from the children's zoo' (12). Like the death of the Los Angeles Zoo's elephant, all these examples of pain at Zoo Atlanta occur out of spectators' range of vision; visitors may not commonly notice such pain at the zoo, but it is nonetheless prevalent behind the scenes. (Zookeepers commonly obscure pain from spectators by temporarily closing exhibits that may reveal animals' suffering.) In another incidence of pain beyond public display, Maple recounts a giraffe's attempt to give birth, unluckily attended by the zoo's staff:

> Daisy labored many hours with a breech birth, and it soon became obvious that it was a stillborn calf, and that Daisy herself would require surgery in order to survive. Since we had no surgical facilities at the zoo, we decided to transport the giraffe to the University of Georgia veterinary school in Athens.

> Transporting a giraffe is difficult even under the best of circumstances. We did not have an adequate transport crate, so the staff spent the next few hours desperately constructing one. Finally, the crate was finished, the giraffe loaded in, and the crate put onto a flatbed truck. The staff began the 65-mile drive to Athens early in the evening, encountered severe thunder and lightning along the way, and did not reach Athens until after midnight. The complicated surgery went well, however, and our keepers elected to bring Daisy back to the zoo early the next morning. But on the drive back just a few miles away from the zoo, Daisy died, a victim of stress and prolonged anesthesia. To make matters worse, the rickety truck and crate had hit some overhead utility wires en route to the zoo.
>
> (16)

Transporting giraffes is difficult, laments the set-upon zoo director, offering further excuses: 'Giraffe births, especially first ones, are no easy endeavor . . . giraffes are notoriously delicate animals' (17). While Maple implicitly blames the victim, we should remember that it is not the *giraffe* that is being difficult. If a zoo cannot manage a giraffe's pregnancy without painfully killing it on the highway, then it ought not stock giraffes.

Finally, zoo animals may suffer in the wake of political or economic circumstances in the culture that runs the zoo – often, conditions embodying such widespread turmoil that the fallout for zoo animals is a negligible consideration. In 1989, amid economic instability, the mayor of Tokat, Turkey, called that town's small zoo 'an unnecessary luxury' and added that 'conditions were not good enough to ensure the animals' comfort and safety'; so he 'closed the zoo and ordered the slaughter of many of the animals. The foxes and wolves were said to have been poisoned and some then drowned because the poison was not strong enough; the zoo's single bear was reportedly shot and its three camels sold in segments as meat. The birds and the ducks were sold to poor but sympathetic local families' (Kelsey, 164).

And again, during civil conflict in Zaire, 'It has been downhill for the zoo here in Kisangani, in central Zaire, ever since some soldiers ate the elephant, and now the keepers are reduced to holding Alphonse's skull, reminiscing about his antics and denying that they had anything to do with his demise,' the *New York Times* reported. 'The zoo, with its elegant gardens and fine tree-lined lane, was founded by the Belgians in 1954 . . . At its peak, it had elephants, lions, jaguars, baboons, antelope, camels and many other species, as well as a popular bar and restaurant. But as Zaire's economy disintegrated over the decades, people had less money to pay the entrance fees' (Kristof). Finally, in 1997, 'the last animal, a crocodile, starved . . . and now the zoo has 22 keepers with nothing but memories and a pile of skulls.' Despite the animals' deaths, the keepers – suspected of having eaten numerous of their charges – 'still show up for work every day, because the zoo is, after all, still open for business.'

Zoo stories reiterate the fact that standard zoo operations involve animals' pain. Alison Baker's 'The Heaven of Animals' (1993) depicts the intermingling of basic support services with (casually understated) egregious barbarity: 'I grew up in the zoo, cleaning out cages, chopping head after head of cabbage in half, hurling unwanted Easter chicks into the pen of Walter, the one-winged eagle, and learning to watch as he tore at them until they died' (69). Valerie Martin, in *The Great Divorce* (1994), illustrates the keepers' impulse to hide even the appearance of zoo animals' pain and disease behind the scenes: the veterinarian is sent 'to examine a blesbok with an ugly hard cyst on the side of his face. Though she concluded he was not in any danger, the keepers wanted him off exhibit at once; he looked bad' (59). Terry Johnson's play *Cries from the Mammal House* (1984) depicts gruesome conditions at a provincial English zoo. Johnson's zoo exemplifies the antiquated, small-scale, poorly run operation that is far more common than the few exceptional 'superstars' zoo proponents commonly tout. If more elite zoos can minimize or hide (but not eliminate) animals' pain, it is ubiquitous and inevitable at the type of zoo Johnson depicts: 'a prison so penniless a third of the cages are empty. The toucan is actually mouldy. Not because Alan's a bad vet, although he is, he is a bad vet, but because the heating's so ancient the humidity's all to pot. There's a dead toad in the reptile house the size of a kitten. It's been there for a week' (150). Eventually, its shareholders declare the zoo economically unfeasible and sell the land for its real estate value; the veterinarian is left to kill the animals. With cool, macabre detachment, Alan gives the rodents lethal injections as a man from the slaughterhouse arrives.

Mick They said we've got a contract here.

Alan The larger mammals, and the whale I think. You're a bit early; we're still on the children's corner. Would you like to come back later; I don't think butchering gerbils would be economically viable, do you?

Mick Don't ask me, it's your zoo. I'm just on contract... There's some big bastards here. Wouldn't it be quicker just to break their necks?

Alan This way's humane.

Mick Wouldn't it be more humane? I'd rather have me neck broken, definitely ... What'll you do with the giraffe and that?

Alan Use a bigger needle.

(193–4)

When it is time to dispatch the elephant, the zoo veterinarian – a doctor of death – addresses the animal:

Alan It's over, I'm afraid. I don't think this'll hurt, but I have no idea really. I'm not sure. I hope it won't. It's this or shoot you and you'd hate the noise ... That leg there would have bothered you soon. It would have been a bad leg. It's a bit quiet around here now isn't it? Let's find a nice wide vein in this ear now, shall we? Time to die, you gentle, gentle girl. (*He injects her.*) Steady. That's it. All over.

(198–9)

The vet's awareness of pain masquerades as humane concern ('I don't think this'll hurt ... I hope it won't'). But the basic ignorance he reveals about what he is doing ('I have no idea really') suggests that his concern is merely a pretense, assuaging his own guilt about providing exactly the opposite of the care he is supposed to furnish.

Isaac Babel's story 'The Beast Grows Silent' describes the pain that befalls animals – in a zoo that, like Johnson's, represents one of the mass of small-time dismal animal prisons – as a result of inability to fund upkeep amid social hardship. The situations depicted in both Babel's and Johnson's stories approximate the real-life account of massacring zoo animals in Tokat, Turkey. Babel's narrative, infused with simple pathos, features the helplessness that many zoo stories project when depicting people who abrogate the commitment to care for animals that they had made when the creatures were inducted into the zoo. A commission surveys the animals to determine how much pain they have suffered, and to decide which can be saved and which must be shot.

> The old men stopped by the cages. In greeting, two hump-backed camels rose on their long legs and licked their hands, bespeaking their humble bewilderment of soul, tranquilized by hunger. The soft, underdeveloped antlers of deer beat against iron bars.
>
> The commission deliberated, and the keeper made a hopeless report.
>
> Over the winter eight of the zoo's lions and tigers breathed their last. They were fed spoiled, rotten horsemeat. The beasts were poisoned.
>
> Only two of the thirty-six monkeys survived. The other thirty-four died from 'consumption' and inanimation. Monkeys don't last more than a year in Petersburg.
>
> One of the two elephants fell – the better one. He dropped from hunger. When the elephant lay down, they realized they should do something. They gave him a pood of bread and a pood of hay. It didn't help.
>
> There are no longer any snakes in the zoo. Their cages are empty. All of the constrictors died.
>
> (62)

In these accounts, a resonant sense of the animals' pain itself is elusive, as if writers find it too difficult to portray the essence and the precise detail of such pain in literal dimensions. Instead, such zoo stories feature mainly the human response to pain (on the part of the characters, the author, the reader) – they indicate how people behave and react (or fail to react) in the presence of suffering. To generalize: people who are actively or passively proximate to zoo animals' pain tend to manifest an understated, debilitated resignation. Stylistically, the stories retreat into cold, stinted, realism at the incidence of pain – they become pragmatic and descriptive, often stripped of emotions (as if, amid such transgressions against nature, human emotion rings hollow, superfluous). Perhaps the stories suggest the need to accept the idea that 'lesser creatures,' when sucked into human culture, will necessarily suffer as the result of human actions and mistakes. Perhaps, too, the human characters in these stories repress empathetic compassion with the animal victims because they are aware of how tenuous and precarious their own safety may be in a world where the disempowered face ubiquitous and arbitrary pain.

In Angus Wilson's *The Old Men at the Zoo*, the zoological society secretary describes 'an old, sick puma that I had watched each morning last winter on my walk to the office, dying out its last days in the uncongenial snow and sleet' (34) – whatever the cause of death (which Wilson does not indicate), the zoo adds insult to injury as the disagreeable clime and habitat exacerbate the puma's terminal suffering. When a mountain lynx that had escaped from its habitat is found, it earns an automatic death sentence for having shown itself capable of subverting the zoo's absolute and impregnable control. Off with its head, the zoo director announces: 'an animal that has found means to escape is properly an object of suspicion. For this reason I have given orders that all such animals shall, on recapture, be destroyed' (205–6). Characterizing this instance of pain at the zoo as an unnecessary and sadistic overreaction, Wilson describes the execution:

> From the cave at the back of the pit emerged the lynx, its tapering ears and slanting eyes, its slender form and dappled colour beautiful even in that dead grey light. It seemed so little ferocious, more like a poor house cat dazed from a glancing blow of a bicycle wheel. It stretched a little in the cold air, then rose, wobbling on its legs. A moment later the young keeper appeared with a rifle on the rocks above. He fired and the beautiful animal coiled back for a second in the air, gave a faint mewing cry, and fell dead.
>
> (206)

John Irving's *Setting Free the Bears* describes zookeepers' responses to animals' pain via their terse, detached ledger entries:

> The giant forest hog has ingrown tusk; is caused some pain. Give aspirinated salt cubes (2), if suffering . . .
>
> The binturong (bearcat of Borneo) has rare disease; better watch out for it.
>
> The bandicoot is dying.
>
> (192)

Siggy, the animals' would-be liberator, discovers these notes as he cases the zoo and reacts with disgust at their bureaucratic, callous demeanor: 'My God. A *rare disease!* Is that all – just watch out for a rare disease? The binturong has nameless, incurable suffering. And the bandicoot is dying! Just like that – dying; the rare little leaper. Keep an eye on it, sweep it out when it's through' (192). Perhaps it is unrealistic to expect keepers to show sincere and engaged concern for ailments that befall animals, or to empathize with their pain: by the same reasoning, doctors cannot cry over every suffering human patient they treat. On the other hand, some believe doctors are socialized to become cold and uncaring, and Siggy clearly thinks the same of the zoo animals' custodians. Irving asserts that when the animals suffer, people shut themselves off from humane response to their pain.

Certainly animals in nature experience pain in their lives just as zoo animals do. Some of wild animals' pain resembles what is present in zoos, and some differs; some wild animals might experience greater pain than animals with at least nominal veterinary care, and some, on the other hand, would probably suffer less than zoo animals. The zoo causes a degree of suffering due to its conditions of captivity and its grossly unnatural feeding and habitat, but also alleviates a degree of pain: for example, zoos diminish the threat of pain from predators and famine (and certainly pain from such sources is part of the animals' natural lifecycles). But my point is simply that animals' pain is part of what happens in the zoo, in significant amounts and with widely varying origins and manifestations. Zoos neglect to report this pain themselves; whenever possible, it is swept behind the scenes.

War causes pain to every element of the biosphere: human and nonhuman, organic and inorganic, geological, atmospheric, environmental. Accompanying human combat is a special variant, or microcosm, of pain reserved for zoo animals amid the forces and clutches of wartime. People drag other species down to our own level of destruction; zoo animals suffer at least as appallingly as people during wartime.

The pain visited upon human noncombatants during wartime is generally considered ethically worse and more ironic than that of soldiers. By the same logic, the pain zoo animals suffer in war should be regarded as even more dismal and unfortunate than that of human bystanders; the animals get caught up in wars for which, of course, they are in no way responsible. An eyewitness from the front lines eloquently explains: 'Many of us are dead and almost everybody is hungry, but I feel more sorry for the animals than for the people.' Adem Hodzic, a taxi driver who tried to help care for the Sarajevo zoo's surviving animals during the war there, continues: 'People made this war, but the animals had nothing to do with it. They're only victims . . . People have people to look after them, to comfort them, but animals in cages . . . can't protect themselves, they can't fend for themselves' (Burns, 'Horrors,' A1, A9).

The Bosnian war is indeed an immense tragedy, for people and zoo animals. Before zookeepers conscripted them, of course, the animals did not have to worry about fending against mortar bombs and sniper strafing, or becoming dependent for their care upon keepers who might have to abandon them. Believing it could care for animals as well as the animals were doing on their own, the zoo deprived them of freedom. Subsequently, however, it abrogated its implicit commitment, violating the moral imperative that Dale Jamieson expresses, 'that if we keep animals in captivity, then what we owe them is everything' ('Zoos Revisited', 63). Although not specifically discussing zoos during wartime, Jamieson's words resonate in this context when he writes that 'these animals are in our custody through no wish or fault of their own. They are refugees from a holocaust that humans have unleashed against nature' (63). In Sarajevo, despite Hodzic's admirable efforts to alleviate animals' suffering, he underplays the situation's pathos. The war is not the first tragedy that has befallen the zoo animals, but the second; their initial misfortune was their induction into the zoo in the first place. I regard the zoo animals' war deaths, which received prominent international media coverage, as epiphenomenal rather than phenomenal. The animals' pain (unlike that of Hodzic and his countrypeople) derives from the *combination* of their twin misfortunes, not the war alone.

Zoo animals commonly suffer pain during war – whether consciously inflicted assault or simply passive neglect, as people find themselves with other things to do than care for captive animals. Animals are not excused from people's social habits just because they aren't directly involved in geopolitics; they suffer along with us. Their pain during war often results in death, and whether they are slaughtered intentionally or 'accidentally,' accounts suggest that considerable pain accompanies their deaths.

Three common rationalizations arise for the intentional killing of zoo animals (as contrasted with accidental, combat-related deaths) in wartime. First, they may be slain for the meat their carcasses can provide to a desperate society. Keeping captive animals alive and on display may be considered worthy during peace, but becomes an expendable luxury when played off against human duress; so instead of consuming scarce provisions, animals may be butchered to increase the food supply. Second, zoo animals may be dispatched for humanitarian reasons: it is deemed better to kill them quickly so they do not starve or incinerate. Third, they may be killed to protect people from the possibility of 'wild' animals running amok on residential streets, in the event that the war deprives the zoo of ablebodied guards to keep animals securely imprisoned. This final eventuality seems improbable, but reinforces the construct (of savagely threatening beasts that would attack people if they were not securely constrained) that helps justify keeping zoo animals in cages. Usually such proactive killing takes place in the thick of combat, as a society anticipates its imminent occupation or defeat; but in at least one incident, the British – ever prepared – began killing animals at the very outbreak of war. In September 1939, at the London Zoo, 'all the poisonous snakes and the black widow spiders . . . were put down. Most of the tanks in the Aquarium were drained and the majority of the fish, other than the rare specimens, were destroyed' (Riddell and Denton, 16).

Besides these reasons, one may detect another covert but compelling explanation for the pain people inflict upon zoo animals during wartime: war engenders a milieu of rampant, unchecked sadism. As human society deteriorates, some people apparently believe zoo animals should not comfortably survive what afflicts our own species; misery loves company. Consider Susan Brownmiller's description in *Against Our Will* of the historical frequency with which (noncombatant) women suffer violence during wartime. While she is specifically discussing rape, her argument equally elucidates violence against zoo animals: 'when killing is viewed as not only permissible but heroic behavior sanctioned by one's government or cause, the distinction between taking a human life and other forms of impermissible violence gets lost.' Further, 'it is a familiar act with a familiar excuse' (24):[4] war provides a cover story for some to exercise the violence and hostility that they fantasize about expressing at other times; codes of acceptable social behavior that normally constrict such aggression are suspended during war.

The indignities that befall zoo animals during wartime are culturally and historically widespread. The exotic sixteenth-century menagerie in Tenochtitlán (now Mexico City) enchanted European explorers when they first visited it. 'But less than a year after Montezuma had graciously shown Cortez the wonders of his zoo, the world's greatest collection of animals suddenly was no more. In 1520 . . . Cortez laid siege to Tenochtitlán and reduced the entire city to rubble. During the course of the battle the starving Indians were forced to kill and eat most of the inhabitants of the zoo' (Livingston, 33).

French monarchs kept a menagerie at Versailles, which declined with royal fortunes. In 1792, 'The revolutionaries considered it shameful that animals should be well fed while people were starving,' so Jacobins demanded the freeing of the animals. The keeper turned over the keys, but noted that the animals might attack; revolutionaries decided, thus, to leave the dangerous animals caged, but sent others to the butcher to feed the city's hungry masses (Cherfas, 34). And in the Jardin des Plantes, during the Prussian siege in 1870, 'expediency proved more important than exhibition, and all the edible animals in the Jardin were slaughtered to provide food for the people of Paris' (35).

After the 1941 Easter Raid of Belfast, when German bombers killed 900 people, the Ministry of Public Security issued the order to '"Destroy all dangerous animals at the zoo immediately." Two RUC [Royal Ulster Constabulary] marksmen were sent to Bellevue Zoo and, the *Belfast Telegraph* recorded, Head Keeper Dick Foster "stood by with tears streaming down his face, as the executioners proceeded from cage to cage and despatched the animals 33 in number, and a vulture." The animals included, unbelievably, two raccoons.'[5]

Hagenbeck's famous zoo at Stellingen, with its celebrated innovations of collection and display, was in many ways the first modern zoo; it is perversely fitting that Stellingen animals should also have suffered the cutting edge of modern warfare as its zoo culture became entwined with Nazi culture. Like Montezuma's menagerie, Hagenbeck's represents an unhappy confluence of state-of-the-art animal captivity and state-of-the-art carnage; the animals suffer the brunt of this irony. 'Thirty-six years after its foundation, Stellingen was destroyed in the night of 25 July 1943, by "a hail of inflammable phosphorus bombs." Hagenbeck's son provides a moving account of keepers humanely shooting cats and bears to save them from death by burning' (Bostock, 31).

Other zoos in which animals suffered extensively during the Second World War include Tokyo's Ueno Zoological Gardens, where 'animal numbers had been reduced to . . . about a fifth of the prewar stock' after the city's extensive war devastation (Zuckerman, 108); the Frankfurt Zoo, where 'neat lawns, ponds and fine buildings were transformed into a wasteland of craters, rubble, and shell' in 1944 (Zuckerman, 78); and the Antwerp Zoo, which, as Zuckerman describes, was nearly obliterated as a result of hostilities:

> Soon after the start of the German occupation in 1940 it became clear that the carnivores would have to be killed because they could not be provided with food. Then it was the turn of those animals that could be killed to provide meat for human consumption. The rare creatures which were preserved lived in a state of near starvation until the liberation of Belgium in 1944. But that was not the end. Antwerp then became a constant target for flying bombs, which the Germans aimed at the port in an attempt to obstruct its use by the advancing Allied armies. The Zoo was hit several times.
>
> (64)

The Berlin Zoo was the site of probably the most extensive pain of any zoo animals during the Second World War. A massive concrete flak tower was built there, 'intended to remind people of medieval fortresses . . . bomb-proof and shell-proof . . . 120 feet or more in height . . . kept stocked with enough food and ammunition to sustain a twelve-month siege' (Read and Fisher, 77–8). The zoo not only failed to provide animals safe haven from the hostilities: because the tower rendered it a primary strategic site, it actually attracted some of the war's most brutal devastation. Even after the war, explosions from the occupying forces' destruction of the tower caused further extensive damage (Zuckerman, 58). (In the Frankfurt Zoo, too, the proximity of munitions augmented the devastation: 'Its destruction was due not only to bombs but to the explosion of ammunition that had been stored in it for the anti-aircraft guns mounted on the roof' (Zuckerman, 78).)

The Berlin Zoo was intensely implicated in Nazi war culture in other ways as well: its director, Lutz Heck, was a close friend of Hermann Göring (Ryan, 62). That zoo consummately exemplifies the potential degradations resulting from the admixture of animals and human sociopolitical culture. People, at our worst, are capable of wreaking a swath of destruction that implicates every element of the planet, in ways that defy logical or ethical comprehension. During the British air raids of 22 November 1943, thousands of bombs rained down on the zoo,

> completely destroying fifteen animal houses . . . In the ruins of the ornate Indian temple that had been the elephant house lay the mangled bodies of seven dead elephants. A rhinoceros lying among them seemed unmarked, but it, too, was dead – the blast had burst its lungs. In the antelope house . . . eighteen dead animals, including two giraffes. Two gorillas and fifteen smaller apes lay dead in the ape house . . . rumours began to circulate almost immediately of man-eating lions and tigers wandering the streets until they were hunted down and shot . . . The truth was that the lions and tigers had all suffocated and burned in their cages.
>
> (Read and Fisher, 139)

Bombing continued for several days. On 26 November, an aerial mine

> exploded in the middle of the 30-yard-long crocodile hall, shattering heavy glass cases and flinging the animals out into the passageways . . . The artificial jungle river, one floor up, where fifteen-foot crocodiles and alligators could be viewed from beneath through thick plate glass, had poured down through gaping holes . . . Most of the crocodiles had also crashed through to the ground, where they now lay, with blood pouring from their nostrils. Two or three were still alive, lashing their tails in agony.
>
> (141)

The raids killed half the zoo's animals; more died later as a result of shock or starvation. Many were eaten: 'Deer, antelope and buffalo were not particularly out of the ordinary for people whose peacetime diet included a great deal of game. But Berliners discovered to their surprise that some unusual dishes were extremely tasty. Crocodile tail, for instance, cooked slowly in large containers, was not unlike juicy fat chicken' (141). Veterinarians spent a week cutting up the elephant carcasses: 'men rattled around inside the giant ribcages . . . often disappearing amid heaps of intestines as they hacked, sliced, and sawed at their tasks' (141); like human victims of the Nazis, the animals were converted into soap.[6]

During the next two years, every surviving animal 'was on less than half-rations – and looked it . . . Siam, his skin hanging in great gray folds, had become so bad-tempered that keepers were afraid to enter his cage. Rosa, the big hippo, was miserable, her skin dry and crusted . . . Pongo, the usually good-natured 530-pound gorilla, had lost more than 50 pounds and sat in his cage, sometimes motionless for hours, glowering morosely at everyone' (Ryan, 170). In the war's waning days, the flak tower attracted intense bombardment during the Battle of Berlin. Anthony Read and David Fisher describe the zoo's condition at the German surrender.

> There were few animals left alive: Siam, the male elephant, Suse the female chimpanzee, Knautschke, a male hippopotamus, a few small monkeys, a few birds. One hippopotamus was dead from blast injuries, another floated in the water of its pool, dead, with the fins of an unexploded shell sticking out of its side. When Soviet troops entered the ape house, they discovered Pongo, the biggest gorilla in Europe, lying dead in his cage, as was a big chimpanzee. Pongo, mysteriously, had died from two stab wounds in the chest. Dark rivers of blood ran from them down the concrete platforms of the enclosure. In front of the platform lay two dead SS men. A third was propped against it, his sub-machine gun across his knees. (463)

As is common in wartime zoo accounts, the scope and processes of animal carnage closely approximate those of human carnage. The scene evokes the depraved, decimated Nazi society represented by the sea of corpses that covered Berlin (and the concentration camps) at the war's end. The tableau of entangled bodies of soldiers and animals that the Allies discover demonstrates the inextricability of captive animals from their captors' self-destructiveness; zoo animals are destined to go down with their human keepers.

The most recent outrage involving zoos and war occurred in Sarajevo's Pionirska Dolina Zoo. During the Bosnian war, its animals' pain paralleled the atrocities against people. In July 1992, the media reported the story of Dragan Curic who risked his life daily to feed six surviving animals. 'His major nemesis is an unseen sniper called "The Jumpy One." Mr. Curic once almost took a bullet in the back, but a 50-pound piece of meat he was hauling for the lions took it . . . A 20-year-old protege of his was shot to death feeding the animals a month ago; another is gravely wounded. Already dead: a Bengal tiger, a panther, eight English ponies, an American bison, a llama, African antelopes, and many ducks, swans and peacocks' ('Crazy Guy'). Note the correspondence between the international range of dead animals and the international array of politicians who impotently watched the slaughter without intervening. From the corners of the earth, animals were collected for display, and then for a lingering death, in an ill-fated corner of Central Europe – caught in the crosshairs of human venality.

By mid-October 1992, six months into the siege of Sarajevo, only one animal – a black bear – remained alive out of the hundred in the zoo's collection before the war.

> She is mangy, perhaps half her weight when her ordeal started, and she barely has the strength to stand upright against the rusting bars of her cage when visitors arrive with a loaf of bread and a few snatches of grass . . . The scene in the animal house is wrenching. A putrid odor pervades the concrete building, and cage after cage is littered with the carcasses of lions, tigers, leopards and pumas. From the skeletal remains of some and the whole carcasses of others, it is clear that some died sooner than others, and that their surviving mates fed on the bodies before they, too, succumbed to hunger.
>
> (Burns, 'Horrors,' A1, A9)

A few weeks later, the *Times* reported the bear's demise. Rescue attempts were stymied by UN officials' refusal to fly the bear to safety on a relief plane. '"We took her some bread and an apple last week, but she was too weak to eat them," Pal Takac, a zoo employee said ... "She died the next day. I was sad to see her go after all these months, but at least her suffering is over"' (Burns, 'Last Survivor').

In zoo stories, fiction correlates with historical accounts of captive animals' wartime pain. One of the most explicit, extensive formulations of the zoo in war appears in Haruki Murakami's story 'The Zoo Attack' (1995), which tells of 'the tigers, the leopards, the wolves, and the bears that were shot by soldiers on a miserably hot afternoon in August, 1945' (68) in Manchuria's Hsinching Zoo. The Japanese soldiers assigned to this mission felt a conviction of impending catastrophe – generating an ironic sense of parallelism between human and animal victims of war – since they assumed they would soon die themselves fighting the Soviet Army; 'But first they had to kill these animals in the zoo' (69). The storyteller, Nutmeg Akasaka, describes the military preparation for the slaughter:

> If possible, they were to kill the animals with poison in order to conserve what few bullets they had left. The young lieutenant in charge of the operation had been so instructed by his superior officer and told that the zoo had been given enough poison to do the job. The zoo's director confirmed that he indeed had orders to 'liquidate' the fiercer animals in case of an emergency and to use poison, but the shipment of poison, he said, had never arrived ... The veterinarian told the lieutenant that the zoo had only a very small amount of poison, probably not enough to kill a horse. The lieutenant telephoned headquarters for instructions, but since the Soviet Army had crossed the border several days earlier, most of the high-ranking officers had disappeared ... The call was transferred from one office to another until a medical-corps colonel got on the line, only to scream at the lieutenant, 'You stupid son of a bitch! The whole goddam country's going down the drain and you're asking me about a goddam fucking zoo? Who gives a shit?' (69)

The lieutenant's mission paradoxically combines intense sadism and, as the colonel indicates, pointless triviality: who gives a shit? In the vacuum of moral and military incoherence that often marks a war's frenzied last days, Murakami's protagonist ponders his options: 'He could forget about killing any animals and lead his men out of there, or they could use bullets to do the job. Either would be a violation of the orders he had been given, but in the end he decided to do the shooting' (69). The soldier rationalizes his actions with the standard excuses:

> If possible, I'd rather not kill any animals, the lieutenant told himself in all honesty. But the zoo was running out of things to feed them, and most of the animals (especially the big ones) were already suffering from starvation. Shooting might even be easier for the animals themselves – a quick, clean death. And if starving animals were to escape to the city streets during intense fighting or air strikes, a disaster would be unavoidable. (69)

Murakami presents the carnage with an impact so directly disturbing that he implicates readers at first-hand – as if bringing us literally into the scene, forcing an intense intimacy.

> Given the layout of the zoo, the first animals to be liquidated were the tigers . . . The lieutenant assigned four men to each tiger and told them to aim for the heart – the whereabouts of which was just another mystery to him. Oh, well, at least one bullet was bound to hit home. When eight men together pulled back on the levers of the Model 38s and loaded a cartridge into each chamber, the ominous, dry clicks transformed the whole atmosphere of the place. The tigers stood up at the sound. Glaring at the soldiers through the iron bars, they let out huge roars. As an extra precaution, the lieutenant drew his own automatic pistol and released the safety. To calm himself, he cleared his throat. This is nothing, he tried to tell himself. Everybody does stuff like this all the time. The soldiers knelt, took careful aim, and at the lieutenant's command, pulled their triggers. The recoil shook their shoulders, and for a moment their minds went empty, as if flicked away. The roar of the simultaneous shots reverberated through the deserted zoo, echoing from building to building, wall to wall, slicing through wooded areas, crossing water surfaces, a stab to the hearts of all who heard it, like distant thunder. The animals held their breath.

> Even the cicadas stopped crying. Long after the echo of gunfire faded into the distance, there was not a sound to be heard. As if they had been whacked with a huge club by an invisible giant, the tigers shot up into the air for a moment, then landed on the floor of the cage with a great thud, writhing in agony, vomiting blood. The soldiers had failed to finish the tigers off with a single volley. They snapped out of their trance and pulled back on their rifle levers, ejecting spent shells and taking aim again.
>
> (69–70)

Murakami strikes the tenor of much of the best literature that I believe can emerge after such abominations as the Second World War (especially from belligerent nations reluctant to acknowledge their transgressions). His story enacts an apologia – exposure, anagnorisis, and atonement – from the culture of the military/imperial aggressors. Murakami asserts that even Nutmeg, a young girl far from any combat, retains some relationship to the war's worst atrocities; in her retrospective story, she attempts to discern exactly how she fits into this past. Similarly, the contemporary reader – even half a century after the war – has to affirm that society must universally share and accept responsibility for history. This suggests a deeper allegorical reading: humanity as a whole represents another aggressor culture, an instigator of pain against innocent animals. 'The Zoo Attack,' then, voices a *mea culpa* for the transgressions our species has committed against other animals.

'The Zoo Attack' suggests the considerable danger and pain animals face as people treat them ignorantly, knowing nothing about the captive inhabitants when they come or when they leave, and ultimately consigning them to merciless, brutal victimization. The namelessness of Murakami's soldier accentuates his symbolic role as a universal type of the zoogoer. The young lieutenant's violence represents just one way people can behave toward the animals held captive in zoos: certainly not the most common way, but – as other accounts confirm – not unique either (nor limited to military situations: remember Hediger's accounts of the constant threat of sadism from deranged zoo spectators). Such assaults upon zoo animals are plausible consequences of the absolute control people exert, and the absolute degradation animals face, when human culture subsumes nature.

Murakami depicts the zoo attack as a continuation of the war on another front – a venue less prominent than Okinawa or Stalingrad or London, but essentially part of the same enterprise, the same sensibility. 'The Zoo Attack' offers an especially poignant account of the confluence between people's and animals' pain in war, situated as it is in the closing moments of the Second World War. The last gasp of a war reveals, simultaneously, its most vivid, depraved chaos, along with an epiphanic insight into its meaning(lessness), its praxis. It shows itself for what it is: complex, well-orchestrated, very much an outgrowth of standard procedures in the sociocultural status quo (as Karl von Clausewitz said, a continuation of political relations, a carrying out of the same by other means).

The end of 'The Zoo Attack' depicts the indigenous Chinese zoo workers cleaning the animals' carcasses, harvesting food and resources: 'We will haul them outside the city and get rid of every last speck,' they tell the soldiers. 'But in exchange we want the hides and meat. Especially the bear meat – everybody will want that. Parts of bear and tiger are good for medicine – they will command a high price' (72). There is no pain here; the scene now is beyond pain. In a macabre way, the Chinese perform a cleansing, a restoration of order. Nutmeg's father, the veterinarian, sees no momentous change after the killings. 'A large number of animals had been liquidated in a moment before his eyes, and yet, for some inexplicable reason, he felt no particular shock or sadness or anger. In fact, he felt almost nothing' (72). He lights a cigarette and takes a nap.

The eerie calm may tempt us to imagine that after the atrocities, life simply goes on. But the story's historical situation precludes such complacency: the reader must juxtapose the fictional account with the dropping of the atomic bombs immediately following the zoo attack. (*The New Yorker* published the story on the fiftieth anniversary of the bombing, in an issue featuring a mushroom cloud on the cover.) While life seemed to go on in the world after August 1945, a suppressed scar, a shame, remained (especially indelible, of course, to a Japanese author). Murakami, finally, depicts pain – the pain of zoo animals, metaphorically representing the pain facing the entire planet – concentrated into a few moments of horrific barbarity, so repulsive that one can barely process it. After the atrocity, everyone returns to business, or so it seems; but the stain endures. A war story/zoo story like this forces readers to confront, intently, the pain people have inflicted. And while 'The Zoo Attack' offers a parable for humanity as a whole, about our capacity for sadistic annihilation, it no less powerfully repudiates, specifically, how people behave in zoos. Murakami depicts what people are capable of doing to zoo animals at the same time that he reminds us of how painfully people are capable of treating each other. 'War is a contagion,' President Franklin D. Roosevelt said.[7] Murakami shows how this contagion spreads beyond the realm of human society, to infect other species.

Other accounts of zoo deaths in war occur in Irving's *Setting Free the Bears* and Wilson's *The Old Men at the Zoo*. Like Murakami, Irving attempts to broach the crimes of the Second World War through a zoo setting; the night keeper, O. Schrutt, is a former Nazi. The story concerns the effort to atone for war, after the fact, by resisting captivity and oppression. While Irving primarily examines Austria's postwar sensibilities, the novel also flashes back in time to the Nazi period, and presents one specific account of the zoo during the Second World War. Siggy, the modern-day animal savior, recalls:

> No one seems to know just what went on in the zoo during the late years of the war. There was a time, though – let's say, early '45, when the Russians had captured the city, but before the other powers had agreed on the terms of occupation – when there wasn't anything to feed the people. There's no telling what the animals did for food. There are some accounts of what the people did for food, though – since there wasn't the manpower, or the concern, to keep the zoo well guarded.
>
> But four men, say, even if they were unarmed . . . could do a pretty slick job of making off with a fair-sized antelope; even a camel, or a small giraffe.
>
> And that happened. There were raids, although some city-guard outfit was supposedly protecting the zoo; they had the future in mind – a kind of emergency rationing.
>
> For you, and you and you – you get the left hindquarters of this here kangaroo. And you get this rump steak of hippo; just remember, you got to boil it a good long while.
>
> But regardless of the city-guard outfit, there were successful

> raids. One bold, hungry crew made off with a wild Tibetan yak. One man, all alone, stole a whole seal.
>
> I suppose there were plans for a full-scale raid. I suppose it was only a matter of time, before some well-organized group of citizens or soldiers, from *any* army, would decide there was a profit to be made in large meat-locker operations in a starving city.
>
> (217–18)

In an attempt to preserve animals from the vicissitudes of war and a citizenry driven to barbarity, one man tried to free them – 'a would-be noble hero, who thought the animals had suffered enough' (218) – but little is known about him, Siggy relates. He broke in and released as many animals as he could, but the animals were so hungry that they ate him. This earlier attempt to free the animals features quite briefly in a novel about the liberation of the same zoo's animals a generation later – perhaps Irving implies that during wartime, little prominence can be accorded acts of valor; war stories are, by and large, stories of depravity. It takes a generation even to begin to expunge and transcend the evil of Nazi Europe; only after some length of time can a story of surmounting oppression emerge, as this novel celebrates setting free the bears in the 1960s. The muddled 1945 attempted zoo liberation ends ignobly:

> And so his good intentions backfired. I don't know if any animals even got outside the main gate, or whether they were all attacked within the general confines. I suppose animals ate other animals too, before the mob got wind of what had happened and swooped into the chaos with old grenades and kitchen utensils . . .
>
> I hope everyone who ate an animal choked on it. Or exploded when his bowels seized up.
>
> After all, it wasn't the animals' war.
>
> They should have been eating all the O. Schrutts.
>
> (218–19)

Although it wasn't the animals' war, it was nevertheless certainly the animals' abasement.

In *The Old Men at the Zoo* (1961), animals' war deaths occur during a conflagration set in the near future. The war is a vaguely comprehensible, massive geopolitical affair (Wilson's anticipation of a Third World War, which, he prophesizes, will be as replete with zoo animals' carnage as the previous war had been). As noted above, Wilson's animals suffer considerable pain even before the war. There is considerable human pain at the zoo as well: at the beginning of the novel, a giraffe suffering from a tumor charges at one of his keepers, trampling him to death; later, wolves maul and kill the director's daughter as she prowls around in their 'natural habitat.' Wilson describes the human deaths in especially graphic and painful detail: in the keeper's death, 'The giraffe trod on young Filson's testicles and crushed them' (60), one zoo employee asserts, though another contradicts him stating, only slightly less horribly, that 'the giraffe trampled on his chest and broke his ribs' (61), also causing the victim to become impaled on a spike lying on the ground. About the other death, the director is informed, 'the wounds in your daughter's throat and in particular the gashes on her cheeks and thighs could only have been made by the teeth and claws of an animal' (230). The combination of people's and animals' deaths in the zoo during peacetime anticipates the intermixture of human and animal pain that occurs during the most extravagant phenomenon of organized pain – war.

As the war heats up, keepers are uncertain whether to implement contingency plans for destroying dangerous animals – exactly the sort of plans recounted in 'The Zoo Attack' – but administrators (the ineffectual 'old men' in the novel's title) are spared the necessity of deciding when the war preempts, destroying the animals for them. The employees hear 'an explosion that filled the universe,' and 'the shrieking and howling of all the captive beasts and birds.' When the smoke clears, the carnage fulfills the prolepsis of shared pain, with intermingled wounded bodies and corpses of human and animal victims:

> Whatever had fallen must have been far off, yet the blast had wrecked and twisted Zoo buildings; the Old Zoo was in flames and from it came the agonizing screams and roars of hippos, rhinos, zebras, apes and trumpeting elephants. The roof had gone from the eagle house and high above it great condors, vultures and golden eagles were circling and spiralling up into the sky. The trees were filled with chattering parakeets, and among the beds of broken, bruised flowers lay the little bodies of a hundred multi-coloured tropical birds; for the aviary had

> been shattered into a thousand pieces. Here and there men were writhing on the turf. In the floodlight the pools of blood stared in technicolour red against an emerald grass. A hundred yards from me lay the body of the boy from the snake house, his head nearly severed by a great sliver of glass . . . Fire had spread too far to save any part of the Old Victorian Zoo and in it died most of the giraffes, rhinos, zebras, deer and elephants . . . Two wounded hippos broke their way down into the canal and we could see them, lashing the bloodied water for a while, until Strawson's assistant picked them off with a gun and they sank to a great tide of mud spilling over the banks.
>
> (276–7)

Employees prepare to slaughter whatever animals survive the bomb, both because keepers can no longer care for them and because their carcasses can provide food to a starving populace. A family comes upon a zoo truck trying to carry the displaced animals to safety:

> 'Monkey!' the labourer cried. 'Now that is a rare old surprise.'
>
> 'Actually,' Harry said, 'I think they're lemurs.'
>
> His grandmother took charge.
>
> 'My dear Harry, whatever they are, I've no doubt they can be eaten.'
>
> 'Ah! No! Monkeys wouldn't go down proper with my stomach . . . That'd be a tough little old dinner.'
>
> 'Oh, nonsense. Palmer,' the girl said grandly, 'it's only a question of boiling the things long enough.' . . .
>
> 'I don't think I'll shoot them all at once, Gran,' Harry said, 'they'll be fresher if we kill them as we need them.'
>
> (302)

Human consumption of zoo animals occurs frequently in accounts of zoos amid war. In *The Sexual Politics of Meat*, Carol Adams discusses the association of war with meat-eating. She focuses on ties between meat and patriarchal dominance: 'People with power have always eaten meat' (26). Zoo stories, on the contrary, depict the eating of zoo animals during war as a sign of desperation amid defeat and deprivation, although perhaps the meat-eating symbolizes a humbled people's last assertion of power

– over zoo animals. In any event, Adams's insights illuminate the connection between war and eating animals (whether by victors or losers, soldiers or civilians). She documents the associations of vegetarianism with pacifism, and meat-eating with war:

> the Vedic word for war means 'desire for cows.' Anna Kingsford, when discussing Women's Peace Conventions of the nineteenth century, bemoaned that 'Those poor deluded creatures cannot see that universal peace is absolutely impossible to a carnivorous race.' Percy Shelley thundered that 'the butchering of harmless animals cannot fail to produce much of that spirit of insane and hideous exultation in which news of a victory is related altho' purchased by the massacre of a hundred thousand men.' (124)

During the First World War an alliance emerged between vegetarian activists and conscientious objectors. The intermingling of human corpses and animal carcasses that pervades *The Old Men at the Zoo* and other zoo stories about war reflects, as Adams writes, the fact that during war, 'soldiers' imaginations became alerted to what Bernard Shaw and other vegetarians had claimed for decades: corpses are corpses. How could the soldier avoid thinking of his commonality with animals as he sat in the trenches watching large black rats consume soldier and horse? The horrors of this war were also to be found in the slaughterhouse' (125). Isadora Duncan, citing the same authority, writes, 'Bernard Shaw says that as long as men torture and slay animals and eat their flesh, we shall have war . . . Who loves this horrible thing called War? Probably the meat eaters, having killed, felt the need to kill . . . From cutting the throat of a young calf to cutting the throat of our brothers and sisters is but a step' (in Adams, 137). Shaw and Adams support my contention that the pain of war evokes a commonality between animal and human suffering.[8]

As the postwar horrors escalate in *The Old Men at the Zoo*, mobs surround and attack the zoo before keepers can proceed with the organized (and, as they believe, humane) animal killing they had planned. The rioters augment the pain that the war has already occasioned, among animals as well as people, with their clumsy, vicious violence. Their cause is obscure: partly, they seem to be protesting the preservation of animals while people are in such dire need, and partly they simply seem to be brawling in an atmosphere of free-for-all chaotic aggression, confirming Roosevelt's observation that war is a contagion. In general, the pain Wilson describes closely resembles other accounts, factual and fictitious. No matter how the story of zoo animals' pain in war is told or who tells it, the correlations repeatedly confirm a horrible authenticity. Wilson adds one unique detail to his account: when the zoo reopens after the war, the vanquishing forces taunt and torture animals native to defeated countries (as symbols of those nations):

> an old mangy brown Siberian bear . . . was tethered by one foot to an iron stake and was disconsolately trying to shake away a cloud of flies. On the railings at the crown of the pit was a large notice which read: 'The Russian Bear in Difficulties.' High above was suspended a large bird cage in which a miserable looking American brown eagle was trying impossibly to spread its wings. The notice here read: 'The American Eagle taught a lesson.'
>
> (333)

The exhibits, where both animals are finally mauled by hounds, show how zoo signs and displays are manipulated to reinforce the prejudices of empowered cultural forces, rather than the objective, scientific, naturalistic, or educational experience of animals.[9]

Like so many other zoo stories, *The Old Men at the Zoo* depicts the zoo as a place where people rampantly exhibit their most oppressive, insensitive attitudes, sinking to a lowest common denominator of Hobbesian brutality. The Romans 'kept animals in order to have living fodder for the games' that resulted in mass slaughter (Jamieson, 'Against', 108). Are modern zoogoers any more enlightened than the Romans? There is certainly a difference in scale and appearance; but essentially, today as in ancient times, people's desire to be entertained obviates concerns about inflicting pain upon captive animals. If animals get injured, or slaughtered, or eaten – if they die during transport, or get sold to circuses by scurrilous keepers, or pace in their cages until they die, or starve when people abrogate their commitment to feed them – zoos hush up the affair behind the scenes, or call for fine-tuning institutional practices. Instead of settling for cosmetic palliatives or ethical rationalization, I argue, we must challenge the institution itself with a determined response to the fact that a profusion of pain has been, and continues to be, inextricably engrained in the display of captive animals.

If zoo stories about war convey animals' pain on the macrocosmic, geopolitical plane, some works, at the other extreme, use images of the pain associated with zoos as metaphors for personal, psychologically interiorized torment. Jerry in *The Zoo Story*, William and Neaera in *Turtle Diary*, and the sisters in 'In the Zoo' all embody such representations. Sylvia Plath's 'Zoo Keeper's Wife' (1961) employs zoo animals' pain as a figurative evocation of personal suffering in a tableau of sadistic relations. The poem vividly depicts the pain a zookeeper inflicts upon his wife, who becomes a fellow sufferer along with the animals: a surrogate victim for the husband to dominate after working hours, an outlet for his stores of cruelty. 'Zoo Keeper's Wife' exudes the pain, pathos, and biting psychological self-maceration that marks Plath's poetic at its most potent. The poem lambastes the zookeeper more critically than any other zoo story I have examined. Plath implies that the keeper has a voracious need for brutal domination (and the title's impersonal reference to the man as his occupation suggests that she intends her imputation to apply generically to any keeper, not just the specific husband in the poem). The keeper's wife, like all the oppressed women who inhabit Plath's poetry, is a self-inscription. The husband figure, similarly, is an incarnation of Plath's husband, Ted Hughes. Since Hughes 'had planned to study zoology,' writes Linda Wagner-Martin, 'the poem has an ironic personal element' (184).[10] The 'particular horrors of her husband's zoo' in this poem, writes Margaret Dickey Uroff, 'recall Hughes's poems' (132).

It is not merely coincidental that Plath depicts zoos' oppressive distortion of natural animals in a poem about men's oppressive misogyny. Indeed, ecofeminist studies feature considerable examination of connections between patriarchal abuse of nature and of women. A 'feminist analysis of social domination,' writes Ynestra King, 'reveals the interconnected roots of misogyny and a hatred of nature' (123).

> We live in a culture which is founded on repudiation and domination of nature. This has a special significance for women because, in patriarchal thought, women are believed to be closer

> to nature than men . . . ecologists, with their concern for nonhuman nature, have yet to understand that they have a particular stake in ending the domination of women because a central reason for woman's oppression is her association with the despised nature they are so concerned about. The hatred of women and the hatred of nature are intimately connected and mutually reinforcing.
>
> (118)

Men's domination of women is the prototype for other forms of domination, King argues, quoting Adrienne Rich from *Of Woman Born*: 'We have been perceived for too many centuries as pure Nature, exploited and raped like the earth' (123). Greta Gaard, too, writes that 'the way in which women and nature have been conceptualized historically in the Western intellectual tradition has resulted in devaluing whatever is associated with women, emotion, animals, nature, and the body' (5).[11] In advance of feminist theorists, Plath shows a keen awareness of similarities between misogyny and the desecration of nature: the devaluation, in tandem, of women and zoo animals. Wagner-Martin calls 'Zoo Keeper's Wife' 'the first of Plath's poems to suggest that what men are capable of doing to animals, they are capable of doing to women' (184).[12]

Plath lived near the London Zoo and visited it regularly (*Collected Poems*, 291). From these excursions, 'Zoo Keeper's Wife' suggests, she observed the pain that marks animal constraint, which she transforms into a metaphor for her experience in a troubled marriage. The poem depicts a murky, threatening, eerie sense of cruelty – plumbing the severity of pain – consequent upon both the institution of zoos and the institution of marriage. The common factor uniting the two is the ethos of the man who ruthlessly controls both. The pain inherent in how zoo animals are kept symbolically represents the pain inherent in how the man in the poem controls – 'keeps' – his wife.

Plath's speaker evokes images of zoo animals which range from merely unpalatable to horrific. The animals become vehicles for the speaker's self-loathing (typical of the poems from Plath's last troubled years) – she depicts them as hideous, by human standards of beauty, so that she can paint herself-as-zoo-animal with a similar ugliness. She appears 'Cold as an eel, without eyelids,' 'lungless / and ugly.' With 'spidery jaws' and 'loose teeth,' she is a pastiche of disembodied deformity: 'this pink and purple plastic / Guts bag' (154); she is an animal, in the most pejorative sense. Plath characterizes the animals as cannibalistic, likening herself to an eel: 'my belly a silk stocking / Where the heads and tails of my sisters decompose' (154).

An odd array of specimens – the speaker's cellmates, to the extent that she is herself one of her husband's captive specimens – inhabit the zoo's hostile environs. These animals are portrayed in variously degraded conditions: bored, soiled, comatose, grotesque; all stand in unfortunate contrast to their natural state. The variegated ark of animals, the diversity typically featured as the zoo's pride, is here awkward and unseemly. The 'sacred baboon in his wig and wax ears' is ridiculous, trivialized and stunted by captivity. The white mice are behaviorally dysfunctional, 'Multiplied to infinity like angels on a pinhead / Out of sheer boredom.' The rhinoceros, 'Dirty as a bootsole' with its 'bog breath,' looks and smells fetid, disgusting. The snails blow 'kisses like black apples,' seeming surreal and haunted like malicious fairy-tale animals. Some animals are depicted as mutilated victims: 'I remember the bloodied chicks and the quartered rabbits' (155), the speaker thinks, presumably referring to creatures slaughtered as food for zoo animals.

The armadillo is 'obscene and bald as a pig' (155), simply ugly – or, rather, ugly in the way that homocentric aesthetics applied to animals would indicate. I do not think Plath suggests that these animals *are* in fact ridiculous, ugly, or obscene, only that they appear that way – or become that way – in the keeper's grips. Again, given the poem's sharply internalized focus, such ugliness evokes the pain people may feel when they perceive themselves as ugly, unloved. It is specifically the profusion of animals gathered together (unnaturally) in a zoo setting that fosters and enables such distorted representations. When the armadillo is derogatorily labeled 'bald as a pig,' two animals are played off each other – as if the dominant animal in this schema, the keeper, contrives to sustain his power by fostering a milieu in which the victims (including the wife herself as an honorary zoo animal) facilitate their degradation by bickering among themselves and bringing each other down. The realm of nature, as distilled and contained within the zoo, thus becomes a house divided against itself. Mastery inheres in the single creature, the keeper, who possesses the power – the keys to the cages, the stores of food, the ability to inflict pain, and (like Adam) the authority to name and to characterize – that holds sway over the fractious anti-Eden he himself has incited to discord. Imagine the keeper (or his vicarious representative, the zoo spectator) seeing an animal that he – wanting to assert his own superiority – determines to regard (to construct, to contextualize) as ugly. Ugly as a . . . what? he muses, seeking an image to confirm his own omnipotence, his subjective embodiment of ultimate beauty. Oh, look there in the next cage: ugly as a bald pig. It is the agglomeration of animals suffering in zoos (like the many women Plath saw suffering in the institution of marriage) that creates the aura of repugnance emanating thence. Indeed, it is literally the large number of animals kept together in artificial proximity and variegation that produces the zoo's profoundly unpleasant smell. Plath refers to the odor only once – 'the moist / Fug of the Small Mammal House' (155) – but this stench pervades the poem, providing a sensory indication as to the totality of the suffocating environment. Plath would develop and enhance this important olfactory reaction more elaborately if she had to, but everyone who has been to the zoo knows from direct experience how the unnaturally concentrated odor festers in its halls, cages, and houses.

Although the poem pegs his character incisively, the zookeeper himself does not figure prominently: the poem is mostly about the animals, their appearances and conditions, and the wife's implication in this scenario. The husband, in the active role of keeper/powermonger, eludes the poem's wrenching focus. He, unlike the animals and the wife, is not caged, and thus moves fast enough and freely enough to evade Plath's poetic of pain unscathed. The wife forcefully realizes her own constraint by the end of the poem, if it was not completely clear to her at the beginning. Perhaps the man is not more clearly drawn because he doesn't need to be – one can infer all one needs to know about him from the victims that litter his domain; or, perhaps, Plath does not look at him head-on because she cannot: he is too tyrannical, and so she displaces the burden of his ineffable horror onto his grotesque animal victims.

Another reason for the keeper's slight presence as only a caricature of abusiveness may be the imperative Plath came to understand, in her late work, of escaping Hughes's influence – his presence, his images, his poetic. In this light, it is illuminating to consider 'Zoo Keeper's Wife' as a reaction or response to

Hughes's own zoo poem written four years earlier, 'The Jaguar' (see Chapter 3). The comparison allows a kind of he-said-she-said insight into their marriage on the imagistic common ground of zoos. If nothing was known of their personal life other than what one can educe from the way these two poems play out the issue of animal captivity, it would be possible to reconstruct a fair approximation of their painful relationship. 'The Jaguar' posits a vision of zoos in which captive animals exist for people's pure imaginative exploitation. The animal's pain (the toll of its deprivation of natural habitat), while self-evident, does not merit the speaker's empathy amid his imaginative flourishes; acknowledging pain would spoil the moment, and the patriarchal insouciance which infuses Hughes's poetic allows him to repress or ignore the pain fully. Plath, by contrast, as she moves from cage to cage in 'Zoo Keeper's Wife,' is tormentingly unable to see anything but pain heaped upon more pain. She cannot eschew its pervasive presence, while her husband, in his zoo story, seems immune to its sting. He, through his power, has achieved the carefree luxury of ignoring the realm of pain in which his wife wholly immerses herself.

In her study of the influences Plath and Hughes exerted on each other, Uroff outlines their creative relationship. The most obvious example of interests they came to share in their poetry, she writes, 'is Hughes's interest in animals, which quickly inspired Plath to write several animal or nature poems.' She finds some of Plath's early efforts weak, overshadowed by Hughes's hand; but 'by the time she wrote "Zoo Keeper's Wife" she had become completely familiar with Hughes's zoo and could use his animals for her own quite separate purposes (in this case, to criticize him)' (9). Uroff's insight suggests an interesting appropriation Plath enacts in 'Zoo Keeper's Wife': taking away the topic, the possessions, the animals, that Hughes the keeper had once controlled, and empowering images of captive animals – contra 'The Jaguar' – by using them against the husband/keeper. Plath marshalls the zoo animals, figuratively, to attack the captor: an exposé of their pain indicts the despot who reigned over this realm. This technique might offer another reason why the man himself is minimally prominent in the poem: Plath is more interested in reclaiming his animals, so she sidesteps the keeper.

The keeper is a collector, a seducer, a trapper. The animals and wife are unappreciated except as tokens, booty – profoundly deprived of any cultural power. But Plath moderates the animals' oppression by transforming their burdens into a potential source of unexpected endurance – as, in many of Plath's other poems, a position of marginalized exclusion and constraint becomes vitalized when the poet makes a virtue of necessity. The animals'/wife's ugliness, for example, embodies a kind of strength to the extent that it allows invisibility, or at least a lessening of (exploitative, leering, voyeuristic) scrutiny, from the male gaze and the capture plot. An ugly woman, as the speaker pointedly proclaims herself, may gain a degree of camouflage (like protective coloration in a wild animal) from male predation. Her stereotypical unattractiveness – 'The spidery jaws, the spine bones' – like that of many animals, embodies a menacing demeanor that may make enemies more hesitant to attack, and collectors less eager to display the subject. This is not to say that the persona seems content in her captive, animalistic state; but if she *is* fated to metaphorical imprisonment, her double-edged association with her grotesquely constructed zoo animals at least mitigates the toll of degradation. Plath's poetic voice enacts a deft fusion of lowly self-pity with a paradoxically growing confidence – a gathering survivalist determination. Uroff calls the voice in this poem 'exhausted . . . but with a new urgency over physical decay and loss' (137). As merely an animal, the wife has a certain freedom to 'act like an animal' – to draw upon zoo animals' otherness, and thus transcend the limiting human-wife script. Zoo animals are forbidden power or integrity, Plath suggests, as is a wife. But a wife who can coopt zoo animals' attributes gains a weird, unexpected dimension, which may allow her to surprise her complacent keeper. If the woman is like an animal that the keeper has caught and caged, she can at least reveal the brutality of keepers and of cages; she can – as Plath's late poetry indeed does – incite a rebellion among the disempowered.

In this vein, Plath subversively transforms the image of the disgusting eel from the poem's beginning into the serpent, the undoer of man, toward the end:

> You checked the diet charts and took me to play
> With the boa constrictor in the Fellows' Garden.
> I pretended I was the Tree of Knowledge.
> I entered your bible, I boarded your ark.
>
> (155)

As the serpent, of course, she possesses the ability to destroy her husband's Eden, his ark, his zoo. Plath's zoo story includes a prophecy of destruction that will punish people's (and specifically zookeepers') transgressions. Her own captivity seems an immediate constraint, but the pain she promises in retribution proves substantial, like the consequences of the animals' revenge against human dominance as embodied in the serpent's actions in Genesis. In most zoo stories, the victims remain mute in their pain; in Plath's, the sufferer has a rare opportunity to voice her condition. Consequentially, the sadist/keeper/husband may have to endure public accusation and exposure, as few people who inflict pain in zoos do. Plath pushes the pain that is so often behind the scenes more insistently into view.

But the poem's conclusion situates the woman more as victim than victor: as Plath herself may have realized, she would eventually surmount Hughes's oppression (via poetry that would prove to be better and more durable than seemed possible in the early 1960s: writing well is the best revenge), but in the shorter term she was foundering and destined to go under, to perish in her keeper's cage. The poem concludes: 'Nightly now I flog apes owls bears sheep / Over their iron stile. And still don't sleep' (155). Ultimately, the keeper destroys the animal-wife's natural behavior irremediably, as a consequence of the unbearable pain suffered in captivity. The poem's end mirrors its opening ('I can stay awake all night, if need be – / Cold as an eel, without eyelids'); agonizing insomnia afflicts the sufferer not just with the lack of sleep but, worse, with tormenting visions of constraint that take the place of sleep. She perverts a pastoral image (counting sheep to bring on sleep) into the infliction of pain upon zoo animals. Plath suggests that zoos drive people to barbarity: that they begin an interminable cycle of sadistic victimization. The abused become abusers, fantasizing about flogging their fellow sufferers. The keeper's impregnable power-fetish is thus solidified by the devolution that his charges manifest, illustrating the self-fulfilling prophecy that creatures treated brutally will become brutes. His zoo's discordant inhabitants prove themselves incapable of self-government – that is, as judged by the keeper's own dominant sensibility, which the poem ruefully projects as the ultimate ethos of the world in which the wife must live (and soon, of course, die). The zoo inmates will continue to require the keeper's oversight to prevent them from flogging each other to death. (The paradigm replicates the fate of the 'primitive' peoples who constituted the 'white man's burden,' the European imperial mission to save non-Westerners from themselves by ruling over them.) The wife, finally, cannot do other than capitulate to the pain of the zoo scenario that victimizes her.

5

Spectatorship

Few if any wild animals . . . would choose to live in full view of human beings, yet in a zoo they must.

A. H. N. Green-Armytage, *Bristol Zoo 1865–1965*

There is no higher use to which a wild bird or mammal can be devoted than to place it in perfectly comfortable captivity to be seen by millions of persons who desire to make its acquaintance.

William Hornaday, Founding Director, Bronx Zoo

The animal scrutinises [man] across a narrow abyss of non-comprehension . . . The man too is looking across a similar, but not identical, abyss of non-comprehension. And this is so wherever he looks. He is always looking across ignorance and fear.

John Berger, 'Why Look at Animals?'

I live only to be stared at.
The throng they call people comes here.
They like to tease me. They enjoy it
when my rage rattles the bars.

José Emilio Pacheco, 'Baboon Babble'

This chapter will examine how spectators watch animals at zoos. What, exactly, do they see? How does the seemingly oxymoronic *activity of spectatorship* affect their consciousness – morally, imaginatively, socially? What does zoo spectatorship fundamentally involve, and how do the characteristics of watching reflect on the enterprise of zoos? What can we see when we watch people watching, and watch *how* people watch? I hypothesize that zoo spectatorship is passive, minimally imaginative, cheaply vicarious, at least slightly distasteful, conducive to a range of socially inappropriate or undesirable behavior, and inhibitive, rather than generative, of the creative experience and appreciation of nature. Both zoo stories and zoo culture suggest that spectators tend to display few of the nobler instincts of inquiry or epistemological and experiential appetite as they pass from cage to cage. S. A. Omrod reflects a sense of the tawdry when he writes, 'Most [zoos] are simply peep-shows, the animals merely goods displayed to the public in return for hard cash' ('Wild Animals in Captivity,' in Magel, 121).

At the extreme, the most audacious spectators may pose tangible harm to animals and to other zoogoers, manifesting aggression and social dysfunctionality. Bob Mullan and Garry Marvin describe accounts of vandalism motivated by, in addition to sadism,

> probably simply the end of being intrusive, or demanding attention or interaction. In Bombay Zoo crocodiles have been stoned to death in futile attempts to stir them . . . Peter Batten . . . observes that it is 'doubtful whether any American zoo has escaped vandalism in some form by sadistic, ignorant, or dimwitted humans . . . zoo animals are maimed, mutilated and killed quite frequently.'
>
> (135)

Bernard Livingston expands upon the potential menaces of spectatorship, recounting keepers' accounts of public nuisances who haunt zoos: among the most common

> are the 'dirty old men' of the zoo . . . These voyeurs hang around the zoo for hours on end hoping to see animals copulate. Every zoo has them and mostly they are harmless except for an occasional exhibitionist . . . Another type of sexual pervert who occasionally plagues zoos is the sodomist. The wild ass, the deer, the aoudad, young llamas and other more or less docile hoofed beasts are usually the choice for this night-visiting predator, chiefly because these animals are similar to the kind of animal he victimized on the farm where the habit often started. [Zoo director Heini] Hediger adds to the sexual perverts mentioned above 'the type who concentrates not on the animals but on women, young people and children, eying them in dark and secluded corners of the zoo. There are also people who apparently are sexually stimulated by the sight of some par-

ticular animal or other, e.g., a long-necked terrapin, and consequently visit it with inordinate frequency.'

(48–50)

Marie Nimier's *The Giraffe* (1993) illustrates similar instances of unbalanced behavior: her zoo visitor reflects upon

> a Sunday I'll remember all my life. I was standing at my favorite vantage point . . . Directly across from me, I saw a man begin to masturbate. It was a fine day and crowds streamed boisterously through the park, but the man seemed completely oblivious. His leather-gloved hand moved back and forth like a forlorn bird, steadily, coldly. His glazed eyes followed the crimson rump of an old female baboon climbing on the boulders.
>
> (29)

The deviant activity is contagious:

> I think he noticed me, for his hand stopped moving when mine reached inside my fly. I ducked behind the wooden shutters. The man removed his jacket and used it to cover himself. I found him attractive . . . I was impressed with the controlled, workmanlike nature of his stroking. Almost involuntarily, I began to copy him, following his rhythm, breathing along with him.
>
> (30–1)

This behavior manifests a kind of spectatorial exuberance gone wild, and probably, too, a warped exertion of power (shocking and offending 'normal' zoogoers, transgressing mores of social propriety). The masturbation betokens exhibitionism (the possibility of being seen by other spectators titillates) as well as voyeurism (part of the men's thrill deriving from masturbating while watching animals and other people), representing a zoo-based variant on the psychiatric characterization of voyeurism:

> The essential feature of this disorder is recurrent, intense, sexual urges and sexually arousing fantasies . . . involving the act of observing unsuspecting people, usually strangers . . . The act of looking ('peeping') is for the purpose of achieving sexual excitement . . . Orgasm, usually produced by masturbation, may

> occur during the voyeuristic activity, or later in response to the memory of what the person has witnessed . . . the person with Voyeurism is aroused by the secretive, illegal nature of his peeping.[1]

In *The Giraffe,* the autoerotic spectators' transgressions result from what Nimier portrays as the objectification of zoo animals: the situation of animals at a great remove from people, and the refusal to dignify their stature in what we regard as our world; the construction of a zoo as a place where normal behavioral guidelines – toward fellow human as well as non-human creatures – do not apply. For example, the narrator muses about a giraffe (the zoo animal that most obsesses him, yet which he still fails to appreciate or respect except as a fetish for his own sensibilities): 'She seemed so different from me, at the time, so distant. I preferred to ignore her, she was only an object, the object of my attentions, nothing more' (25–6). Here and in other zoo stories, spectators' perceptions that the zoo does not nurture or require considerate standards of deportment facilitates misbehavior. It is as if offending spectators perceive the zoo's abrogations of social/natural beneficence (its sadistic strain, hegemonic chauvinism, constraint) that make transgressive behavior seem less proscribed than in ordinary society. The zoo, in such cases, fosters sociopathy – or, at least, provides people with sociopathic tendencies an amenable environment for their expressions.

Another zoo voyeur appears in Brigid Brophy's *Hackenfeller's Ape* (1953), where the interests of science provide a cover for Professor Darrelhyde's study of the apes' sexuality. 'There was no record that any white man had witnessed the mating of Hackenfeller's Ape' (19). The professor becomes as obsessed with these animals as Nimier's spectator is with the giraffe, sublimating his emotions to the advancement of biological knowledge. 'When he observed the mating fervour seize the apes, he came as near as his temperament allowed to ambition,' imagining that he would be cited in 'a footnote in every future monograph on the species. What he hoped was to replace the confused, anonymous, undated tradition, which had been preserved among untrained minds, by a couple of sentences, packed and precisely descriptive' (19), describing the animals' copulation. Brophy depicts voyeurism masquerading as a quest for scientific insight, order, truth.

Certainly most zoo spectators are not latent perverts; but many do behave badly, inappropriately, in less extreme ways than the overt degenerates. Spectators' opportunity to watch everything animals do resembles on some level the power and pleasure that characterizes the disorder of voyeurism. Peeping – watching everpresent and compliant subjects, *carte blanche* – encompasses zoo visitors' role, their *raison d'être*. 'Staring,' writes Stephen St C. Bostock, 'is in a way the essence of a zoo' (100).

Yet if zoo spectatorship taps into subconscious cravings for voyeuristic arousal by tantalizing patrons with exotic and forbidden stimuli, it can also frustrate visitors' fantasies and cravings. John Berger writes:

> The zoo cannot but disappoint. The public purpose of zoos is to offer visitors the opportunity of looking at animals. Yet nowhere in a zoo can a stranger encounter the look of an animal. At the most, the animal's gaze flickers and passes on. They look sideways. They have been immunised to encounter, because nothing can any more occupy a *central* place in their attention. Therein lies the ultimate consequence of their marginalisation. That look between animal and man, which may have played a crucial role in the development of human society, and with which, in any case, all men had always lived until less than a century ago, has been extinguished. Looking at each animal, the unaccompanied zoo visitor is alone. As for the crowds, they belong to a species which has at last been isolated.
>
> (26)

The spectators' position is circumscribed by paradox: the zoo promises it will allow them to see everything, but they may really see nothing. The spectatorial role, people presume, privileges us magisterially. But according to Berger, animals deflate the human gaze we conceive as so puissant, by cutting us in return – refusing to dignify or acknowledge our self-important ritual of looking. A king may look at a cat, but perhaps a cat disdains to look back at a king. The zoo situates spectators in a position suggesting that they will regard unimpeded, imperiously, omnivorously, masters of all they survey. But the actual visual pickings may prove less grand: eager for quick and lurid thrills, spectators may instead discover isolation and frustration.

Michel Foucault's ideological insights further despoil spectators' purportedly innocent pleasures. The logical extrapolation of the zoo, Foucault writes in *Discipline and Punish*, is the prison; in both, authority figures exercise power via surveillance. He discusses Jeremy Bentham's model for the panopticon prison, an architectural enterprise famously devoted to regulation, discipline, separation between a figure of power and a subjugated other, and the enforced imposition of order upon unwilling subjects. 'Bentham does not say whether he was inspired, in his project, by La Vaux's menagerie at Versailles: the first menagerie in which the different elements are not, as they traditionally were, in a park' (203); but Foucault infers that La Vaux exerted an institutional influence upon Bentham.

In the Versailles menagerie, 'At the centre was an octagonal pavilion which, on the first floor, consisted of only a single room, the king's *salon*; on every side large windows looked out onto seven cages . . . containing different species of animals' (203). Both zoo and panopticon show 'a similar concern with individualizing observation, with characterization and classification, with the analytical arrangement of space' (203). For the prisoners always potentially under scrutiny – who know always that the guardian *could be* watching, although not that he necessarily is – 'Visibility is a trap' (200). The major effect of this 'trap' is 'to induce in the inmate a state of consciousness and permanent visibility that assures the automatic functioning of power . . . Surveillance is permanent in its effects, even if it is discontinuous in its action' (201). Whether or not someone happens to be watching, the caged creature is there to be exhibited, and thus endures the constant servility of the subject under surveillance. Via surveillance, the institution ensures 'that the perfection of power should tend to render its actual exercise unnecessary' (201). In the prison, the ramifications of such surveillance obviously assist the processes of keeping prisoners captive. In the zoo, Foucault's analysis implies, people watch animals as a means of symbolically celebrating (or supplanting, or satisfying vicariously) a desire to exert power over them more explicitly.

The institutional dynamics of spectatorship as a power stance inhere in the zoo whether or not its patrons consciously opt to exercise them. Foucault suggests how zoo spectatorship reiterates the prison warden's position with its power of unbounded, one-way surveillance. Other appraisals of zoo culture, too, confirm the praxis he describes as operant in zoos. 'The problem with staring,' writes Bostock, is 'that staring with many species, including ourselves, is a threat' (100). 'The traditional menagerie,' as Mullan and Marvin describe, 'allow[ed] the humans the closest visual experience of the animals. The notion that an animal was entitled to some sort of privacy, that it could absent itself from the human gaze, was totally alien to this sort of exhibition. It was on display, the public had paid to see it and therefore it should be visible' (70). As unfortunate as this scenario is for animals, I am more interested in what this incessant sense of entitlement to absolute spectatorial control says about the people who relish the power that accompanies total visual access. If, as Foucault suggests, zoos resemble prisons semiotically and institutionally, it is unsurprising that the relationship between the watcher and the watched should embody antagonism.

One of the most popular spectatorial activities is feeding time at the zoo – both keepers' scheduled feedings and visitors' *ad hoc* offerings. A 1930 *Cook's Handbook to London* notes, under its entry for the London Zoo: 'The feeding time of the lions and tigers is 4 p.m., except from November to February, when it is one hour earlier; the sea lions and seals are fed at 4.30 (November to February 3.30); pelicans 2.30' (238).[2] And still, in 1996, the zoo distributes a brochure, 'London Zoo: Your Day in Our Life,' listing special events including '1.30: Pig out! You are welcome to come and watch our rare breeds make pigs of themselves at lunch. Better than that, you can even help feed them!'; '2.30: Fast food. It's down in one when the penguins p-p-p-pick up a fish and generally make a meal of feeding time. See for yourself why it's one of the Zoo's top attractions'; '2.30: Fishy goings-on. Piranha pounce, sharks attack, archer fish aim and angel fish angle for a bite in the aquarium.' (An advertisement in that brochure, headlined 'Feeding Time at the Zoo,' promotes several restaurants and kiosks where *people* can eat; outside the cages as well as inside, ingestion features as a prominent zoo activity.) 'Eating, especially for animals, is still an act overlaid with magical associations,' argues Boria Sax, explaining the appeal of watching animals feed. 'In a very visceral way, people have always been inclined to judge types of animals by the things and manner in which they eat.'

Louis MacNeice's *Zoo* (1938) depicts what a spectator at the Regent's Park lion house sees at feeding time:

> the heavy rumbling of the meat-trolley, an outburst of growls, general galvanization . . . The keeper began with the jaguar in the cage at the west end, undoing the slat at the bottom of the bars and thrusting in a joint of horse. The animals struck at him with left hooks through the bars, growling breathily. Some went on growling even when the meat was in their mouths. Most of the leopards took their pieces up to their high shelves, like a cat jumping on to a table, but most of the lions subsided plumb in the front of their cages facing the crowds behind the barrier and, bending their heads to one side, lazily ground up the bones.
>
> (100–1)

MacNeice may or may not intend the unsavory and unsettling tinge I perceive in his account. While the activity of eating is literally natural and common, it appears colored here with a subliminal guilty embarrassment, even repulsion. The antagonistic oppression Foucault identifies, and the disappointing emptiness Berger posits, indeed seem present – in terms of a pervasive and otherwise inexplicable sense of anger, and an almost grotesque viciousness – as MacNeice describes spectators watching animals eat.

E. F. Benson's essay 'The Zoo' (1893) provides a more explicitly critical and disturbed reaction to Regent's Park feeding displays:

> I once saw the snakes fed; the public are now no longer allowed to see it, and quite rightly. There were about a dozen people in the snake-house, at the time, and I think we were all silent as we went out, when the feeding was over. The snake I watched was a live python from South America . . . and he was given a live rat, for they will not eat the dead food. The rat was let in through a small wire grating, and seemed quite at his ease at first, for the snake was asleep. He ran about the cage for a little while, and eventually walked across two of the reptile's coils. At that moment the other opened his eyes and saw the rat. He was in no hurry, and stretched himself slowly . . .
>
> The rat was still unconcerned, he was sitting in a corner, performing his last toilet, which was not worth while, and it

> was very pitiful. Presently he looked up, and saw that which made him drop down on all-fours, and tremble. The snake had fully awoke, he was hungry, and it was dinner time; two small eyes were looking towards the living meal . . . it was horrible.
>
> It is many years since I saw that sight. It was, I think, the most terrifying thing I ever beheld. In sleep, the horror of it sometimes still reaches me. I am in a dim unfamiliar room, alone at first, but as I sit there, something wakes into existence which is horrible, evil, not understood, and I cannot get away.
>
> (158–60)

My point – and I believe Benson's as well – is not that animals eating is disgusting; obviously it is a fundamental facet of natural behavior. But something seems askew, inappropriate, about feeding rituals as they occur at the zoo, and about spectators' presence. Both MacNeice's and Benson's accounts (but more explicitly the latter) project a sense that it is wrong for people to be watching – yet spectators queue up nevertheless, as directed by timetables, to see. Benson's final passage extends beyond describing the feeding, focusing ultimately on himself: his own troubled memory of the event. He indicates, as I argue, that what happens in zoos is essentially not about animals but about people, and that it is about us in disturbing ways. Despite the copious anthropomorphism, I do not think Benson means to address the situations of the rat or the snake: they are on their own as predator and prey, just as they would be in nature. Rather, he expresses the troubling qualities of *human* behavior, the spectator's traumatic anagnorisis. What is significant (and most disturbing) about the feeding scene as he describes it is, specifically, the human presence.

Penelope Lively's *Moon Tiger* (1987) offers a tawdry depiction of how feeding the animals generates revenue and spectatorial attraction at the Cairo Zoo: 'The hippos share a small lake with flamingos and assorted duck; a keeper stands alongside with a bucket of potatoes – five piastres buys a couple of potatoes which you then throw into the pink maw of the hippo. The adult hippos wallow with their mouths permanently agape while two young ones, who have not yet got the idea, cruise fretfully up and down, occasionally struck by inaccurate potatoes'; a spectator remarks that the display resembles 'an exotic form of hoop-la' (106).

In Edward Kamau Brathwaite's 'The Zoo' (1989), feeding animals explicitly represents one element in the repertoire of degradation that spectators exert: the poem catalogues dozens of animals, who

> are merely gathered here so we can gape &
> celebrate their public idiosyncrasies –
> so we can pause, point, peel oranges,
> buy buns to throw
>
> (48)

Another account of public feeding appears in John Irving's *Setting Free the Bears*:

> I watched them feed the Big Cats. Everyone in the zoo seemed to have been waiting all day for that . . . First, this keeper came and flipped a horse steak through the bars to the lioness; the keeper flipped it right in a puddle of her pee. Everyone snickered . . . the keeper was more professional with the cheetah; he slid the meat in on a little tray, shook it off, and the cheetah pounced on it, snapping it around in his mouth. Just the way a house cat breaks a mouse's neck. But the cheetah shook his meat too hard; a big hunk flew off and plopped on the ledge outside the bars. Everyone was hysterical. You see, the cheetah couldn't quite reach it, and being afraid someone would steal it, the poor animal set up this roar . . . Someone pranced in front of the cheetah, pretending to make a grab for the meat on the ledge. The cheetah, must have lost his mind, trying to jam his head between the bars.
>
> (107–8)

When the animal finally grabs the food, 'he ate up that meat in two terrible bites and swallows – not one bit of chewing – and sure enough, he gagged, finally spewing it all back up. And when I left the Cat House, the cheetah was bolting down his vomit' (108). Irving infuses the scene with the spectators' tawdry, sadistic glee: the people act entertained by the animals' difficulty in eating, titillated by the visceral incontinence of their gross appetites. What the spectators watch, of course, hardly resembles animals' natural feeding behavior – Irving's emphasis on the cage, the bars, the animals' difficulty reaching the food, the food's proximity to urine and vomit all specifically connote how animals eat in zoos; *wild* animals eat without these obstacles. Irving implies that people come to zoos precisely to see the antics of a public feeding spectacle. Mullan and Marvin describe the sensational appeal of watching animals feed: 'members of the public . . . seem to be fascinated by the spectacle of [a lion] eating portions of [a cow]. Many zoo directors have stopped such public feeding of the big cats as they feel that the snarling, growling and generally agitated behaviour which is displayed by the animals at this time is a poor ethological representation of their true behaviour and merely panders to popular misconceptions' (6).

Many zoos today attempt to ban spectators' attempts to feed animals themselves, 'because of what we know of the harm done to animals' health by uncontrolled public feeding' (Bostock, 183). In Chile's Santiago Zoo, for example, 'An African elephant died after undergoing numerous operations to remove plastic bags, nails, and other items from its stomach. Zoo workers said visitors, who until recently were allowed to feed the animals, often gave the elephant lighted cigarettes' (Sims). Even if prohibitions exist, throwing popcorn through bars remains a highlight of a zoo visit for many spectators, as irrepressible as tossing pennies in a fountain. Despite the nutritional dangers, write Mullan and Marvin, understimulated animals will often beg for food simply to alleviate boredom, which 'the public often responds to positively because it allows them to interact with the animals' (134). While no zoos that they studied encouraged public feeding, 'so concerned are most zoo visitors to influence what goes on in an enclosure and to cause activity among the animals, that in all but a few zoos, we found a variety of animals are fed' (134). They conclude, 'rather than the animals needing to be fed, it is humans wanting to feed them. Zoos are ostensibly about going to view animals, an activity in which the people are not important except as passive viewers. But this is not how it works in practice. In the zoo the humans *demand* to be noticed by the animals' (134).

A. A. Milne illustrates Mullan and Marvin's observation in *When We Were Very Young* (1965), showing how feeding represents spectators' attempt to bridge an otherwise absolute division between people and animals:

If you try to talk to the bison he never quite understands;
You can't shake hands with a mingo – he doesn't like
  shaking hands,

> And lions and roaring tigers hate saying, 'How do you do?' –
> But I give buns to the elephant when I go down to the Zoo.
> (46–7)

And Yi-Fu Tuan describes zoo visitors' spontaneous feeding in a vein that recalls the Foucauldian model of the spectator as authority: 'One of the pleasures of visiting a zoo is feeding the animals. The act is generous and the pleasure is innocent, although both derive from a base of superiority and power. Making another being eat out of our hand – *that* yields a special thrill all the greater if the animal is first made to beg and if it is large enough to crush us in another setting less structured in our favor' (80).

In fact and fiction, dating provides a common occasion for zoo outings, although zoo stories depict zoos as strange places for dates. Zoo dates offer insight into how spectatorship may relate to human passions and libido; part of the attraction, and the strangeness, of a date at the zoo derives from watching animals' sexuality – their own 'dating' behavior, the socio-sexual interaction between cagemates. The San Diego Wild Animal Park attempts to tap into (and profit from) the zoo's putative romantic allure. It offers a tour called 'Night Moves' on Saturdays, lasting three hours, for $150 – as a promotional announcement promises –

> focusing on the wild courtship and mating rituals of the facility's exotic – and erotic – residents. Did you know that lions can mate fifty times a day, and that the gorilla who's smitten gets bitten if he tries to force his affections? These are just a few of the examples of what goes on 'behind closed gates' at the San Diego Wild Animal Park.
>
> A unique dating experience, the Night Moves tour includes a romantic evening drive into the park's huge field enclosures . . . Safari guides share anecdotes, show some of the gadgets used by matchmaking zookeepers, and take memento photos of tour participants.
>
> After sunset, the truck stops at romantic Amani Point, a secluded spot offering panoramic, moonlit views . . . Here guests can snuggle with their sweeties as they enjoy liqueur-spiked coffee and choose from a selection of sinful desserts. A Wild

Animal Park expert is on hand to talk about reproductive behavior in the animal kingdom.

The tour is tasteful but guaranteed to put one in the mood.[3]

The Animal Park (part of the San Diego zoo) markets the cheap thrills of sexually tinged zoo voyeurism as an erotic aphrodisiac for spectators. As the publicists suggest, animal sexuality may inspire people on a date to kindle their own steamy adventures; but at the same time, things can become too close for comfort. If zoo animals provide potential models for human couples (perhaps, subliminally, inducements for 'natural,' unfettered sexuality), they can also divide rather than unite a courting couple if the pair respond differently to a given display – if, that is, animals project an aura of sexuality that highlights the two spectators' conflicting attitudes. Contrary to the romantically arousing backdrop that the San Diego Wild Animal Park promises, zoo stories by e. e. cummings and Alberto Moravia illustrate variants of bad dates at the zoo, which figure as an inexpedient backdrop for successful romantic interaction. cummings's Poem XVIII from *ViVa* (1931) tells of a Radcliffe student, Miss Gay, visiting New York, whom the narrator offers to entertain:

> when Miss G touched n.y. our skeleton stepped from his
>   cupboard
> gallantly offering to demonstrate the biggest best busiest city
> and presently found himself rattling for that well known suburb
> the bronx

where the pair visits the zoo.

> arriving in an exhausted condition,i purchased two bags of
>   lukewarm peanuts
> with the dime which her mama had generously provided
>   (despite courteous protestations)
> and offering Miss Gay one(which she politely refused)set
>   out gaily for the hyenas
> suppressing my frank qualms in deference to her not
>   inobvious perturbations

cummings's parodically starched clichés of social decorum (generous provision, courteous protestations, polite refusal, frank qualms, not inobvious perturbations) foreshadow a brewing gender conflict that will erupt at the zoo. The spectacle displayed to the dating couple proves especially inimical to polite etiquette, setting up the poem's flagrant peripeteia:

> unhappily,the denizens of the zoo were that day inclined to
> be uncouthly erotic
> more particularly the primates – from which with dignity
> square feet turned abruptly Miss Gay away:
> 'on the whole' (if you will permit a metaphor savouring
> slightly of the demotic)
> Miss Gay had nothing to say to the animals and the animals
> had nothing to say to Miss Gay

The date is a bust. Miss Gay rejects the animals (and thus her zoo date itself) apparently because the uncouthly erotic zoo denizens make her uncomfortable. The poem hints that her displeased escort regards Miss Gay's squeamish reaction to animal sexuality as evidence of a similarly reticent sexuality on her own part. Nothing remains but a period of awkward small talk until the couple can be disentangled:

> during our return voyage,my pensive companion dimly
> remarked something about '*stuffed*
> fauna' being 'very interesting' . . . we also discussed the
> possibility of rain . . .
> (328; author's emphasis and ellipses)

The man seems to have enjoyed his zoo visit perfectly well (except for Miss Gay's snit of propriety); he implicitly appreciates life in all its varied color, while she instead prefers dead taxidermic specimens. When they part, the man considers himself well done with his abortive date: as soon as Miss Gay vanishes into a YWCA, 'I thereupon loosened my collar / and dove for the nearest l.' In her absence, and apparently bitter because she has not played the dating game according to his script (having satisfied neither his ego nor his drives), he mocks her for being 'a certain Young Woman unacquainted with the libido.' In a tone implying castigation, he further charges her simply with 'pursuing a course of instruction at radcliffe college,cambridge,mass.' – that is, for educating herself above what he considers appropriate for her gender. Presumably, he regards her desexualized deficiency as a consequence of her being an intelligent woman; it sets her definitively apart from the life of pure, raw, natural libido that he and the zoo animals share. At the end of the poem, he bids good riddance to Miss Gay and the whole unfortunate zoo date with a final superfluous aspersion on stereotypically 'overeducated' women:

> i try if you are a gentleman not to sense something un poco putrido
> when we contemplate her uneyes safely ensconced in thick glass
>
> (328)

The narrator of Moravia's 'The Chimpanzee' (1959) is also on a first date, with a cashier named Gloria. 'My only worry was that I had very little money,' he thinks, regretting that he cannot afford to take her to a cinema or dance-hall. 'I had so little that all I was able to offer Gloria was a visit to the Zoo, and afterwards, at most, a cup of coffee standing in a bar' (8). 'But I have a passion for animals and I fooled myself into thinking that Gloria shared this passion with me,' he thinks – and in any case, if they are truly compatible, his lack of money should not matter. As soon as he sees her, however, he realizes from her outfit and her demeanor 'that I had made a mistake: this was not the girl for me' (8); still, he resigns himself to going through with the date. As he feared, she wants to dance or see a movie, but he resists, and instead:

> 'There's always the Zoo . . .' I began. But immediately, curling her lip, she replied: 'Like a servant-girl and a soldier on leave. Thank you very much, I think I'll go home.' And she made as if to go away. So then, almost hoping, secretly, that she really would go: 'All right,' I said, 'good-bye.' But now she was afraid I would leave her. 'Very well then,' she said, 'let's go there. There's nothing else for it.'
>
> (9; author's ellipsis)

So despite the unpromising arrangement, they head off on their zoo date. The event fulfills the inauspicious presentiments, as the two prove unceasingly combative. When the narrator buys two bags of nuts, he gives one to his date. '"What's this for?" she asked. "For the Monkeys." "Well, you can give them to them. I can't bear monkeys"' (9). At the elephant enclosure, he hands Gloria some grass to feed the animal:

> She did not want to do so, but then agreed unwillingly. The elephant put out its trunk, took the grass from Gloria's hand, curled back its trunk very slowly and put the grass into its mouth. Gloria was unable to restrain a cry of pleasure: 'Look, it's eating, it's eating!'; and for a moment I hoped that she was beginning to enjoy herself. But she immediately regretted what she had said. 'Just look!' she cried: 'I've dirtied my hands with mud . . . look at that!' And she wiped her hand, with a look of disgust, on my waterproof.
>
> (10; author's ellipsis)

When they go to look at the rhinoceros, which the narrator characterizes as ugly but with a nice character, Gloria responds 'contemptuously: "What ever can you find interesting about the creature? It looks as if it was all stitched together like a football"' (10). In the hippopotamus house, Gloria waits impatiently for the slow-moving animal to come out of the water, finally leaving before it has emerged and complaining about what she considers a wasted display. The narrator catches up with her at the bear cage, where he sees furry, peaceful sleeping creatures, but 'Gloria refused even to look at them because, she said, bears reminded her of a bearskin rug belonging to an old aunt of hers . . . She was even more disagreeable when we came to the gazelles, those highly attractive creatures, with their slim legs and beautiful black eyes and their curly horns. "Goats?" she said; "have I come here to look at goats?"' (11).

Fed up, Moravia's narrator finally decides to cut the date short, but now Gloria perversely determines to persevere, insisting on visiting the monkey house: she 'was now anxious to prove to me that she liked monkeys; but set about it with such an obvious effort that I should almost have preferred her to go on being as ill-mannered as before' (13). They regard the animals there as the story reaches its climax. It is probably not accidental for Moravia's plot design that the final animals looked at are the ones most closely resembling people; like cummings, Moravia features primates as a litmus test for human gender relations during a zoo date – perhaps representing an ironized mirror-image of ourselves.

> The chimpanzee on the swing came down and stood upright against the bars. He stretched out his mouth, which was black outside and pink inside, as if he were going to speak, and made a queer, yelping sound; and all the time he was scratching his paunch at the point where the hair was thinnest. Gloria held out a nut towards him but the chimpanzee did not even notice it. 'I wonder what's the matter with him?' said Gloria: 'doesn't he like nuts?' The chimpanzee gave a kind of whistle and walked off, bent and tired-looking, towards the back of the cage, then turned round all of a sudden, picked up a handful of some sort of filth from the floor and rushed back and hurled it in our faces.
>
> The only one of us to be hit was Gloria: I myself was standing behind her, and . . . two young men jumped nimbly to one side. It all happened in a second: Gloria looked at her beautiful red coat splashed from top to bottom; the two young men burst out laughing; Gloria cried: 'Curse the Zoo and curse these filthy animals,' and ran away sobbing. I started to follow her but she warned me off. 'Don't come near me! Go away! Leave me alone!' And so I gradually slackened my pace and finally stopped altogether. Gloria slipped through the gate and vanished.
>
> (13–14)

The narrator resumes his solitary musings, irritated and resentful of women's power to ruin men's potential pleasures. The story's final sentence, gratuitously nasty, resembles the narrator's kiss-off to the absent woman at the end of cummings's poem. Both men need to have the cutting last word after their dates have rejected and abandoned them: 'Ah, why is it that women have the power to make us happy, yet they don't know it, and they spoil everything with their abominable characters?' (14).

In 'The Chimpanzee,' as in cummings's Poem XVIII, the socialization of dating delineates the man's responsibility for where the couple go. In each case *he* has chosen the zoo, and at the end of both works, after the failed dates, the zoo seems to be the man's turf in a way that it is not the woman's. It is a place where he, more than she, belongs; more hospitable to his demeanor, and more hostile to hers. If the woman does not get literally shat upon at the zoo, as in Moravia's story, then she suffers a figurative approximation of that humiliation via character slander, as cummings's narrator dubs Miss Gay 'un poco putrido'; both works invite the reader to affirm that the filth-spattered woman has received her just desserts. These zoo stories suggest that whatever the man shows the woman on a conventional date somehow reflects his own performance; and whatever the woman looks at, she is at least indirectly looking at the man who brought her to the zoo.

Moravia and cummings evoke the zoo's situation as a sort of battleground, or dividing line, between men and women – perhaps metaphorically evocative of how zoos serve as a dividing line between people and other animals. The gender contentiousness becomes especially volatile when the musth of human courtship is in the air (exacerbated, or somehow weirdly skewed, by the coincident presence of animal musths: as if a chaotic interspecies hormonal fugue ricochets wildly around the compound). These zoo stories illuminate the difference between men's and women's perceptions of zoos, and the consequent negative impact that the gender gap exerts upon an inchoate romantic interlude. The zoo confirms the narrators' (and writers') apparent prejudices about women, evoking their reputed proclivities for prudishness, false modesty, petulant and arbitrary resistance to men's romantic drives. Poem XVIII and 'The Chimpanzee' confirm Sylvia Plath's expression in 'Zoo Keeper's Wife' of how a zoo can be a very different place for men and women, for the empowered and the disempowered.

Indeed, many zoo stories seem predicated on a cultural sense that zoos are somehow inherently 'manly': more attractive to men and more repellent to women. The zoo's semiotic resonances of aggressive adventure, patriarchal control/exploitation, and imperial bravado probably appeal more to men than women; perhaps women are more sensitive than men to the suffering of animals, and to the inauthenticity of a construct shaped by the stereotypically male sociocultural provenances of capture, imperial bravado, and elaborate testimony to physical mastery. Significantly gendered attitudes are discernible in numerous zoo stories. For instance, consider Jerry's unsociable, anti-domestic hostility from Albee's *The Zoo Story*, a play tinged with homosocial misogyny. In Stafford's 'At the Zoo,' constraining, autocratic zoo imagery metaphorically threatens the sisters' integrity and autonomy; the resonance of a zoo seems especially constrictive to young girls. The futile, driven machismo of the hunger artist's ego in Kafka's story seems specifically masculine, like Yank's blundering self-destructiveness in O'Neill's *The Hairy Ape*; zoos pointedly affect both characters' outlooks. Drabble's Jane Grey, in *The Waterfall*, manifests maternal instincts that resist zoos. Doyle's Paddy Clarke and Edgar from Doctorow's *World's Fair* express uneasily ambiguous feelings about zoos shaped by their awkward adolescent sense of 'proper' gender behavior: the socially prescribed masculinity script, dissuading acknowledgment of sensitivity, conflicts with more sympathetic boyish strains, resulting in their inability to situate themselves comfortably, definitively, with respect to the zoo. Zoos offer men sanctuary from women they perceive as threats, as in Garnett's *A Man in the Zoo* and *The Hairy Ape*. The personae in Hughes's 'The Jaguar' and Dickey's 'Encounter in the Cage Country' exhibit particularly masculine spectatorial stances of entitlement and heedlessness of the disempowered.

Zoo 78, Victor Burgin's photographic exhibition depicting Berlin, presents more variations on the theme of spectatorship, evoking blatantly exploitative and tawdry sexual zoo associations colored by voyeurism, oppression, and constraint. Like Leonard Woolf, Viktor Schklovsky, and Nicolás Guillén, Burgin represents zoos' politically allegorical resonances: for example, juxtaposing zoo cages with the Berlin Wall. *Zoo 78* features eight diptychs about 'the idea of enclosure,' comprising photographs of zoo animals in a prison-like compound, dwarfed and barely visible amid several sets of cages, obscured by signage; voyeuristic shots of a bored-looking nude woman posed degradingly in a commercial sex show; a scene of impassive patrons at a café counter, who look as displaced and decontextualized as if they were zoo animals; and forbidding images of a tattered, claustrophobic, industrially foreboding Cold War Berlin (which, like the zoo photograph, feature excessive and ominous signage). The photographs include an overlaid text with phrases describing various processes of surveillance, but the texts conspicuously mismatch the photographs on which they are printed. The photograph of the peep-show, for example, includes a caption describing a panopticon:

> The plan is circular: at the periphery, an annular building; at the centre, a tower pierced with many windows. The building consists of cells; each has two windows: one in the outer wall of the cell allows daylight to pass into it; another in the inner wall looks onto the tower, or rather is looked upon by the tower, for the windows of the tower are dark, and the occupants of the cells cannot know who watches, or if anyone watches. (72)

And on the zoo photograph:

> A circular revolving stage, within four walls of booths, the size of telephone boxes. A window in each booth looks onto the stage, but only when a coin is put in a slot, causing a blind to be withdrawn: 1 Minute – 1 Mark. The stage is lit, exposed; the cells are in darkness, their occupants concealed. (70)

Describing the thematic connections between all these images, Burgin explains:

> the centre, where the main railway-station is, is called 'Zoo' – Zoologischer Garten – the actual zoo is right alongside the station – and all around the same area are sex shows called 'peep-shows,' where a naked girl dances on a small revolving stage with booths all around it which you can enter and, by putting a coin in a slot, get a peep at the girl. Of course, not so far away there's the Wall with men peeping through slits in concrete boxes. I was interested in the possible links between these different forms of surveillance.
> (78)

Burgin's aesthetic fuses several themes associated with zoo spectatorship: the Foucauldian power dynamics, the voyeuristic perspective, the zoo as a venue for symbolically playing out issues of human sexuality – straightforwardly or ironically. The disparate scope of images in *Zoo 78* suggests that the sensibility the zoo represents (or exudes) transcends zoos, manifesting a milieu, an ethos, detectable in numerous diversely oppressive situations. If Burgin's 1978 exhibit is identified as '*Zoo 78*,' then presumably there exists also a Zoo 77, a Zoo 79, and so forth. The misplaced textual descriptions of surveillance make the point that they are all interchangeable – variations on a theme. Burgin's exhibition argues for the importance of appreciating spectatorship's manifold range of apparitions. Most important, his photographs explicitly identify the central perspective of this zoo sensibility as being associated with his camera, with the viewer's stance, with the relationship of the seer to the seen. The activity of watching may seem innocent and harmless, but Burgin's vision situates it as archly powerful, ominous, deadening – an element of totalitarianism. Burgin does not elucidate or prove the zoo's specific implication in these dark forces; he simply observes, suggestively but vaguely, 'possible links between these different forms of surveillance' that his photographs depict. His work points toward a network of relations growing out of the spectatorial paradigm, wherein his titular zoo represents the overarching exemplar of a nefarious milieu.

Julio Cortázar's 'Axolotl' (1967) demonstrates metaphorically the dangers of watching – of getting too close and falling through the looking glass (or in this case, the aquarium tank glass): spectators who see too much get caught. At the end of Kafka's 'A Hunger Artist,' the audience hovers enthralled outside the cage: on the verge of becoming implicated in, or infected by, ignominies comparable to what the creature on display experiences. 'Axolotl' picks up from that point, and also recalls the sensibility from Jacques Tourneur's film *Cat People*, where a person obsessed with a zoo animal becomes somehow fused with that animal – interconnected, even interchangeable.

'There was a time when I thought a great deal about the axolotls,' begins the narrator of Cortázar's surrealist story. 'I went to see them in the aquarium at the Jardin des Plantes and stayed for hours watching them, observing their immobility, their faint movements. Now I am an axolotl' (3). Almost immediately, 'I knew that we were linked, that something infinitely lost and distant kept pulling us together' (4). As he watches, the narrator perceives the misery of the animals' constraint, seeing the 'axolotls huddled on the wretched narrow (only I can know how narrow and wretched) floor of moss and stone in the tank' (4).

His empathy only makes him feel guiltier about watching them. 'Disconcerted, almost ashamed, I felt it a lewdness to be peering at these silent and immobile figures heaped at the bottom of the tank' (4). While he perceives that his spectatorship, in some way, involves the pain of those animals he finds so compelling, he is nevertheless powerless to stop watching: trapped, as if obsessed or addicted. (He might have profited from the insight Russell Hoban's character Neaera, in *Turtle Diary*, reaches at the aquarium: 'The fish all look bored to death but of course fish aren't meant to be looked at closely, will not bear close examination' (30).)

The narrator finds the axolotls beautiful – 'I saw a rosy little body, translucent (I thought of those Chinese figurines of milky glass) . . . what obsessed me was the feet, of the slenderest nicety' (5) – illustrating how zoo spectators may *intend* the most eloquent enterprise of aesthetic appreciation: savoring beautifully sublime facets of nature. But his train of thought undercuts a stance of respectful, imaginative homage to natural beauty: 'And then I discovered its eyes, its face. Inexpressive features, with no other trait save the eyes, two orifices, like brooches, wholly of transparent gold, lacking any life but looking, letting themselves be penetrated by my look' (5). The spectator's experience deteriorates from his contemplation of the pure, delicate splendor of biological existence. His description of the fish as inert and insensate (inexpressive . . . transparent . . . lacking any life) belies his initial sensitivity to their attractiveness. The simile comparing the animals' eyes to gold brooches invokes a reference to a mineral that has become appropriated as the consummate currency of human cultural power: something that represents not nature but human exploitation and usurpation of natural beauty. (Imaginative cultural imagery rarely extols gold in its natural condition: it acquires its allure only after it has been mined, smelted, artificed – only after humankind has transformed it almost unrecognizably.) The spectator perceives (or fantasizes about) the lizard acquiescing passively to his appropriation, his control. A golden lifeless mass is 'penetrated *by my look*' – indicating its submissive vulnerability. Power permeates Cortázar's praxis of spectatorship: to see is to penetrate, to violate, to determine the subject's condition.

The narrator watches, with the most extreme intensity of attention possible. He reaps the rewards of spectatorship, and eventually, more than he bargained for – he begins to get sucked in: 'Once in a while a foot would barely move, I saw the diminutive toes poise mildly on the moss. It's that *we* don't enjoy moving a lot, and the tank is so cramped' (5, emphasis added). He slips, accidentally using the wrong pronoun: first-person plural instead of third-person (-animal?). The more he stares, the more he realizes how much he resembles them: 'Above all else, their eyes obsessed me . . . their handsome eyes so similar to our own' (6); and 'They were not human beings, but I had found in no animal such a profound relation to myself' (7). As Cortázar narrows in on the essence of spectatorship – intensively scrutinizing the spare, elemental tableau that his story situates, of a man outside a tank staring at a reptile within – a reversal becomes gradually apparent: 'The golden eyes continued burning with their soft, terrible light; *they continued looking at me* from an unfathomable depth which made me dizzy' (6, emphasis added). And the act of looking, the narrator intimately realizes – all the more keenly as he begins to become the spectatorial subject – is keenly loaded, dangerous. '"You eat them alive with your eyes, hey," the guard said, laughing . . . What he didn't notice was that it was they devouring me slowly with their eyes, in a cannibalism of gold' (7).

The story's power, and danger, derive from its eventual uncertainty about exactly who watches whom. Cortázar challenges the zoo spectator's traditional position of absolute privileged supremacy. Turnabout is fair play: the watchers in Cortázar's fantastic story become the watched, in a Möbius-strip version of spectatorship. His point is that spectatorship, which he depicts as evil in its exploitative consumption of an objectified animal, debases the watcher as well as the watched. The culmination of spectatorship, as Cortázar sees it – the most acute condition of watching something, visually devouring the subject, obsessively craving to see the animal in captivity – is to become what one is looking at. The narrator exerts spectatorship so fiercely that he becomes the subject of his own visual subjection. This narcissistic strain implies that zoos are more about people than animals: it is in some way as if this spectator is finally looking at himself – seeking the spectacular beauty of life, he ultimately discovers an incarnation of his own reflection to be the most stunning image of all.

Cortázar's zoo story suggests a disturbing allegory: temporarily, zoos celebrate people's power over animals – our *penetrating* ability to keep them and watch them. Human control over zoo animals celebrates an imperial relation toward the realm of nature, and its subordination to our whims. But in the long term, a human society that expresses its relationship to the natural world via the institution of zoos risks foundering amid our imperious ecological ethos. At the apex of modern Western culture, we act as if we control everything in the world; but the tables will turn. As the bumper sticker puts it, Nature bats last. Eventually, people risk finding ourselves victims of the lifestyles and habits we have enjoyed (of which zoo spectatorship is one isolated symbol, or symptom). Indeed, by many accounts, we are already beginning to suffer the toll of a reckless exploitation of nature; we may become as disempowered, in a biotic meltdown, as the creatures we now revel over in the zoo.

In the narrator's waning final moments of privilege as a spectator, he imagines the axolotls' cry: 'Save us, save us.' (7) The irony is thick: it is still not too late for him. If only the spectator (and by implication, I posit, all zoo spectators) could appreciate the moral import of what he is seeing in the zoo; if only he (*we*) could *truly* empathize with the animals; if only he could perceive the dangers of zoos. But he cannot, so he is sentenced, in the mode of Dantean *contrapasso*, to suffer what he has consigned others to. (I suggest that *contrapasso* is not just a literary motif, but a law of nature.)

Finally, Cortázar depicts the narrator's metamorphosis from man to amphibian, from spectator to specimen in the tank, as inevitable – the necessary culmination of the aquarium construct, of spectatorship, 'that had to occur':

> there was nothing strange in what happened. My eyes were attempting once more to penetrate the mystery of those eyes of gold without iris, without pupil. I saw from very close up the face of an axolotl immobile next to the glass. No transition and no surprise, I saw my face against the glass, I saw it on the outside of the tank, I saw it on the other side of the glass. Then my face drew back and I understood.
>
> (7–8)[4]

The narrator's transformation into a zoo exhibit resembles the denouement of *The Hairy Ape*, when Yank becomes like the escaped zoo animal to whose place he was relegated. However, in Cortázar's zoo story, the human–animal exchange occurs not just spatially but physically as well: 'He was outside the aquarium . . . I was an axolotl,' or, more specifically, 'prisoner in the body of an axolotl, metamorphosed into him with my human mind intact, buried alive in an axolotl' (8). The story ends with the narratorial consciousness, now stuck in the aquarium tank, watching a man outside the tank who watches the axolotls. 'He returned many times, but he comes less often now' (9). Who is 'he' – a shade of the former human self now trapped in the reptile's body? A replacement spectator, the next generation of exploitative watcher-cum-victim? The last words of 'Axolotl' identify 'him' with the story's author: 'in this final solitude to which he no longer comes, I console myself by thinking that perhaps he is going to write a story about us, that, believing he's making up a story, he's going to write all this about axolotls' (9).

'Axolotl' illuminates a tension between zoo and zoo story – one that, I find, infuses most zoo stories. Cortázar's final frame pronouncedly privileges the zoo story over the zoo. This zoo devours the integrity of all – whether caged animal or human spectator – inside its inviolable clutches. It might (to invoke Dante again) fittingly bear on its gates the legend from the gates of hell: Abandon all hope, you who enter here. The only antidote to the existentially vacant despair festering at the end of this parable lies in the writer's presence: 'he's going to write all this about axolotls' (as, obviously, he just has). Like a missive smuggled out of prison, this story embodies the only possible transcendence of the subjugation suffered by those stuck inside. It is the zoo story alone that can attempt to make sense of, or order, or mediate, or expose, the miasma Cortázar describes. What happens in the zoo here is nightmarish, deadening; but what happens in the zoo story is at least decipherable, comprehensible – even clever, neat, symmetric, vital in its artifice – within, and by recourse to, certain conventions of avant-garde narratology. However much the *fabula* (i.e., what happens in Cortázar's zoo *per se*) is unsettling, horrible, deadening, ineffable, the *sjuzet* – the narrative working of the *fabula* – flourishes within a rich tradition of imaginative expression. The zoo story often posits a kind of contest between itself and the zoo, and – unsurprisingly – here, as often, the zoo story wins.

The rampant dysfunctionality surrounding Cortázar's spectator invites further attention to the psychiatric condition of voyeurism, which resonantly underlies the trope of spectatorship. Mass zoo spectatorship relates to the clinical occurrence of voyeurism in a way that cannot quite be literally categorized as such, according to the technical psychiatric definition; but the spectator is a voyeur in much more than simply a metaphorical sense. In 'Representation, Voyeurism, and the Vacant Point of View,' Joel Rudinow establishes a model that elucidates a potent strain of voyeurism inherent in spectatorship. He delineates a network of symptoms and sensibilities common to voyeurism and spectatorship, arguing 'that the consumption of representations generally is voyeuristic' (179), and advancing a paradigm I find neatly applicable to the 'consumption of representations' (i.e., spectatorship) at zoos.

Rudinow's definition of what he terms a 'voyeuristic project' resembles my characterization of zoo spectatorship. 'The voyeur seeks a spectacle, the revelation of the object of his interest, that something or someone should be open to his inspection and contemplation; *but no reciprocal revelation or openness is conceded*' (176, author's emphasis). This criterion applies to zoos: animals are there for people to look at, but, as Berger writes, the look is not returned. Zoo stories rarely describe a reciprocity of watching: instead, they depict caged animals ignoring the public scornfully (Smith's 'The Zoo'); or offending spectators, as if to discourage further watching (cummings's Poem XVIII, Vonnegut's 'Welcome to the Monkey House,' Edgar's 'The Lion and Albert'); or serving as impassively victimized subjects incapable of exchanging glances (Johnson's *Cries from the Mammal House*, Babel's 'The Beast Grows Silent,' the beginning of Cortázar's 'Axolotl,' and Rilke's 'The Panther' – where the animal becomes literally blind). Berger asserts that spectators want their looks returned, while Rudinow suggests they do not; but both cases finally demonstrate a lack of reciprocity in the viewing arrangement. I regard the zoo's fundamental, imperial inequity to be its absolute establishment of a *one-way* power-based relationship between viewer and subject, which is undesirable in and of itself, and, more dangerously, sets the tone for manifold other human practices that exploit animals and nature based upon principles of non-reciprocity.

'The voyeur understands his act of viewing as an act of aggression, specifically invasion,' Rudinow continues, 'and accordingly as something ideally to avoid suffering himself' (176). The invasiveness of bona fide voyeurs is apparent – they look at things (people's personal and private behavior) that the victims would not wish to be seen. The parallel invasiveness of zoo spectators features in copious zoo stories: in Neaera's admission of guilt about watching zoo animals in Hoban's *Turtle Diary*, and in the extensive meditation on his invasiveness Cortázar's spectator conducts in 'Axolotl.' Voyeuristic invasiveness is a kind of aggression, Rudinow asserts, and – from Albee's Jerry to O'Neill's Yank – manifestly aggressive zoogoers are legion. I believe at least some zoo spectators, like participants in Rudinow's more generic voyeuristic projects, *do* indeed understand the aggressive, invasive elements of their behavior. Indeed, this consciousness may even increase the experience's flattering appeal. Many activities in a society predicated upon the ethos of capitalist/imperialist exploitation accrue cachet in proportion to the ensuing toll borne by others.

The consciousness of aggression in spectatorship/voyeurism leads Rudinow to argue:

> viewing is understood by the voyeur to be destructive, to spoil the view. I believe this understanding to be based on the voyeur's profoundly accurate perception that to treat something as a voyeuristic spectacle is to ruin it for other more fundamental human purposes: it cannot be touched, one cannot be touched by it, one cannot reveal oneself to it. In general, one cannot enter into any relationship with it which is mutual, reciprocal, or symmetrical, insofar and so long as one treats it voyeuristically.
>
> (176)

If we find this assessment an apt approximation of zoo spectatorship, we must recognize how impossible it is for zoos to fulfill their nominal goals of facilitating natural appreciation and ecological ethics. Some zoo stories explicitly delineate the destructiveness in which spectators are implicated, as in Murakami's 'The Zoo Attack,' where the soldiers' sole function as zoo visitors is to kill every animal, or Lispector's 'The Buffalo,' featuring a woman thinking 'of the carnage she had come in search of in the zoological gardens . . . she would have destroyed these monkeys leaping around inside the cages,' she fantasizes, 'with fifteen sharp bullets' (147–8). But even in the absence of such extreme spectatorial destruction, many zoo stories suggest that people who look at animals in zoos do not leave the visual subject unaffected, uninjured: viewers somehow corrupt what they view. Spectators regarding a herd of Asian animals in their local zoo see, in addition to the animals present, immediate physical/visual confirmation that they have spoiled a comparable view in Asia. Cutting-edge zoos pride themselves on offering *recreations* of natural biotas; semantically, recreating implies having destroyed.

Rudinow asserts that the voyeur manifests a 'paradoxical care for the spectacle which he would destroy' (177), which explains why the zoos I characterize as such retrograde institutions are nevertheless enveloped with a thick discourse of solicitous concern on the parts of patrons and keepers. The workings of voyeurism, Rudinow explains, involve voyeurs' 'attempts not only to consume and destroy the spectacle, but also, and in the same gaze, to preserve it as a continuing object of view' (176–7). His theory illuminates the apparent paradox of strong public support for zoos that coexists with our destruction of the natural world – whether willfully and sadistically, or through benign neglect, laziness and selfishness – at an unprecedented pace. Zoos capitalize on spectators' commitment to lovingly preserving what they simultaneously destroy. Indeed, as I have suggested earlier, token support for preservation may be a way of repressing awareness of, or alleviating guilt about, large-scale ecological desecration.

Voyeurs, finally, have 'not a chance of gaining satisfaction' (178), Rudinow writes, however determinedly they embrace their voyeuristic project. This seems instinctively true of psychiatrically certified deviant voyeurs: at least we (the nondeviant) would like to believe that such invasive, withdrawn, antisocial, nonreciprocal relationships as voyeurs crave cannot prove gratifying. Cortázar's spectator offers one example of the zoo voyeur's absolute frustration; and I believe he stands metaphorically for many more spectators in zoo stories and zoos alike. Spectators may look as intently as possible, in zoos that are as good as they can be, and still the experience may well prove unfulfilling. This strain infuses zoo stories consistently, explaining the sordid, unpleasant proclivities that repeatedly tend to indict zoos. As evidence of the voyeur's constant frustration, Rudinow cites 'the multitude of genuine innovations and finicky adjustments which continue to be made in the devices and settings for voyeuristic observation and in the descriptions and formulations of what constitutes the voyeur's satisfaction' (178). The voyeurs' view, their experience, is never quite good enough: they can never see as much as they want for as long as they want, or derive from the sight as much pleasure as they want, so they fidget to grasp more of what continues to elude satisfaction. And keepers tinker with innovations and adjustments, trying to make zoos better places to see more authentic, appealing, stimulating, 'natural' vistas of animals. The view in the zoo is not good enough, and never can be; but keepers and patrons obsessively continue striving simply (and impossibly) to establish a more satisfying spectatorial experience.

There are other ways of watching animals besides in zoos or in their native habitats: two popular modes are television programs and Internet sites. The genre of nature shows dates back even before the advent of television – in the 1930s Marlin Perkins hosted a live radio nature show ('until the day he brought on an electric eel that got a little overexcited and sent a charge through him, his assistant, and the microphone, blowing out the entire network' (Siebert, 'Artifice', 47–8)). In the early days of television, Charles Siebert writes, 'most people's idea of a nature show was still *The American Sportsman*: Curt Gowdy and Mickey Mantle duck hunting on Saturday afternoons' (46); such shows, and even Perkins's later *Mutual of Omaha's Wild Kingdom* series, featured what Siebert calls 'television's cowboy naturalists' (47). Hosts chased, trapped, and often physically grappled with the animals they filmed, sometimes shooting them with tranquilizers; the television personalities who mediated the viewer's relationship to the animals were very interactive with them, in a way I consider inappropriately intrusive: hindering an understanding of how animals live when people are not around them; conveying an undesirable sense of how people should behave toward animals; reinforcing the habits of what Jim Mason calls a dominionist sensibility toward nature.

A rich tradition of nature programming has grown out of these early ventures (comprising a significant portion of American Public Broadcasting, and a cable network, the Discovery Channel, that devotes a considerable amount of its schedule to productions about animals and nature). Perkins's successors include Jacques Cousteau in the 1970s – 'our first existentialist naturalist,' as Siebert terms him, featuring 'the hushed, somber, guilt-tinged tone that has become the hallmark of nature-show narration' (45) – and 'today's definitive nature-show host' Sir David Attenborough, 'escorting us like a knowledgeable and omnipresent museum guide, his voice respectfully trailing off into gaspy whispers whenever he gets very close to the proceedings' (49). Another mainstay of the genre comes from National Geographic productions, which embody the vintage Smithsonian naturalistic discourse of precise, encyclopedic coverage.

I find documentaries about wild animals potentially appealing – many are of high quality, educationally profuse, sensitive to a range of issues about animals' lives and interrelated ecological concerns regarding the shared world of people and other species. They can help offer viewers exposure to animals' worlds in ways that I believe zoos cannot. At the same time, nature shows remain vulnerable to many of the criticisms (or close variants thereof) that I launch against zoos.

Cliff Tarpy, who advocates new and improved zoos (as he regards them), credits television with uplifting spectators' standards. He quotes a zoo director who says: 'In the '70s you could see a shift in the public's attitude toward zoos. Wildlife shows on television were a big influence. They showed you animals running free in the wild, their behavior, the importance of ecosystems' (11). This zoo director is probably correct that nature shows have made spectators more intolerant of the most egregious zoo conditions; and I regard this as a point in their favor, illustrating how they enlighten viewers about desirable and undesirable ways of representing and experiencing nature. But on the other hand, I worry that Tarpy's scenario coopts the ideal consequences of ecological education: that is, I would hope such awareness would lead viewers to oppose not just 'bad' zoos but all zoos. Indeed, I think some people do respond to nature shows with a wholehearted dismissal of the approach to nature embodied in zoo culture. Personally, as I began to find zoos increasingly unpalatable, I turned to nature shows; finding it possible to satisfy my interest in wild animals through this outlet (among others) coincided with my conviction that zoos were not necessary or even adequate providers of natural education. Zookeepers, like the proprietors of any mass-oriented industry with a long-term record of success, cannily note changes in the winds among target audiences, and reposition/repackage themselves to maintain their market share. The phenomenon Tarpy describes – zoos making themselves look a bit more like animals' natural worlds as nature programming makes people increasingly familiar with natural biotas, and aware of how vastly they differ from zoo cages – represents an example of such consumeristic adaptation geared toward the industry's survival. Nevertheless, I think that continued exposure to effective nature shows can lead audiences beyond tolerating old zoos with a new facade. Television alone cannot be a universal panacea for artificial, convenient misrepresentations of nature – the education must occur along several fronts; but nature documentaries can offer one effective effort in this regard.

Two compelling critiques come from Siebert and Steve Baker. Baker's *Picturing the Beast* examines numerous incidences of what he calls the manipulative and inauthentic appropriations of animals' integrity that inhere in the semiotics of cultural representation. One false type of animal representation, he argues, is the nature show, in which

> the desired truth or reality of the animal seems to elude the viewer, forever slipping out from the edge of the image. A television reviewer writes wistfully: 'Wildlife programmes have grown to become such a televisual industry that . . . you can watch more than a dozen over any seven days. All beautiful, all leaving you frustrated at the brief and distant glimpses you get, at best, of the real thing.' Umberto Eco says much the same thing about the role of the realistic fake wild animal in Disneyland. The crucial thing is its 'obedience to the program': it is there when viewers want to see it, and it stays there.
> (194)

Although television representations of wild animals offer viewers close, insightful approximations of animals' lives, Baker argues, their problem

> is that we can hardly know in any very meaningful way what we are seeing (or rather, merely glimpsing). Tim Ingold puts it plainly: 'for the Western television viewer, observing the antics of a strange and exotic animal on his screen, he might as well be watching a work of science fiction as a nature documentary.'
> (194)

Siebert, making arguments resembling mine against zoos, rejects television nature shows because he believes they domesticate and distort the real world. (Indeed, he notes at least one example of an explicit connection between nature shows and zoos, recounting an episode of *Wild Kingdom* from the early 1960s in which Perkins 'is thrashing about in a South American river with an anaconda around his neck, his face going red as he tries to get the snake into a burlap bag for some zoo in Europe' (46–7).) Siebert objects to an unnatural convenience: 'to sit here in front of a nature show is to have one's ego fed shamelessly,' he writes, 'via the distilled essence of that original place whose indifference and gradualness we can no longer abide' (48). That is, nature is too slow and undramatic for the modern temperament; the television-age sensibility demands that nature conform to the narratives, the pace, the style, that audiences expect of any stimuli emanating from television sets. The discourse of nature shows, Siebert writes, is 'above all else, extravagant animal opera, dramatizing, scoring, voicing in human terms the vast backdrop of inhuman action' (43). Actual and televised nature 'have little to do with each other. The woods are so wide, old, and slow as to be dismissive of me . . . and what I might wish and wait to see. The show, by contrast, is rapid, focused, and framed, a potent distillation of someone else's waiting designed precisely for me' (44). The profusion of shows has made us 'a race of armchair naturalists,' and even when we do venture into the wilds to visit 'the places and creatures whose stories we've watched,' what we have seen on television conditions our expectations: 'We go as nature tourists . . . expectant of seeing those characters, as though visiting the various sets of a Universal Studios theme park' (50). Just as I consider zoos, with their artifice and contrivance, inauthentic because they are a subset of human culture, Siebert accuses television nature shows of lacking their own integrity and being a subset of television culture.

A modern nature show offers 'a clean and well-lighted simultaneity of the unseen; of things you'd never see in a thousand walks in the wild,' while nature's wonders themselves are remarkable 'for precisely the reasons a nature show cannot convey. It is the mostly hidden and non-reflective enormity of their life forces, behemoth and belittling, that has most to show and tell us' (48). Siebert parallels my main objection to zoos when he argues that television transforms real nature into *our* nature, distanced and distinct from the original: 'The more facts we compile about the animals' days, the more human the tales we tell of them. We've come so far from actual nature' (45).

But finally, while I cannot wholly dismiss Siebert's provocative and well-reasoned objections, I consider nature shows much the lesser of two evils. It is crucial for people to learn about animals and their natural settings, their native worlds, and it is both unreasonable and undesirable to expect that this understanding could be achieved at first-hand on a mass scale. Some sort of sociocultural mediation, therefore, is necessary, and such mediation should be as unobtrusive as possible; if representations are destined to distort reality in some way, they should strive to do so as little as possible. If the process of interacting with animals must occur within a system of commercial capitalism, it should strive to be as little as possible tainted by this. (In America, nearly all nature shows appear on public broadcasting stations or low-key cable outlets, rather than the big business networks; those who create and produce nature shows are at the low-status end of the television and film industry; financial support for such documentaries comes from government grants, public-interest foundations, and ecologically attuned educational and advocacy organizations, rather than mainstream commercial interests.)

Zoos are one response to people's need and desire to know animals, and nature shows are another; I side with nature shows. Both are artificial constructs, profoundly ensconced in human discourse: but I believe the documentaries offer a greater potential for people to understand how animals really exist (while doing less damage than zoos to animals and their habitats). Animals shown on nature shows almost always appear *in situ*, behaving naturally, and – in today's shows, which have evolved beyond Perkins's wrestling matches – depicted in a condition unmediated by human contact (or, if human proximity *is* involved, the implications of such proximity are explored, instead of ignored and repressed as in zoos). If an element of dominionist bravado remains ('Look at the amazing places a few people can visit and document with cameras') it is much less dangerous than what zoos celebrate ('Look how many millions of "us"; can enjoy easy access to something we have spirited away from "there"'). Granting Siebert the shortcomings and distortions inherent in the neat editing, the musical background, the contextualizing 'nature voice' with its cultural biases, and the artificial concentration of action, I still finally believe that benefits outweigh drawbacks. Television shows about animals explicitly acknowledge the distance between us and them, unlike zoos, which pretend that animals are very close to us. Certainly it could be argued that television sucks its viewers into a vicarious fantasy world where armchair spectators are induced to pretend they can transport themselves magically to all the places the documentaries show, and are, even more than zoo visitors, in a position of ultimate (and delusory) mastery. But I think that for most viewers, the literal inaccessibility of what documentaries show is clearly presented and understood, in a way that the zoo fudges, finesses.

Television depicts the difference between the animals' world and ours. Nature shows teach people about animals, usually in great detail, with careful scientific and ecological information of weighty content, which dwarfs the zoo's main educational medium, signs. One of the chief functions zoos invoke to justify their existence is arousing audiences' sympathies for the plight of endangered species and habitats, and spurring financial/sociopolitical motivation to support conservationism. I believe television shows can accomplish ecological advocacy as effectively as zoos – probably even more so, since the medium of television is so conducive to promotion.

But if television seems to offer a palatable technocultural medium for watching animals, the heir apparent to its media prominence – the computer – offers less sanguine prospects. Internet sites and CD-ROMs offer a new postmodern twist to reading zoos: watching, via the isolated distance of the computer terminal, something that isn't there. Computers promise ultimate control over the subject; compared with zoos, they distance viewers even further from animals, but compensate with more (and instant) data and knowledge. Animals are trapped not in a cage, but in the net, which represents the logical consequence, and at the same time the *reductio ad absurdum*, of zoo spectatorship. Wild animals are infinitely decontextualized, to the point where spectators enjoy complete access to what is physically absent. Viewers retain cultural/cognitive mastery over animals, without the smell of shit.

In Sue Townsend's *The Queen and I* (1992), the splendid high-tech vacuousness of a computerized zoo appears in a brief zoo story tableau. The novel presents a comic prophecy of Britain in the near future, after the Queen has been sacked and a populist Republican government transforms the country into a place less like traditional merrie England and more like the rest of the homogeneous modern global village. One of the innovations in this brave new world:

> The Council were investing their money in buying a windswept thousand-acre site on the outskirts of town where they planned to build a theme park: a zoo without animals. Instead of the mess and the smell and the necessity to feed real wild animals, the Council had been persuaded by a private company to build a series of huge windowless edifices. Inside, electronic imagery and sophisticated sound systems were to replicate the continents of the world and their indigenous animals.
>
> (107)

Townsend's virtual zoo is not, alas, a fictive fantasy: numerous real ventures are exploring the potential for computer animals to augment or replace zoo animals. A 1995 program launched by Atlanta's Fernbank Museum of Natural History, described by the chairman of its Board of Trustees, L. L. Gellerstedt III, promises 'enormous potential ... in the use of interactive TV broadcasts with schools across Georgia ... that will benefit the children of Georgia. Zoo Atlanta, for example, has an interactive program that is beaming lions and tigers and bears into dozens of classrooms on a weekly basis.'[5] The Internet, it appears, promises to broaden the range and scope of zoos. (To undertake just a quick semiotic analysis of the museum chairman's discourse: I find it interesting, and probably not irrelevant, that when he describes the panoply of computer zoo offerings his catalogue of animals is borrowed from Dorothy in *The Wizard of Oz*. Media worlds collide: as Gellerstedt unintentionally implies, his computer zoo probably *is* closer to the Technicolor fantasy entertainment universe of cowardly lions than to the world of nature; his lions and tigers and bears are more creatures of a make-believe Internet–Hollywood–Munchkinland forest than a real one.)

In 1992, Software Toolworks produced a computer program called 'The San Diego Zoo Presents ... The Animals! A True Multimedia Experience.' A review from *CD-ROM Professional*[6] gives a sense of how it works and what people expect of new technology for watching animals. Note how heavily computer discourse circumscribes this spectatorial experience, resulting in exponentially obscure subjects: animals are already overwhelmed by the zoo milieu, which is in turn further overwhelmed by the computer milieu.

> The Main Menu screen of Animals! is a colorful map of the entire zoo. By moving the mouse over various sections and pressing the right mouse button, a brief summary of that section of the zoo will appear . . . The Main Menu shows the various 'biomes' that represent the world's ten bioclimactic zones. Other Main Menu features are the Research Center, Library, Tours, Stories, and Information . . . The Biome sections are interesting and filled with information, pictures, video segments, and sounds . . . Each Biome contains a number of exhibits that can be explored by choosing the Jump to Exhibit button on the Navigational Palette . . . Within the exhibit you may be able to choose an Information Profile, A Kid's Planet (an easier overview of the exhibit for younger users), Facts & Figures, or a Text Topic. Icons of a camera, world, speaker, and movie clip provide users a visual way to open pictures, maps, sounds, and movies related to the exhibit.
>
> (170)

What the reviewer identifies as the software's flaws are all computer- (rather than content-) oriented: its major drawback

> is that the linking of multimedia elements (text, graphics, sound, motion, pictures) seems to be lacking. Most of the program is extremely linear in nature and proceeds page-by-page instead of being 'linked' so that a more interactive experience can be had by the user. A major oversight is the lack of a comprehensive index to the disc so that you can find any animal you want. There is an alphabetical section for finding animals, but there is no cross-referencing.
>
> (169)

The attributes of the animals themselves, and the effectiveness of the program's natural education, do not rate any comment. The computer-age virtual zoo's appeal is expressed and measured in computer specifications: linked multimedia text and graphics, and so forth. When spectators look at a terminal, they are watching a computer program – not a zoo, and not animals.

Today's cyberspectator need not go from cage to cage to glimpse animals; instead, one simply goes from screen to screen. The epistemological fantasy of control over distant wild animals and their provenances was once expressed in simple physical and literal terms, as when Sir Stamford Raffles brought his Sumatran monkeys to London as proof that England had subdued the Orient. Now the fantasy takes the form of net surfing, pointing and clicking, linking, snarfing, configuring, loading and reloading. In the computer age, the enterprise of reading zoos must become ever more attuned to technical language, terms, keystrokes and keywords, hardware and software: the language of human discourse (disintegrating into computer discourse) as a mediating force privileged over animals. More than ever before, zoos are about people – our systems of processing information, experiential habits, technological fetishes, cutting edge high-resolution color screens and sound systems and fantasies of infinite instant global data transmission – rather than animals. Spectators cannot read a virtual zoo if they are not well-versed in the proper computer syntax; if they type in the wrong commands, they get no animal.

Another reaction to the San Diego Zoo software comes from Laurent Belsie,[7] who compares and contrasts the actual zoo with its electronic offshoot (which had sold over *1 million copies* and was forthcoming in an updated and expanded version: the phenomenon of computer spectatorship is far from negligible). He sees the two realms interacting complementarily. The real zoo obviously offers real sensory experiences –

> Just one splash from an aviary's waterfall, and you'll never try to compare CD-ROM virtual reality with the real thing. 'There's a lot of interesting stuff at the San Diego Zoo that's not going to get captured on a CD-ROM,' says James Coggins, a computer-science professor ... 'You won't smell anything that is there. You won't realize just how tall that giraffe really is.'

– but the software has its own virtues: 'While the real zoo was more enjoyable, I nevertheless found it was far easier to learn from the CD-ROM. No matter how many plaques one might read, the information flowing from the virtual zoo was far more ample and accessible. And that is the point of virtual reality. It is not intended to replace the real world. It's designed to give people a better way of interacting.' As Belsie presents it, computers aid the acquisition of knowledge, data, science. The conquest of ignorance, which the zoo initiates and the computer database greatly enhances, implies a kind of omnipotent control of nature – reiterating the processes inherent in the earliest formulations of European zoos during the imperial age, when visiting a zoo signified power over the subaltern provinces of primitivism.

Beyond the popular San Diego Zoo software, the Internet offers everything anyone ever wanted to know about zoos and more. Or, perhaps, less. It may seem contradictory to laud television nature shows for providing a profusion of information while castigating cybermedia for the same thing. The difference is that television nature shows dissociate themselves from the institutional clutches of zoos and transcend the constriction of what zoos offer (animals in a subordinate perspective, cast as a subset of human culture). But computer animal information is, in a nutshell, glitzy pap, with little sense of awareness of the ethical foundations and implications of its knowledge base. There is no evidence, as there is in television nature programming, that the purveyors of data have thought very deeply about where the information is coming from and going to – how it is conveyed, what it should teach, how its audience might ideally use it, and how it will improve the environmental consciousness of the community it reaches. Instead, its discourse embodies the random incontinence of many Internet communicators. Web site creators realize that they can reach a new and larger audience via computer, and that seems to be their sole motivating energy: more spectators!

To give just a sample of the pickings: the American Zoo and Aquarium Association's Home Page lists (at this writing) over 100 sites about specific zoos. The world of animals is literally at one's fingertips, from Bardu, Norway's Polar Zoo to Albany, Georgia's Chehaw Wild Animal Park to San Jose's Happy Hollow Park and Zoo. (The panoply of appellations suggests changing currents, or uncertainties, in the identity of zoos, as evidenced in the Bronx Zoo's nominal transformation into a Wildlife Conservation Park. A web site lists Victoria, Australia's Healesville Sanctuary; Torino, Italy offers Zoo in the Wild; Verona, Italy has Parco Natura Viva; Stockholm offers the Skansen Open-Air

Museum and Zoological Gardens. Broxbourne, England, lists – a modern-day Eden? – the Paradise Wildlife Park.) Related world-wide web pages posted in the WWW Virtual Library for Zoos range from soup to nuts: Aquaria in Japan, DeerNet, Zany Zoo cartoon strip, Arctic Wildlife, Butterfly Web Site, Dog Related Web Sites, Cyber-Pet, Attwater's Prairie Chicken, Laurence Monroe Klauber Memorial Rattlesnake Homepage, World Wide Raccoon Web, Primate Gallery, Sounds of the 4-H Farm, Great Penguin Count on Gabo Island, Tiger Tails, Skunk and Opossum Page ('Two great varmints which go great together').

The material awaiting the virtual zoogoer, after all the graphic flourishes, includes lots of pictures of animals, fairly indistinct and unremarkable, certainly much less satisfying or detailed or informative than what one could find in any of dozens of basic reference books about animals. There are short movies of animals in zoos, which involve (at least for this user) an inordinately complex process to access and load, and which play for a few seconds without providing any momentous insights. One depicts monkeys feeding – a new way of looking at the same old things people have always looked at in zoos. These clips remind me of my grandfather's home movies from the 1940s – out of focus, haphazard, not really showing anything very comprehensible, but just reveling in newly available technology for its own sake.

It's interesting to flip from the Tallinn, Estonia Zoo, to the Oklahoma City Zoo in a matter of seconds – the computer concentrates, and exaggerates, the world-at-one's-fingertips thrill of zoos that allows spectators to see, for example, Asian water buffaloes followed by Arctic reindeer. But finally, as with so many aspects of the Internet, the experience becomes overwhelming; an unposed question behind all this material is, does anyone really need such vast access to 'information'? What do we do with it? There's so much data that the *process* of information access becomes vastly more striking, more foregrounded, than the subject of what one accesses. The animals become an even smaller part of the whole equation – even more than in zoos, pawns; necessary but trivialized and overshadowed elements in some larger cutting-edge activity. They are not what's new and exciting here: after all, captive animals have been around for thousands of years, but it's only in the last two or three that we can do *this* with them. '*This*,' in this case, indicates Internet technology; in the last generation, *this* was something else, and so on back throughout history ... but now, as always, institutionalized animal captivity and display involves predominantly not the represented (the animals) themselves, but the *phenomenon of representation* – what we can do with them.

As wary as I am about succumbing to the lure of vapid infocravings, I nevertheless want to convey exactly what sort of material is out there, and how insidiously, weirdly diffuse, polymorphously perverse, the zoo and the idea of the zoo become as they get sucked into computer culture. What follows is an indiscriminate cross section of the bits and bytes of data that might whiz past the eyes of a virtual zoogoer:

> **Tallinn Zoo Home Page**: Shortly about the Tallinn Zoo. It is generally accepted that one of the indicators of a country's cultural life and standard of living is the establishment of zoological gardens, their level of development and importance in the society. In Estonia, it was not before the 1930s that the idea of founding a zoo became repeatedly discussed and fiercely argued in the leading circles of the republic ... In 1937, a World Championship of shooting took place in Helsinki where the Estonian team was most victorious. They returned home with the Argentine Cup and some other traditional prizes but to crown all, they also brought with a live baby lynx. At that time it was a very rare animal in Estonia where only some 20 specimens were counted. It was an unusual present and had to be well received. Without much ado a place was found for it in the park of Kadriorg ... On the territory of the tree nursery of the Department of Tourism and Nature Preservation a cage for the lynx was erected. The news quickly spread and the young lynx, hardly adapted to the new home, had to get accustomed to curious visitors. The problem of establishing a zoological gardens grew more acute and discussions in the press became more matter-of-fact. The indispensability of a zoo was not questioned any more, now it was planned where and how it should be built ... On August 25, 1939, the inauguration of a state zoological gardens took place ... The war left its traces on the life of the zoo. At that time, the most valuable animals of the collection, the young polar bears, were exchanged for an old sickly specimen from Germany. It was inevitable that bombardments took their toll. The last bombing killed the lynx called Ilu (Beauty), who later became the emblem of the zoo ...

San Diego Zoo Home Page: Center for Reproduction of Endangered Species:

Society Conservation Projects: Butterfly Farming in Costa Rica. Butterfly farming is an example of sustainable resource use. Farmers are taught how to plant the correct nectar and host plants. Butterflies are drawn out of the forest and into the garden, where they breed and lay eggs . . . Eighty per cent of the pupae or butterflies are harvested and shipped to a clearinghouse. The other 20 per cent are allowed to return to the forest, providing breeding stock for the next generation. The San Diego Wild Animal Park purchases thousands of tropical butterfly pupae for its Butterfly Encounter Exhibit.

Frozen Zoo: The first laboratory set up in . . . 1976 dealt with cytogenetics. This lab immediately began growing fibroblast (skin) cell cultures from various exotic species for chromosomal studies. These cells were frozen in liquid nitrogen at −320 degrees Fahrenheit. Today the Frozen Zoo is housed in 4 storage tanks, which hold viable cell lines from more than 3,200 individual mammals, representing 335 species and subspecies.

CRES Wish List: . . . Ten trees for the lion-tailed macaque corral at the Wild Animal Park – $12,000. These trees will provide arboreal enrichment for the macaques . . . Automatic Pipetting Station – $20,000. Extremely time-saving and accurate equipment used to transfer small quantities of liquid samples for hormone analysis of endangered species.

Paradise Wildlife Park: Meet our lion cubs and help save lions in Africa! The Opportunity of a Lifetime! How would you and your family like to meet with a lion or tiger cub? They are hand-reared and very friendly. You can bring your cameras and video camera to capture a truly memorable experience. A lion or tiger session costs £40, or for the ultimate experience, have a lion and tiger for £60.

National Zoological Park Home Page: You are visitor 4409 since June 3, 1996. Your cyber-ticket has been collected by webcounter. Zoo Highlights. Zoo Views. Zoo News. Animal Photos. Tracking Elephants in Malaysia. Crossword Puzzle. Word Searches. National Zoo Cinema: Visit CoolFusion and Download the Plug-In. Mopie and Mesou Picnicking on the Grass. Sobat Enjoys a Meal. Melba and Dennis Preparing Breakfast in the Small Mammal House . . .

> Please take a few moments to fill out this short questionnaire. Your answers will help us to improve the quality of the information we provide through the National Zoo Web Site. Have you ever made an electronic visit to the National Zoo before? . . . Have you ever visited the National Zoo in person? If yes, what did you like most about your visit to the 'real' zoo? What did you like most about your visit to the E-Zoo? Do you plan to return to the E-Zoo? If yes, what other information would you like to see on your next visit to the E-Zoo? Do you plan to tell others about this service?

(At this last question, I snicker to my research assistant, who is escorting me through the cyberswamp: do I ever!)

As intellectually and culturally shabby as I find conventional zoos, the Internet zoo outstrips their vapidity. It's all so obviously insubstantial and artificial, so vastly degraded a representation of the wild animals with which it purportedly concerns itself. (Am I the only one who hears echoes of a brothel entreaty when the Paradise Wildlife Park beckons: 'for the ultimate experience, have a lion and tiger for £60'?) At the end of Chapter 2, I regretted the prospect that the zoo's future seemed to lie, institutionally, in the land of Disney. Here, similarly disenheartened, I worry about what Internet zoogoing indicates, on the individual level, regarding the future of this cultural habit – what people want to see today, and how spectators may be watching zoo animals in the next century. It's as bad as ever, to paraphrase Pogo, but more so. My point, simply – turning again to the discourse of Oz (which seems, for some reason, to embody an oddly appropriate tone for dealing with all this) – is that we're not in Kansas anymore. Perhaps if I were less of a novice at Internet exploration I would not find myself so completely boggled by such spectatorial solicitations as the National Zoo Cinema offers: 'Visit CoolFusion and Download the Plug-In.' Maybe it means something to someone; but to me, as I take a detour from print-culture zoo stories to spend a morning flipping through computer screens, it seems as if the anxious cacophony that hovers at the margins of so many 'old-fashioned' representations of animals and captivity escalates into a full-scale high-tech Babel of computer gibberish – sound and fury signifying nothing, or at least, nothing that has anything to do with animals – when the zoo comes to us via the pixilated glory of the information superhighway.

Through the miracles of modern science, a user in Asia might learn of the San Diego Wild Animal Park's fundraising drive to 'provide arboreal enrichment' for a troop of macaques, refugees from northern Africa on display in Southern California. As I wait for the computer to download, I muse about monkeys and trees . . . about how macaques' arboreal enrichment was provided before computers, and before zoos. Probably the process worked pretty well on its own, without the elaborate networks of intervention people have constructed to surround and surmount nature. Is the information system we have superimposed upon monkeys and trees an improvement? I think not. Can we even see the forest (a *real* forest, where real macaques live) for all the trees of cyberspace? To approach the zoo, the modern spectator must cut through so many accreted layers of technological discourse, cultural mediation, capitalistic commodification of nature (at $1200 a tree, a hefty price tag). By the time one finally gets to an animal, I suspect – as Gertrude Stein said about Oakland – there's no there there.

6

Kids and Zoos

the child wept with pity for the poor captive animals
Isabel Allende, *The House of the Spirits*

Gina didn't give a fuck about the animals.
Roddy Doyle, *The Van*

'In the main, people visit zoos in family or social groups, rather than alone,' write Bob Mullan and Garry Marvin, often as 'an outing for the kids' (132). What do children experience from a visit to the zoo? Why do people take children to zoos? The latter question generates a variety of responses; I begin with one of the more unusual, from Henri Cole's poem 'The Zoo Wheel of Knowledge' (1989), describing a family's decision one afternoon to go to the zoo:

How strange to hear in the fading sun
the little girls from Sacred Heart scream
and rush against each other when the lions
in the park let go their convulsive roar,

awakening in us, as with the addict,
a spasmlike hunger to please the beast.
So we set off, all of us, guiding our stroller . . .
(63)

The girls' rowdy screaming and rushing connotes the violence Cole connects implicitly with the threatening noise from a nearby zoo. This unsettling fusion of sounds would seem to indicate a fairly unpromising relationship between children and zoo animals. But in a disjunctive response to these noises, the speaker nevertheless decides to bring his family to the zoo. His compulsion to go, colored by the ominous clamor, does not portend a pleasant visit; the venture seems involuntary (the addict's drive), not freely chosen.

With this paradox, Cole suggests adults take children to zoos not because they want to but because they feel they have to: parents capitulate to some sociocultural force, as if addicted to the idea of such family outings. The image of addiction indicates a craving for guilty, decadent, unhealthy, even dangerous pleasures – the 'spasmlike hunger to please the beast.' The speaker's involuntary zoo visit provides a loaded metaphor: who or what exactly figures as this 'beast' of addiction, and how does a zoo visit satiate it? Do zoo stories construct a trip to the zoo as a pilgrimage to appease the beastly lion – an angry god served by the family's submissive obeisance to its convulsive roars? Or are the children the beasts who must be pleased, compelling parents (against their inclinations) to visit zoos? Cole recognizes an uneasy danger consequent upon mixing people and animals in zoos. He highlights his wariness with the fearful image of the girls' screams, a terror evoking Christians (from Sacred Heart) sacrificed to the lions. As the poem subsequently relates, the zoo holds dark tidings for children; but some force other than rational appraisal of a zoo visit seems to drive this family off on their excursion: some mysterious, ill-fated influence. I will return to explore the tragic consequences Cole sees for children at the zoo.

Several years ago, I lived near Brooklyn's Prospect Park Zoo, and occasionally cut through it while walking in the park; I remember it made me queasy. As a boy, I made obligatory zoo excursions like most American children. My reactions were not what kids were apparently supposed to think about zoos – a trip to the zoo was fun, and anyone who disagreed was weird. But I recall the pervasive odors of excreta and fetid animal fur, flesh, feathers; an odd, surreal mixture of different animals and habitats; disconnected images of brick houses, dirty windows, nasty halls. John Hawkes's story 'In Dante's Forest' (1974) presents a sensory reaction that resembles and expresses my own memories:

> on the dead air was a smell that I recognized at once as belonging only to the reptile houses in the zoos of childhood and, further, as having been secreted through the waste ducts of rodents and cold-blooded creatures lying in dry coils. The smell

> was like that of venom or urine or black ink in a context of crushed peanuts.
>
> (64)

William Carlos Williams offers similar images in his story 'The Zoo' (1950): 'The smell was appalling. Dead fish, dead something, anyhow foul, it gripped you right in the throat, you could taste it . . . Once you got used to the fetid odor of the place, the din hit you. Shrieks and catcalls on all sides' (334–5). In *The Liars' Club* (1995), Mary Karr remembers a childhood zoo outing where 'we ate burgers on round concrete picnic tables, which were oddly placed to get the full stink of the nearby monkey pits . . . The big cat cages also stank in the heat' (54). My childhood memories of zoos are, of course, filtered through my mature consciousness. I *think* I remember zoos along the lines of Hawkes's, Williams's, and Karr's descriptions; such passages feel familiar, although perhaps they create rather than recall memories. To some extent, I now realize things about zoos that I didn't as a child; and to some extent, my present perspective has emerged from sensibilities I experienced as a child but couldn't articulate.

The societal conviction that kids should be taken to zoos relates to other general beliefs and assumptions about children and animals. 'Received wisdom has it that the tendency to like, to care for and to identify with animals is essentially a childhood phenomenon, or, as it might often be more condescendingly expressed, a childish thing,' Steve Baker writes (123); he cites Bruno Bettelheim's theory that children innately embrace animism, believing that all living things have lives much like our own.[1] Children see affinities between themselves and things that adults find quite different, Bettelheim believes. If zoos embody distancing, inauthentic relationships, as I argue, Baker's theory of 'received wisdom' may exempt children from these perceptions. Zoos' shortcomings might be less noticeable to children than to adults – even wholly indiscernible – because youngsters connect and identify more closely with animals they perceive as akin to themselves and, consequently, might overlook the institutional constructs surrounding zoo animals. On the other hand, if children feel themselves so closely allied to animals, they could be even more upset than adults by the indignities and displacement suffered in the zoo. In fact, I believe children *are* attuned to the affronts experienced by the animals that fascinate them; a considerable uneasiness many children exhibit in zoo stories reflects a heightened sensitivity authors ascribe to them.

In either case, Baker and Bettelheim imply that taking children to zoos offers them an experience whose value might elude adults – reflecting predilections and sensibilities that are disparate in children and adults. Adults, who may or may not enjoy going to zoos themselves, endure it for their children's betterment. Even if they don't like zoos, they may believe that children's experience of it is different from their own; a zoo visit is one of the many sacrifices parents make for their children. Zoos, then, may serve to indicate and delineate children's perceptual *otherness* from adults; and perhaps this correlates to the way zoos affirm animals' otherness from people. I have argued that the speciesist distinction the zoo projects (subject animal as other, caged for display; people regarding the spectacle as confirmation of empowerment) distorts our biological role as one part of an interrelated ecosystem, and panders to anthropocentric fantasies of natural supremacy. The assumption that children's perceptual experiences are essentially and qualitatively different from those of adults – that young zoo visitors are oblivious to the dynamics of oppression and constraint – may be similarly erroneous.[2] Adults may nurture such beliefs to dismiss or rationalize zoos' manifestly distasteful aspects: parents would like to imagine that their children, suffused with the pure wonder of beholding exotic animals, tune out the foul smells and the unnatural, exploitative context of constraint afflicting the animals on display. Many zoo stories, however, undermine the notion that children are oblivious to unpleasantness; the stories suggest that even if children do not raise immediate objection to vexing conditions during a zoo visit, they are nevertheless liable to recall the experience as disturbing later in life. (In several works I examine, a zoo memory from childhood festers for years until finally the subject comes to terms with it as an adult.) In her study of children's perceptions of environmental concerns and crises, Donna Lee King writes that children *do* have a sophisticated consciousness about a range of green concerns (which would presumably include animal welfare). 'Children are not social incompetents when it comes to understanding and interpreting environmental messages,' she writes. 'Most children are responding to social messages about environmental crisis with a clear and confident sense that they can do something about the problem'

(115). It is disingenuous for parents to assume their children are immune to, or unaffected by, the ecologically retrograde sensibilities that zoos embody.

Cultural patterns and stereotypes collude to enhance the zoo's appeal: 'Children in the industrialized world are surrounded by animal imagery: toys, cartoons, pictures, decorations of every sort,' John Berger observes (20). Such imagery reifies the natural world as constituted for human entertainment or mass consumption. Although one might suppose children have always been interested in animals, 'it was not until the 19th century that reproductions of animals became a regular part of the decor of middle class childhoods,' he reports. At that time a new demand arose for verisimilitude in animal toys such as stuffed animals and rocking horses, and this 'manufacture of realistic animal toys coincides, more or less, with the establishment of public zoos . . . Adults take children to the zoo to show them the originals of their "reproductions" [toys], and also perhaps in the hope of re-finding some of the innocence of that reproduced animal world which they remember from their own childhood' (21). But if toy animals and zoo animals somehow reinforce each other representationally, as Berger argues, they may also deconstruct each other. In 'The Last Bear' (1982), Andrei Bitov writes:

> Isn't it strange that we make more and more books with fairy-tales and pictures about wild rabbits and wolves and foxes, and we still make fish and reindeer and teddy bears out of rubber and plastic and stuffing and realize less and less what it is we are doing. And our children already live in a world where there are thousands of times more toy animals than there are animal animals. Animals are no longer objects of first-hand knowledge and acquaintance with which to spend your life. They are objects of mythology.
>
> (278)

Besides toys, a range of other cultural constructs augments the centrality of the zoo, and the idea of the zoo as unassailably appealing and appropriate for children. Copious children's games, songs, storybooks, and alphabet primers feature zoos as pleasant, apolitical spectacles akin to playgrounds or parks; almost universally, such representations of zoo animals geared toward children lack any intimation that the animals have been wrenched out of their natural habitats or are at all constrained by their life in captivity. Zoo animals are rarely contextualized as being related to natural animals or unconstrained wild habitats; rather, zoos appear as ends in themselves, as self-sufficient cultural institutions. Visits to zoos and other pedagogical activities that are outgrowths of zoo culture feature prominently in curricula at all age levels for schools, environmental awareness programs, and other educational enterprises. Zoo attractions, especially at children's and petting zoos, include carnival-like amusements and other recreational stimuli that would seem to ensure their unassailable wholesomeness. But such indications that zoos *should* be appealing, while often compelling, are not infallible: 'The animals seldom live up to the adults' memories, whilst to the children they appear, for the most part, unexpectedly lethargic and dull' (21), Berger writes, raising issues that pervade zoo stories about children (or children and adults) watching captive animals: disappointment, inauthenticity, cultural diminution and failure, and the ephemerality of what makes wild animals important and fascinating. 'The Last Bear' describes the inadequacy a man perceives as he visits the zoo with his daughter:

> You become unaccountably sad and dull. The false desire to be enlivened with the help of your child, to look at everything with motion-picture eyes, remains sterile. They are simply attentive, children. Their eyes are on the borderline of fear. Fear, not of an animal's frightfulness – how could the poor thing be frightening? In a cage? But of life itself.
>
> (275)

In Williams's 'The Zoo,' the characters find their outing distasteful. Elsa, a maid, takes the two children in her charge to the zoo, where she must occupy them for five hours. The noises, smells, and general atmosphere unsettle her; the children, too, find the zoo unappealing. The lion 'Opened his jaws. And split the air with a terrifying voice of thunder. The baby clung to the maid's neck and began to whimper. Lottie clung to her skirts . . . I want to go home! said Lottie whimpering' (339). When another bellow startles them, 'Lottie, bewildered, put her hands up to her ears and ran – forward into the room as Elsa clutched the baby which suddenly had again clutched her . . . Another deafening roar. In terror the little maid and the children escaped through the door nearest them' (340). It is difficult for Elsa to dispel the assumption that a zoo visit is guaranteed to be enjoyable, even in the face of obvious evidence to the contrary; indeed, it seems as if such assumptions hold the characters captive (in a symbolic parallel to the animals' captivity?) and prevent them from following their natural inclination to quit the zoo. Only after the long visit, completed, has proven a unilateral failure can Elsa assert the unpalatability that must have been subconsciously clear to all three of them the entire time. 'Well, some day you can go again, said the Missus. No, said Elsa. Schtinks! I see once, I see too much' (342). In light of numerous zoo stories depicting children's dissatisfaction, one can posit a proposition running counter to a widespread presumption: children *may not* enjoy going to zoos. Certainly it is untrue to generalize that children unilaterally hate zoos or are traumatized by visiting them; I want to argue only that considerably more complicated dynamics accompany the mixture of kids and zoos than most people are prone to acknowledge. A major facet of zoos – children's exposure to them – traditionally considered straightforward and unproblematic, is, in fact, quite polyvalent.

Representations of children at zoos frequently juxtapose the child's constricted range of 'appropriate' reactions and the adult's potentially more complicated responses. This opposition may be constructed as a dialectic between a child's view of the zoo and an adult's simultaneous experience, or a single character's memory of the zoo as a child versus the consideration of it as an adult, or some combination of these. Childhood is a vitally engaging topic, because of its volatile cache of vacillating and intensely felt emotional extremes: exuberance, fear, trauma, achievement, despair. Literature offers adults the chance to revisit the events and temperament of childhood, and thereby to understand the world (as mediated by the text) in a way that may have eluded them as children. The adult can confront issues that the child lacked the self-confidence to do, and can somehow, perhaps, retroactively remedy the tribulations of youth. As Tom Robbins promises in the last words of *Still Life With Woodpecker*: 'It's never too late to have a happy childhood.'[3] Experiencing youth vicariously, adult readers can liberate themselves from the tyranny of ideas that may deny the validity of children's own thought processes. But at the same time, an inherent powerlessness affects the adult who writes or reads of childhood. However vitally one explores, analyzes, or exorcises the nuances of youth, one cannot step in the same river twice. Childhood, that tantalizing repository of formative experience and imagination, can never be recaptured. The more adults come to understand our childhood, the more we realize how *little* we actually understood or controlled what was going on then. This tension infuses writing about kids at the zoo.

In her collection *Zoo* (1996), Britta Jaschinski's stark black and white photography, often grainy and blurry, accuses the institution of a cold, harsh otherworldliness: resonances of constraint, disembodiment, artificiality, the unknowability and unreality of zoo animals, infuse her vision. Her postscript suggests a paradigm of how an adult's zoo representation may draw upon childhood memories and feelings, fusing several themes that recur in accounts of kids and zoos: the ineffability of her deepest feelings about visiting zoos, and the lack of a discourse to protest; the heightened sensitivity to obviously unpleasant details children perceive, mixed with the frustrating inability to actualize resistance; the confusing carnival of sensory overloads (ranging from the trivial trappings of entertainment to the tragedy of displaced animals) rendering clear cognitive perception and action all the more complicated for children; and finally, the adult's troubling residue of distant childhood visits:

> I felt it as a child. It was some indefinable feeling, a sense of hopelessness staring out from behind the glass. Perhaps as children, standing on the brink of understanding, we have all felt a vague embarrassment. It may be that we instinctively recognize the unnatural minutiae of incarcerated life or the abnormal behaviour: perpetual pacing, bar biting and swaying. In the end the big event, the ice cream and the novelty of new sights and smells wins out. Eventually, on our progress to adulthood, that malaise recedes and ossifies in the recesses of our awareness. What remains is a kind of primitive regret.

In *The Waterfall* (1969), Margaret Drabble explores the experiences of children and adults as Jane Grey takes her son Laurie (about three) and newborn daughter Bianca to the London Zoo; she thinks, 'I had not been to the zoo for years . . . I must say I had forgotten how unnatural some animals are. If I had remembered, I might have been more chary about introducing Laurie to them' (194). During her visit, Jane perceives zoos to be of dubious value for children, but this hadn't occurred to her before she came. She is in the process of formulating her adult perceptions of zoos (and confronting 'forgotten' childhood memories that she fleshes out to augment her adult perceptions) at the same time she introduces her children to zoos. There is something of the essential human irony here: we discover disturbing things, but too late to avoid them – perversely, we repeat rather than escape their influences. Jane herself learns a lesson about zoos in this passage, but cannot avoid sentencing her children to reenacting the zoo visits she remembers with distaste from her own youth.

Jane had felt compelled to take Laurie and Bianca to the zoo because the standard rites of child development fundamentally include zoos. 'I had been promising the zoo for months, ever since Laurie had learned to say the word. He had a book with animals in it, a zoo book, and he knew all the names – giraffes, elephants, camels, panda bears, monkeys. I thought he ought to see them' (191–2). But Jane's feeling of normative social compulsion regarding children directly conflicts with the more private and individual sentiment that surfaces once she arrives: 'I do not like the zoo,' she realizes.

> I still feel sorry for the animals, as I used to feel as a child: I feel they are caged and bored and lonely. This may be a pathetic enough fallacy, but I can't get rid of it. And this time, pausing in front of the gorilla, I noticed that it was sitting on its small square floor idly tossing up and down, up and down, a piece of straw from its bedding. From time to time it sighed. It was sick with true human boredom, that animal, I would swear it. The crowd was laughing a little at these familiar, recognizable gestures, but nervously, without pleasure, without amusement. (195)

In a pattern common to zoo stories about adults' recollections of childhood, Jane can only belatedly express the antipathy she felt many years earlier. Once her voice emerges, it is cogent and fluent: in a few condensed sentences, Jane touches upon many of the themes evinced in more elaborate considerations of animals and captivity – issues of animal consciousness, human empathy, the semiotics of captivity, the implications of spectatorship. But despite her insights, Jane retains guilt about depriving children of an experience socially construed as an entitlement of childhood, and a lack of confidence in the validity of her feelings – as if they are too irrational to act upon, not obviously corroborated anywhere in the outside world, and better repressed. Thus, she continues to attend the zoo. The trope of delayed return to a zoo by someone who harbors uncomfortable childhood memories recurs in other stories. Perhaps the adult confrontation is necessary to allow a catharsis of the repressed thoughts from childhood; there is at least the possibility that this visit is the last one Jane will make – that Laurie and Bianca will not return, and will not become indoctrinated into zoo culture.

Marianne Moore describes the tension between childhood experience of zoos and adult reminiscence in 'The Monkeys.' In the first stanza, she mentions briefly various animals she had once seen in a zoo – monkeys, elephants, small cats, a parakeet; then, in the second stanza,

> I recall their magnificence, now not more magnificent
> than it is dim. It is difficult to recall the ornament,
> speech, and precise manner of what one might
> call the minor acquaintances twenty
> years back.
>
> (40)

Moore goes on to detail a remembered conversation (discussed further in Chapter 7) with one animal she does recall, a large cat. But the poem begins with her regret about loss of recollection, imagination, appreciation – overshadowed now by dimness. The poem was written in 1917; twenty years earlier, Moore was ten years old. One may wonder why Moore, always extremely careful about her poetic details, seems not to have revisited the zoo to refresh her memory. Perhaps she thinks of zoos primarily as places one visits as a child, and accepts that such 'dim' recollection is necessary for an adult.

Dimness, for Moore, is a severe flaw. She predicates her poetry upon the presentation of 'magnificence' – magnificent perspectives and sights, in magnificent language and prosody. Moore thus indicates a shortcoming associated with zoos, and with childhood experience versus adult recollection. The things that are now difficult for her to recall – ornament, speech, precision of manner – are the types of details so vividly honed elsewhere in her poetry. The zoo may indeed have appeared magnificent to Moore as a child; but we cannot be assured of this, for there is no imaginative document to 'prove' it. If she remembers only one of the many animals, one must consider her zoo visit mostly a washout; her poetic bestiary shows her fascination with *every* animal she comes across. Her animal poetry generally preserves this fascination, this magnificence, eternally; but her experiences of zoo animals have mostly dissipated, she informs in 'The Monkeys.'

The persona in 'The Monkeys' suggests an autobiographical element, although one must be wary about simplistically conflating author, voice, and persona/character. Novels by E. L. Doctorow and Roddy Doyle highlight more explicitly the significance of autobiographical elements in adults' writing about kids at the zoo. The authors address what happens to children at the zoo, and how the adult who reflects back mediates and shapes childhood zoo visits, tinged with what seems a more mature consciousness.

I approach Doctorow via Frank Buck, a popular 1930s figure who provided a prominent bridge between children and animals. An exotic animal collector, trader, showman, and publicity hound, Buck featured in many flattering (and only loosely factual) characterizations of his exploits in the wild. His books include *Bring 'Em Back Alive* (1930), *Wild Cargo* (1932), *Fang and Claw* (1935), and *On the Jungle Trails* (1937). (Vicki Croke notes that *Bring 'Em Back Alive* 'might have more aptly been titled, "Kill Most of Them along the Way." Countless adult animals were slaughtered so that offspring could be collected, and more died from harsh conditions and stress during travel . . . Throughout his career, Buck delivered . . . all in all, 10,000 mammals and 100,000 birds. The number of animals who didn't make it is incalculable' (156).) Several of Buck's books also became films, in which he starred; he gained further exposure through comics, magazine articles, lectures, and radio talks. His stories describe adventures stalking wild animals (Indian pythons, Malay tigers, crocodiles, antelopes) in far-flung settings, capturing them, fending off 'natives', and deftly transporting his 'wild cargo' back to America. All his media undertakings celebrate his heroic character: the film of *Fang and Claw* opens with titles describing it as the 'official and authentic motion picture record of Frank Buck's wild animal collecting expedition in the Asiatic jungles.' Buck's publicity photographs depict the stereotypically intrepid tamer/master of wild animals and natives, down to the pith helmet. The author's note in *Bring 'Em Back Alive* boasts:

> He has crossed the Pacific forty times, circumnavigated the world five times, knocked out an orang-utan in a fair fight, walked practically the entire width of the island of Borneo . . . He is internationally famous for having brought back to this country an amazingly large number of 'firsts' or unique specimens. These include the only authentic man-eating tiger ever seen in this country, captured on a rubber plantation in Johore, Malaya, by Buck and his native helpers after it had killed and partly eaten a coolie . . . [and] two rare Indian rhinos which he transported from the jungles of Nepal where no white man is allowed.

This account considerably exaggerates Buck's actual involvement with the capture and procurement of wild animals. He was essentially a middleman: from his Singapore headquarters, he sold to zoos and circuses animals he had acquired from other traders.

Buck exhibited animals at the 1939 New York World's Fair, where we pick up his trail in a zoo story. In *World's Fair*, Doctorow depicts his protagonist's reaction to the cultural icon. Eight-year-old Edgar, who devours Frank Buck comics, is Doctorow's autobiographical inscription, so this story illustrates an adult remembering his childhood zoo visit, and thus represents – as in many other zoo stories – two people in one visiting the zoo: the present-day author along with the child who is the father of the man.

Edgar's initial response to Frank Buck shows the boy's concern about animal abuse, along with his naive approval of the adventurer's methods: 'he didn't kill animals, he brought them back by ship to the zoos and circuses. He was kind to the animals, which I liked' (218). The young boy knows that Buck's cultural arena – big game hunters, white men in the dark wilds

– often involves violence and cruelty toward animals as testimony to the hero's bravery, and he appreciates the trapper's restraint. While Edgar values animals' humane treatment, he does not (yet) make the inference that zoos are potentially abusive of animals. As he reads about Buck's adventures in the unreality of comic books, he does not consider the ethics of zoos or what happens to the real captive animals after they are delivered to their purchasers.

But Edgar's feelings become more sophisticated, more critical, when he attends the World's Fair and confronts in person what Buck actually does and what he represents, beyond the flattering comic book account. When they visit the extravaganza, Edgar and his friend Meg visit every exhibit, from the sleek Plaza of Light, Constitution Mall, and World of Tomorrow, to the more banal, carnival-like exhibits of the Amusement Zone. There, they discover Frank Buck's Jungleland:

> It was a zoo technically, he had lots of different animals, but the railings were wood and the cages were portable, so it was more makeshift than a zoo, more in the nature of a camp. There were three different kinds of elephant, including a pygmy, and there was a black rhinoceros standing very still, as still as a structure, and who obviously understood nothing about where he was or why; there were a few sleeping tigers, none of them advertised as a man-eater; and tapirs, an okapi, and two sleek black panthers.
>
> (336)

Edgar demonstrates an interesting concern with the definition of the zoo as genre: he grapples with what precisely denotes a zoo in terms of animal inventory, physical attributes of the compound, and institutional character (portable versus permanent, makeshift versus established). His careful deliberation is appropriate to this exhibition of animals for two reasons: first, Buck is a polymorphous phenomenon – trapper? animal aficionado? explorer? film star? And second, the World's Fair is itself an amalgam of cultural genres integrating entertainment, education, science, politics, advertising, and sociological indoctrination. Throughout the Fair, as at Jungleland, Edgar exerts considerable reflection trying to discern what is what; he probes the implications of its sleek, harmonious vision of the world. Insightfully,

Edgar finds the Fair's confident, cocky outlook somewhat eerie, sometimes unconvincing, in light of the real world around him – turbulence in his family, the social hardships of the Depression, and the imminence of war. (His cynical father teaches him how to read through the Fair's propaganda – pointing out, for example, that the General Motors exhibit features an ultramodern vision of highways because it wants people to demand that the government build these, which will stimulate demand for GM cars.) With regard to both Buck and the Fair, there is much that needs to be interpreted.

Like Buck and the Fair, the zoo invites decoding. The more Edgar thinks about it and looks at the animals, the more emerges beneath the surface, beyond the obvious. Determining the formal and generic constitution of the zoo – contextualizing it – is Edgar's first step toward deconstructing it. The black rhinoceros he sees, paralyzed and disoriented, 'obviously understood nothing about where he was or why.' This observation seems to provoke Edgar, paradoxically, both to pity the caged creatures and to resist his own implication in their condition. He must figure out for himself what is going on in the Fair, in his life, and in the world, in 1939; he must prevent himself from becoming associated with the animals' confusion; he must, for both ethical and epistemological reasons, avoid being sucked into the World's Fair/ Frank Buck fantasy world. His thoughts continue:

> You could ride on a camel's back, which we didn't do. On a miniature mountain, there lived, and screamed and swung and leaped and hung hundreds of rhesus monkeys. We watched them a long time. I explained Frank Buck to Meg. He went into the wilds of Malaya, usually, but also Africa, and trapped animals and brought them back here to zoos and circuses and sold them. I told her that was more humane to do than merely hunt them. In truth, I had worshipped Frank Buck, he lived the life I dreamed for myself, adventurous yet with ethical controls, he did not kill. But I had to confess to myself, though not to Meg, that I had now read his book twice and realized things about him I hadn't understood the first time. He complained a lot about the personalities of his animals. He got into scraps with them. Once an elephant picked him up and tossed him away. An orangutan bit him, and he nearly fell into a pit with a certified man-eating tiger. He called his

> animals devils, wretches, pitiful creatures, poor beasts and specimens. When one of them died on the ship to America, he felt sorry for it, but he seemed sorrier to lose the money the specimen would have brought.
>
> (336–7)

Doctorow thus depicts Edgar's awakening to the reality of relations between people and animals within the dynamics of captivity and display. No matter how dashing Buck appears on celluloid, his heroism cannot endure Edgar's confrontation with the real-life manifestation of Buck's adventures. Edgar thinks his insights derive from having 'read his book twice,' noticing things he missed the first time. To a degree, this seems true (and metaphorically indicates how reading and probing more closely debunks flimsy cultural constructs). Additionally, however, it seems clear that Edgar's personal experience at the zoo precipitates the change of heart. Seeing the victims of Buck's heroic enterprises first-hand – the poor rhino, the exploited camel, the hordes of displaced monkeys – directly affects Edgar. Personal, immediate exposure to the Frank Buck myth subverts, rather than affirms, the cultural conjunction of children and captive animals.

Doctorow depicts children as capable of interpreting zoos' subtexts, and fleshing out contradictions that undermine the surface (the Derridean aporia). Edgar demonstrates keen critical sensitivity to issues of language (performing a close textual reading of the Frank Buck comic: 'He called his animals devils, wretches, pitiful creatures . . .'), refusing to take Buck at face value. Even if Edgar – imbued with the sensibility of a budding novelist – isn't fully a true-to-life eight-year-old, he thinks things Doctorow must at least wish youngsters could express. Edgar realizes that the man who captures wild animals, although he appears suave, doesn't hold up under closer consideration. Buck's motives seem self-serving, and the animals bear the burden of this selfishness. Further, Edgar sees that the implications of Buck's endeavors transcend the man and his persona: they extend to the institutions of zoos, and relate particularly to his experience as he mulls all this over, at a zoo. As he watches captive animals and becomes uncomfortable, Edgar continues to probe:

> I looked around for Frank Buck, knowing full well he wouldn't be here. I understood his legendary existence depended on his

> not being here, but I looked anyway. The truth was, I thought now, Frank Buck was a generally grumpy fellow, always cursing out his 'boys' or jealously guarding his 'specimens' or boasting how many he had sold where and for how much. He acted superior to the people who worked for him. He didn't get along with the authorities in the game preserves, nor with the ships' captains who took him on their freighters with his crated live cargo, nor the animals themselves. I saw all that now, but I still wanted to be like him, and walk around with a pith helmet and a khaki shirt and a whip for keeping the poor devils in line.
>
> (337)

Through a child's perspective, Doctorow examines zoos' origins – what practices underlie them, and how the animals are acquired. He makes the reader confront the ethos of captivity and imperialism head-on.[4] Edgar devotes relatively minor attention to the animals themselves (although they are obviously at the heart of what troubles him). He focuses instead on Frank Buck: his behavior, his politics, his motives, his role in the captive animal industry. Edgar unflinchingly attacks the zoo at its roots, performing a radical and fundamental exposé. Doctorow deflates children's supposed single-minded fascination with zoo animals. When Edgar looks at animals, he sees in the foreground not the animals themselves but the dynamics that have resulted in their oppression – both on the part of producers (zoos, and Buck specifically) and consumers (the audience Buck cultivates with his cultural showmanship). Edgar 'sees' what he knows isn't literally there: Frank Buck, in the spirit if not in the flesh. Doctorow shows that children are not the literalists people assume when they think a child will regard a zoo specimen divorced from its natural context as authentic.

Edgar realizes that it's all a scam – Buck, Jungleland, and the whole artificial vision of the world neatly packaged at the World's Fair. Although the last line ('I still wanted to be like him . . .') seems to undercut Edgar's critique, I think it serves rather to indicate the magnitude of dissonance he is experiencing – the difficulty any child faces in attempting to rebut cultural hegemony. Edgar's contradictory coda resembles Jane Grey's behavior in *The Waterfall*, when she brings her children to the zoo despite her misgivings. By the novel's end Edgar knows the Fair and

Jungleland are basically charades, but still their mythos has an undeniable attractiveness – perhaps, as Cole characterized it in 'The Zoo Wheel of Knowledge,' an addictiveness – and he cannot look away.

Paddy Clarke Ha Ha Ha (1993), Roddy Doyle's depiction of life through a ten-year-old's eyes, affirms the serious depths of a child's psyche. Doyle conveys the exuberance and intricacy of Paddy's imagination, combined with the pre-adolescent's sometimes frustrating limitations of expression. The novel is considerably self-referential, so its tensions reflect a pull between the writer as an adult and his childhood memories. 'The vividness of the young Paddy's observations has prompted readers to wonder just how autobiographical the novel is,' writes John Rockwell, who interviewed Doyle. 'Paddy Clarke is 10, the book takes place in 1968 and Mr. Doyle was born in 1958. But the author, who grew up in a north Dublin suburb not unlike his fictional Barrytown . . . said his latest book recalls his own life only in details, not in its plot.' Rockwell quotes Doyle as saying, 'The place is mine; the time is mine. There are memories of my own . . . But the story [painfully recounting the tyranny of Paddy's abusive father] isn't mine, I'm glad to say.' One episode concerns Paddy's ruminations about a zoo visit. Irrelevant to the plot, it reflects 'place,' 'time,' and 'memories,' so it is presumably autobiographical. Like Doctorow, then, Doyle produces an atemporal fusion of adult and childhood responses by describing childhood reactions as colored by the mature sensibility of the writer.

In a casual discussion with his mother, Paddy meanders toward the subject of zoos, apropros of nothing, as a child's comments often arise (or at least seem to adults):

> – I'm going to Africa.
> – Are you? Why?
> – I just am, I said. – I have my reasons.
> – To convert the black babies?
> – No.
>
> I didn't care about the black babies; I was supposed to feel sorry for them, because they were pagans and because they

> were hungry, but I didn't care. They frightened me, the idea of them, all of them, millions of them, with stick-out bellies and grown-up eyes.
>
> (139)

When his mother asks why he wants to travel abroad he cannot answer fully or honestly. It is not that he lacks a purpose, but he cannot explain himself, or chooses not to. He assumes his mother will not understand; children learn that their own logic – the rambling thought process Doyle captures masterfully – differs from adults', and most adults will privilege their own over children's. Why, she repeats, is he going to Africa?

> – To see the animals, I said.
> – That'll be nice, she said.
> – Not to stay, I said.
> She wasn't to give my bed away.
> – What animals? she said.
> – All of them.
> – Especially.
> – Zebras and monkeys.
> – Would you like to be a vet?
> – No.
> – Why not?
> – There's no zebras and monkeys in Ireland.
> – Why do you like zebras?
> – I just do.
> – They're nice.
> – Yeah.
> – We'll go to the zoo again; would you like that?
> – No.
>
> Phoenix Park was brilliant – the Hollow and the deers; I wanted to go back there again. The bus, where you could see over the wall into the park when you were upstairs. We went there on my Holy Communion after we were finished with my aunties and uncles; on buses all morning, before my da got his car. But not the zoo, I didn't want to go there.
> – Why not? said my ma.
> – The smell, I said.
>
> It wasn't just the smell. It was more than the smell; it was what the smell had meant, the smell of animals and the fur

on the wire. I'd liked it then, the animals . . . But I remembered the smell and I couldn't remember the animals much. Wallabies, little kangaroos that didn't hop. Monkeys' fingers gripping the wire.

I was going to try to explain it to my ma, I wanted to; I was going to try. She remembered the smell; I could tell by her smile and the way she stopped it from getting too big because I hadn't said it for a joke. I was going to tell her.

(139–40)

But he doesn't. Just as Paddy cannot initially explain his African plans, he fails or refuses to explain to his mother how he regards zoos. His stumbling attempts illustrate how children may be unable to argue and receive a validating response for their reactions to zoos. It goes without saying that Paddy does not enjoy seeing zoo animals, or interact with them beneficially, or delight in their exoticism oblivious to the conditions of captivity. He struggles to isolate small particulars from the larger phenomenon. No language available to him will suffice to explain his resistance to the zoo, or to encompass his revulsion; he resorts to fragmentary signs and expressions of distaste: the foulness of a smell, the odious image suggested by fur hanging on the wire, torn off an animal. Such fragments evoke the image of a caged creature, lacerated, suffering, and perhaps – since the fur has not been removed from the cage – unassisted in its pain or even unnoticed.[5] It is incredible that anyone could imagine children failing to observe such traumatic details or piece together what is going on in zoos; probably many more children perceive such things, and are troublingly affected by them, than adults realize.

Ultimately, Paddy cannot communicate his feelings about zoos explicitly (although Doyle does so eloquently, demonstrating a simultaneous tension and collusion between adult and child). He simply knows intuitively that he doesn't like them: they stink, and the stink denotes some greater disturbing aspect of animal captivity that he cannot name. As yet, he lacks a vocabulary to rebut attitudes about zoos that society forces upon children.

Paddy clearly likes animals, exotic and local. They intrigue him, and he displays innate respect for them and their natural habitats. He has, as well, a child's inconsistency or immaturity of character: his sophisticated appreciation of animals contrasts with an inability to empathize with suffering Africans (but at least he knows he *should* feel compassion; extrapolating from Paddy's humane sensibility toward animals, we may hope for him to develop into a more sensitive adult despite some limitations in the novel's present). Paddy's feeling for animals is one of pure imaginative fascination, defying any practical context his mother tries to impose: for example, he doesn't like them because he wants to be a veterinarian. He wants to see real animals, as opposed to zoo animals, and realizes that to do so he would have to go to Africa because zebras and monkeys really live there, not in Dublin.

Other animals, deer for example, *do* exist in Ireland uncaged, and can be seen in local contexts – the expansive urban retreat of Dublin's Phoenix Park. The Dublin Zoo is also in Phoenix Park, but the area of the park Paddy recalls appreciatively is where people mix with free-ranging deer; he distinguishes between this part of the park ('the Hollow,' he calls it – also known as the Furry Glen, where deer have lived since the seventeenth century) and the zoo. Both deer and people occupy amenable habitats in Phoenix Park, interacting naturally on common ground; it is not a place where one species gawks at another in captivity. In zoological terminology, Phoenix Park offers natural or free-living conditions – 'a habitat so attractive that the animals . . . drop in and stick around by choice' (Bostock, 103) – approximating the deer's native environs. Paddy finds this interaction between people and animals 'brilliant,' the ideal way to experience animals. Africa would offer similarly genuine experiences if he ever went there. For Paddy, an African expedition is the only way to see monkeys and zebras; animals in a zoo are not the next best thing – they are wholly unacceptable. Paddy's imagination is still fresh enough to revel in the possibility that he might someday get to Africa to see the animals there, although he realizes such a journey is not imminent. Still, the possibility of never seeing some animals *in situ* does not diminish his fascination with them. If he can go to Africa, brilliant; if not, then he will not see monkeys and zebras. He does not suffer from the cultural constriction – the petulant, spoiled imagination – of those who demand to see animals locally, conveniently, immediately.

Paddy directly rebuts the most common argument for zoos, and especially for taking children to zoos. Stephen St C. Bostock summarizes this rationale, while first conceding zoos' drawbacks: 'that animals are not living their natural lives. Or if in some degree they are . . . they are clearly not living (by definition) in their natural environment. And even if their conditions simulate or substitute for their natural environment very effectively, this is only because of our human management: the animals are living, as it were, by our favour and in the state we have arranged for them' (180–1). 'However, this doesn't make very much difference,' Bostock continues, dismissing the problems he has enumerated and arguing that a zoo visit can be meaningful – that the end, even a less than ideal end, justifies the means. 'A horse is a different kind of being from ourselves, in a way something 'other,' something that is closer than us to the natural world,' even if we are observing it in captivity; 'I don't say that a wild horse would not be still better, even a great deal better; but we couldn't get close to the wild horse, and most certainly we normally couldn't get close to a tiger in the wild . . . With some animals, meeting them in the zoo and in the wild aren't alternatives. Most of us will meet them . . . in the zoo or not at all' (181). Paddy rejects Bostock's pragmatic epistemology; he forgoes direct experience of non-native animals, and exhibits instead what Lawrence Buell in *The Environmental Imagination* calls the aesthetics of relinquishment, the 'relinquishment . . . of material trophies'; such renunciation 'supplies perhaps the commonest plot scenario in environmental writing' (144) and dramatizes a crucial stage of green consciousness, 'the passage from society to environment' (180). Paddy's outlook illustrates the kind of ideal ecocentric moral zoo stories can convey.

Just as Moore characterized her childhood memories of zoos as generally 'dim' in 'The Monkeys,' Paddy thinks, 'I remembered the smell and I couldn't remember the animals much.' For both Moore and Doyle, this inability to remember the animals indicates a cultural deficiency inherent in the zoo visit. If the experience does not endure in the mind (or endures only in its negative aspects), then it is worthless. Paddy's thoughts also recall those of Drabble's Jane Grey, who wished she had not exposed her son to the unnaturalness of zoo animals. Paddy is disturbed when he sees 'kangaroos that didn't hop' – exactly what Jane feared her son would notice, zoo animals' abnormality and behavioral dysfunction. Bostock explores such qualms about animals' behavior and consequent indications about the appropriateness of captivity. 'We can judge the well-being of an individual animal . . . by knowledge of that species' natural behaviour, and this would apply still more, if anything, in the case of a relatively wild animal in a zoo . . . We can hardly avoid taking that species' wild behaviour as a norm' (83). One of Bostock's criteria for judging unnatural behavior is 'characteristic forms of locomotion' (86); Paddy realizes that the abnormality indicated by 'Wallabies, little kangaroos that didn't hop' – a loss of their characteristic locomotion – signals a perversion of the animals' nature and an indictment of the zoo. Paddy feels, as I do, that these zoo animals are simply not real wallabies; he would likely agree with animal management experts who argue that abnormal behavior is 'the clearest possible indication of bad captive conditions' and that 'where this sort of thing occurs, conditions must be improved until at least the abnormal behaviour ceases, or else the animals must just not be kept' (87).

It must appall kids to realize that animals displayed for them suffer abnormality because of exhibition conditions. Paddy's determined antipathy toward zoos results in his mother's at least appreciating his seriousness ('she stopped it from getting too big because I hadn't said it for a joke'), if she does not fully understand his views. Although Paddy fails to verbalize his feelings fully, he ensures that his mother will not press the point; most importantly, it seems unlikely that he will be cajoled to go to the zoo in the future.

An earlier novel of Doyle's, *The Van* (1991), also features kids at the zoo. The Rabbitte family, whose day-to-day adventures the novel chronicles, takes a pleasant and unmomentous outing:

> They all went to the zoo. Darren and the twins wouldn't come, but the rest of them did; Jimmy Sr and Veronica, Sharon and Gina, and Jimmy Jr and his mot, Aoife. They'd a great day. Gina didn't give a fuck about the animals; she just wanted to go on the slide all day. Jimmy Sr and Jimmy Jr laughed their way around the place. Aoife laughed at nearly everything they said, but especially when Jimmy Sr said that the hippo smelt like Veronica's mother used to, and Veronica agreed with him. She was a lovely girl, Aoife; lovely. They'd a picnic with them. Jimmy Jr slagged Jimmy Sr because he wouldn't sit on the grass cos he's his new suit on him.
>
> (229)

(Jimmy Sr and Veronica Rabbitte are the parents of Darren, the twins, Sharon, and Jimmy Jr; Gina is Sharon's daughter, about three years old.) The expedition is a genial gathering as far as it goes, but the zoo itself seems irrelevant. In depicting the family's lack of interest in animals, Doyle conveys a casual disregard for the zoo's supposed function. For the Rabbittes the zoo does not educate or enlighten; it simply offers someplace to pass the time. Mullan and Marvin's survey of zoogoers corroborates the Rabbittes' attitude: 'Most zoo visitors around the world see the zoo as a cheap place for a day of fun,' they write, 'and do not come predisposed to learn about the animals' (127). Even if visitors realize that zoos are supposed to be intellectually stimulating, their behavior belies this: 'zoos have been successful in communicating a message of what the zoo should be about. Visitors are able, when questioned, to reproduce the arguments that zoos are important educational establishments where one goes to learn about animals. But the pattern of their activities during the course of a zoo visit leads us to conclude that they are acting with a different model in mind' (135). Zoos offer an idealized version of why they exist and what visitors may garner, but a zoo story such as *The Van* suggests an actual cultural role considerably more diminutive than the zookeepers would have it. Children, especially – for whom the zoo visit is supposed to be so entrancing – are prone to resist the proper, prescribed enthusiasm. The father worries in Graham Swift's *Shuttlecock* (1981) when he gives his children money for their zoo outing: 'I could see all this money being spent on candy-floss and rides on dodgem-cars, and so I said: 'You won't forget to look at some animals too.' They looked puzzled – weren't they going to a zoo? But I could imagine them looking for a while at the leopards and antelopes, getting bored and then heading for the ghost train' (152–3). In *The Liars' Club*, Mary Karr remembers an unpleasant (and mostly animal-free) childhood trip to the zoo: 'No sane person would have chosen to spend the afternoon outdoors in that heat. There was a miniature train running through it for free back then, and we climbed on. But it was crammed with the kind of spilling, chewing, farting farm kids who made Mother nuts, so we got off at the gift shop' (53–4). And the father in Martin Amis's *The Information* (1995), on the way to the zoo with his sons, asks them, '"Where shall we go first? The reptile house? . . . The aquarium?" "The gift shop," said Marius' (337).

Doyle's forte lies in the speakers' lexicons, their habits and rhythms of speech. Evocative of Joyce, the voices resound genuinely in their grunting, slangy commonness. It is especially noteworthy when Doyle attributes to cute little Gina the idea that she 'didn't give a fuck about the animals.' While Doyle's characters swear profusely, three-year-olds, at least, mostly refrain from profanity. But Gina doesn't really use dirty language so much as Doyle himself does: 'fuck' is his word more than the girl's. Doyle's adults often sardonically don't give a fuck about something in a way that a three-year-old is probably still too innocent to do. Doyle takes creative license here, however, to depict what he indicates as Gina's thought. (In a kinder, gentler age, the heroine of Ludwig Bemelmans's children's book *Madeline* shares Gina's outlook, but evinces more delicacy: 'To the tiger in the zoo Madeline just said, "Pooh-pooh."'[6]) Or perhaps Doyle believes Gina does possess the worldliness he imputes to her: out of the mouths of babes . . . Paddy Clarke could not fully explain why zoos offended him, but was at least able to indicate his general dislike in a way his mother understood. Gina cannot be as suggestive, so Doyle helps her with a flourish of language. If she could really verbalize her opinion as *The Van* describes, Doyle may have imagined with a satisfied smirk, *she* would be one little girl who wouldn't get dragged to zoos any more. As occurs in other zoo stories, Doyle bestows upon children a sophistication of voice to help them resist the nearly immutable fate of being taken to zoos.

In *The House of the Spirits* (1986), Isabel Allende describes the courtship of Blanca, whose suitors 'attempted to win her heart by bribing her daughter,' six-year-old Alba; they showered the little girl with expensive gifts and dolls

> and took her to the zoo, where the child wept with pity for the poor captive animals, especially the seal, who stirred dreadful omens in her soul. These visits to the zoo holding on to the hand of some conceited spendthrift suitor gave her a lifelong horror of enclosures, walls, cages, and isolation.
>
> (276)

Alba's florid empathy for zoo animals contrasts with the flippant dismissal of Doyle's Gina. The two girls represent disparate models for children's objections to zoos. Gina simply denies the zoo any value in the child's universal challenge: how much fun is it? Alba, on the other hand, is deeply moved by the inequity she perceives. Gina reacts by rejecting wholly the idea of visiting the zoo, while Alba shows poignant engagement with the 'poor captive animals,' typifying the abundant compassion children may possess before it becomes socialized out of them in favor of more self-centered qualities. Alba embodies a spiritual hypersensitivity in Allende's magical realist parable: she feels and emotes profusely, reacting on a heightened level – with more prescience than those around her who bumble through their lives untouched by a vision of enchantment. She relates to the plight of captive animals vibrantly, and finds her zoo visit keenly significant: not at all the sort of thing she can easily dismiss as Gina did. She sees that the animals' circumstances imply or foretell something – perhaps the depravity of which people are capable; such a supposition is consistent with Allende's noirish vision of human social behavior.

Alba's 'lifelong horror' corresponds with other accounts of children in zoo stories who remain significantly affected by a childhood zoo visit. The horror testifies to the intensity with which zoos may disturb a child emotionally. Adults may trivialize or compartmentalize what occurs when a child visits the zoo, believing children experience no more than the observation of a certain animal with certain physical characteristics. Allende's portrait rejects the idea of a zoo visit as a discrete and inconsequential experience for children. *The House of the Spirits* suggests that parents are mistaken when they assume zoos represent guaranteed fun for every young child, serving (like candy or toys) to elicit cheap, easy appreciation. Alba relates to the animals, perceives their injustice, and resents their captivity in ways that transcend logical rhetoric (as Doctorow's Edgar and Doyle's Paddy, too, incorporate attitudes that are illogical, by adult standards, in their opposition to zoos); she simply feels an instinctive pang of commiseration. Allende intimates that children, with such vividly incisive moral visions as Alba exhibits, could puncture the ways adults think about zoos, if we paid more careful attention to them.

Like *World's Fair* and *Paddy Clarke Ha Ha Ha*, *The House of the Spirits* depicts a child who has an instinctual, deeply felt aversion to zoos. The authors present this aversion not as a silly whim or imagined bogey, but as dignified with a force of conviction often unrecognized in children. In all three novels, the zoo trauma accompanies other serious threats in the child's life. In *The House of the Spirits*, the mother's undesirable suitors and the prospect of her remarriage threaten Alba, as does Chile's social turmoil; in *Paddy Clarke Ha Ha Ha*, the family's dissolution as a result of the father's violence provides constant distress; in *World's Fair*, Edgar's apprehension concerns his parents' arguments as well as the prospect of impending war. In these children's troubled lives, negative feelings about zoos intersect with other immediate concerns. To some extent, perhaps, they transfer their anxieties onto the zoos – or, the zoos serve as inkblots that evoke their troubledness. In any case, zoos prove well-suited as a vehicle for children's anxiety, fear, insecurity; zoos evoke these unsettling psychological reactions more prominently than they inspire (as zoo proponents would claim) fun, education, or imagination.

Paul Goodman's *The Empire City* (1959) has a resonant psychological sensibility that suggests a paradigm for the manifest affinity, but subliminal antipathy, with which children may regard zoos. A young boy expresses emotions of attraction to the zoo, but his dreams betray the interlacing of subconscious anxieties and fears:

> He went to sleep and the same dream came, of the animal biting little Gus or eating him up. Now it was a crocol-dile; formerly it had been the tiger, or other large beasts seen at the zoo. He was mad for the zoo. Sometimes the wolf ate up the dog, while Gus looked on petrified with fear. Once it was a tin tiger that swallowed him . . . He woke screaming, and with sealed eyes saw the striped tiger burning bright, and the saw-tooth crocol-dile, and the elevum with proboscis awrithe. What a thing it was to have seen the beasts in cages! Would they not, precisely, come *out* of their cages? And re-establish the continuity between the man and the other generations, and on both parts teeth and lust? . . . But now in a quite normal way, with hysterical excitement, he loved gingerly to pet animals both large and small. And he was mad for the zoo, but he was willing for them to be in their cages. He was not asleep, but lying calmly awake with open eyes and thinking. 'It's mean. They're mean to come out and bite me.'
>
> (191–2)

Gus's intermingled, opposed sensations of enticement and repulsion elucidate the paradoxical reactions of several other young zoo story protagonists.

The zoo is a background image in Dylan Thomas's 'The Hunchback in the Park' (1941), a poem that recounts a group of boys' callous cruelty toward a crippled man they taunt: 'And Mister they called Hey mister / The truant boys from the town.' When he responds, they run away

> Past lake and rockery
> Laughing when he shook his paper
> Hunchbacked in mockery
> Through the loud zoo of the willow groves
> Dodging the park keeper.
>
> (123)

The 'zoo' initially connotes simply a type of garden, almost a synonym for a park; compare the common terms 'zoological garden' and 'zoological park.'[7] At first glance, this figurative zoo seems unencumbered by the usual associations of captivity, oppression, voyeurism. A 'zoo of the willow groves' invites a harmless reading – restricted to flora rather than fauna, the zoological garden seems akin to a botanical garden.

But Thomas's language flourishes and complicates itself. If the zoo is only a park or garden, why is it 'loud'? (Willow trees are never loud – they only whisper as the wind blows through.) It is the boys who are loud; they puncture the park's tranquility and recall zoos' intrinsically jarring qualities. A playfully innocent facade unravels to expose unruly, vicious interaction. Complicated syntax and hazy imprecision make the scene initially ambiguous, but what seemed simply benign boyishness in the park grows more insidious as one looks more closely. Thomas's loud zoo indicates the boys' raucous uproar. They act as if they are in a zoo, Thomas suggests: this means, possibly, that they are like zoo spectators, haughtily watching the hunchback who resembles a zoo specimen because of what they perceive as his grotesque otherness. Or perhaps Thomas posits a zoo-like scenario to indicate that the savage boys themselves are like zoo animals: they behave misanthropically, as if influenced by the distortions endemic to zoo culture. Either way, the zoo association signifies inconsideration, oppressiveness, abuse, taunting of others (to sustain a gratuitous sense of mastery and superiority), failure to appreciate every creature's innate dignity. Ultimately, this poem confirms the negative connotations inherent in the image of a 'zoo' – exactly the kinds of associations Bronx Zoo director William Conway tried to repress by removing the word 'zoo' from the institution's title.

As they gambol on, sadistically energized by their jeering, 'the boys among willows / Made the tigers jump out of their eyes / To roar on the rockery stones' (124). They simultaneously imagine, construct, and inhabit a zoo of their own design, where they can freely express their ferocity. They exhibit children's propensity for magical realism, somewhat akin to Allende's Alba; however, the boys' magical power in their 'zoo' is antisocial and nasty, unlike Alba's considerate empathy. Alba becomes a better person after her zoo visit; she feels compassion for animals and resists forces of constraint in her own life. Thomas's boys, on the other hand, become tainted by the zoo's inherent cruelty. They think zoos are fun; they also think tormenting hunchbacks is fun. 'The Hunchback in the Park' conveys a conventional image of zoos as places that captivate children's eager attention, an atmosphere where boys can be boys. Subliminally, Thomas associates zoos with degrading treatment of fellow creatures; they bring out the worst in people. At the end of the poem, night falls on what Thomas calls an 'unmade park,' his rendition of a fallen Eden. The poem's park, like the biblical ur-park, reveals the fallacy of an assumed innocence. Thomas evokes a zoo to reinforce his park's lapsarian spirit; as in most zoo stories, zoo imagery calls forth the delusory, self-destructive nature of human dynamics – the misconstrual of the rules, processes, and order of our ecosystem, for which Genesis 1:3 provides the template of dysfunctionality and disobedience. The biblical serpent – a fitting symbol, indeed, for the modern zoo – temptingly promised a too-easy form of knowledge with which humankind, in its pervasive ignorance (about nature), could not cope. If we fail to recognize the seductions of erroneous epistemology today, we are fated to reenact the fall and face expulsion from what tenuously endures of this planet's biospheric garden.

In zoos, parents mediate the natural world for their children. Ostensibly, the setting affords adults the opportunity to render education efficiently as families traipse from cage to cage, but zoos may still offend their patrons in this enterprise. Despite the rigorous control of zoo culture, exhibits may have to be censored or sanitized to hide perceived threats to children's idealized innocence. For example, some animals are wont to play with their genitalia while on public display in their cages: in *The Liars' Club*, for example, Mary Karr remembers seeing at the zoo, as a child, a spider monkey that 'stood at the edge of the pit with his bright red penis in his hand, screaming and jacking off furiously' (54). Kurt Vonnegut, Jr's 'Welcome to the Monkey House' (1968) parodies the anthropocentric reaction to natural animal behavior which disregards human social codes of propriety. The story illustrates the rigidity of expectations about what zoos should provide, especially when children are involved; animals that undermine their assigned function of putting on a wholesome show challenge human control. If some vestige of animals' natural behavior is deemed vulgar, it must be eliminated. Control is fundamentally important to zoos, and when monkeys assert self-determination by exercising their habits, zoos must squelch this natural proclivity. 'Welcome to the Monkey House' describes the creation of 'ethical birth control' (32), a pill that obviates any sexual drive by making people numb from the waist down. Universally mandatory in Vonnegut's totalitarian futuristic society plagued with overpopulation, the pill was invented by a man named J. Edgar Nation, who discovers the need for it after a zoo visit with his children:[8]

> He didn't have the slightest idea his pills would be taken by human beings someday . . . His dream was to introduce morality to the monkey house at the Grand Rapids Zoo . . . He and his eleven kids went to church one Easter. And the day was so nice and the Easter service had been so beautiful and pure that they decided to take a walk through the zoo, and they were just walking on clouds . . . So we went on to the monkey house together, and what do you think we saw? . . . We saw a monkey playing with his private parts! . . . And J. Edgar Nation was so upset he went straight home and he started developing a pill that would make monkeys in the springtime fit things for a Christian family to see.[9]
>
> (32–3)

As in other zoo stories, Vonnegut's zoo differentiates between adult and youthful sensibilities. Sexuality is limited to adults, Nation believes, so he attempts to shelter children from exposure to such aspects of adulthood.[10] (Children are as familiar with their genitals as adults or monkeys, of course, but Nation refuses to acknowledge this.) Another zoo story about children's sexuality (and the confluence with animals' sexuality) is Steve Watkins's 'Critterworld' (1991). The narrator, a high school student, watches his friend lecturing to a group of younger children at the zoo about elephant penises.

> He told those kids that an elephant penis weighs sixty pounds, and it gets four feet long when the elephant gets aroused, and sometimes, if the elephant is chasing a cow, he might even step on it. And he told them about how the penis is shaped sort of like an S, and the muscles at the end work on their own to poke around under the cow's belly to find the hole, which is way up underneath, not right there between the hind legs.
>
> For some reason it really bothered me that George was telling them all that. I knew it, too, of course – Jun had given both of us the same book to read – but George was just showing off how much he knew, and what a dirty mind he had. Those kids, though, they didn't deserve to know that stuff. They hadn't earned the right like we had. It didn't seem appropriate, or fair, or something, that they should get it so cheaply. (352–3)

Vonnegut and Watkins depict zoo animals' sexuality as potentially corrupting of innocent minds: it is considered unsuitable, somewhat incomprehensible for young spectators. Adults want children to see things at the zoo, but not *too* much, and not precisely what adults see. In 'Welcome to the Monkey House' the distinction between adults' and children's perceptions specifically concerns sexuality, but I think this double standard applies more broadly: adults, for example, may perceive the zoo's tawdriness and oppression and similarly seek to hide or transform this fact to protect their children.

Vonnegut describes the warped society that emerges in the aftermath of Nation's pill – a world where the government curbs natural human drives in the service of blandly Orwellian biological and cultural regulation. As in *Slaughterhouse-Five*, Vonnegut's comment about animal captivity in 'Welcome to the Monkey House' is not explicitly a diatribe against zoos. His attitude, although indirectly expressed, characterizes them as dangerous institutions that are implicated in other nasty things that occur in society. The story's title is wholly ironic: Vonnegut's brave new world is hardly one readers feel 'welcome' or eager to approach; a more straightforward title might be 'Enter at Your Own Risk,' or 'Abandon All Hope.' The 'monkey house' metaphorically represents the reactionary society Nation's pills have spawned. This society's cultural order obliges people to regulate and restrict their most innate personal drives, and subject themselves to autocrats' depraved control – and that, according to Vonnegut's social and political symbolism, is what it means to live in a zoo.

Underlying the self-righteous bluster in Nation's attempt to exert absolute control over zoo animals is a hypocritical bluff. The despots pretend their suppression benefits children. (If everybody takes Nation's pills, of course, there won't *be* any more children.) Tyrants often shield themselves behind children's interests when acting so unscrupulously as to defy any other rationale; children's welfare has traditionally offered a cover story for egregious moral violations. If autocrats can effectively spin-doctor outrageous policy so it appears to benefit children, resistance becomes untenable. But Vonnegut suggests the dangers inherent in such social self-deception: if we begin by tampering with our children's reality – numbing monkeys below the waist to prevent kids from discovering that it is fun to touch their genitals – the consequences snowball. When monkeys offend Nation's repressed sexual sensibility, the inventor uses children as an excuse to justify what is unnatural and ridiculous. By the same token, I think people could not rationally justify zoos without recourse to the commonly accepted (though dubious) assumption that they are good for children.

Except when such prurient censors as J. Edgar Nation block the view, zoos invite children to get very close to animals, promising that this interaction will be stimulating and beneficial; but sometimes children get too close. A prime function of a family zoo outing is for children to get closer – metaphorically, experientially – to animals; but there is latitude for disaster when efforts to facilitate this proximity go awry due to overeagerness or ignorant misappraisal of animals' real behavior. It is difficult 'to suppress a shudder,' writes John C. Edwards, when 'shown photographs of children embracing a subadult male chimpanzee (capable of ripping them limb from limb) in the Children's Zoo at the London Zoo in 1938' (143–4); the photographs show how even at one of the world's most distinguished zoos, and apparently with the keepers' full complicity, children may be exposed to ludicrous dangers because of a naive compulsion to foster closeness. An ancient account of children interacting with dangerous animals appears in Isaiah 11:6–8.

> The wolf also shall dwell with lamb, and the leopard shall lie down with the kid; and the calf and the young lion and the fatling together; and a little child shall lead them . . . And the suckling child shall play on the hole of the asp, and the weaned child shall put his hand on the cockatrice' den.

Similar to what modern zoos promise, the biblical utopian topos portrays children's intimate interaction with wild animals – controlled and subdued – as testimony to their society's talents, blessings, virtues. It is depicted as desirable for children to do things with animals that they rationally shouldn't.

Accounts of dangerous encounters between kids and zoo animals range from absurdity to tragedy. First, the ridiculous: a 1907 poem by Hilaire Belloc, from his *Cautionary Tales for Children*, launches a tradition of zoo stories about young zoo visitors who get eaten by lions. The title encapsulates its plot: 'Jim who Ran Away from his Nurse, and was Eaten by a Lion.'

> on this inauspicious day
> He slipped his hand and ran away!
> He hadn't gone a yard when – Bang!
> With open Jaws, a Lion sprang,
> And hungrily began to eat
> The Boy: beginning at his feet.
>
> (260)

Belloc describes the attack without stinting on gory details:

Now, just imagine how it feels
When first your toes and then your heels,
And then by gradual degrees,
Your shins and ankles, calves and knees,
Are slowly eaten, bit by bit.
No wonder Jim detested it!

(260–1)

The keeper runs to interrupt the carnage, but arrives too late. When he commands the animal to desist

The Lion made a sudden Stop,
He let the Dainty Morsel drop,
And slunk reluctant to his Cage
Snarling with Disappointed Rage.
But when he bent him over Jim,
The Honest Keeper's Eyes were dim.
The Lion having reached his Head,
The Miserable Boy was dead!

When Nurse informed his Parents, they
Were more concerned than I can say: –
His Mother, as she dried her eyes,
Said, 'Well – it gives me no surprise,
He would not do as he was told!'
His Father, who was self-controlled,
Bade all the children round attend
To James' miserable end,
And always keep a-hold of Nurse
For fear of finding something worse.

(261)

In the same tradition, Marriott Edgar's 'The Lion and Albert' (1933), the comic ballad popularized by music-hall star Stanley Holloway, tells of a family on a Blackpool holiday; the Ramsbottoms become bored of the seaside attractions, and

seeking for further amusement
they paid and went into the Zoo,

Where they'd lions and tigers and camels,
And old ale and sandwiches too.
There were one great big Lion called Wallace;
His nose were all covered with scars.
He lay in a somnolent posture,
With the side of his face on the bars.
Now Albert had heard about Lions;
How they was ferocious and wild.
To see Wallace lying so peaceful;
Well it didn't seem right to the child.
So straightway the brave little felller,
Not showing a morsel of fear,
Took his stick with his 'orses's 'ead 'andle
And pushed it in Wallace's ear.
You could see that the Lion didn't like it,
For giving a kind of a roll,
He pulled Albert inside the cage with 'im,
And swallowed the little lad 'ole.

(2–3)

In the burlesque mode, Mr and Mrs Ramsbottom handle the incident with English aplomb: they register a complaint with the keeper, who 'was quite nice about it; He said "What a nasty mishap. Are you sure that it's *your* boy he's eaten?" Pa said "Am I sure? There's his cap"' (4). When the manager is summoned, 'He took out his purse right away, Saying "How much to settle the matter?" And Pa said "What do you usually pay?"' (5). Finally, when the Ramsbottoms appeal to higher authorities,

The Magistrate gave his opinion
That no-one was really to blame,
And he said that he hoped the Ramsbottoms
would have further sons to their name.
At that Mother got proper blazing,
'And thank you sir, kindly,' said she,
'What waste all our lives raising children
To feed ruddy lions? Not me!'

(5)

In a sequel, 'The Return of Albert' (1935), the lion regurgitates the boy just as the insurance firm issues a reparations payment.

Faced with the return of his son but the loss of nine pounds four and two, Mr Ramsbottom gives it one last go: 'The young feller from the Prudential, to pick up the money began, And father says "Eeh! just a moment, don't be in a 'urry young man." Then giving young Albert a shilling 'e said "Pop off back to the Zoo. 'Ere's yer stick with 'orses's 'ead 'andle, go and see what the Tigers can do!"' (17).

Belloc's light verse and Holloway's music-hall ballads would be pleasantly diverting zoo stories if they embodied no more than innocent frivolity. But turning to real life, these farces provide a macabre counterpoint to the literal and freakish horror that has actually befallen children who come too close to zoo animals. On 19 May 1987, two polar bears mauled and killed 11-year-old Juan Perez in Brooklyn's Prospect Park Zoo. A woman called 911 after hearing screams coming from the zoo; police who responded discovered that Juan had sneaked into the bear enclosure with two friends by scaling a spiked fence. When they first arrived, police saw bears mangling the boy's body. In an effort to save him (although he was probably already dead), police fired shotguns and revolvers 26 times, killing the two bears which stood eight feet tall and weighed over 900 pounds. Parks Commissioner Henry J. Stern said of the bears' shooting: '"They were not executed ... There seems to be no question but the police did the right thing in the circumstances." When asked what might provoke such an attack, Mr. Stern said, "The mere presence of people in their cage." He said polar bears are territorial and vicious by nature, but that these two – Teddy and Lucy – had never attacked anyone before' (Barron, 'Polar Bears'). Stern added that this fatality was the first involving a bear in a New York City zoo since 1982, when a man was found dead inside Central Park Zoo's polar bear cage after having climbed a series of fences to enter that compound.

Two days after the death, the *New York Times* reported that Juan had entered the bear enclosure after he and two companions, who escaped unharmed, had dared each other to go swimming inside the fence; they were wading in a shallow moat near where the bears were sleeping. 'The two animals, apparently awakened by what they considered to be intruders, clambered down a rocky cliff toward the moat, where one lunged at Juan, dragged him into the den and engaged in a tug-of-war over the body before being shot' (Rangel). Stern reported that more than a dozen illegal entries into the zoo had occurred since 1984, and that keepers regularly chased off children who tried to scale the fence after closing. He hoped the incident would reshape public attitudes about bears: '"People see bears as honey eating, tender loving creatures," he said. "But polar bears are carnivorous animals and highly protective of their territory. In romance, we've overlooked the fact that they are highly dangerous animals."'[11] The *Times* also reported hundreds of irate callers to the police and parks department protesting the animals' shooting, but a police spokesperson said most were not well informed about the circumstances.

The following day's news account concluded the story's high-profile coverage, which had fascinated and saddened the city, by reporting concern about what the incident signified for zoos: 'Many zoo patrons and animal lovers are questioning whether it is advisable to keep wild animals in city zoos. They also wonder whether anything can be done to guarantee safety, other than to lock the animals in secure cages at night . . . "This should never have happened," said Virginia Chipurnoi, the president of the Humane Society of New York. "The child is the heartbreak, of course, but it's also a heartbreak that three lives were lost. Those animals were in their own territory and the children should not have been in the zoo at night"' (Barron, 'Officials').

Were the bears really 'in their own territory' – in *Brooklyn*? Certainly, as she says, the children should not have been in the zoo at night. But should the bears have been there either? Without trivializing the tragic waste of Juan's death, one must extend the scope of tragedy even further. As Chipurnoi admits, the bears' shooting compounds the pathos; and beyond this, the animals' mere presence in Brooklyn in the first place must be considered part of the nexus of events that augments the misfortune. The boy and the bears were all in the wrong place at the wrong time, and all suffered for it. The incident discloses an etiology that indicts the cultural construct of zoos. Juan was the victim of a confluence of factors, including the fact that the bears had been brought to a Brooklyn zoo; that he and his friends were drawn to the captive animals; that the boys dared each other, for an adventure, to get too close to bears and to disregard the cage separating children from animals; that they failed to understand the extent of the danger inside the enclosure.

The scene must have been gruesome; in Juan's case, the horror is self-evident. But a zoo story account may help elucidate the bears' fate. In 'The Zoo Attack,' Haruki Murakami describes Japanese soldiers shooting bears in a zoo, slaughtering the animals in anticipation of their Second World War defeat. The circumstances, of course, differ vastly from the Brooklyn Zoo incident, but Murakami's story provides a perspective that may usefully complement news accounts of the New York bear killing. The aesthetic *focus* inherent in fiction conveys an action's essence, significance, and magnitude, in a way that may elude nonfictional representations. The fiction, a contrivance, may not necessarily shed light on an actual historical incident, but potentially it can supply a resonant moral sensibility and a thorough overview from a carefully crafted viewpoint, as immediate journalistic accounts may not. Of course fiction may be as susceptible as journalism to propaganda, cultural blind spots, and other distorting biases; but arraying parallel journalistic and literary investigations of a phenomenon may provide mutual checks and balances: one medium may illuminate elements of truth which another obscures, and so the end result of such a conjunction may provide insights that transcend any single discourse. Zoo stories invite readers to consider their representations and decide whether they correlate with reality, how they enlighten us, if at all. Murakami's depiction of killing bears in the zoo may or may not relate to the NYPD's killing bears in the zoo – readers may judge for themselves.

> They killed the leopards. They killed the wolves. They killed the bears. Shooting the bears took the most time. Even after the two gigantic animals had taken dozens of rifle slugs, they continued to crash against the bars of their cage, roaring at the men and slobbering, fangs bared. Unlike the cats, who were more willing to accept their fate (or who at least appeared to accept it), the bears seemed unable to comprehend the fact that they were being killed. When, at long last, the soldiers finally succeeded at extinguishing all signs of life in the bears, they were so exhausted they were ready to collapse on the spot. The lieutenant reset his pistol's safety catch and used his hat to wipe the sweat dripping from his brow. In the deep silence that followed the killing, several of the soldiers seemed to be trying to mask their feelings of shame by spitting loudly on the ground. Spent shells were scattered about their feet like

> so many cigarette butts. Their ears still rang with the crackling of their rifles. The young soldier who would be beaten to death by a Soviet soldier seventeen months later in a coal mine near Irkutsk took several deep breaths in succession, averting his gaze from the bears' corpse. He was engaged in a fierce struggle to force back the nausea that had worked its way up to his throat.
>
> (72)

Juan Perez was not the only child who ever tried to enter a zoo cage: as Stern said, the type of illicit zoo activity that led to Juan's death occurs regularly. I agree with Stern that this incident highlights people's ignorance about wild animals, but I break ranks with his implication about how people *should* come to know a bear's actual nature. Stern implies that people should try with increased determination to learn about animals in zoos and to respect cages. I would think, on the other hand, Juan's death informs that people should *stop* regarding zoos as places where people and animals can learn to interact better: the enterprise has been a failure. A week after the deaths, in a coda to the misadventure, the city issued a report finding that the zoo should increase its security:

> uniformed guards trained in security measures and using vehicles with searchlights, two-way radios and a public address system should be immediately assigned on each of the evening and night shifts . . . the incident requires that the entire planning standards for the zoo be re-examined. 'No longer can exhibits be designed with the intention of keeping the animals in,' it said. 'Such exhibits must now be designed with an eye to keeping the people out.'
>
> ('Report')

Zookeepers and city administrators responded to the child's death by augmenting communications technology and institutional bureaucracy, assigning more guards, increasing the efficiency and intricacy of animal captivity. Such responses, however, treat the symptoms rather than the underlying essence of the situation.

Henri Cole's 'The Zoo Wheel of Knowledge,' discussed at the beginning of this chapter, describes a parent's decision to bring his children to the zoo – a resolution tinged with a proleptic vision of tragedy. Later in the poem, an oddly muted, almost understated scene eerily evokes the fate of Juan Perez. The family visits

> the dark, arctic tanks where the bears
> glide, monsterlike yet sultry,
> their eyes opening, brown as mother's,
> at the viewing window, their phosphorescent
>
> trunks so white and godlike
> a neighbor's sons, one night, scaled the wall
> to dive and kick among them.
>
> (63)

Like many other zoo stories involving children, 'The Zoo Wheel of Knowledge' registers the scary, macabre milieu that zoos can engender. The bears in their tanks are eerie, unreal, ghastly – almost like aliens in a science-fiction B-movie – figuratively reinforcing the reasons for fearing and resisting zoos, as Doctorow's Edgar, Doyle's Paddy, and Allende's Alba do. For Cole's boys, like the boys in Thomas's 'The Hunchback in the Park,' the zoo projects a dangerously seductive allure. Its unnatural air, as both poets represent it, has the ironic and harmful effect of enticing the children to act in ways they should not: relatively harmlessly (albeit nastily) in Thomas's poem, but appallingly in 'The Zoo Wheel of Knowledge,' as the boys are drawn, like Juan and his friends, into the bear cage. I do not completely understand the details of the boys' misfortune as Cole depicts it – what exactly about these odd-looking bears lured the boys into the cage – but then again, a rationally coherent explanation for what led to the real-life Brooklyn zoo deaths was similarly elusive.[12]

Cole's boys – nameless in the poem itself, but identified in the dedication *'for Christopher Bram and Draper Shreve'* – meet the same fate as Juan Perez. Cole confirms their deaths later in the poem, offhandedly, when he refers to the zoo by evening light as a 'crazy fantasia / of the unconscious where we all collect / eventually, even . . . the souls / of the boys found in the polar tank' (64). Cole avoids confronting Christopher and Draper's tragedy head-on; oddly, he skews his narrative by embedding their deaths in a poem that devotes more attention to the quotidian details of a family zoo visit and that omits literally identifying them in the body of the poem. Perhaps Cole presents the events this way because it is too horrible for him to describe directly the tragedy of 'a neighbor's sons' (which augurs the calamities that might befall one's own children). Perhaps he realizes that the boys' deaths do not have to be highlighted more prominently: the horror speaks for itself, even in the muted way it appears here. Perhaps he regards the deaths as unremarkable, simply business as usual at the zoo. If one transposed the boys from 'The Hunchback in the Park,' one could easily imagine that they, too, given the chance to cavort with bears, would have been eager 'to dive and kick among them.'

Very few children, thankfully, are killed in zoos, but Cole's poem raises the prospect of how people's deaths may serve as emblems of the range of dangers zoos embody. O'Neill's Yank dies in a zoo cage at the end of *The Hairy Ape*, and in Goodman's *The Empire City*, a tiger kills Gus – the little boy whose nightmares belie his supposed attraction to the zoo – when the animals are set free. Albee's Jerry dies simply in the attempt to confront and express a zoo story. Zoo deaths, while rare, are possible and therefore enter into the moral discourse in which we debate the existence of zoos; they provide an endpoint – and not just hypothetical, but real – of the continuum on which we appraise the value of zoos. Juan Perez is not the only victim: as Parks Commissioner Henry Stern said, the last *bear-related zoo death* in New York City occurred five years previously. How many zoo deaths had there been in that time involving *other* animals, I wonder? How many bear-deaths, and other-than-bear-deaths, and non-lethal maulings, occurred in zoos outside New York City? In fact, it is not difficult to uncover such information case by case, now that every contemporary event is accessible on-line. Simply call up a database such as InfoTrac or ProQuest, search for zoos, and read the body count of people – often, kids – who get *too close* to animals. March 1996: eight people are hospitalized, including a six-year-old boy near death from dehydration, when they contract salmonella bacteria after stroking a Komodo Dragon held by a zoo employee. March 1995: a homeless woman thought to be mentally ill is mauled to death by lions at Washington's National Zoo after crossing several barriers and entering their cage; ruled a suicide. January 1995: a lion in the London Zoo is killed after mauling two men who climbed into its enclosure. December 1994: a two-and-a-half year old boy loses most of his right arm after being attacked by wolves in Wisconsin's Manitowoc

City Zoo; the wolves were destroyed immediately. In 'Sunday at the Zoo' (1986), Stuart Dybek writes:

> Just that week the newspapers had carried an account of how a small girl had an arm gnawed off – she'd reached in to pet them and one wolf held it while the other ate. It was, in fact, what had led us, along with the crowd, relentlessly to the wolves' cage.
>
> (128)

Dybek suggests that such horrific encounters between children and animals at the zoo perversely accord with – or even augment – whatever it is that makes the zoo appealing. Such perversity exaggerates, but reiterates, the subtler paradox that underlies the opening of Cole's 'The Zoo Wheel of Knowledge,' when the family heads for the zoo despite the sense of danger it projects.

In 1987, I lived in the same Brooklyn community as Juan Perez. While I never knew him, he was, as Cole describes Christopher and Draper, a neighbor's son. I determined to write this book, as Cole was inspired to write 'The Zoo Wheel of Knowledge,'[13] partly as a response to Juan's death. Afterwards, I stopped walking through the Prospect Park Zoo, and I resolved that when I had my own children, I would never take them to the zoo.

7

Animals and their Contexts: Beyond Zoos

All animals are entitled to respect ... All wild animals have the right to liberty in their natural environment ... Deprivation of freedom, even for educational purposes, is an infringement of this right ... No animal shall be exploited for the amusement of man. Exhibitions and spectacles involving animals are incompatible with their dignity.

Universal Declaration of the Rights of Animals

He did not care for zoos.

Janice Elliott, 'The Noise from the Zoo'

I conclude by examining two types of zoo stories that distance the zoo from the story. The first of these features a zoo frame: the work begins and ends with reference to a zoo, but in a way not particularly integral to the narrative's main thrust. This may be a strategy for invoking and then sidestepping the morass that seems endemic to zoo stories – perhaps reflecting writers' cognizance of the zoo's stultifying cultural influence. Marianne Moore and Albrecht Dürer epitomize the second type: they determine to transcend captivity in their representations of animals.

Janice Elliott's 'The Noise from the Zoo' (1991) relates a drily absurdist and loosely existentialist account of a man, Felix, who digs a hole for no reason, in an action he intends to be wholly pointless. When the unremarkable hole and its *raison d'être* (or lack thereof) are discovered, the interest of the press is aroused; the authorities are suspicious, threatened, antagonistic to the hole's existence; the public is curious, amused, and, in some quarters, fiercely determined to defend what they see as casual anarchy, or silly season diversion. Felix is dismayed when opposing camps ultimately come to violent confrontation: Parks Committee workers attempting to fill in the hole become engaged in a full-fledged riot with the Save the Hole group (bearing slogans such as 'AN ENGLISHMAN'S HOLE IS HIS CASTLE'). Elliott's point seems to be that we live in such a fractious, thoughtlessly combative world that any gesture, however innocuous, can incite our prejudices to violence.

The story has nothing to do with a zoo aside from its title and an opening and closing zoo frame. The opening paragraph:

> From where he dug in the night Felix could hear the zoo. As the last visitor left the murmur began; these were the smaller, familiar animals, the gossips, but by midnight the larger and the rarer gave voice and Felix paused to listen to the bellows, moans of complaint, and wild laughter. At first this seemed to him an hysterical conversation between insomniacs, later, as weariness and fancy overtook him, the Passion of the beasts, the desperate cry of martyred innocents. He did not care for zoos. The animals appeared to him prisoners without hope of release or redemption. Those not captured but born there were like the blind born without sight. For himself, if he were a beast and could choose he would prefer capture, if only to have something to remember, to talk about at night.
>
> (184)

Elliott makes no further reference to zoos or animals until the conclusion. During the riot:

> A passing and oblivious dog, his mind perhaps on burying bones, paused, was astonished by the hole and set up a piercing howl. From the zoo a hyena answered . . . When the crowd had been dispersed and the injured carried away Felix, who was not the kind of man you would notice in a riot, came out from the trees and stood by the hole. He hardly recognised it. In the fighting the edges had been broken and it had already begun to fill with rain. He saw it . . . as a grave; soon it would be a pond. If you looked long enough you could make anything you liked of it. Someone had left a lamp. Kneeling, the rain trickling down his neck, he held it close to the rising surface of the water and saw, reflected, a face he recognised to be his

> own. He stood, awkwardly, and found that he was crying. He stayed for a while listening to the noise from the zoo.
> (189)

The zoo contextualizes the framed story, at the same time the intervening narrative resists it. The zoo, while close to the scene of this story, is nevertheless definitively separate. It never appears, nor do the animals, except in the noises that cross the barrier from the zoo to Felix; between people and zoo animals there is no intercourse (reiterating the theme common to zoo stories that people interact poorly with captive animals).

The title, 'The Noise from the Zoo,' raises but then subverts readers' expectations that the story will involve a zoo. Similarly, many zoo stories depict zoos as places that raise but then disappoint people's expectations about experiencing animals. The zoo's absence in Elliott's story may arouse curiosity about what is happening there, but at the same time the narrative declines to venture inside the zoo. Its physical absence despite its formal presence (in title and frame) makes its effect more loaded, perhaps more sinister.

In part, the zoo's symbolic effect is somewhat obvious: writers often invoke a zoo in juxtaposition with the world outside to connote a character's supposedly 'free' (vibrant, sophisticated) life as being, in fact, caged, degraded, dreary.[1] At the end, when Felix hears the noise from the zoo, recognizes himself, and cries in the same moment, it seems to evoke the common association of zoos with constraint. Felix is like a trapped zoo animal, driven to his meaningless action of digging a pointless hole because the 'cage' of his own world limits him so greatly that any significant gesture is unimaginable.

'The noise from the zoo' suggests (but does not literally portray) the cruelty of animal captivity. Felix hears the noise and assumes it corresponds to animals' pain,[2] but – because of the zoo's absence from the story – cannot confirm or refute his supposition by first-hand experience. At the beginning of the story the noise evokes for Felix troubling imagery of deranged, tortured prisoners; at the end it accompanies his awareness of the Hobbesian brutality of life, and the fact that for the zoo animals (as for him and his society?) nothing has changed throughout the course of the story – animals and people have all simply spent a bit more time in jail.

What if we could 'hear' this noise more clearly and make sense of it? Connect the noise with animals (*real* animals, not zoo animals)? Communicate and interact with creatures expressing something momentous, something that might alleviate people's destructive instincts and somehow inform our suffering? Elliott provokes such deliberations for the reader, and perhaps subliminally for Felix himself as he listens to the animals' sounds. The incomprehensible noise confirms the gulf between species, between all creatures; confirms, too, the futility of attempting to transcend this gulf. Elliott's zoo informs us of impossibility, of unimplementable ideals; it fails as a place of communication, education, or interaction. She reinforces this message in terms of the disjunctive frame. The animal noise finally fails to connect (except in so far as the reader conjecturally attempts to work out possible implications) with the 'human noise,' the story, the narrative. The *frame* would better fit the *picture*, the rest of the story, if Felix had some sense of how he relates to the zoo and its noises – if, for example, he consciously realized his affinity to the captive animals and, as in Russell Hoban's *Turtle Diary*, dug the hole as a symbolic escape, a 'jailbreak' from his own cage, or as a vicarious gesture for the animals whose cries evoke his sympathy.

But, Elliott stresses, Felix doesn't know why he is digging the hole; his action has no meaning. The frame finally doesn't fit the picture, just as, in the zoo, the frames (in the form of cages) do not 'fit' the animals inside – do not do justice to them; in fact, they obscure and distort them in a way that frames should not do. Henri Cole's poem 'The Zoo Wheel of Knowledge' describes the gulf between people outside a cage looking at animals inside: 'the cage-bars / frame us apart' (64). Theoretically, a frame should support and enhance the work inside, unobtrusively, but in zoo stories, the frame tends rather to *challenge* that which is framed. John Berger deconstructs frames and cages at the zoo:

> as many species and varieties of animal as possible are collected in order that they can be seen, observed, studied. In principle, each cage is a frame round the animal inside it. Visitors visit the zoo to look at animals. They proceed from cage to cage, not unlike visitors in an art gallery who stop in front of one painting, and then move on to the next . . . Yet in the zoo the view is always wrong. Like an image out of focus. One is so used to this that one scarcely notices it any more . . . However you look at these animals, even if the animal is up against the bars, less

> than a foot from you, looking outwards in the public direction, *you are looking at something that has been rendered absolutely marginal*; and all the concentration you can muster will never be enough to centralise it.
>
> (21–2; author's emphasis)

The frame in 'The Noise from the Zoo' evokes the problematics that mark numerous other zoo stories: the difficulty of meshing a human context with the distorting contexts zoos impose on animals, in venues where we aspire, unpromisingly, to combine stories of people and animals; and the near-impossibility of hearing – coherently, meaningfully – the 'noises' animals emit from their cages in places where they shouldn't be. As he digs his hole on the street outside the zoo, Felix cannot understand the noise from inside the animal compound as anything more than just noise because, in the natural order of things, there shouldn't be such noise infusing his world, and both his and the animals' worlds are the poorer (anguished, existentially inauthentic) for this.

Jean Stafford also uses the zoo to frame her story 'In the Zoo' (1953); as in Elliott's story, the zoo appears marginally relevant to the rest of the narrative despite its presence in the title and as an opening and closing frame. The story relates two middle-aged sisters' reminiscences of an emotionally stinted childhood with a dour and manipulative foster mother, Mrs Placer, in Adams, Colorado: an experience so painful that 'you only have to say the name of the town aloud to us to rip the rinds from our nerves and leave us exposed in terror and humiliation' (285). Stafford begins by making her reader look (uncomfortably) at animals in the Denver zoo:

> Keening in his senility, the blind polar bear slowly and ceaselessly shakes his head in the stark heat of the July and mountain noon. His open eyes are blue. No one stops to look at him; an old farmer, in passing, sums up the old bear's situation by observing, with a ruthless chuckle, that he is a 'back number.' Patient and despairing, he sits on his yellowed haunches on the central rock of his pool, his huge toy paws wearing short boots of mud.
>
> (283)

After further descriptions of animals, the focus wanders to the narrator and her sister, Daisy, who are sitting on a bench at the zoo. The blind bear reminds them of Mr Murphy, a strange codger from Adams but one of the few people the girls counted as a friend; this connection triggers their memories of the past. The bear evokes recollections of Mr Murphy both because the man (habitually drunk, prone to odd displays of behavior, functionless in his world), like the zoo animal, was strikingly pathetic, and because Mr Murphy kept what the narrator calls a 'small menagerie' with several animals including a skunk, a parrot, two monkeys, and a coyote. 'In the Zoo' touches on the subject of animals but, like 'The Noise from the Zoo,' it is more about people's problems – our cruelty, oddness, and dysfunctionality.

The opening zoo frame depicts an insistently disturbing cavalcade of images. The polar bear's habitat is grossly inappropriate 'in the stark heat of the July and mountain noon.' Its ceaselessly shaking head indicates what a zoologist would diagnose as the abnormality of stereotypy (repetitive animal behavior that does not naturally occur and that indicates a disturbed state). As in the scene from Galsworthy's *The Man of Property* where unpleasant people mock similarly unpleasant looking animals in a spectacle that degrades both zoo animals and visitors, an old farmer here taunts the polar bear with ruthless cruelty. Most other zoogoers ignore the bear, confirming the frequent observation in zoo stories that, by and large, sloppily unobservant spectators *miss* more than they see of the specimens assembled for them. The bear is in despair; the display allows no modest retreat – instead, it mercilessly spotlights the animal on a central rock. With its 'huge toy paws' and 'boots of mud,' the bear's tragic humiliation is sealed with grotesque overtones. (Zoo stories frequently depict animals unflatteringly bedraggled and disheveled, as, for example, in Irving's *Setting Free the Bears*: 'we saw the giraffe's head tottering on its neckpole. The shambly heap of the giraffe followed its neck; bucket-hooved, its legs tried to keep up. There was a raw, hairless spot on its thin chin, where it had scraped the high storm fence' (12); and the bears' 'coats looked oddly slept on, like a series of cowlicks' (18). In Penelope Lively's *Moon Tiger*, 'The polar bear, its dark yellow flanks heaving, its coat tufted like a badly mown lawn, lies in a basin of dirty water' (105). And in *The Liars' Club*, Mary Karr passes a cage where 'The Bengal tiger had flies creeping all over its eyelids, and he didn't even blink' (54); a vampire bat 'seemed so awkward trying to arrange his frail-looking wings that I kept thinking of a broken umbrella' (55).)

The bear's evocation of Mr Murphy leads into the story of a dog he gave the sisters. Mrs Placer renamed the dog, making it her own ally, and Mr Murphy angrily confronted her upon discovering this. During their argument, the dog attacked and killed the monkey Mr Murphy had brought with him; in revenge, he poisoned the dog. The zoo setting serves no apparent narrative function except to evoke Mr Murphy, and even the incident involving him is not very significant except as a vehicle for the sisters to recall, and attempt to confront and exorcise, their animosity toward Mrs Placer. The dog story in the foreground of their rambling memories indicates the lunacy amid which the girls were raised. At the end of the story, the sisters conclude their reminiscences and return to the immediate moment. As they try to distance the painful memories from Adams, their crazy childhood friend Mr Murphy metamorphoses back into the present-day animal that sparked the reverie: 'Even if we were able to close our minds' eyes to the past, Mr Murphy would still be before us in the apotheosis of the polar bear' (302). The sisters are back in the zoo, where they began, completing the zoo frame that opened the story; the narrator boards the train to return home, leaving her sister until their next reunion.

At the same time that the zoo seems literally irrelevant, however – little more than a construct or springboard for an unrelated kind of story – it has a figurative resonance as in 'The Noise from the Zoo.' The zoo animals set up, or symbolically parallel, the sisters' disturbing youth. The frame features 'the narrator ironically describing the animals in distinctly human terms,' writes Mary Ann Wilson, to suggest that the animals' 'little community here in the zoo is riddled with all the cruel social snobberies plaguing their human counterparts' (52); and the deadening pathos of the animals' unfortunate constraint symbolizes the human tragedy Stafford dramatizes, of 'an insidious destruction of the spirit that rendered [the sisters'] anxious souls ill equipped to face the world' (54). Mrs Placer, metaphorically resembling a heartless zookeeper, lacks any concern for her charges' well-being, fundamentally incapable of appreciating their needs and sensibilities.

'This zoo is in Denver, a city that means nothing to my sister and me except as a place to take or meet trains,' Stafford writes (284). The two sisters do not belong in the zoo, or in Denver; they have no meaningful connection to the place. Formally, the zoo frame reenacts this misplacement with its apparent irrelevance to the narrative. And by the same token, zoo animals themselves lack any reason for being there – certainly the senile polar bear cannot fathom why it is in the harsh Colorado sun – just as the younger girls had no reason for being in Adams, no sense of fitting in congenial environs there. Unlike Elliott's story, with its discordance between frame and story, the frame 'fits' for Stafford. The sisters realize, in the zoo, that they cannot fully escape their unhappy memories; they are, in a sense, 'caged' like the sad zoo animals they regard. The zoo is an appropriate backdrop for this story, although it initially seemed tangential. Elliott's character Felix, wallowing in his existential mire, probably could not explain, if asked, why he happened to dig his hole near the zoo, but these sisters *should* be able to discern the relation of the zoo setting to their own unfortunate history. In both cases, the zoo functions as a frame – whether perceived or not – to our own human sense of constraint and our own versions of stereotypy. On the most basic level, both authors suggest, the way people treat animals bears some relation to the way people treat other people, and if we consider our lives to be miserable we could perhaps look for fellowship to zoo animals, whose lives are similarly (by our doing) miserable. Certainly we have the power to alleviate their captivity, their suffering; perhaps, too, we have the power to ameliorate ourselves.

Two writers, Countee Cullen and Conrad Aiken, produced similar volumes of children's poetry about animals (both accompanied by profuse color illustration, and both representing obscure elements of their oeuvres). Like Elliott's and Stafford's stories, both works have a zoo title and a zoo frame but do not really describe zoos; they depict, instead, imaginary animals in what may be considered a kind of 'anti-zoo,' since the creatures do not really exist and even if they did, they are portrayed as inhabiting an unconstrained realm of imaginative fantasy, not a zoo. As in the stories by Elliott and Stafford, there is a complicated interplay between the zoo frame and the non-zoo or anti-zoo interior. Within the zoo frames of both books, animals explicitly go beyond zoos, transcending the frames; yet both works also in some ways reinforce the primacy of zoos as the conventional setting for experiencing animals. The books essentially negate the constraint of animals as a prerequisite for experiencing them, encouraging instead the exercise of the imagination; yet they retain at least a slender connection to animal captivity in zoos.[3]

Aiken's *Who's Zoo* (1977, published posthumously) depicts fanciful combinations of animals such as the 'Rhinocerostrich' and the 'Camelephant.'[4] Aside from the title, there is minimal reference to zoos *per se*. The first animal, the 'Alligatorangutan,' is described as 'reading in his cage,' but all other animals are completely free of zoo restraints: the 'Guineapiguana,' for example, travels widely as he 'voyages to Havana, / or, occasionally, Savannah'; the 'Tigermine' lives in arctic nature, in a 'lonely luminous palace / of Aurora Borealis.' Contrasting with the relative homogeneity of zoo animals' contexts, Aiken's imaginary animals manifest widely varied behavior, activities, habitats, and exploits: the 'Octopuss,' for example, spends all night roistering with oysters, gets them drunk, and steals their pearls (which it uses to solicit the attention of Hula girls on the beach at Waikiki); the 'Chimpanzebra' spends his days drinking Cuba Libres in baths of Coca Cola and reading 'Mr Eliot's Five Foot Shelf' of great literature.

But a final poem, 'Epilogue,' imposes a zoo frame on *Who's Zoo*. The speaker of all the other poems announces, in the final lines, that the fantastic collection of animals presented herein *is* a zoo, if not a normal one:

> Where do I keep my Zoo? My child,
>   these creatures are so *very* mild,
> so tame, so shy, so sensitive,
>   they could not for a moment *live*
> if people came, and paid a penny,
>   and then just stared, and said How funny!
> That, I'm afraid, would *never* do.
>   But *some* day, I might take *just you*
> to see this quite unrivalled Zoo.
>   Till then, I sign myself, good-bye,
>   Yours truly
>   Giddyun Butterfly.

Via Giddyun, Aiken briefly but unmistakably condemns the institution of zoos, at least for these 'special' sensitive animals which could not survive in a conventional zoo – they would die or wither under the gazes of ignorant spectators if they lived in captivity. But when the butterfly tells its reader that someday maybe *'just you'* will see *this* zoo, Aiken at least nominally affirms the construct of zoos and their potential allure. Aiken asserts that these animals, 'quite unrivalled,' are immensely more fascinating than conventional zoo animals; the corollary implications are, first, that these animals do not exist in captivity – readers can never experience them except by reading about them in this book; and, second, that zoo spectators oppress animals. In the main, this book offers an anti-zoo. A child who read this book and later visited the zoo might well be disappointed by the zoo's offerings, and affirm that the poet has splendidly imagined an unbridled exoticism that the zoo cannot capture. The 'Epilogue' conveys the idea that zoos are bad, but implies that an ideal zoo could exist – although anything resembling a zoo would be irreconcilable with the imaginative richness of Aiken's animals.

Like Aiken's poetry, Cullen's *The Lost Zoo* (1940) describes animals that do not exist in nature, and certainly not in zoos – specifically, animals that missed the boat for Noah's ark, the seminal zoo archetype in Western culture.[5] Cullen's animals are all imaginary: supposedly extinct, and of course literally nonexistent; so like Aiken's, these poems do not manifestly affirm the exploitation or appropriation of animals. Cullen's animals are as fancifully extravagant as Aiken's, and as unfettered by any human constraint: they include the haughty and graceful 'Snake-That-Walked-Upon-His-Tail', the frisky, mirthful 'Ha-Ha-Ha', and the 'Wakeupworld', a surreal creature with an omnipotent control of time.

A prose introduction to the collection features an account of the relationship between a first-person narrator and his cat friend, Christopher. A zoo frame – a prose frame to a mainly verse work – opens as Cullen informs that he frequently visits the zoo because he likes looking at astonishing animals, but conceals these visits from his friend because he thinks Christopher would want to go with him, and it would be difficult to take a cat to the zoo. (We may infer an unacknowledged reason for Cullen's concealment:

guilt at letting his animal friend know about his excursions to gape at fellow animals behind bars.) Finally, one day, the narrator has such a fine time at the zoo that he cannot keep it to himself, and begs Christopher to guess where he has been.

> 'I give up,' purred Christopher contentedly, without making even the slightest attempt to guess. 'Tell me. Where *did* you go?'
>
> 'To the Zoo!' I answered very importantly, looking him straight in the eye to see how he would take it, for I was sure he would be beside himself with excitement!
>
> You can imagine my disappointment when all he said was, 'Oh, *that* place!'
>
> 'Is that all you have to say, Christopher?'
>
> 'No,' he answered, gazing at me sadly. 'How I pity all those poor animals.'
>
> (14)

The cat listens briefly to the narrator's account, unimpressed by stories of antic monkeys and majestic lions. '[I]t seems to me that you didn't see anything or anyone very exciting. Wasn't there anything new?' (15). Uncompromisingly, the animal deflates its friend's naive excitement at the zoo experience, construing it as commonplace and formulaic. Resisting the narrator's enthusiasm, the cat redirects attention to the plight of the 'poor animals.' Christopher straightforwardly does what animals in other zoo stories attempt more obliquely: the cat informs that zoos are bad places for people to interact with animals.

Most animals in zoo stories are depicted as less successful than Christopher at getting their message across. With the exception of fabulous fantasy literature such as *The Lost Zoo*, literary animals tend not to speak human language to people, so – despite the anthropomorphic flair infusing many zoo stories – they are incapable of precisely communicating their feelings about captivity. Zoo animals are mainly unvoiced, I conjecture, in deference to a prejudice that projects upon nature a mute cultural impoverishment. 'Nature *is* silent in our culture,' writes Christopher Manes, 'in the sense that the status of being a speaking subject is jealously guarded as an exclusively human prerogative . . . It is as if we had compressed the entire buzzing, howling, gurgling biosphere' into a subservient silence (15). (Alternative perspectives exist, he notes: 'for animistic cultures,' for example, 'animals, plants, and even "inert" entities such as stones and rivers are perceived as being articulate and at times intelligible subjects . . . In addition to human language, there is also the language of birds, the wind, earthworms, wolves, and waterfalls – a world of autonomous speakers whose intents . . . one ignores at one's peril' (15).) Steve Baker examines the phenomenon of talking animals, mainly with respect to cartoons, and develops an 'insight of [Ursula K.] Le Guin's: that something in the structure of the talking-animal story makes it inherently subversive of patriarchal culture' (137). Talking animals can subvert the 'denial of the animal' (125), and can exploit their gift of human speech 'in order to turn the tables on the society which so readily marginalizes them' (152). In a zoo story, a talking animal is well poised to become what Baker calls 'the avenging animal' (154). It makes sense to assume talking animals might be eager to tell people, directly and unmistakably, their unflattering reactions to what we have done to them in zoos. If the zoo's own discourse generally stifles debate or critical examination of zoo practices, then the prospect of talking animals figures to threaten this; could zoos defend themselves in response to animals' direct broadsides?

As an animal, Christopher is more sympathetic than the narrator to the predicament of zoo animals. Animals are depicted as being more receptive than people to the condition of other animals – even if one is a zoo animal and the other a domesticated pet. Bonds of animal connection endure (unified in opposition to the dominant human oppressors). The reader's sympathies align with Christopher, who seems more likely than his zoogoing human friend to be sensitive to the authentic experience of animals.

Christopher continues to undercut his friend's zoo visit by showing him how much he missed. The theme of how (ironically) oblivious zoo spectators can be to animals recurs frequently. *The Lost Zoo* offers Christopher the opportunity to make the point that zoos offer a paltry approximation of the vast fascination animals can embody. The cat asks, '"Did you, by any chance, . . . see a Squilililigee?" . . . "No, Christopher," I replied as calmly as I could. "No, I didn't see a Squilililigee." "You bet you didn't, and you bet you never will," said Christopher' (16–17). The cat goes on to describe numerous animals the narrator did not see at the zoo, and never could see, because they do not exist in captivity; they come to life exuberantly in *The Lost Zoo*, rather, via the processes of imaginative depiction. The cat taunts his friend about the impossibility of his seeing these 'lost' animals and, simultaneously, whets his desire to find out more about them – obviously, necessarily, in some other way than in a zoo. The ensuing poetry (for which Christopher is accorded co-authorship), displacing zoos, represents a better way of thinking about animals. Introducing the poetry, the zoo frame suggests that people who want to experience awesome animals have to go beyond habitual ways of seeing them: beyond zoos.

Cullen's (and Christopher's) poetry begins by describing the process of collecting animals before the flood, giving playful accounts of the peccadilloes of the animals we know today – those that made it onto the ark. The section ends depicting them on board, 'safe and sound,' leading into the title of the next section (the heart of the book): 'Except These Very Unfortunate Few / We Never Shall See in Any Zoo' (45). *Are* they really unfortunate? Cullen, in fact, grants them much more imaginative potency than the animals preceding them. The 'unfortunate' animals had considerably more exciting lives than they would have had in a zoo. He shows the ark-animals to be bickering and petty: the elephant demands not to be lodged near the mice, and bees resent the bears' expectations of free access to their honey. The animals on the ark were saved to live in captivity, in zoos, so perhaps those who escape this fate are indeed fortunate.

For each species, *The Lost Zoo* explains why the animal didn't get on the ark. Two had wanted to go but missed the proverbial boat: the 'Snake-That-Walked-Upon-His-Tail' got a tardy start; it had wanted to be the last animal to arrive, fashionably late, to create a stir, but overestimating its rate of locomotion, it was left behind. The 'Ha-Ha-Ha,' ever silly and playful, never got around to the serious business of planning for the impending deluge. Two other animals consciously chose not to live the life proscribed by human 'captivity' that the ark betokened. The 'Treasuretits,' whose mission is to find lost things, regarded the prospect of a post-flood life as onerous and tedious; they envisioned a life of disempowerment consequent upon salvation at the hands of people:

> those two for the Ark's trip chosen,
> With horror at the thought were frozen!
> Oh, what a dismal, dreary fate
> Theirs was, they shook to contemplate.

Thousands of animals would be there,
And they of their kind the only pair!
Millions of things would go astray,
And who would find them? They, only they!
They'd have no time to dance or sing,
Or play, or rest, or anything!
They looked ahead . . . and forty days . . .
They looked ahead . . . and forty nights . . .
Of work and weariness met their gaze,
A future stripped of all delights.
Though every passenger might pretend
He was their one and only friend,
Behind this friendliness would lurk
Only the wish to make them work!
The prospect pleased them not a whit;
That's why we have no Treasuretit!
(63–4; author's ellipses)

The 'Hoodinkus,' a land creature, absolutely refused to follow Noah onto the sea, preferring extinction to salvation in an alien habitat. These animals refute the idea of ark (and, implicitly, zoo) as benevolently preservationist: some opt *not* to be preserved under terms of subservience. The Treasuretits and the Hoodinkus, choosing not to be saved themselves, also implicitly choose for their descendants to avoid the fate of a zoo (evocative of the way Sethe chose to end her line, and the perpetuation of generations oppressed in slavery, in Toni Morrison's *Beloved*).

As in Aiken's *Who's Zoo*, the anti-zoo in Cullen's *The Lost Zoo* advances the idea that animals reject captivity and human domination. And like Aiken, he calls his fantasy animal collection a zoo, although such an institution is inherently incompatible with the specific animals that inhabit both sets of poems. Cullen undercuts the zoo's cultural hegemony by highlighting the allure of animals that pointedly do not exist any longer for our easy viewing pleasure. For Cullen and Aiken, the idea of the zoo sets a kind of limit, a boundary, a margin (*marginalized* by the compelling anti-zoo animals) just as a frame limits a canvas. But the canvas is – conventionally, at least before postmodernism – supposed to be more interesting than the frame. Despite the fact that the frame represents, on some level, an ultimate control over the process of art, announcing that the picture stops *here*, it is the picture that wins our hearts and minds. Even within the confines of a frame, the interior can offer unbounded fascination that is figuratively infinite albeit physically limited. A zoo frame functions similarly: the zoo, the predominant venue where people experience animals, is limited in what it can offer and, in tandem, limits the experience of animals pervasively throughout our culture. A zoo is a boundary: literally, a jail – another strict social and physical boundary – for animals, and figuratively a limiting set of boundaries for people's experiences of animals. But within this frame a determined artist, can achieve (and inspire) transcendence of the frame – as happens in many zoo stories. (If this is so, some might challenge, then why can't a zoo animal transcend its frame, its cage, and exude its natural fascination? Supporters of zoos would argue that this is exactly what happens. I would counter, however, that this paradigm of frames and interiors is applicable only to art, not life; there is a difference.)

The idea of a zoo frame may have wider application to many zoo stories. One could consider Albee's *The Zoo Story* to have a kind of zoo frame. Or possibly, extending the idea of Aiken's and Cullen's anti-zoos, Albee presents an anti-frame: Jerry's zoo that frames the beginning and end of the play actually never appears at all. Still, the dynamics between zoos and transcendence of zoos, between frame and interior, apply to *The Zoo Story*. Indeed, a considerable number of zoo stories embody at least some part of the model I have described: their reference to the zoo comprises a sort of frame, or backdrop, or metaphorical parallel, to a disconnected, or disjunctive, or somehow unrelated human story 'inside' – necessarily unrelated, on some level, because of the unbridgeable gap between people and animals that most zoo stories affirm, and that belies the zoo's ability to facilitate interaction between human and nonhuman species. In Jarrell's 'The Woman at the Washington Zoo,' Woolf's 'Fear and Politics: A Debate at the Zoo,' Guillén's *The Great Zoo and Other Poems* – perhaps in all incidences of the zoo as political metaphor – we might see the zoo as a frame which is meant to be overcome (with the implication that one must work to prevent political realities from becoming 'zoo-like').

BEYOND ZOOS

Marianne Moore's poetry stands as a striking example of art that teaches a great deal about animals without necessitating their constraint, and without involving (even figuratively) people's spectatorial presence, as all zoos and most zoo stories do. A stay-at-home type who never ventured to exotic foreign habitats (she infrequently even left Brooklyn, making friends from Manhattan cross the river to see her), Moore read about animals and looked at pictures of them. She nurtured her imagination – and, in turn, her audience's – creating poetry about animals without recourse to animal captivity. Others who write about animals may share Moore's attitude, determining to integrate animals into art from a distance and without disturbing their natural existence, but Moore is remarkable for the extent and determination with which this ethos explicitly informs her poesis. With one exception, her animal poems do not derive from or relate first-hand encounters with animals, but rather, from a bestiary of her mind.

Moore's poetic bestiary is the best-known component of her oeuvre.[6] Animals are 'Moore's most frequent concrete subject,' writes Margaret Holley. 'She wrote approximately forty poems featuring animal subjects from "A Jelly-Fish" in 1909 to "Tippoo's Tiger" in 1967' (128). Animals featured in these poems include the buffalo, pigeon, arctic ox, ostrich, snail, elephant, rat, horse, lizards, porcupine, ibis, goose, vulture, and loon. In a letter to T. S. Eliot, Moore referred to some of her poems as 'animiles'; Holley writes that this term 'means literally "pertaining to animals," but it is also loosely perhaps an echo of something like "Anglophiles," the form of affinity' (79).

Moore found her animals in books, magazines, libraries, pictures: and she makes these sources unequivocally clear. A headnote to 'The Arctic Ox (or Goat),' for example, informs that the poem is '*Derived from "Golden Fleece of the Arctic," by John J. Teal, Jr., who rears musk oxen on his farm in Vermont, as set forth by him in the March 1958 issue of the* Atlantic Monthly' (193). The first reference to the title animal in 'The Jerboa' carries an endnote reading: '"There are little rats called jerboas which run on long hindlegs as thin as a match. The forelimbs are mere tiny hands." Dr. R. L. Ditmars, *Strange Animals I Have Known* (New York: Harcourt, Brace, 1951), p. 274' (263).

Endnotes to 'The Plumet Basilisk' cite an *Illustrated London News* article titled 'The Chinese Dragon,' describing the behavior of such lizards and folklore about them, and a discussion in *Animals of New Zealand* about another lizard called the tuatara. 'The Frigate Pelican' cites Audubon's work, while 'An Octopus' cites an *Illustrated London News* article as the source for the poem's colorful descriptions ('ghostly pallor changing / to the green metallic tinge of an anemone-starred pool' (71)). George Jennison's *Animals for Show and Pleasure in Ancient Rome* provides a source (at one remove) for Xenophon's observation in *Anabasis* of an ostrich, used in 'He "Digesteth Harde Yron."' The image of 'a chameleon with tail / that curls like a watch spring' and vertical tiger-stripes in 'Saint Nicholas' (196) carries an endnote reference: 'See photograph in *Life*, September 15, 1958' (293).

Moore's frequent use of direct quotation in her poetry parallels her 'use' of animals. She uses the raw material out of which she crafts her verse without *appropriating* it. She does not exhaust her imaginative fodder in any way, nor affect the way other people may later wish to use that material: it remains just as she found it in her sources. The same cannot be said of zoo animals. In response to an interviewer's question about her extensive quotations, she said, 'I was just trying to be honorable and not steal things. I've always felt that if a thing had been said in the *best* way, how can you say it better? . . . If you are charmed by an author, I think it's a very strange and invalid imagination that doesn't long to share it. Somebody else should read it, don't you think?' (*Reader*, 260). Moore is explicitly referring to plagiarism when she says people shouldn't steal things, but this sensibility also explains her proclivity to borrow (or 'share') animals rather than 'steal' them – as, I believe, zoos steal both the physical animals and their more metaphysical essence and integrity. She seems happy to share things, not needing to own them – a characteristic antithetical to the dominionist ethos that underlies zoos.

Moore presents her poetic animals on the same level as people; we perceive them directly, reciprocally, one-on-one. The intellectual and aesthetic experience her poetry offers is antithetical to the non-reciprocal paradigm of the spectator as voyeur. As she brings animals into the realm of human art, she does so with a wariness about what that action means and what presuppositions it embodies: Moore does not 'anoint' her animals with the benevolent gift of our culture; she does not presume that the animals who enter her ken are necessarily ennobled by the poet's touch. 'Critics and Connoisseurs,' for example, contrasts an ant's natural behavior oblivious to the human artist's attention – what she calls 'unconscious fastidiousness' – with the more consciously fastidious people who are stiffly precise, able to produce artworks that are 'well enough in their way' but no match for the insect's innate, ineffable splendor (38). She realizes that the introduction of animals into human art may well result in an awkward discomfiture, a clash of cultures; and that human culture may very well show itself to have less integrity, less inherent stability and appropriateness, than the animals' world. Pamela White Hadas proposes that Moore believes 'animals and animal nature . . . present a definite threat to art' (103).

Moore's poetry tempts one to surmise that she preferred animals to people. 'She consistently used animals to represent desirable qualities,' writes Bernard F. Engel; 'it is man who is guilty of greed, falseness, misuse, and other errors that she condemned' (9). Her animals often deflate human presumptions to intellectual superiority. (Such an 'unpatriotic' comparative analysis of species would seem impossible at the zoo: the people who pay to attend them would hardly accept the suggestion that they are not the imperial animal.) People have none of the power over Moore's poetic animals that we do over zoo animals – if anything, the animals in her human–animal encounters have the advantage over us in their free-spirited, natural, unfettered complexity. In 'The Plumet Basilisk' she calls the Malay Dragon 'the true divinity / of Malay' (21), and she seems to feel most of her animal subjects warrant a similar tribute, enjoying a kind of supreme perfection in their own setting. The dazzling difficulty of Moore's poetic and her diction increases in proportion to the magnificence of an animal's attributes and insights. The reader has to work hard, and not always with assured success, to appreciate her animals; we have to position ourselves carefully, sometimes awkwardly and uncomfortably, to find a point of view that allows us to see Moore's animals. This situation offers a direct antithesis to the construct in which caged zoo animals wait for people to walk by and ogle them, easily, for as long (or short) a time as the spectator wishes.

Only when Moore's animals come into contact with people do they appear less than majestic. 'The Jerboa' links human treatment of animals with nationalist bravado and slavery: the way we use animals – as beasts of burden harnessed to amuse us, to satiate our appetites, to appease our superstitions – betrays our basest behavior. The poem describes how people kill animals and harvest their resources to indulge our follies, using goose-grease paint and ground rhinoceros horn in frivolous rituals. People appropriate the natural world like thieves, without appreciating its harvest, out of a sense of entitlement: believing that 'The bees' food is your / food' (12). Our relation to animals is characterized by cruelty, possessiveness, and competitiveness:

> They had their men tie
> hippopotami
> and bring out dappled dog-
> cats to course antelopes, dikdik, and ibex;
> or used small eagles. They looked on as theirs,
> impala and onigers.
>
> (10)

'He "Digesteth Harde Yron"' dramatizes the barbarity of conspicuous consumption. In 'The Arctic Ox (Or Goat),' people are ridiculed for the way we exercise the seminal act of imperial dominance over animals, naming them (as Adam did in Genesis): 'The musk ox / has no musk and it is not an ox – / illiterate epithet' (193). When animals have the misfortune to become engaged with human society, Moore warns throughout her animal poems, their dignity and essential existence are put at great risk. She echoes the sentiment from the closing words of Stevie Smith's poem 'The Zoo': when animals are implicated in our insensitive and perverse cultural practices, their 'talents are misusèd.'

Moore attended Brooklyn's Prospect Park Zoo, as she mentions in her essay 'Brooklyn from Clinton Hill,' relating a brief uncritical objective description. Her single poem about a zoo, however, more intricately problematizes the zoogoing experience. In 'The Monkeys,' Moore laments the dissipation of experience from a youthful zoo visit: the dimness of the poet's recalled sensation implicitly contrasts with the eternal vividness of her own literary bestiary. The rarity of zoos as a source for her animal poetry probably indicates disaffection or disapproval – a sense that zoos did not provide the kind of stimulating and usable inspiration that printed reference sources did.

Besides being her only zoo poem, 'The Monkeys' is unusual among Moore's animal verse in several ways. The differences between this poem about captive animals and her others suggest how she feels zoos distort the cultural examination and representation of animals. The title, for example, is misleading:[7] the poem mainly features not a monkey but a large cat. Normally Moore's poetry – especially her animal poetry – is marked by a focal sure-handedness: she knows what she wants to examine, and sets sharply about the business of doing so; if there are preliminary digressions (as, for example, 'The Steeple-Jack' begins with an odd evocation of Dürer), they are structurally and poetically functional. But the monkeys in this poem are only a distraction. The speaker must plod through a panorama of animals – monkeys, zebras, elephants, small cats and a parakeet – before discovering the one she seeks.

Winnowing out a single zoo animal from the crowd is mimetic of a zoo experience, with its overwhelming profusion of animals. Bob Mullan and Garry Marvin observe that for most zoo visitors, their experience

> is not intensive or of a long duration . . . watching consists of merely registering that they have seen something as they move quickly past it. For example, in a recent study of visitors to the Reptile House in the National Zoo, Washington DC, the average time recorded for people in the entire house was 9.7 minutes, with an average of only 0.44 minutes spent in front of each enclosure.
>
> (133)

Perhaps as a way of evoking this dizzying overload, zoo stories commonly build up, indirectly, the approach to the central animal; zoo visitors must first briefly encounter and bypass an array of other clattering animals vying unsuccessfully for attention. In Hoban's *Turtle Diary*, for example, William comes to the zoo to see an octopus, which he finds the zoo does not stock; his attention is only then accidentally captivated by the sea turtles, whose plight consumes him for the rest of the novel. Cortázar's narrator in 'Axolotl' goes to the zoo and finds 'The lions were sad and ugly and my panther was asleep. I decided on the aquarium, looked obliquely at banal fish until, unexpectedly, I hit it off with the axolotls' (4). Before his narrator arrives at the bear's cage in 'The Last Bear,' Andrei Bitov conveys a spectator's glib and anticlimactic response to the zoo cavalcade:

> You come to the horn-and-hoof section – colorlessly heaped-up nonlikenesses of cows . . . Here, too, are the northern reindeer, whose cage you pass by especially quickly – for some reason this very reindeer is nothing new to you. Then a few gnus and some sort of llama. And a bison, shall we say, which won't come out from the darkness of its shelter. You quickly leave this lowly cattleshed behind, almost without having registered in your brain the surprisingly unimposing quality of the reindeer and the roe deer and without having switched your consciousness to the land of savannahs and selvas.
>
> (274–5; author's ellipsis)

In Ted Hughes's 'The Jaguar,' the viewer does not come to the jaguar's cage until the third of five stanzas – forced, first, to negotiate what Hughes characterizes as bored apes, boring snakes, slutty parrots, lazy tigers and lions, and an unidentified assortment of other stinky inhabitants. The spectator 'runs . . . past these' (3) noting the distracting animals only momentarily, and gaining no rewarding experience, but only suffering the tiresome burden of dismissing their existence. Moore seems to regret the smorgasbord, an embarrassment of riches with too many animals for the viewer to appreciate properly – as Bitov puts it, one doesn't even have time to switch one's consciousness to the biota on display; one doesn't begin to appreciate its essence. Zoo animals in bulk, as these writers present them, are mostly distasteful, unmemorable, unstimulating; under such circumstances, a pleasantly edifying zoo visit seems unlikely. Even though Moore, Hoban, Bitov, and Hughes all feature a 'highlighted' animal in their zoo stories, its vitality is diminished because it is contextually introduced as existing amid an unremarkably slovenly crowd.

In 'The Monkeys,' Moore negotiates the animals that obscure her vision from the animal that will not appear until the middle of the poem, 'that Gilgamesh among / the hairy carnivora – that cat with the // wedge-shaped slate-gray marks on its forelegs and the resolute tail' (40). An unusual distance and hesitancy marks her foray among the other animals, and those relegated to the role of minor characters appear uncomfortable, undignified. The monkeys 'winked too much and were afraid of snakes.' That is all Moore says about them, despite the poem's title; it is as if the monkeys had made a sort of desperate showy bid for attention, for prominence, but were jostled out of the spotlight by the competing hordes of animals.[8] The monkeys seem dissatisfied – as does Moore – because the zoo does not allow each animal its due attention or proper appreciation. The awkwardness in this opening deluge reflects Moore's inability to approach these animals as she does in all her other animal poems.

The parakeet appears 'trivial and humdrum on examination,' which is not to say that it *is* essentially trivial and humdrum, only that it looks that way – people perceive it that way – in the zoo. The elephants, 'with their fog-colored skin / and strictly practical appendages,' are not explicitly 'humdrum' like the parakeets, but manifest a blasé colorlessness, or fog-like murkiness, atypical of Moore's bestiary. (Her poem 'Elephants' does these animals more justice; those compelling elephants were inspired not by zoo animals but by Cicero's observations and a lecture-film entitled *Ceylon, the Wondrous Isle*.) The zebras are 'supreme in / their abnormality'; describing their coloration as abnormal implies a normative context – that is, they are unlike any of the other zoo animals; a zebra wouldn't seem abnormal in its natural habitat, surrounded by other zebras. 'Abnormal' carries a pejorative connotation, and again, Moore does not apply such characterizations to animals outside the zoo bestiary. (The zebra is also 'supreme,' but the mitigated, paradoxical nature of this compliment diminishes her usually effusive admiration for animals.) Contrast the self-assured immodesty of a free animal in 'The Buffalo,' which 'need not fear comparison / with bison, with the twins, / indeed with any / of ox ancestry' (28). The zebra's 'abnormality' suggests that people burden captive animals with an unnatural self-consciousness, and an unfortunate rivalry with their artificial zoo neighbors, that derive from human standards and perceptions.

After Moore observes all these animals, her attention finally settles on the cat (not identified by any more precise zoological nomenclature or popular name, unlike nearly all the other animals in her poetry – suggesting that captivity has stinted its identity). That cat makes what the poet calls an astringent remark, a single (82-word!) sentence – about the nature of people, the nature of animals, art and epistemology, the workings of human society, the condition of the natural world, the relation of people to animals, the relation of art to the natural world, the relation of human society to the natural world, the vanity of human society – expansive in its philosophical resonance and profundity. Moore's animals do not speak human language elsewhere; the cat's monologue indicates another difference between this and her other animal poems. Perhaps she feels that the unique depiction of a captive animal in her oeuvre justifies the animal's unique recourse to human language, to make sure people don't overlook what this zoo animal has to say.

The aggressive, confident certitude of the cat's speech is a slap in the face, certainly not what people would expect a captive animal to be telling us from behind zoo bars, especially after Moore has depicted the cat against the backdrop of unremarkably diminutive animals – twitching monkeys, trivial birds. This ironic effect is certainly intentional: Moore implies that people can contain and suppress some of the animals some of the time, but not absolutely. The caged animals were tamed for the first half of the poem; in the second half, the cat (on behalf of the natural animal kingdom) explodes in the reader's face and gives immensely more than one bargains for in the zoo. What the cat has to say is bitingly incisive, uncompromisingly brutal. It is as if one has ambled too close to the cage and has been gouged and bloodied by the cat's lashing out, although the metaphorical 'assault' is ideological rather than physical. Surprising us with a stark departure from a conventional, predictable zoo experience, Moore warns against the unexamined presupposition of dominionist complacency people bring to the zoo. The poem suggests she has not returned to this zoo in the twenty years since the encounter; understandably, one would not repeatedly subject oneself to such unsettling outbursts.

The cat says:

> 'They have imposed upon us with their pale
> half-fledged protestations, trembling about
> in inarticulate frenzy, saying
> it is not for us to understand art; finding it
> all so difficult, examining the thing
>
> as if it were inconceivably arcanic, as symmet-
> rically frigid as if it had been carved out of chrysoprase

> or marble – strict with tension, malignant
> in its power over us and deeper
> than the sea when it proffers flattery in exchange for hemp,
> rye, flax, horses, platinum, timber, and fur.'
>
> (40)

Critics have amply discussed what they perceive as the poem's main brunt, the critical manifesto that happens to emanate from a cat. But they dissociate this weighty dictum, privileging intellectual abstraction over the poem's precise reference to the physical context of the zoo. Bonnie Costello realizes the cat 'may be speaking on behalf of nature or on behalf of the artist,' but finds a human aesthetic dictum finally more interestingly complex and pertinent. 'As the voice of the isolated artist it speaks against a public, including critics, who put art in a special category. As the voice of the public it speaks against critics and their high-sounding interpretations' (31). Hadas believes the cat describes and then rebuts the frenzied protestations of a critical-artistic voice which asserts that art must be difficult. The animal

> does not agree that art has power over us simply because it offers flattery (insincere words or difficulty that flatters the initiated 'understanding' of the self-ordered priests of interpretation) in exchange for the raw materials of life, the commodities of world-market exchange. The artist must offer flattery, fulfillment of arcanic expectations, in exchange for the necessities of life. Whereas it should be the other way around? The cat attacks vain literary work and the suspect livelihood of a conspiracy of artist-critics. Quite rightly.
>
> (122)

Engel writes that the poem is about Moore's 'preference for criticism that has an emotional basis and her scorn for merely intellectual methods' (45). The poem's zoo setting has remained largely unexplored – regarded as tangential, irrelevant, simply preliminary. Costello notes that the opening zoo construct has metaphorical and structural functions: this opening and the cat's speech 'depend on each other, in several ways,' she writes. 'In the first half the images are presented primarily as literal ones . . . The figure in the second half is obviously allegorical, bearing only a secondary relation to the creaturely setting from which it is drawn'

(30). Engel, too, perceives the zoo as symbolically functional, seeing the animals as 'a parliament of literary critics' (43).

But a fundamental and also fairly obvious aspect of 'The Monkeys' is its direct zoological and ecocritical commentary. Critics have too quickly glided over the implications of a caged zoo animal discussing art, other than to observe that the irony of this unexpected reversal typifies Moore's poesis, and they miss her fascinating consideration of the cat and art, and of the cat *as* art (in a derogatory, formulaic, affected sense of 'art' as cloistered artifice). Human culture, zoo culture, and nature all converge here (and battle things out) at a weird Sophoclean crossroads. In 'The Monkeys,' Moore addresses how we treat our planet – comprising minerals, plants, and animals as well people and human art – and what zoos signify about our record. Art is, indeed, one component of what exists in the world, but a fairly small one, and certainly not the only one – other entities such as rye, hemp, flax, platinum, and timber, similarly comprise a substantial part of the ecostructure in which we exist. And art is made out of several of these raw materials, such as flax, platinum, and timber, but art is not the *only* thing they can be used for. Ultimately the raw materials that overflow the poem's last line are important in their own right, not just because art, or anything else, can be made out of them.

Moore is, partly, trying to decenter an adulatory fixation on art, trying to contextualize more rationally the relative function of the materials, resources, artifacts, that surround us. The cat inscribes itself into this catalogue of raw materials via the horses, fellow animals. The caged animal pontificates so prolifically because the stakes are so direct: it is literally trapped, captive, within one version of our cultural practices, the zoo. The cat realizes, not theoretically but from first-hand experience, the dangers of people's conceptions of their right to use, fashion, manipulate, contrive the resources in the world around them – whether timber, horses, or zoo animals – for their own 'artistic' education and delight. The cat's theoretical pronouncement boils down to this: Art exists in a manipulable, contrived, and undesirable realm. But this statement is most significant in its relevance to the cat's larger ecological statement about its condition (and the condition of all other animals, trees, minerals, resources): given that art exists in this ingenuine, corrupt condition, there are victims, of which the cat itself is one. Anything used in the cause and processes of art is 'imposed' upon (to use the cat's own word), and stripped of its integrity, stripped of its power to determine how it is regarded and constructed as subject. In the tyrannical hands of its manipulators, art is 'malignant / in its power over us.' The cat is simply told, 'it is not for us to understand art' – that is, that its function as subject on the canvas (in the cage) where it now finds itself is beyond its comprehension. The artists, the controllers, the manipulators, know what they're doing; shut up and smile. We people are doing the hard work, practicing upon the other (in Stephen Greenblatt's terminology), 'examining the thing' (as the cat says).

The poet and the cat share a voice in 'The Monkeys.' Their ultimate point, above and beyond the other injunctions, is, don't desecrate the planet; don't contrive with its hemp, platinum, and horses (and implicitly its cats, monkeys and other zoo animals) the way you do with art. Respect the essence and integrity of rye, flax, and fur, without having to *make* something out of them, or transform them into (what people would erroneously believe to be) some higher condition. 'Fur,' as the poem's last word, neatly embodies the dialectic opposition between the idea of an animal as a unique living creature and as a commodity – it is a reader-response challenge: if we recognize the fur not as an animal but only as a commodity, then we have failed Moore's test.[9] Art perverts natural existence if it serves as a medium whereby a valueless material, 'flattery,' can be exchanged for real things such as rye and timber, and such perversion betokens a world in which people have lost sight of the inherent value that natural objects possess.

Moore's cat warns that people should not delude themselves by believing that just because we can make dense, clever art, we can ignore the costs and victims of our culture. She presents spectacular animals made dull and abnormal by cages at the poem's opening; at the end, she shows the natural bounty of plants, animals, and minerals dully represented as merely ingredients for appropriation by industrial/commercial human culture, like items on an inventory sheet. People must regard our own cultural and artistic achievements, Moore suggests, against the more important backdrop of nature and the unfortunate mark we have left on it. Zoos typify our failure to perceive the proper perspective within our macrocosm: we see caged animals as a kind of 'art,' but we remain oblivious to costs and dangers that far outweigh any value of our art.

People behave badly in our world: abusively appropriating its resources, imprisoning its animals, and justifying such habits by the conceit that we are doing something very intricate, and something the victims that inhabit the natural world cannot begin to understand because they are too stupid, too unhuman. Animals' inability to engage in art except as subjects, as fodder, then implicitly legitimizes their relegation to the passive, captive role of raw material. The Western imperial sensibility resonates in the background of this ethos. As John Berger describes the ideology that constrains the animal as cultural subject to passivity: 'animals are always the observed . . . They are the objects of our ever-extending knowledge. What we know about them is an index of our power, and thus an index of what separates us from them. The more we know, the further away they are' (14).

Marian Scholtmeijer describes how people often dishonestly consider and portray animals, in order to reassure ourselves about our relation to the world in a way that Moore's ethically probing consideration would disallow:

> Refusal to recognize animal reality is a hedge against the guilt we would feel as we make use of their bodies were we to see them as sentient individuals rather than commodities . . . as Richard Tapper (citing Claude Lévi-Strauss) observes, animals 'are good to think with.' As living beings, whose content we have decided is inaccessible, animals are peculiarly primed to vitalize thought without – so we think – impeding its freedom. We have a liking for the effect of animals upon our thoughts, as long as they do not challenge their instrumentality as mediators of culture. In all cases, there is a certain presumptuousness behind the philosophical position that the human mind constructs reality. That presumptuousness reaches a critical point, however, when we involve other living beings in our cultural projects.
>
> (5)

Moore recognizes what Scholtmeijer calls the cat's 'animal reality' as few people, certainly very few zoogoers, do. She does not force her cat into a subservient role as a passive mediator of culture, but rather depicts the cat as challenging this role eloquently. The cat deflates what Scholtmeijer calls the cultural presumption that the human mind constructs reality; conversely, the cat *deconstructs* human reality as it is posited in the zoo.

Earlier, I briefly noted a reference to Albrecht Dürer in Moore's poem, 'The Steeple-Jack':

> Dürer would have seen a reason for living
>   in a town like this, with eight stranded whales
> to look at; with the sweet air coming into your house
> on a fine day, from the water etched
>   with waves as formal as the scales
> on a fish.
>
> (5)

The Renaissance artist recurs in Moore's writing. Darlene Williams Erickson identifies several points of connection:

> Dürer's works rank among the treasured 'old things' from 'When I Buy Pictures.' Moore had been fascinated by Dürer since her trip to Paris in 1919. References to the German painter turn up in two other of Moore's poems, 'Then the Ermine' ('like violets by Dürer') and 'Apparition of Splendor' ('Dürer's rhinoceros'). For the July 1928 issue of the *Dial*, Moore wrote an important review of an exhibition of Dürer prints at the New York Public Library. The seeds of 'The Steeple-Jack' can be found in that review . . . Moore makes the point that the 'reliquary method of perpetuating magic' is ordinarily to be distrusted, but not so with Dürer . . . [and] that seeing such work 'commits one to enlightenment if not to emulation, and recognition of the capacity for newness inclusive of oldness.'
>
> (74)

Costello notes that Moore, like Dürer, 'was absorbed by the particular'; they shared 'a passion for observation' and a 'fascination with the strange in the real.' (194)

Just as Moore based her depictions of animals on secondary sources rather than the creatures themselves, Dürer, too, began his study of engraving in his father's goldsmith shop, from 'pattern books – albums filled with all sorts of designs of birds and beasts, flowers, and exotic peoples' (Eisler, 9). A later influence was the writing of Erasmus of Rotterdam, a scholar whose 'Latin correspondence and literature are enlivened by references to animals' and who advocated 'appreciation for the gifts of the animal as teacher' (26). Erasmus believed animals could enlighten people in such wide-ranging disciplines as art, architecture, domestic economy, and social values. The same faith in animals' pedagogical wisdom permeates Dürer's and Moore's art: Colin Eisler writes that Dürer's prints 'may have been used by teachers following Erasmian progressive ideals . . . Supreme imitator of the way animals look and live, [Dürer] also became teacher of human ways along with those of the squirrel or hare, lion or stag beetle' (27). Moore, too, teaches human ways along with animals' ways and via animals' ways – the cat's lesson to people in 'The Monkeys' epitomizes an Erasmian model.

Out of Dürer's hundreds of animal works, I focus on the one Moore alludes to in 'Apparition of Splendor,' his 1515 woodcut. *Rhinoceros* testifies to the ability to create art about animals at a remove, without directly exploiting them. Further, it indicates how great the power of such nonexploitative animal art can be. The fascination with this work in later art and culture attests to how widely such art can be recycled, and how much energy is stored in such representations. Zoo stories tend to draw on and perpetuate the negative energy surrounding zoo animals; zoo stories tend to be sad stories. Moore's and Dürer's animals combat this negativity with an imaginative panache that offers an exemplary ideal for cultural interaction with animals. Moore specifically admires Dürer's *Rhinoceros* in her essay on him, noting 'that in the best pictures he has obtained his sense of fact second hand, filtered through prior representations, a tendency of course akin to her own drawing of the particular from books, pictures, films. She writes of Dürer that "liking is increased perhaps when the concept is primarily an imagined one – in the instance of the rhinoceros, based apparently on a traveller's sketch or description"' (Costello, 194).

Dürer never saw a live rhinoceros (as Moore presumably never saw a live plumet basilisk or arctic ox). His source was another picture and a description, by the Moravian printer Valentine Ferdinand, whose text Dürer reproduces on his woodcut:

> They call it a rhinoceros. It is represented here in its complete form. It has the color of a speckled turtle. And in size it is like the elephant but lower on its legs, and almost invulnerable. It has a sharp strong horn on its nose, which it starts to sharpen whenever it is near stones. The stupid animal is the mortal enemy of the elephant.... Because that animal is so well armed, the elephant cannot do anything to it. They also say that the rhinoceros is fast, lively and clever. The animal is called 'Rhinocero' in Greek and Latin. In India it is called 'Ganda.'
> (Eisler's translation; 269)

In some ways, Ferdinand contextualizes this rhinoceros unfortunately – calling it 'stupid' (although he contradicts himself subsequently) is an irrelevant exertion of human presumptions to superiority. Ferdinand experienced the animal under conditions of imperialist domination and captivity, 'in Lisbon when the great beast was shipped there in May 1515, sent from the farthest reaches among Portuguese Maritime conquests, Cambay in northwest India' (Eisler, 269). Dürer is implicated to a degree in this context – at a remove, so less damningly, but nevertheless Ferdinand's experience affects Dürer's cultural interaction with the animal. But I think the cultural outcome finally invokes praise, rather than condemnation, of Dürer's ethics of representation. I acknowledge that this ethical stance may have been unconscious or unintended: drawing animals from life was not considered a necessary technique in the aesthetic of this period, so Dürer was not necessarily rejecting the ethos of the immediate captive animal subject;[10] but nevertheless, especially in the legacy of Dürer's representation, we can (as Moore did) acclaim his art as an important ethical statement for *our own* time if it was not as clearly so for his own. The rhinoceros had already been caught, and Dürer's disseminated image allowed people to experience a rhinoceros without any others having to be caught, imprisoned, and exhibited. Dürer himself (who often travelled under difficult conditions to get to something he wanted to draw) *could have* done what Ferdinand did – witnessing and recording as a spectator the display of a captive animal as imperial booty – but chose not to.

Dürer's audience, the vast majority of which had never seen a rhinoceros, was 'shown' one by the artist, who similarly had never seen one. An important transmission, a recycling, of culture has thus taken place, concerning animals, without the direct implication in the dynamics of captivity by either producer or consumer. If Ferdinand was implicated at second-hand because he went to see the animal an imperialist had captured, then Dürer is implicated at third-hand, and his viewers at fourth-hand: this complicity is not negligible, but at least it lessens at each remove. Dürer's picture and text do not in any way apologize for this remove from nature, or attempt to atone for it or conceal it. On the contrary, the work proudly proclaims its distance from the original subject – proudly, because the artist is all the more talented for having produced this representation out of his own mind, without direct experience.

The enduring popularity of Dürer's *Rhinoceros* further testifies to the power of an aesthetic representation derived wholly from the artist's mind. The rhinoceros as Dürer depicts it has striking idiosyncracies: 'the complicated cut of the fierce beast's covering recalls those of courtly armor,' writes Eisler. 'The animal has a strangely "dressed" look, like some revolting pet lovingly clad by a proud owner.' But 'this personal quality is one of the many reasons why Dürer's print remained the definitive image of a rhinoceros centuries after its many inaccuracies and strange little additions – such as the spiral dorsal horn above the shoulders . . . – had been noted' (270). A contemporary of Dürer's, Hans Burgkmair, also made a rhinoceros print the same year, but without the extra horn and stylized armor: 'Burgkmair's more accurate rhino never caught on. People wanted to believe in the rhinoceros just as Dürer first showed it. If nature was demonstrably different, he was right and reality was wrong' (271). Joan Barclay Lloyd confirms that 'Dürer's beautiful, but largely imaginary, figure . . . became the standard picture in Europe of a rhinoceros for nearly two hundred years' (91). The cause of art triumphs in Dürer's work, and most importantly (as Moore and her cat would appreciate), without cost to nature.

Rhinoceros had eight printings; by the seventeenth century, when the woodblock was showing signs of decay, two Dutch printers restored the image by preparing 'an additional woodcut, inked in grey to be printed over the first one to create a chiaroscuro effect, lengthening the old block's life and enhancing the image's rich graphic quality to suit the new Baroque style' (Eisler, 271). Dürer's work thus shows one of the consummate indications of enduring art, the modification by artists of subsequent eras who combine both the original and more contemporary attributes. Other subsequent representations of a rhinoceros indebted to Dürer's – situating viewers at a fifth-hand remove from the original animal imprisoned by Portuguese imperialists – include appearances in Maximilian's *Hours* and the triumphal arch on his coat of arms, as a statue in Paris celebrating the ascension of King Henri II (1547), in sculptured reliefs in Schönborn castle, in white china for the Porcelain Palace in Dresden (1731), in Jan Joesten's 1660 book *Curious Descriptions of the Nature of Four-Footed Animals, Fish and Bloodless Water Animals, Birds, Crocodiles, Snakes, and Dragons*, and in a silk painting based on Joesten's drawing (thus, at sixth-hand remove from the original), by the Japanese artist Tani Buncho in 1790 (Eisler, 271–4). Dürer's image demonstrated an energy of recirculation and proliferation, exhibiting a vitality generally absent from the cultural representation of zoo animals (as Moore's predominantly dim recollection in 'The Monkeys' typifies). When a zoo animal dies, it is dispatched to the prosector or the glue factory and another is acquired to replace it, whereas Moore's and Dürer's animals have an enduring power and worth that testify to the strength of animals' cultural potency in a context free from captivity.

I like Costello's characterization of both Moore and Dürer as 'realist[s] of the imagination and not of nature' (194). I do not mean to argue that an animal of the imagination is inherently *better* than a natural animal. Rather, an animal of the imagination is a more fitting thing to expect from artists, from people and for people, as a representation of nature, than an imperial appropriation of the thing itself. Moore and Dürer recognize the vast potential and also the limits of human perception, cognition, and appreciation. They give their audience as much as they can in the realm of the imagination, forgoing as irrelevant and inappropriate any attempt to 'capture' the natural.

Moore herself provides a fitting terminus to the centuries of recycling Dürer's animal representation (and the dual aesthetic and environmental connotations of 'recycling' are appropriate – both are ways to conserve our planet's resources). Her 'Apparition of Splendor,' about the attributes of the plain old porcupine, begins by recalling Dürer's fabulous creature:

> Partaking of the miraculous
>   since never known literally,

Dürer's rhinoceros
  might have startled us equally
  if black-and-white spined elaborately.
(158)

Moore does not mean to deny the imaginative sense of rhinocerosness Dürer achieved when she suggests it could have been just as amazing if it were a porcupine. Rather, she implies that *any* animal transformed through art into the realm of vivid aesthetic consciousness has an equally fabulous potential. The zoo animals I have examined throughout this book, mired in the dynamics of captivity, tend to embody the stench of cultural inauthenticity. I would like to end by contrasting Moore's homage to the 'miraculous' power of animals in purely imaginative art – a miracle in which she invites like-minded readers to partake – with, in reprise, two representations of animals and captivity:

> I went to the zoo to find out more about the way people exist with animals, and the way animals exist with each other, and with people too. It probably wasn't a fair test, what with everyone separated by bars from everyone else . . . But, if it's a zoo, that's the way it is.
>
> (Edward Albee, *The Zoo Story*)

> Few if any wild animals . . . would choose to live in full view of human beings, yet in a zoo they must.
>
> (A. H. N. Green-Armytage, *Bristol Zoo 1865–1965*)

Notes

CHAPTER 1 ZOO STORIES

1. Solly Zuckerman, President of the Zoological Society of London, describes the rise of zoos in modern urban culture: 'In the early part of the nineteenth century a demand arose for zoological gardens that were open to the public by right, or at least to a company of subscribers or to people who paid for admission . . . Most were founded by prominent citizens who felt that no great city should lack a good zoo' (10–11). The President of Zoo Atlanta, Terry Maple, affirms the contemporary conviction that a good city needs a good zoo: in the 1980s, when deplorable conditions and a series of mishaps at that zoo attracted national attention, 'These events were a terrible embarrassment to our ambitious city. Aspiring to greatness, Atlanta in 1984 was a city humbled by the image of its hapless zoo. After the zoo crisis, the city slipped from first in 1983 to eleventh in Rand McNally's 1984 *Most Liveable Cities* index, wherein the zoo crisis was identified as a factor contributing to its degraded image' ('Agenda', 20).
2. Jim Mason's book, *An Unnatural Order: Uncovering the Roots of Our Domination of Nature and Each Other*, extensively explores the preconceptions and prejudices that color contemporary attitudes toward nature and that underlie such questions as these. He defines what he calls dominionism – 'Western peoples' proud, basic view of the world and our most sacred, fundamental policy on how to live on it' (25) – and explores the ramifications of this attitude, as well as alternatives. 'The dominionist ethos is not the natural order of things,' Mason argues. 'However old and well settled it may be, it had a beginning; and thus it can have an end' (48). An antecedent for this concept of dominionism appears in *A Sand County Almanac*, where Aldo Leopold characterizes what Mason calls dominionism as 'our Abrahamic concept of land,' and criticizes those who perpetuate it: 'We abuse land because we regard it as a commodity belonging to us. When we see land as a community to which we belong, we may begin to use it with love and respect. There is no other way for land to survive the impact of mechanized man, nor for us to reap from it the esthetic harvest it is capable . . . of contributing to culture' (xviii–xix). In *Ishmael*, Daniel Quinn offers a fictional representation of two social types: Takers, who selfishly appropriate the earth's resources, positing an antagonistic relationship toward nature and attempting to transgress its laws; and Leavers, who live in harmony with natural cycles and dynamics, respecting the natural order and acknowledging that they are only one of many

species with an equal claim to existence. The title character, a liberated zoo gorilla, attempts to enlighten a human student about the need to reject the Takers' mythos (which approximates Mason's dominionism and Leopold's Abrahamism). 'The premise of the Taker story is *the world belongs to man*,' Quinn writes; 'The premise of the Leaver story is *man belongs to the world*' (239).

3. Nature: the realm most prominently characterized by living things and a support system of inanimate elements, in an environment relatively (compared to some other, less 'natural' condition) more conducive to their existence, prosperity, and functional sustainability, and which relatively enhances rather than diminishes biodiversity; that physical reality which people have relatively (again, a comparative indicator) less despoiled, or exploited, or tampered with, or manipulated, or artificed. A working definition (with a disclaimer: I cannot claim to have mastered the concept of nature; if anything, I aim for inductive enlightenment over the course of this book). And I add a self-cautionary pledge to avoid the simplistic idealization and the easy misanthropy that Stephen Budiansky parodies when he characterizes the predominant popular environmentalist sensibility today, of 'nature as a pristine world, spoiled only by modern man, the klutz in the heavy boots trampling the flowers.' Budiansky importantly reminds us that 'The truth, as ecological research struggles so often in vain to tell us, does not admit of any simple lines between that which is man's and that which is wild . . . that which is wild is not always heroic and beautiful. Man has always been a part of nature, a fact we can ignore now only at the peril of man, animals, and the world' (4–5).
4. 'The term has come to summarize the response of literary study and analysis to the ecological consciousness of the last two decades and to the recognition that human culture is inextricably involved with, and ultimately subordinate to, the physical, natural world,' writes Glen A. Love. 'The word "ecocriticism" was originally coined in 1978 by William L. Rueckert, in his important essay, "Literature and Ecology: An Experiment in Ecocriticism [*Iowa Review* 9.1 (Winter 1978): 62–86]"' (*'Et in Arcadia'*, 196).
5. Jamieson argues that zoos' ideal educational mission – teaching facts about animals' physiology and behavior, providing information about and advocacy for endangered species, developing a sense of compassion for wild animals' fate – does not justify keeping animals in captivity. 'Couldn't most of the educational benefits of zoos be obtained by presenting films, slides, lectures and so forth?' ('Against', 111–12).
6. Terry Maple, Rita McManamon, and Elizabeth Stevens describe the ideal formulation of a zoo's contribution to an enlightening understanding of the natural world. They extol what they term 'the motivational zoo,' which 'realizes that its mission is to conserve wildlife and natural habitats through changing the attitudes of its visitors' (230). An encounter with unusual captive animals 'can be so stimulating that the visitor will want to learn more . . . In the best-case

scenario, the visitor will be moved to the point of taking some tangible form of conservation action . . . The zoo experience can be that initial spark that motivates a member of the general public to become more responsible about conserving the environment' (231–2). I dispute this ideal: I believe that the sensibilities the zoo promotes hinder human appreciation of the natural world far more significantly than they inspire a proper respect.

7. See letters to Molly McCarthy (22 November 1924), Lady Ottoline Morrell (22 June 1932), and Quentin Bell (26 July 1933).
8. Besides *Three Guineas*, another inspirational 'fusion' text is Aldo Leopold's *A Sand County Almanac*. Combining naturist writing with the formulation of ecological rhetoric and doctrine, Leopold produces what Lawrence Buell calls 'a symbiosis of art and polemic, such that environmental representation and lyricism exist for their own sakes yet also, ex post facto, as a means to make the reader more receptive to environmental advocacy' (40).
9. 'Whipsnade is not my idea of a zoo,' writes MacNeice dismissively (245). Valentine Cunningham cites a handful of literary references to this zoo: 'Gladys Davidson's *At Whipsnade Zoo* (1934) finds a natural slot in the . . . series of Nelson Discovery Books for Boys and Girls . . . It was a trip to the newly opened Whipsnade in his brother's motorbike side-car in September 1931 that helped tip C. S. Lewis finally over into the Christian faith. He "liked bears," he says in his autobiographical *Surprised by Joy* (1955) . . . There can't have been anything specifically godly about Whipsnade, even its bears: still, T. S. Eliot does, in the second chorus of *The Rock*, describe the Church settling "all the inconvenient saints, / Apostles, martyrs, in a kind of Whipsnade"' (87).
10. Harriet Ritvo describes prejudicial cultural images of tigers among Victorian audiences: 'About the tiger there were no two ways of thinking. It epitomized what man had to fear from the animal kingdom . . . It was greedy, reputed to stop feeding on one carcass in order to kill another animal and to slaughter an entire flock of sheep, leaving them dead in the field. Like the wolf, the hyena, and some other big cats, it was often called "cowardly," which apparently meant unwilling to face men with guns. The authors of *The British Museum* used the language of redemption to lament that "no discipline can correct the savage nature of the tiger, nor any degree of kind treatment reclaim him"' (Ritvo, 28). Such sensibilities underlie the expressions of Galsworthy's characters.
11. Galsworthy's concern for animal welfare is evidenced outside his fiction as well: his essay 'For Love of Beasts,' published by London's Animals' Friend Society in the 'A.F.' pamphlet series (1912), protests exploitations of animals as pets, beasts of burden, sources of material for fashion (e.g., birds' feathers to decorate hats), and so forth.
12. 'Cuddling Up to Quasimodo and Friends.' *New York Times* 23 June 1996: 2.1, 26–7.
13. Mason attempts to estimate the impact Americans make on our

environment: 'Taking into account all the buildings, machines, highways, and other products used, the typical American... probably drains more material and energy from the environment in a week than a Paleolithic forager did in a year... Biologists and population experts Anne and Paul Ehrlich have compared person-demand' – the use of energy and material that measures the human toll on the planet – 'in America to that in the world's poorest nations. The average American has, for example, roughly 50 times the environmental impact of an average Bangladeshi. And, the Ehrlichs say, the American causes 70 times the environmental damage of a Ugandan or Laotian' (46). A commonly cited statistic is that Americans, comprising 6 per cent of the world's population, consume 40 per cent of its resources.

14. I am indebted to Birkeland's critical overview of ecological schools and philosophies. For more information about deep ecology, she suggests a book by Bill Devall and George Sessions, *Deep Ecology: Living As If Nature Mattered* (Salt Lake City: Peregrine Smith, 1985); and Arne Naess's *Ecology, Community and Lifestyle* (trans. and ed. David Rothenberg. Cambridge: Cambridge UP, 1989). For further reading about social ecology, see Murray Bookchin's *The Ecology of Freedom: The Emergence and Dissolution of Hierarchy* (Palo Alto, CA: Cheshire Books, 1982).
15. Lawrence mentions other animals that are victims of cultural prejudices: 'Americans, for example, generally hate and fear bats due to their extreme otherness and defiance of the perceived natural order. Because they are active at night, frequent deserted areas, hang upside down with their wings folded about their bodies like witches' cloaks, are associated with vampires, and seem to be an eerie mixture of mouse and bird that confounds classification, they have been routinely persecuted. Their important ecological role, though beginning to be appreciated, has never been valued enough to overcome connotations of evil. Pigs, because of characteristics like their corpulence, their habits of wallowing in mud and rooting in the dirt, their voracious appetite for garbage, their ugly squeal, their alleged stupidity and sloth, their biblical status as unclean, and perhaps the projected disgrace of their exclusive role as meat providers, are almost universally derided in our society' (184).
16. 'Is it really better to confine a few hapless Mountain Gorillas in a zoo than to permit the species to become extinct?' asks Jamieson. If people attempt to preserve a dwindling species at any cost, 'aren't we using animals as mere vehicles for their genes? Aren't we preserving genetic material at the expense of the animals themselves? If it is true that we are inevitably moving toward a world in which Mountain Gorillas can survive only in zoos, then we must ask whether it is really better for them to live in artificial environments of our design than not to be born at all' ('Against', 115–16). And in 'Zoos Revisited,' Jamieson adds, 'Increasingly zoos have attempted to position themselves as the guardians of wild nature, as the boy with his thumb in the dike trying to hold back the floodwaters. I

do not believe that zoos can successfully play this role. Establishing genetic warehouses is not the same as preserving wild animals. Highly managed theme parks are not wild nature' (53–4). In 'The Trouble With Zoos,' Michael W. Fox argues: 'As to the claim that the best zoos are helping save species from extinction by breeding them in captivity, it may be best to let these animals become extinct if there is no place for them in the wild . . . To put animals on exhibit as 'specimens' and 'social groups' torn from the very fabric of the ecosystems and bio-fields in which they evolved and which shaped their being as an inseparable part of the seamless web of creation, is a violation of the biological and spiritual unity of all life' (in Magel, 144).

17. I touch only briefly on an issue with immense ecological, scientific, and philosophical complexities, and about which much has been written on both sides. I mean to indicate my general sympathies and convictions on this topic: it is beyond my scope to develop a complete argument about animal conservation. For an incisive discussion of an opposing viewpoint to my own, see Chapters 8 and 9 in Bostock's *Zoos and Animal Rights*.

CHAPTER 2 EXHIBITING IMPERIALISM

1. See, for example, Stephen Slemon's 'Unsettling the Empire: Resistance Theory for the Second World,' *World Literature Written in English* 30.2 (Autumn 1990): 30–41; Jenny Sharpe's 'Figures of Colonial Resistance,' *Modern Fiction Studies* 35.1 (Spring 1989): 137–55; and Edward Said's chapter, 'Resistance and Opposition,' in *Culture and Imperialism* (191–281).
2. Eugene Hargrove calls the modern zoological garden an outgrowth of the botanical garden, which emerged 'during the transition from the late medieval to early modern periods, when natural history scientists began classifying new-world biota' (13). Imperial influences are obvious as Hargrove explains the gardens' origins: 'Botanical gardens were created to display the plants discovered worldwide during the period of European exploration that began with the voyages of the Spanish and the Portuguese in the fifteenth century'; they presented 'celebrations of human dominion over nature' (13–14).
3. For a historical survey of early zoos and their precursors over the last five millennia, see R. J. Hoage, Anne Roskell, and Jane Mansour, 'Menageries and Zoos to 1900' in Hoage's *New Worlds, New Animals: From Menagerie to Zoological Park in the Nineteenth Century*, 8–18. The earliest modern historical overview of zoos is Gustave Loisel's seminal work, the three-volume *Histoires des ménageries de l'antiquité à nos jours* (Paris: Octave Doin et Fils, 1912).
4. On the rise of American zoos, see Vernon N. Kisling, Jr's essay 'The Origin and Development of American Zoological Parks to 1899,' and Helen Lefkowitz Horowitz's 'The National Zoological Park: "City

of Refuge" or Zoo?' both in Hoage's *New Worlds, New Animals: From Menagerie to Zoological Park in the Nineteenth Century.*

5. The *OED* lists an interesting colloquialism derived from the Tower of London animal displays. Under the definition of 'lion,' item 4:

> Things of note, celebrity, or curiosity (in a town, etc.); sights worth seeing, esp. in phr. *to see,* or, *show, the lions.* In early use, *to have seen the lions* often meant to have had experience of life. This use of the word is derived from the practice of taking visitors to see the lions which used to be kept in the Tower of London.

6. V. I. Lenin. *Imperialism: The Highest Stage of Capitalism.* Lawrence & Wishart. London, 1942, page 81; first published 1916.
7. Michael Hutchins, Betsy Dresser and Chris Wemmer write that 'scientific investigation was an explicit objective of many early institutions' of animal captivity:

> For example, the ancient zoo in Alexandria was built to satisfy the scientific curiosity of Emperor Ptolmey II. The menagerie of the Museum National de Historie Naturelle in Paris was established primarily for zoological investigation in 1793 . . . Stamford Raffles, the founder of Singapore, had suggested the 'need for a collection of animals for scientific purposes as well as the general interest,' and this led ultimately to the creation of the Zoological Society of London. The society's charter aspired to create 'a collection of living animals such as never yet existed in ancient or modern times . . . to be applied to some useful purpose, or as objects of scientific research, not of vulgar admiration.'
>
> (253)

The design of early zoos, according to Alexander Wilson, emphasized taxonomy as a way of highlighting their function as venues of scientific education. Zoos' 'models, like those of botanical gardens, science museums, and aquariums, were medicine and the old natural sciences. To each species a separate cage, the better to observe and know' (250).

8. *Heart of Darkness and The Secret Sharer.* New York: Bantam, 1981, page 9; first published 1902.
9. Although I am concerned mainly with the rise of the London Zoo and its correlation with the ascendant British Empire, it is worth noting that the fall of the British Empire has been accompanied by the Zoo's decline. In 1991, the Zoo announced it might have to shut down unless government support was increased, and threatened to destroy animals for which new homes could not be found. The next year, it again announced its impending closure, but found a last-minute reprieve in a large gift from the Emir of Kuwait. Despite a spate of managerial troubles that a *Nature* editorial called 'mainly self-inflicted' – 'the public was beginning to suspect [the Zoo] of crying wolf over its financial troubles. Projected closing dates have

come and gone with alarming frequency in the past two years, averted by a series of relaunches and rescue bids' – the London Zoo continues clinging to life ('Last-chance zoo?' *Nature* 361 (25 February 1993): 668).

10. *Atlanta Journal Constitution* 11 October 1994: C2.
11. 'Ivan's isolation ends today.' *Atlanta Journal Constitution* 26 June 1995: C2.
12. *Atlanta Journal Constitution* 27 June 1995: C2.
13. *Atlanta Journal Constitution* 30 June 1995: A10.

CHAPTER 3 CAGES

1. See Cliff Tarpy's article 'New Zoos: Taking Down the Bars' on refinements in zoo exhibits and habitats; Judith E. Rinard's *Zoos Without Cages* (Washington: National Geographic Society, 1981) is also informative on this topic.
2. 'Today the inhabitants of zoos are often the last remnants of a species or community,' writes Alexander Wilson. 'Their exoticism is an exoticism of immanent loss' (247). He calls near-extinct species that are institutionally sustained in zoos or reserves 'the living dead.'
3. In 'The Trouble with Zoos,' Jonathan Barzdo explicitly criticizes zoos along the lines of what *Creature Comforts* faults more indirectly. Opposing the common and naive belief that zoo animals simply need a certain *quantity* of space, Barzdo writes:

> what is now obvious is that, although some animals do need large areas for their living quarters, the quality of the space is more important. Otters and hippos must be able to swim, crested porcupines and badgers need earth in which to burrow, bats need room to fly and perches to cling to, and so on. All this is only common sense, but examples are rife in British zoos of animals that are prevented from behaving naturally by a thoughtless lack of adequate accommodation and facilities.
>
> (19)

4. 'The experiment of exhibiting a man had been a much greater success than any of the Committee had dared to hope,' writes Garnett near the end of the story; 'such a success, indeed, that it had decided to follow it up by having a second man, a negro . . . The intention of the Committee was eventually to establish a "Man-house" which should contain specimens of all the different races of mankind, with a Bushman, South Sea Islanders, etc., in native costume' (78). The planned Man-house resembles the sorts of displays common in nineteenth-century London, as described in Chapter 2. While Garnett makes no explicit reference to this cultural antecedent, the brief discussion of the second man's exhibition in the zoo is tinged with a racist flair befitting the sensibilities of imperialist England a century earlier. An interesting corroboration of racism involving the

London Zoo is MacNeice's revelation in *Zoo* (1938) that its black leopard's name was 'Nigger' (101); as in Garnett's novella, there is no condemnation expressed.

5. A modern incidence of people in zoo cages is recorded in Duncan Smith's graphic art exhibition 'Images of Captive Animals.' One panel shows a photograph of three people sitting in a cage surrounded by spectators, journalists, and photographers. Titled '*Homo Sapiens*, Chessington Zoo, UK,' the text reads: 'The presentation of the classifications of known animals in zoos was fully completed in 1969 when three examples of the species *Homo Sapiens* were exhibited to the public at Chessington Zoo' (43). The Chessington specimens are of the same race and culture as the spectators, unlike the construct integral to earlier displays, of featuring 'exotics' from far-flung lands. Another recent human exhibition at a zoo is described in a *New York Times'* article (29 August 1996: A 10), 'Zoo in Copenhagen Exhibits New Primates (Fully Clothed)': 'Living out their daily lives in a plexiglass-walled apartment between the baboons and a pair of lemurs, Henrik Lehmann, an acrobat, and Malene Botoft, a newspaper employee, say they hope to make visitors think about their origins.' The two-week-long display included a conventional zoo sign listing details of Homo sapiens's habitat, diet, and other basic facts. Spectators watched the couple fix motorcycles, work on a computer, and use the telephone and fax.
6. This is clearly the case in Helen Zenna Smith's *Not So Quiet . . .* (1930), when a zoo metaphor illustrates her reactions to being in a bizarre and unpleasant situation. During the First World War, the English narrator attends a concert in a German prisoner-of-war compound. For her protection, she is

> seated in a big cage with bars – iron bars – exactly like the Zoo. I shall never stare at an animal in a cage again; I shall feel too sorry for it. If it experiences half the embarrassing sensations I experienced, its life must be one long torture. Five minutes passed before I dared glance up from my programme, to meet hundreds of staring eyes. Brown eyes, blue eyes small eyes, large eyes – curious eyes all of them . . . I went scarlet. Once I dreamed I was travelling in an Underground carriage minus a stitch of clothing; I felt exactly now as I did then. Naked and exceedingly ashamed. The prisoners circled round and round the cage whispering and pushing the front ones away when they had stared long enough. It was the first time most of them had ever seen an Englishwoman, and . . . their remarks were distinctly uncomplimentary.
>
> (142)

7. Graham Swift's 'Hoffmeier's Antelope' (1982) features a keeper, like Nimier's, fanatically dedicated to the animal he oversees, who similarly moves into its cage as he becomes increasingly detached from reality. The animal is destined to be the last of its species, as the last male has died; but the keeper 'was under the illusion . . . that,

like children who believe that mere "loving" brings babies into the world, he could, solely by the intense affection he bore the female antelope, ensure the continuation of its kind' (41). Like Joseph from *The Giraffe*, Swift's keeper manifests a deranged passion for this animal with which he cohabits in a zoo cage. In Valerie Martin's *The Great Divorce*, a troubled person fantasizes about being in a zoo cage. Camille, a keeper assigned to the large cat house, is emotionally unstable: her mental health is plagued by low self-esteem and suicidal tendencies, and a therapist diagnoses her as having personality disorder. Camille represents another instance of a psychologically afflicted person associated with a zoo cage when she lies in bed at night and thinks about a 'fantasy – or was it a plan – that she would spend an entire night in the night house' (where the zoo animals sleep) to escape from unpalatable living arrangements in her mother's house (25).

8. Plath's poetic suggests that her images of her husband, Ted Hughes, might offer another depiction of the fascist as zoo keeper if her oeuvre is considered as a composite work: the husband-figure (who is a type of 'animal keeper,' given his extensive canon of animal poetry) appears as a keeper in 'Zoo Keeper's Wife' and a Nazi in 'Daddy.' Daniel Quinn's *Ishmael* tells of a gorilla liberated from a zoo by a man whose family perished in the Holocaust: 'he decided to rescue me from my cage and fashion me into a dreadful substitute for the family he had failed to rescue from the cage of Europe' (20), the animal thinks. In Vonnegut's *Slaughterhouse-Five* the general devastation of the Second World War – though without specific reference to the Holocaust – is constantly present as a force suggesting the omnipresent *Zeitgeist* of social madness loosely associated with the depiction of people in a zoo. Also of interest on this topic, although probably *à propos de rien*: 'During the 1936 Berlin Olympics all competitors were obliged to give the Nazi salute, but the British contingent would have none of it. Whilst giving a fair impression of acknowledging the Führer they chanted, not "Heil Hitler!", but the immortal phrase: "Whipsnade Whipsnade, Zoo, Zoo, Zoo!"' (Riddell and Denton, 15).
9. Such enfranchisement is not strictly limited to the dominant species. Certain other animals, in certain conditions, may enjoy protection under the social compact: for example, under laws preventing cruelty to (some) animals. I would argue that such laws should be extended to cover zoo animals but this rarely happens, except in extremely appalling cases, because they have been contextualized in such a way that they are denied the social consideration given other domesticated animals. See Harriet Ritvo's chapter, 'A Measure of Compassion,' in *The Animal Estate*, on the capricious history of animal protection. In *Animals, Property, and the Law*, Gary L. Francione describes how American social and legal systems have historically regarded animals as property belonging to people, thereby obviating claims for animals' legal rights or protection.

10. Lucina P. Gabbard explores numerous significant similarities between *The Hairy Ape* and *The Zoo Story*. She notes the 'striking parallel' between O'Neill and Albee, 'that each, in one of his earliest literary efforts, wrote a play based on the same metaphor' (365) – the zoo.

> In *The Hairy Ape* and *The Zoo Story* this common metaphor leads to similar situations, settings, and plots. Both plays feature a character who visits the zoo to contemplate his desperate isolation. Both characters travel the same path – from Fifth Avenue to the exact same New York Zoo. They are, of course, both outcasts, 'have-nots,' who struggle for acknowledgment. Yank and Jerry have had emotionally deprived childhoods; their mothers were alcoholics who died before their sons had reached manhood. Neither boy felt loved by his father. Both Yank and Jerry confront the 'haves' of society . . . Both outcasts are willing to die to gain proof of their existence, and both do die in relatively suicidal acts.
>
> (366)

11. A subsequent novel, *Doctor Dolittle's Zoo* (New York: Frederick Stokes, 1925) features a zoo designed and run by animals, and containing only animals native to England because, Dolittle realizes, the climate is not healthy for non-native animals.
12. Smith examines relations between animals and people in other poems as well. 'This is Disgraceful and Abominable' reacts against animals' abuse in a circus rather than a zoo, but its moral resembles Smith's point in 'The Zoo.' 'Of all the disgraceful and abominable things,' the poem begins, 'Making animals perform for the amusement of human beings is / Utterly disgraceful and abominable.' She laments the inane spectacle, the cruel training, and the substandard living conditions that circuses necessitate, and concludes the poem: 'Oh, away with it, away with it, it is so disgraceful and abominable. / Weep the disgraces. Forbid the abominations' (338). Smith's poems often address animals' rights: 'Death Bereaves our Common Mother / Nature Grieves for my Dead Brother' provokes sympathy for vegetarianism. 'Nature and Free Animals' lambastes people's attitudes toward domesticated pets:

> I will forgive you everything,
> But what you have done to my Dogs
> I will not forgive.
> You have taught them the sicknesses of your mind
> And the sicknesses of your body
> You have taught them to be servile.
>
> (42)

And 'Parrot' also laments the condition of pets; like 'The Zoo,' it protests the indignity of caged captivity:

He has croup. His feathered chest
Knows no minute of rest.
High on his perch he sits
And coughs and spits,
Waiting for death to come.
Pray heaven it wont be long.
(104)

13. In *Zoo*, MacNeice offers another account of the jungle animal's wistful memory of the deprivation of its natural life, in terms virtually identical to those used by Lofting, Smith, and Rilke: 'instincts creep about inside him which will never again be realized in action. His cage is a train carrying him through the jungle that was but is no more his; now it is night and when he looks into the window all he can see is himself in the cage reflected there' (104). Masson and McCarthy offer a comparable account of a young gorilla imported to Europe: 'Hum-Hum had lost all joy in living. She succeeded in living to reach Hamburg, and from there, the Animal Park at Stellingen, with all her caretakers, but her energy did not return again. With signs of the greatest sadness of soul Hum-Hum mourned over the happy past . . . She died of a broken heart' (100). And Felix Salten's 'Prisoners' describes a newly arrived orang-utan:

> For twenty years he had lived in freedom in Sumatra. But one day they caught him with some kind of narcotic, perhaps opium. He swallowed it in bait that had been laid out, and sank into a heavy sleep. When he awakened, his freedom was gone . . . With his full red beard he looked like some frightening figure from a fairy tale – an evil wood spirit. But when I saw the deep depression of his face, his eyes, I knew that instead it was he who was under the spell of evil enchantment. For he was as if bewitched. As soon as he had taken a bite of the food that was thrown through the bars he shuffled back to his corner. With one overlong arm he clutched a branch, and with the knuckle of an enormous finger painted figures on the wall. Silent, sad, quivering. He'd hardly get used to this. Nor would he ever be domesticated. His wildness was too passionate, his pain too deep. He would simply die, quietly, sadly, slowly.
>
> (106–8)

Finally, e. e. cummings, in his typically enigmatic poem number 30 from *50 Poems* (1940), depicts the same sense of a caged animal's melancholy, when he describes an elephant in the zoo as

   vanishing from a this world into bigger
much some out of(not visible to us)whom only his dream
ing own soul looks
and
the is all floatful and remembering
(516)

14. Another striking account of a zoo animal's pain is occasioned by the same zoo and cage as Rilke's poem: 'The first time that I ever really *saw* an animal in a cage was in a small zoo at the Jardin des Plantes,' writes Michael W. Fox.

> I entered a large, ornate Victorian rotunda that housed a few animals in small wrought iron cages. I now recall seeing only one animal there. At first it appeared not to see me even though I stood beside its cage for a long time . . . Its liquid form brushed across the front of the cage. After insinuating itself around some artificial rocks and a body-polished tree stump toward the back of the enclosure, it ricocheted off a ceramic-tiled wall to again caress the front of the cage . . . And then I saw the blood – a streak of blood down her left thigh, draining from an open sore that would never heal until the cat was freed from the hypnotic lines she traced and was so inexorably bound to execute. Each scraping turn around the tree trunk kept the sore open, like a broken heart bleeding for the loss of all that was wild and free. I wondered if she felt any pain. Her yellow-green eyes were like cold glass, with neither fire nor luster. Perhaps this was a slow ritual form of suicide, gradually grinding and rubbing and shredding the body to pieces to free the wild spirit within. I saw the glint of white bone – or was it tendon – through the cat's thigh muscles winking as she turned and paced before me.
>
> (147–8)

Like Rilke, Fox bemoans the animal's loss of natural existence:

> The panther body, denied freedom of expression and fulfillment of purpose, had become a prison for the creature spirit within . . . Confined in such limited space, how else could this boundless spirit of the jungle respond? Her rhythmic, trancelike actions were more than thwarted attempts to escape. Was her compulsive animation designed simply to help her cope with the emptiness of existing in body without any purpose for the spirit, a kind of living death?
>
> (148–9)

Although three-quarters of a century separates the caged animals in Rilke's poem and Fox's animal rights treatise, the two complement each other uncannily.

15. MacNeice's account of the same zoo three decades later confirms the generally unpalatable atmosphere Rilke depicts. The zoo in the Bois de Vincennes had replaced it as the city's preeminent zoo: 'there *were* still animals in the Jardin des Plantes but nothing to write home about' (229). MacNeice was 'Exhausted by the dank, overloaded, rather seedy atmosphere of the menagerie,' which he calls 'a melancholy relic of history' (243).
16. The following discussion considers both Hoban's and Pinter's versions

of *Turtle Diary*; while the screenplay is fairly close to the novel, it is not identical, and contains some of its own uniquely significant details.

17. In the chaotic military conflagration at the end of Angus Wilson's *The Old Men at the Zoo*, some of the zookeepers are actually maimed and killed which is, indeed, even more radical than freeing the caged animals if it is meant in the spirit of retribution – but it seems unlikely that Wilson consciously advocates the murderous overthrow of keepers. Rather, I believe he simply loses his grasp of that novel's muddled conclusion; things often get bloody when a writer's control lapses.
18. Another liberation story of related interest is Caralyn and Mark Buehner's *The Escape of Marvin the Ape*, a children's story. An ape escapes from its cage when the keeper isn't watching, and eludes the police as it frolics through New York City doing all sorts of things that were impossible in captivity: dining in fancy restaurants, romping in Central Park, visiting the art museum, attending movies and ball games, riding the Staten Island Ferry. Marvin is thrilled with his newfound freedom (and young readers will certainly empathize wholeheartedly with his escape from constraint and his fulfilling new life); on the last page, Helvetica the hippopotamus sneaks out of her cage, inspired by Marvin. The story instills a pointedly anti-zoo sentiment, as an antidote to the vast number of children's stories that extol zoogoing.
19. See Brigid Brophy's *Hackenfeller's Ape* for an extensive consideration of this theme. In that novel, a professor develops an extreme attachment to an ape in the zoo while studying its mating habits; when he learns that the animal is scheduled to be launched into space atop a rocket, he helps the ape escape.
20. On the risks and frequent failures of reintroducing zoo animals to a natural environment, see Benjamin Beck's essay 'Reintroduction, Zoos, Conservation, and Animal Welfare' in *Ethics on the Ark*, 155–63.

CHAPTER 4 PAIN

1. Heini Hediger suggests using electric restraints in his chapter on confinement in *Wild Animals in Captivity*. 'It really is surprising how little imagination has been shown up till now in research into methods of confinement,' he writes; electrical barriers used in conjunction with mechanical barriers offer 'the advantage of a combination of different negative stimuli' (58–9).
2. Will Travers catalogues the pain suffered by the London Zoo's elephants from 1946–83, when seven elephants died or were killed, at an average age of 20 (as compared to the natural lifespan of 50–60). One was shot after injuring keepers; two died from falling into moats; one suffered a heart attack and was found dead hanging by a chained leg in the moat. One, Pole Pole, became a *cause célèbre* after it was killed by lethal injection; it had lived in captivity for 15 years, consigned to a concrete habitat and manifestly unhappy throughout

that period, and was finally subject to euthanasia, when keepers accepted their failure to ameliorate its misery (McKenna, Travers and Wray, 204).

3. Given zoos' frequently outdated and decrepit facilities, such fire deaths are not unusual. The same year, 'four giraffes burned to death in a fire that is believed to have been caused by faulty electrical wiring' at the Santiago Zoo (Sims); in a 1996 fire in the Montgomery Zoo that killed a dozen animals, again an electrical problem was suspected as the cause.
4. New York: Bantam, 1976.
5. Bardon, Jonathan. *A History of Ulster*. Belfast: Blackstaff Press, 1992, pages 568–9.
6. Consider a comparable zoo story account: Steve Watkins's 'Critterworld,' describes the inept, macabre disposal of the carcass of another elephant, Stash. 'It became like a big joke there in the Critterworld parking lot: people saying, "How do you get rid of a dead elephant?" then cracking up, as if it was the funniest thing in the world.' A tree surgeon appears with a chainsaw. 'On the third pull it coughed around and caught, and the noise was so loud that the little kids covered their ears. He went for a leg first, aiming carefully just above the knee where the skin was taut, but I guess he should have checked how tough the flesh was because the chain saw kicked back on him and took a bite out of [his] own leg.' A crowd gathers: 'some pulled out knives and poked at him with their blades. I saw a guy sawing Stash's tail, and a couple of kids tugging on a tusk. Somebody else went for a piece of the ear' (357). Football players arrive with axes, chopping away at the elephant accompanied by school cheers. 'It must have gone on for a long time, guys passing off the axes when they got tired, always somebody new to step in for a few more whacks at Stash. A couple of people left, offended, but more came, and the Critterworld parking lot turned black with blood' (358). At day's end, 'For all their chopping and their pep rally and everything, Stash was still there. Sure, he was cut to hell and bleeding everywhere, and his trunk and his tail were gone, and the ears were tattered, and all like that, but he was still there. They could have swung their axes for another whole day and Stash would still have been there. Even dead he was too much elephant for them' (359). The elephant is finally dragged into a field, pushed into a hole dug by a bull dozer, doused with gasoline, and incinerated. The noirish demeanor suggests that if zoo animals are badly treated when they are alive, the misuse is even more flagrant when they die.
7. 'Quarantine the Aggressors' speech, Chicago, 5 October 1937.
8. Harriet Schleifer explicitly links meat-eating and animal captivity: 'the attitude that allows us to raise animals for food colours our treatment of all other creatures . . . Once we have accepted that we may utilize animals for so trivial a reason as our enjoyment of the taste of their flesh, it is easy to use them for any purpose which is equally frivolous, such as . . . confining them in zoos to amuse us' (70).

9. In *Cat People,* Irina identifies strongly with a black panther in the zoo. That animal, the film explains, symbolizes the troubled history of Irina's Serbian heritage. Both Irina and the cat, with their scary, hostile natures, evoke Serbia's historical predicament; the depiction resembles Wilson's attention to zoo animals' nationalistic connotations in *The Old Men at the Zoo.*
10. While it is not about zoos, the title of another poem by Plath, 'The Beekeeper's Daughter' (1959), suggests that it may be a companion poem to 'Zoo Keeper's Wife.' Each poem sketches out Plath's relation to a male oppressor (and see 'Daddy' for an example of how she yokes the two men together in their tyranny). In 'The Beekeeper's Daughter,' Plath's father – an entomologist who specialized in bees – is 'Hieratical in your frock coat, maestro of the bees . . . My heart under your foot' (118). Both poems portray the men's degrading uses of animals, and their comparable degradation of the speaker. The woman, like the animal, ends up objectified – just 'wife' or 'daughter': the property of the 'keeper,' who treats his specimen as he pleases, without regard for its happiness.
11. See also Jim Mason's chapter, 'Misogyny and the Reduction of Women and Female Power' in *An Unnatural Order,* which explores the links between men's oppression of women and social structures that exploit animals.
12. Another prominent example is 'The Rabbit Catcher.'

CHAPTER 5 SPECTATORSHIP

1. *Diagnostic and Statistical Manual of Disorders,* 3rd edn. Washington: American Psychiatric Association, 1987, pp. 289–90.
2. *Cook's Handbook to London.* London: Simpkin, Marshall, 1930.
3. Press release issued by the San Diego Wild Animal Park; reprinted in *Harper's* 292.1749 (February 1996): 33
4. Cortázar's focus on eyes throughout the story draws attention to the instruments, the organs, of spectatorship. The device is metonymic: the part – the eye – represents the whole – the spectator.
5. 'Despite trouble, a bright future for Fernbank.' *Atlanta Journal Constitution* 15 March 1995: A11.
6. Linda Rosen. *CD-ROM Professional* January 1994: 168–70.
7. 'How Virtual Reality Stacks Up With the Real Thing.' *Christian Science Monitor* 24 January 1995: 11.

CHAPTER 6 KIDS AND ZOOS

1. More radically than Bettelheim, Gary Snyder claims, 'Children know . . . that *they are little animals.* That is why they so vigorously oppose the forces of domesticity and civilized education. They know quite well they would be better off in the forest, the mountains, the deserts, and the seas' (in D. King, 12).

2. This is not to deny that children and adults perceive the world around them differently. Andrei Bitov describes a father's reflections about his daughter's experience on their zoo visit: 'I lifted her up at every cage at which she couldn't see well enough. She experienced everything deeply, which is to say in silence . . . But – and this is at the heart of the matter – she experienced something *different*, and what it was I really am unable to say' (277–8). While children's and adults' perceptual processes and analysis are not identical, the differences do not justify the notion that children are naively unconscious of the more 'sophisticated' issues of inequity and inauthenticity that pervade zoo culture. Perhaps Bitov's conclusion is the most sagacious one: adults really do not know, finally, what children are thinking.
3. New York: Bantam, 1980, p. 277.
4. Solly Zuckerman confirms Edgar's suspicions about the moral tenuousness that infused Buck's industry. The proliferation of zoos in the mid-twentieth century, he writes, was

   > a heyday for animal dealers. Safari parks also started to mushroom as opportunist ventures in which dealers and circus proprietors joined forces with big land-owners for their mutual financial benefit . . . Exotic animals were now being exploited to make money which was going to be used neither for the advancement of knowledge nor for the well-being of the animals themselves. Wild beasts had become a kind of currency. They could help to keep roofs on country houses, and to buy mansions for dealers.
   >
   > (19).

5. Another account of the same zoo reiterates its unpalatable milieu: 'the Dublin lions disappointed me, looked a shade moth-eaten,' writes Louis MacNeice in *Zoo*. He recalls watching 'a keeper spraying the feet of an elephant who had foot-rot – bantering him in a brogue for the diversion of the visitors. I remember a common donkey in a heavily barred cage marked "This Animal is Dangerous," and several cages which were empty, overgrown with grass' (70).
6. Ludwig Bemelman. *Madeline*. New York, Viking, 1967, unpaginated (first published 1939).
7. 'It is significant that the modern Anglo-Saxon name is the "zoological garden,"' write Mullan and Marvin, 'for a garden is an artificial and controlled reconstruction of elements from the natural world which have been chosen and then ordered for presentation in an alien context' (68).
8. In the following passage, the voice fluctuates between third and first person as the speaker, an anti-pill activist, steps in and out of Nation's character.
9. Wondering why monkeys are traditionally such popular zoo attractions, Yi-Fu Tuan writes, 'One reason, no doubt, is that they resemble humans . . . Some visitors are especially attracted by the

easy sexual behavior of the monkeys. Voyeurism is forbidden except when applied to sub-humans.' But as in Vonnegut's story, monkeys may transgress against standards of acceptable conduct: 'in one of the largest zoos in the world a spacious open-air enclosure had to be pulled down because its inmates had behaved "indecently"' (82).

10. John Hawkes depicts another explicit instance of zoo animals' erotic display in 'In Dante's Forest.' In a reptile house cage,

> two waking bats, like a pair of old exhibitionists, were holding open their black capes and exposing themselves . . . The faces of the two aroused and wakeful bats were grinning. Their penises, each one perhaps the size of a child's little finger, looked like slender overlong black mushrooms, leaping all out of proportion from the tiny loins . . . in unison the two bats slowly rolled and stretched upward from mid-body until grotesquely, impossibly, the two eager heads were so positioned that in sudden spasms the vicious little mouths were engaged in the slow jerky calisthenics of auto-fellatio.
>
> (66–7)

No children are present, but the adults' response confirms J. Edgar Nation's fears about inciting impressionable minds. 'See how much pleasure they give themselves' (67), a woman approvingly remarks; she and a man who 'clearly, had himself become uncontrollably aroused by the sight of the bats' (67–8) proceed to copulate on the reptile house floor.

11. Stephen Budiansky further explores the cultural misperception of bears in zoos:

> The favorite animal in a survey of visitors to the National Zoo in Washington, D.C., was the giant panda, typically described by zoogoers as 'cute, cuddly, and adorable.' It actually is solitary, ill-tempered, and aggressive, but never mind. Some zoologists suggest that the influence of generations of teddy bears . . . appeal to our naive sense – innate or learned – of parental protectiveness. Mere facts cannot compete with perception.
>
> (2)

12. Charles Siebert writes of the same tragedy at the Prospect Park Zoo:

> I remember the incident casting a strange spell over the neighborhood and people expressing confused emotions: sorrow for the boy who'd been killed, befuddlement over his and his friend's intentions, and, most vociferously, anger and remorse about the fate of the bears. It was never made clear what exactly those boys were thinking – there was talk of one of the boys making a dare – but it occurs to me now that when they climbed over those bars, they were, in a sense, stepping into the story of the bears, the idea and the aura of the old zoo animal. City kids in the

> summer will take the caps off hydrants, anything, to escape the heat, and if they sneak into the zoo for a swim, there are a number of less threatening moats . . . in which to swim. They, however, sought out not the coldest pool but the pool of the *coldest animal*, the animal that *stands for* coldness: the ice bears in some children's book; or the ones who ride blocks of ice across soda-bottle labels and menthol cigarette packs.
>
> ('Gone', 53)

13. Personal correspondence with the author.

CHAPTER 7 ANIMALS AND THEIR CONTEXTS: BEYOND ZOOS

1. Saki's 'The Mappined Terrace' exemplifies this dreariness. A woman and her aunt discuss the positive and negative aspects of the new style of cageless animal enclosures (called 'Mappin Terraces') at the zoo, and then turn to a consideration of their own lives: 'we are able to live our unreal, stupid little lives on our particular Mappin terrace, and persuade ourselves that we really are untrammelled men and women leading a reasonable existence in a reasonable sphere' (188), the niece says.

> Lack of initiative is the thing that really cripples one, and that is where you and I and Uncle James are so hopelessly shut in. We are just so many animals stuck down on a Mappin terrace, with this difference in our disfavour, that the animals are there to be looked at, while nobody wants to look at us. As a matter of fact, there would be nothing to look at. We get colds in winter and hay-fever in summer, and if a wasp happens to sting one of us, well, that is the wasp's initiative, not ours; all we do is to wait for the swelling to go down.
>
> (189)

2. John Irving portrays a similar array of the zoo's night noises in *Setting Free the Bears*, and even more strongly than Elliott, indicates that the noises denote animals' pain. Siggy, hiding in the zoo to stake out plans for releasing the animals, observes night watchman O. Schrutt walking through the zoo:

> I heard a wail from some lost aisle of the Small Mammal Maze. A cry cut off at full force, as if O. Schrutt had flung open a door on some poor beast's nightmare and slammed the door shut again as quickly as he'd opened it . . . But the wail was contagious. The Small Mammal House whimpered and moaned. Oh, the screams blared and were cut off again, muffled but not altogether gone. As if a certain zoo train had passed you somewhere, going fast, and the frightened animals' cries had slashed out at you like a passing buggy driver's whip; and the cries hung for a moment

> all around, like the sting of the whip lingering on your neck after the buggy driver had slashed and passed on.
>
> (170)

Later the same night: 'I can't imagine what O. Schrutt could be doing to them. I still hear them; the whole zoo is listening. Now and then there's a door that opens suddenly on some awful animal music, and just as suddenly closes – muffles the cry. I can only guess: O. Schrutt is beating them, one by one.' (178). David Garnett, in *A Man in the Zoo*, describes the night noises as disembodied and unsettling to John Cromartie (who is locked in the zoo with the animals): 'At intervals he could hear the cries of different beasts, though he could rarely tell which it was from the cry. Several times he made out the howl of a wolf, and once the roar of a lion. Later the screaming and howling of wild animals became louder and almost incessant. Long after he had . . . gone to bed, he lay awake listening to the strange noises' (15).

3. Another children's book, A. A. Milne's *Winnie-the-Pooh* (1926), loosely fits the model of zoo frames seen in Aiken's and Conrad's works: a brief introduction informs that the London Zoo displays the original of the fanciful fuzzy bear. Milne characterizes the zoo in the standard mode of uncritical adulation: because his son, Christopher Robin, loved going to see the polar bears there, he created/embellished the lovable animal that became a childhood favorite. But the stories never refer to the zoo again after the introduction, and the fictional Pooh is so engaging precisely because his rambles through the hundred acre wood embody a *joie de vivre* that would certainly elude a captive animal. Milne's story, like Aiken's and Cullen's poetry, raises the idea of a zoo to subvert it (implicitly) via a narrative about a creature that is very loosely a zoo animal, but that could never enjoy the range of experiences it is depicted as having if it actually lived in the zoo.
4. Aiken's coinages evoke the combinative medieval term for a giraffe, 'camelopard' – so named, according to Robert A. Palmatier, because its long neck resembles that of the camel and its brown spots on a lighter background resemble those of the leopard (61). The word 'leopard' itself is a fusion of lion (*leo*) and 'pard,' an archaic form of panther. The *OED* cites usages of 'camelopard' from 1398 to 1840. In *Zoo*, Louis MacNeice writes that in the early nineteenth century 'the giraffe was almost unknown in England; in 1810 a man had painted spots on a white camel and exhibited it as "a camelopard just arrived"' (116).
5. For example, in *Citizen Kane*, the newsreel narrator describes the mogul's menagerie: '*Xanadu's livestock: the fowl of the air, the fish of the sea, the beast of the field and jungle – two of each; the biggest private zoo since Noah*' (114); the zoo director in Marie Nimier's *The Giraffe* is first described as looking 'like Noah before the flood' (2). But Dale Jamieson points out differences: 'Zoo professionals like to say

that they are the Noahs of the modern world and that zoos are their arks. But Noah found a place to land his animals where they could thrive and multiply'; endangered animals supposedly being preserved in zoos are not so much like Noah's charges as they are 'like passengers on a voyage of the damned, never to find a port that will let them dock or a land in which they can live their lives in peace and freedom' ('Zoos Revisited', 62).

6. 'Why an inordinate interest in animals and athletes?' Moore asked in the foreword to *A Marianne Moore Reader*.

> They are subjects for art and exemplars of it, are they not? minding their own business. Pangolins, hornbills, pitchers, catchers, do not pry or prey – or prolong the conversation; do not make us self-conscious; look their best when caring least . . . 'The fabric of existence weaves itself whole,' as Charles Ives said (*Time*, August 22, 1960). 'You cannot set art off in a corner and hope for it to have vitality, reality and substance.'
>
> (xvi)

7. The poem's original title was 'My Apish Cousins.' Engel suggests that the title change offered a neater and more subtle irony. The new title explicitly informs that an animal is conveying the message; 'the poem's original title . . . made somewhat more obvious the ironic comparison of human and animal' (43).
8. Other zoo stories, too, describe zoos' agglomeration of animals as leading to a kind of combativeness, or competition among species, with the effect of casting certain animals as inferior to others. Zoos implicate animals in a human model of a zero-sum system of castes and hierarchies: some animals' glamor or attractiveness necessitates other animals' perception as being unattractive. In 'In the Zoo,' Stafford describes a bear's neighbors, a cage full of monkeys, which she anthropomorphically portrays gratuitously criticizing the surrounding animals: 'stealthily and shiftily, they are really watching the pitiful polar bear . . . and the windy black bear ('Life of the party. Gasbag. Low I.Q.,' they note scornfully on his dossier), and the stupid, bourgeois grizzlies ('It's feed the face and hit the sack for them,' the monkeys say)' (284). In *A Man in the Zoo*, Cromartie's neighboring primates are extremely hostile to him, the keeper explains, because

> 'They are wild with jealousy . . . that you should have drawn such a large crowd.' At first Mr. Cromartie found this very hard to credit, but afterwards, when he got to know the characters of his fellow captives better, it became the most ordinary commonplace. He learnt that all the monkeys, the elephants, and the bears felt jealous in this way. It was natural enough that the creatures that were fed by the public should feel resentment if they were passed over, for they are all insatiably greedy . . . The wolves felt

> a different jealousy, for they were constantly forming attachments to particular persons among the crowd, and if the chosen person neglected them for a neighbour they became jealous.
>
> (19)

9. 'The Arctic Ox (Or Goat)' expresses Moore's feelings about fur: 'To wear the arctic fox / you have to kill it. Wear / *qiviut* – the underwool of the arctic ox – / pulled off it like a sweater; / your coat is warm; your conscience better' (193).
10. I thank Macmillan's anonymous reviewer for this observation.

Bibliography

PRIMARY SOURCES (ZOO STORIES)

Aiken, Conrad. *Who's Zoo*. Illus. John Vernon Lord. New York: Jonathan Cape, 1977. Unpaginated.
Aillaud, Gilles. Catalogue of painting exhibition, introduced by John Berger. In Barzdo, 26–34.
Albee, Edward. *The Zoo Story*. 1959. New York: Coward-McCann, 1960.
Allende, Isabel. *The House of the Spirits*. Trans. Magda Bogin. New York: Bantam, 1986.
Amis, Martin. *The Information*. New York: Harmony, 1995.
Babel, Isaac. 'The Beast Grows Silent.' In *Isaac Babel: The Forgotten Prose*. Trans. Nicholas Stroud. Ann Arbor, MI: Ardis, 1978.
Baker, Alison. 'The Heaven of Animals.' In *How I Came West, and Why I Stayed*. San Francisco: Chronicle, 1993. 62–75.
Baxter, Charles. 'Westland.' In *A Relative Stranger*. New York: Norton, 1990. 19–41.
Belloc, Hillaire. 'Jim who Ran Away from his Nurse, and was Eaten by a Lion.' 1907. In *Complete Verse*. London: Duckworth, 1970. 260–1.
Benson, E. F. 'The Zoo.' 1893. In *Six Common Things*. London: Osgood, McIlvaine & Co., 1895. 153–65.
Bitov, Andrei. 'The Last Bear.' In *Metropol: Literary Almanac*. Eds Vasily Aksyonov et al. Trans. George Saunders. New York: Norton, 1982. 273–8.
Brathwaite, Edward Kamau. 'The Zoo.' In *Sappho Sakyi's Meditations*. Mona, Jamaica: *Savacou* 16, 1989. 45–50.
Brophy Brigid. *Hackenfeller's Ape*. London: Allison & Busby, 1953.
Buck, Frank. *Bring 'Em Back Alive*. New York: Simon & Schuster, 1930.
Buehner, Caralyn and Mark Buehner. *The Escape of Marvin the Ape*. New York: Dial. n.d.
Burgin, Victor. *Zoo 78*. In *Between*. Oxford: Blackwell, 1986. 61–87.
Capote, Truman. *Other Voices, Other Rooms*. New York: Random House, 1948.
Chaucer, Geoffrey. *The Manciple's Tale*. In *The Works of Geoffrey Chaucer*. Ed. F. N. Robinson. Boston: Houghton Mifflin, 1957.
Cole, Henri. 'The Zoo Wheel of Knowledge.' In *The Zoo Wheel of Knowledge*. New York: Knopf, 1989.
Cortázar, Julio. 'Axolotl.' In *End of the Game and Other Stories*. Trans. Paul Blackburn. New York: Pantheon, 1967. 3–9.
Cullen, Countee. *The Lost Zoo*. 1940. Illus. Joseph Low. Chicago: Follett, 1968.
cummings, e. e. 'The Secret of the Zoo Exposed.' In *E. E. Cummings: A Miscellany*. Ed. George J. Firmage. New York: Argophile P, 1958.

cummings, e. e. '[Poem] XVIII.' From *ViVa*. 1931. Poem 30. From *50 Poems*. 1940. In *Complete Poems: 1904–1962*. Ed. George J. Firmage. New York: Liveright, 1991. 328, 516.

Dazai, Osamu. 'Monkey Island.' In *Crackling Mountain and Other Stories*. Trans. James O'Brien. Rutland, VT: Tuttle, 1989. 80–90.

Dickey, James. 'Encounter in the Cage Country.' In *Poems: 1957–1967*. Middletown, CT: Wesleyan UP, 1967. 274–5.

Doctorow, E. L. *World's Fair*. New York: Ballantine, 1985.

Doyle, Roddy. *Paddy Clarke Ha Ha Ha*. New York: Viking, 1994.

Doyle, Roddy. *The Van*. London: Secker & Warburg, 1991.

Drabble, Margaret. *The Waterfall*. New York: Knopf, 1969.

Dunbar, Paul Laurence. 'Sympathy.' 1913. In *The Collected Poetry of Paul Laurence Dunbar*. Ed. Joanne M. Braxton. Charlottesville, VA: UP of Virginia, 1993. 102.

Durrell, Gerald. *A Zoo in My Luggage*. Illus. Ralph Thompson. New York: Viking, 1960.

Dybek, Stuart. 'Sunday at the Zoo.' In *Sudden Fiction: American Short Short Stories*. Eds Robert Shapard and James Thomas. Salt Lake City, UT: Peregrine Smith, 1986. 128.

Edgar, Marriott. 'The Lion and Albert.' 1933. In *The World of Stanley Holloway*. London: Francis, Day & Hunter. 1972. 2–5.

Edgar, Marriott. 'The Return of Albert (Albert Comes Back).' 1935. In *The World of Stanley Holloway*. London: Francis, Day & Hunter. 1972. 14–17.

Elliott, Janice. 'The Noise from the Zoo.' In *The Noise from the Zoo and Other Stories*. London: Hodder & Stoughton, 1991. 184–9.

Galsworthy, John. *The Man of Property*. 1906. New York: Scribner's, 1969.

Garnett, David. *A Man in the Zoo*. Illus. Ray Garnett. London: Chatto & Windus, 1924.

Ginsberg, Allen. *Howl and Other Poems*. San Francisco: City Lights, 1956.

Goodman, Paul. *The Empire City*. 1959. New York: Macmillan, 1964.

Greenaway, Peter (writer and dir.). *Zoo: A Zed and Two Noughts*. 1985.

Guillén, Nicolás. *¡Patria O Muerte! The Great Zoo and Other Poems*. Trans. Robert Márquez. New York: Monthly Review P, 1972.

Haanstra, Bert. *Zoo*. 1962. In *Experimental Avant Garde Series, Vol. 22*. The New York Film Annex.

Hawkes, John. 'In Dante's Forest.' *American Review* 20 (April 1974): 60–70.

Hoban, Russell. *Turtle Diary*. New York: Random House, 1975.

Hughes, Ted. 'The Jaguar.' 1957. In *New Selected Poems*. New York: Harper, 1982. 3.

Irving, John. *Setting Free the Bears*. 1968. New York: Pocket, 1979.

Jarrell, Randall. 'The Woman at the Washington Zoo.' In *The Woman at the Washington Zoo*. New York: Atheneum, 1960. 2–3.

Johnson, Terry. *Cries from the Mammal House*. 1984. In *Plays: One*. London: Methuen, 1993. 137–209.

Kafka, Franz. 'A Hunger Artist.' 1922. In *The Complete Stories*. Ed. Nahum N. Glazer. Trans. Willa and Edwin Muir. New York: Schocken, 1983. 268–77.

Karr, Mary. *The Liars' Club*. New York: Penguin, 1995.

Khlebnikov, Velimir. 'Menagerie.' In Schklovsky, Viktor. *Zoo, or Letters Not About Love*. Trans. Richard Sheldon. Ithaca, NY: Cornell UP, 1971. 5–8.

Laffan, K. B. *Zoo Zoo Widdershins, Zoo*. 1968. London: Faber, 1969.

Lispector, Clarice. 'The Buffalo.' 1960. In *Family Ties*. Trans. Giovanni Pontiero. Austin: U of Texas P, 1972.

Lively, Penelope. *Moon Tiger*. New York: Grove, 1987.

Lofting, Hugh. *The Voyages of Doctor Dolittle*. New York: Frederick Stokes, 1922.

MacNeice, Louis. *Zoo*. Illus. Nancy Sharp. London: Michael Joseph, 1938.

Mankiewicz, Herman J., and Orson Welles. *The Shooting Script*. In *The Citizen Kane Book*. Boston: Little, Brown, 1971. (Film released in 1941.)

Martin, Valerie. *The Great Divorce*. 1994. New York: Bantam, 1995.

Milne, A. A. *When We Were Very Young*. London: Methuen, 1965.

Milne, A. A. *Winnie-the-Pooh*. 1926. New York: Penguin, 1992.

Moore, Marianne. 'Brooklyn from Clinton Hill.' In *A Marianne Moore Reader*. New York: Viking, 1961. 182–92.

Moore, Marianne. 'The Monkeys,' 'Apparitions of Splendor,' 'He "Digesteth Harde Yron."' In *The Complete Poems of Marianne Moore*. New York: Macmillan, 1981.

Moravia, Alberto. 'The Chimpanzee.' 1959. In *More Roman Tales*. Trans. Angus Davidson. London: Secker & Warburg, 1963. 7–14.

Murakami, Haruki. 'The Zoo Attack.' Trans. Jay Rubin. *The New Yorker* 71.22 (31 July 1995): 68–74.

Nimier, Marie. *The Giraffe*. 1993. Trans. Mary Feeney. New York: Four Walls Eight Windows, 1995.

O'Neill, Eugene. *The Hairy Ape*. 1922. In *Complete Plays* Vol. 2 (1920–31). New York: Library of America, 1988. 119–63.

Pacheco, José Emilio. 'Baboon Babble.' In *An Ark for the Next Millennium*. Trans. Margaret Sayers Peden. Austin, TX: U of Texas P, 1993. 69.

Park, Nick (dir. and animator). *Creature Comforts*. Aardman Limited production for Channel 4. 1989.

Park, Nick. 'Inside *The Wrong Trousers*.' Interview broadcast with *The Wrong Trousers*, PBS, 1995.

Pinter, Harold. *Turtle Diary*. Dir. John Irvin, 1985. Screenplay text in *The Comfort of Strangers and Other Screenplays*. London: Faber, 1990. 101–63.

Plath, Sylvia. 'Zoo Keeper's Wife.' 1961. In *The Collected Poems*. Ed. Ted Hughes. New York: Harper & Row, 1981. 154–5.

Quinn, Daniel. *Ishmael*. New York: Bantam, 1992.

Riddell, Jonathan, and Peter Denton. *By Underground to the Zoo: London Transport Posters 1913 to the Present*. London: Studio Vista, 1995.

Rilke, Rainer Maria. 'The Panther,' 'The Gazelle,' and 'The Flamingos.' In *The Selected Poetry of Rainer Maria Rilke*. Trans. Stephen Mitchell. New York: Viking, 1989.

Saki. 'The Mappined Life.' 1919. In *Selected Short Stories of 'Saki.'* Harmondsworth: Penguin, 1939. 187–91.

Salten, Felix. 'Prisoners.' In *Good Comrades*. Trans. Paul R. Milton. New York: Grosset & Dunlap, 1942. 100–8.

Sansom, William. 'Among the Dahlias.' In *The Stories of William Sansom*. London: Hogarth P, 1963. 382–9.
Schklovsky, Viktor. *Zoo, or Letters Not About Love*. Trans. Richard Sheldon. Ithaca, NY: Cornell UP, 1971.
Scott, Sarah. *A Description of Millenium Hall and the Country Adjacent*. London: J. Newbury, 1762.
Simon, Paul. 'At the Zoo.' In *Classic Paul Simon*. New York: Amsco, 1991. 136–40.
Smith, Duncan. 'Images of Captive Animals.' Catalogue of graphic arts exhibition. In Barzdo, 35–44.
Smith, Helen Zenna. *Not So Quiet* . . . 1930. New York: Feminist P, 1989.
Smith, Stevie. 'The Zoo.' In *The Collected Poems of Stevie Smith*. New York: Oxford, 1976.
Stafford, Jean. 'In the Zoo.' 1953. In *The Collected Stories of Jean Stafford*. New York: Farrar, Straus and Giroux, 1968. 283–303.
Stoker, Bram. *Dracula*. 1897. New York: Penguin, 1986.
Struther, Jan. *Mrs. Miniver*. New York: Harbrace, 1940.
Swift, Graham. 'Hoffmeier's Antelope.' In *Learning to Swim*. New York: Poseidon, 1982. 29–43.
Swift, Graham. *Shuttlecock*. London: Penguin, 1982.
Thomas, Dylan. 'The Hunchback in the Park.' In *The Collected Poems of Dylan Thomas: 1934–1952*. New York: New Directions, 1956. 123–4.
Tourneur, Jacques (dir.). *Cat People*. Writer, DeWitt Bodeen. RKO, 1942.
Townsend, Sue. *The Queen and I*. London: Methuen, 1992.
Vonnegut, Kurt, Jr. *Slaughterhouse-Five*. 1969. New York: Dell, 1971.
Vonnegut, Kurt, Jr. 'Welcome to the Monkey House.' In *Welcome to the Monkey House*. New York: Delacourte P, 1968. 27–45.
Watkins, Steve. 'Critterworld.' 1991. In *The Pushcart Prive XVII: Best of the Small Presses*. Wainscott, NY: Pushcart P, 1992. 348–60.
Williams, William Carlos. 'The Zoo.' 1950. In *The Farmers' Daughters: The Collected Stories of William Carlos Williams*. New York: New Directions, 1961. 333–42.
Wilson, Angus. *The Old Men at the Zoo*. London: Secker & Warburg, 1961.
Woolf, Leonard. 'Fear and Politics: A Debate at the Zoo.' In *In Savage Times: Leonard Woolf on Peace and War*. New York: Garland, 1973. 5–24.
Woolf, Virginia. *The Letters of Virginia Woolf* Vol. 2, 1912–1922. Eds Nigel Nicolson and Joanne Trautmann. New York: HBJ, 1976.
Woolf, Virginia. *The Letters of Virginia Woolf* Vol. 3, 1923–1928. Eds Nigel Nicolson and Joanne Trautmann. New York: HBJ, 1977.
Woolf, Virginia. *The Letters of Virginia Woolf* Vol. 5, 1932–1935. Eds Nigel Nicolson and Joanne Trautmann. New York: HBJ, 1979.
Woolf, Virginia. *To the Lighthouse*. 1927. New York: HBJ, 1955.
Woolf, Virginia. *The Voyage Out*. 1915. New York: Harcourt, 1948.
'Zoological Gardens.' P[eter] C[halmers] M[itchell]. *Encyclopedia Britannica*, 11th edn. Cambridge: Cambridge UP, 1911. 28: 1018–21.

SECONDARY SOURCES

Adams, Carol J. *The Sexual Politics of Meat: A Feminist-Vegetarian Critical Theory*. New York: Continuum, 1990.

Altick, Richard D. *The Shows of London*. Cambridge, MA: Harvard UP, 1978.

Angier, Natalie. 'Flouting Tradition, Scientists Embrace an Ancient Taboo,' *New York Times* 9 August 1994: B5, B8.

'A Zoo by any Other Name . . .' *New York Times* 5 February 1993: A 11.

Baker, Steve. *Picturing the Beast: Animals, Identity and Representation*. Manchester: Manchester UP, 1993.

Barron, James. 'Officials Weigh Tighter Security At Zoos in Parks.' *New York Times* 22 May 1987: B3.

Barron, James. 'Polar Bears Kill a Child at Prospect Park Zoo.' *New York Times* 20 May 1987: A1, B9.

Barzdo, Jonathan. 'The Trouble with Zoos.' In Barzdo, 19–23.

Barzdo, Jonathan, John Berger, Chris Rawlence, et al. *Zoos*. London: Institute of Contemporary Arts, 1982.

Batten, Peter. *Living Trophies*. New York: Crowell, 1976.

Beck, Alan M. 'The Common Qualities of Man and Beast.' *The Chronicle of Higher Education* 17 May 1996: B3.

Bell, Quentin. *Virginia Woolf: A Biography*. 2 vols. New York: Harcourt, 1972.

Berger, John. 'Why Look at Animals?' In *About Looking*. New York: Pantheon, 1980.

Birkeland, Janis. 'Ecofeminism: Linking Theory and Practice.' In Gaard, 13–59.

Blunt, Wilfrid. *The Ark in the Park: The Zoo in the Nineteenth Century*. London: Hamish Hamilton, 1976.

Bogdan, Robert. *Freak Show: Presenting Human Oddities for Amusement and Profit*. Chicago: U of Chicago P, 1988.

Bostock, Stephen St C. *Zoos and Animal Rights: The Ethics of Keeping Animals*. London: Routledge, 1993.

Bradford, Phillips Verner and Harvey Blume. *Ota: The Pygmy in the Zoo*. New York: St. Martin's, 1992.

Brophy, Brigid. 'The Rights of Animals.' In *Don't Never Forget: Collected Views and Reviews*. New York: Holt, Rinehart & Winston, 1967. 15–21.

Budiansky, Stephen. *The Covenant of the Wild: Why Animals Choose Domestication*. New York: Morrow, 1992.

Buell, Lawrence. *The Environmental Imagination: Thoreau, Nature Writing, and the Formation of American Culture*. Cambridge, MA: Harvard UP, 1995.

Burns, John F. 'At Sarajevo Zoo, the Last Survivor Dies.' *New York Times* 4 November 1992: A18.

Burns, John F. 'In the Sarajevo Zoo, Only a House of Horrors.' *New York Times* 16 October 1992: A1, A9.

Bustad, Leo K. 'Man and Beast Interface: An Overview of Our Interrelationships.' In *Man and Beast Revisited*. Eds Michael N. Robinson and Lionel Tiger. Washington: Smithsonian Institution P, 1991. 233–63.

Cherfas, Jeremy. *Zoo 2000: A Look Beyond the Bars.* London: British Broadcasting Corporation, 1984.
Clines, Francis X. 'What's 3 Letters and Zoologically Incorrect?' *New York Times* 4 February 1993: A1, B10.
Conway, William. 'Zoo Conservation and Ethical Paradoxes.' In Norton, 1–9.
Costello, Bonnie. *Marianne Moore: Imaginary Possessions.* Cambridge, MA: Harvard UP, 1981.
'The Crazy Guy Who Feeds the Animals.' *Atlanta Constitution* 28 July 1992: A2.
Croke, Vicki. *The Modern Ark.* New York: Scribner, 1997.
Cunningham, Valentine. *British Writers of the Thirties.* Oxford: Oxford UP, 1988.
Edwards, John C. 'The Value of Old Photographs of Zoological Collections.' In Hoage, 141–50.
Ehrenfeld, David. Foreword to *Ethics on the Ark: Zoos, Animal Welfare, and Wildlife Conservation.* In Norton, xvii–xix.
Eisler, Colin. *Dürer's Animals.* Washington: Smithsonian Institution P, 1991.
Elder, John. *Imagining the Earth: Poetry and the Vision of Nature.* Urbana, IL: U of Illinois P, 1985.
Engel, Bernard F. *Marianne Moore.* Boston: Twayne, 1989.
Erickson, Darlene Williams. *Illusion is More Precise Than Precision.* Tuscaloosa, AL: U of Alabama P, 1992.
Fiske, John. 'Cultural Studies and the Culture of Everyday Life.' In Nelson, 154–65.
Foucault, Michel. *Discipline and Punish: The Birth of the Prison.* Trans. Alan Sheridan. New York: Pantheon, 1977.
Fouts, Roger. 'Arrogance of Knowledge versus Humility of Ignorance.' In Norton, 277–85.
Fox, Michael W. *Inhumane Society: The American Way of Exploiting Animals.* New York: St. Martin's, 1990.
Francione, Gary L. *Animals, Property, and the Law.* Philadelphia: Temple UP, 1995.
Gaard, Greta, ed. *Ecofeminism: Women, Animals, Nature.* Philadelphia: Temple UP, 1993.
Gaard, Greta. 'Living Interconnections With Animals and Nature.' In Gaard, 1–12.
Gabbard, Lucina P. 'At the Zoo: From O'Neill to Albee.' *Modern Drama* 19.4 (1976): 365–74.
Giddings, Robert, ed. *Literature and Imperialism.* London: Macmillan, 1991.
Glotfelty, Cheryll. 'Introduction: Literary Studies in an Age of Environmental Crisis.' In Glotfelty, xv–xxxvii.
Glotfelty, Cheryll, and Harold Fromm, eds. *The Ecocriticism Reader: Landmarks in Literary Ecology.* Athens: U of Georgia P, 1996.
Green-Armytage, A. H. N. *Bristol Zoo 1865–1965.* Bristol: Arrowsmith, 1964.
Greenblatt, Stephen. *Marvelous Possessions: The Wonder of the New World.* Chicago: U of Chicago P, 1991.

Griswold, Wendy. *Renaissance Revivals: City Comedy and Revenge Tragedy in the London Theatre, 1576–1980*. Chicago: U of Chicago P, 1986.
Hadas, Pamela White. *Marianne Moore: Poet of Affection*. Syracuse, NY: Syracuse UP, 1977.
Hancocks, David. 'So Long, Old Zoo.' *BBC Wildlife*. June 1991: 424.
Hargrove, Eugene. 'The Role of Zoos in the Twenty-First Century.' In Norton, 13–19.
Hediger, Heini. *Wild Aninals in Captivity: An Outline of the Biology of Zoological Gardens*. Trans. G. Sircom. London: Butterworths, 1950.
Hoage, R. J., and William A. Deiss, eds. *New Worlds, New Animals: From Menagerie to Zoological Park in the Nineteenth Century*. Baltimore, MD: Johns Hopkins UP, 1996.
Holley, Margaret. *The Poetry of Marianne Moore: A Study in Voice and Value*. Cambridge: Cambridge UP, 1987.
Hutcheon, Linda. 'Colonialism and the Postcolonial Condition: Complexities Abounding.' *PMLA* 110.1 (January 1995): 7–16.
Hutchins, Michael, Betsy Dresser, and Chris Wemmer. 'Ethical Considerations in Zoo and Aquarium Research.' In Norton, 253–76.
Jamieson, Dale. 'Against Zoos.' In Singer, 108–17.
Jamieson, Dale. 'Zoos Revisited.' In Norton, 52–66.
Jaschinski, Britta. *Zoo*. London: Phaidon, 1996. Unpaginated.
Kelsey, Tim. *Dervish: The Invention of Modern Turkey*. London: Hamish Hamilton, 1996.
Kheel, Marti. 'From Heroic to Holistic Ethics: The Ecofeminist Challenge.' In Gaard, 243–71.
King, Donna Lee. *Doing Their Share to Save the Planet: Children and Environmental Crisis*. New Brunswick, NJ: Rutgers UP, 1995.
King, Ynestra. 'Toward an Ecological Feminism and a Feminist Ecology.' In *Machina Ex Dea: Feminist Perspectives on Technology*. Ed. Joan Rothschild. New York: Pergamon P, 1983. 118–29.
Kohlstedt, Sally Gregory. 'Reflections on Zoo History.' In Hoage, 3–7.
Kristof, Nicholas D. 'Alas, Poor Alphonse! Was He His Keepers' Supper?' *New York Times* 24 April 1997: A4.
Lawrence, Elizabeth Atwood. 'Conflicting Ideologies: Views of Animal Rights Advocates and Their Opponents.' *Society and Animals* 2.2 (1994): 175–90.
Leopold, Aldo. *A Sand County Almanac*. 1949. New York: Ballantine, 1970.
Leppmann, Wolfgang. *Rilke: A Life*. New York: Fromm, 1984.
Livingston, Bernard. *Zoo Animals, People, Places*. New York: Arbor House, 1974.
Lloyd, Joan Barclay. *African Animals in Renaissance Literature and Art*. Oxford: Clarendon, 1971.
Lopez, Barry. *Arctic Dreams: Imagination and Desire in a Northern Landscape*. New York: Bantam, 1987.
Love, Glen A. '*Et in Arcadia Ego*: Pastoral Theory Meets Ecocriticism.' *Western American Literature* 27 (1992): 195–207.
Love, Glen A. 'Revaluing Nature: Toward an Ecological Criticism.' *Western American Literature* 25 (1990): 201–15.

Lutwack, Leonard. *Birds in Literature*. Gainesville, FL: UP of Florida, 1994.
MacDonald, Robert H. *The Language of Empire: Myths and Metaphors of Popular Imperialism, 1880–1918*. Manchester: Manchester UP, 1994.
McFadden, Robert D. 'Birds Flee Wreckage of Bronx Zoo Aviary.' *New York Times* 6 February 1995: B12.
McKenna, Virginia, Bill Travers, and Jonathan Wray, eds. *Beyond the Bars: The Zoo Dilemma*. Wellingborough, Northamptonshire: Thorsons, 1987.
McNeil, Donald G., Jr. 'Where Roving Circus Goes, Rare African Species Vanish.' *New York Times* 29 November 1995: A1, A13.
Magel, Charles R. *Keyguide to Information Sources in Animal Rights*. London: Mansell, 1989.
Manes, Christopher. 'Nature and Silence.' In Glotfelty, 15–29.
Maple, Terry. 'Toward a Responsible Zoo Agenda.' In Norton, 20–30.
Maple, Terry, and Erika Archibald. *Zoo Man: Inside the Zoo Revolution*. Atlanta, GA: Longstreet P, 1993.
Maple, Terry, Rita McManamon, and Elizabeth Stevens. 'Defining the Good Zoo: Animal Care, Maintenance, and Welfare.' In Norton, 219–34.
Mason, Jim. *An Unnatural Order: Uncovering the Roots of Our Domination of Nature and Each Other*. New York: Simon & Schuster, 1993.
Masson, Jeffrey Moussaieff, and Susan McCarthy. *When Elephants Weep: The Emotional Lives of Animals*. New York: Delacourte P, 1995.
Midgley, Mary. *Animals and Why They Matter*. New York: Penguin, 1983.
Mighetto, Lisa. *Wild Animals and American Environmental Ethics*. Tucson, AZ: U of Arizona, P, 1991.
Molotsky, Irvin. 'National Zoo Puts Six Orangutans to Work in a High-Wire Act.' *New York Times* 21 August 1995: A11.
Mullan, Bob, and Garry Marvin. *Zoo Culture*. London: Weidenfeld & Nicolson, 1987.
Navarro, Mireya. 'Disney Announces Plans for a Wildlife Theme Park.' *New York Times* 21 June 1995: B9.
Nelson, Cary, 'Cultural Studies: An Introduction.' In Nelson, 1–16.
Nelson, Cary, Paula A. Treichler, and Lawrence Grossberg, eds. *Cultural Studies*. New York: Routledge, 1992.
Norton, Bryan G., Michael Hutchins, Elizabeth F. Stevens, and Terry L. Maple, eds. *Ethics on the Ark: Zoos, Animal Welfare, and Wildlife Conservation*. Washington: Smithsonian Institution P, 1995.
Nossiter, Adam. 'Escaped Birds Seen Everywhere (Even Zoo).' *New York Times* 7 February 1995: A1, A9.
Nyhuis, Allen W. *The Zoo Book: A Guide to America's Best*. Albany, CA: Carousel P, 1994.
Palmatier, Robert A., ed. *Speaking of Animals: A Dictionary of Animal Metaphors*. Westport, CT: Greenwood P, 1995.
'Philadelphia Zoo Guards Smelled Smoke, but Did Nothing About It.' *New York Times* 28 December 1995: C18.
Pratt, Mary Louise. *Imperial Eyes: Travel Writing and Transculturation*. London: Routledge, 1992.

Rangel, Jesus. 'Boys Entered Bears' Area On a Dare.' *New York Times* 21 May 1987: B1, B8.
Rawlence, Chris. 'Jungle Lore.' In Barzdo, 12–17.
Read, Anthony, and David Fisher. *The Fall of Berlin*. New York: Norton, 1992.
Regan, Tom. 'Are Zoos Morally Defensible?' In Norton, 38–51.
Reichenbach, Herman. 'A Tale of Two Zoos: The Hamburg Zoological Garden and Carl Hagenbeck's Tierpark.' In Hoage, 51–62.
Rensberger, Boyce. *The Cult of the Wild*. Garden City, NY: Anchor, 1977.
'Report Recommends Increase In Security at Brooklyn Zoo.' *New York Times* 30 May 1987: 35.
Richards, Thomas. *The Imperial Archive: Knowledge and the Fantasy of Empire*. London: Verso, 1993.
Ritvo, Harriet. *The Animal Estate: The English and Other Creatures in the Victorian Age*. Cambridge, MA: Harvard UP, 1987.
Roberts, John. 'From Discipline to Discovery.' In Barzdo, 59–64.
Rockwell, John. 'Is it Autobiography or Fiction? But Then Does it Really Matter?' *New York Times* 20 December 1993: C11.
Roddick, Anita. *Body and Soul*. New York: Crown, 1991.
Ross, Andrew. *The Chicago Gangster Theory of Life: Nature's Debt to Society*. London: Verso, 1994.
Ross, Andrew. 'New Age Technoculture.' In Nelson, 531–55.
Ross, Andrew. *Strange Weather: Culture, Science, and Technology in the Age of Limits*. London: Verso, 1991.
Roudané, Matthew. *Understanding Edward Albee*. Columbia: U of South Carolina P, 1987.
Rudinow, Joel. 'Representation, Voyeurism, and the Vacant Point of View.' *Philosophy and Literature* 3.2 (Fall 1979): 173–86.
Ryan, Cornelius. *The Last Battle*. New York: Simon & Schuster, 1966.
Ryder, Richard D. *Animal Revolution: Changing Attitudes Towards Speciesism*. Oxford: Blackwell, 1989.
Said, Edward. *Culture and Imperialism*. New York: Knopf, 1993.
Sax, Boria. 'The Zoo: Paradise or Utopia: Are there Predators in Paradise?' *Terra Nova* 1.2 (Fall 1996).
Scarry, Elaine. *The Body in Pain: The Making and Unmaking of the World*. New York: Oxford UP, 1985.
Schleifer, Harriet. 'Images of Death and Life: Food Animal Production and the Vegetarian Option.' In Singer, 63–73.
Scholtmeijer, Marian. *Animal Victims in Modern Fiction: From Sanctity to Sacrifice*. Toronto: U of Toronto P, 1993.
Siebert, Charles. 'The Artifice of the Natural: How TV's Nature Shows Make All the Earth a Stage.' *Harper's* February 1993: 43–51.
Siebert, Charles. 'Fear of Zoos.' *New York Times* 9 February 1993: A 15.
Siebert, Charles. 'Where Have all the Animals Gone? The Lamentable Extinction of Zoos.' *Harper's* May 1991: 49–58.
Sims, Calvin. 'Chile Zoo Called Hostile Setting for Man and Beast.' *New York Times* 23 June 1996: A4.
Singer, Peter, ed. *In Defence of Animals*. Oxford: Blackwell, 1985.
Slack, Jennifer Daryl, and Laurie Anne Whitt. 'Ethics and Cultural Studies.' In Nelson, 571–92.

Spiegel, Marjorie. *The Dread Comparison: Human and Animal Slavery*. Philadelphia: New Society, 1988.
Stevens, William K. 'Bugs Help Keep the Planet Livable But Suffer From an Image Problem.' *New York Times* 21 December 1993: B5, B9.
Tarpy, Cliff. 'New Zoos: Taking Down the Bars.' *National Geographic* 184.1 (July 1993): 2–37.
Tester, Keith. *Animals and Society: The Humanity of Animal Rights*. London: Routledge, 1991.
Thiher, Allen. *Franz Kafka: A Study of the Short Fiction*. Boston: Twayne, 1990.
Tiffin, Chris, and Alan Lawson. 'The Textuality of Empire.' In *De-Scribing Empire: PostColonialism and Textuality*. Eds Chris Tiffin and Alan Lawson. London: Routledge, 1994. 1–11.
Tuan, Yi-Fu. *Dominance and Affection: The Making of Pets*. New Haven. CT: Yale UP, 1984.
'Universal Declaration of the Rights of Animals.' Adopted by the International League of the Rights of Animals, London, 1977. In Magel, 233–4.
Uroff, Margaret Dickey. *Sylvia Plath and Ted Hughes*. Urbana, IL: U of Illinois P, 1979.
Veltre, Thomas. 'Menageries, Metaphors, and Meanings.' In Hoage, 19–29.
Wagner-Martin, Linda. *Sylvia Plath: A Biography*. New York: Simon & Schuster, 1987.
Wilson, Alexander. *The Culture of Nature: North American Landscape from Disney to the Exxon Valdez*. Oxford: Blackwell, 1992.
Wilson, Mary Ann. *Jean Stafford: A Study of the Short Fiction*. New York: Twayne, 1996.
Wuichet, John, and Bryan Norton. 'Differing Concepts of Animal Welfare.' In Norton, 235–50.
Zuckerman, Solly, ed. *Great Zoos of the World: Their Origins and Significance*. Boulder, CO: Westview P, 1980.

Index